The Early Modern Englishwoman: A Facsimile Library of Essential Works

Series III

Essential Works for the Study of Early Modern Women: Part 1

Volume 7

Women and Murder in Early Modern News Pamphlets and Broadside Ballads, 1573–1697

The Early Modern Englishwoman: A Facsimile Library of Essential Works

Series III

Essential Works for the Study of Early Modern Women: Part 1

Volume 7

Women and Murder in Early Modern News Pamphlets and Broadside Ballads, 1573–1697

Selected and Introduced by
Randall Martin

General Editors
Betty S. Travitsky and Anne Lake Prescott

Routledge
Taylor & Francis Group
LONDON AND NEW YORK

First published 2005 by Ashgate Publishing

Published 2016 by Routledge
2 Park Square, Milton Park, Abingdon, Oxon OX14 4RN
711 Third Avenue, New York, NY 10017, USA

Routledge is an imprint of the Taylor & Francis Group, an informa business

British Library Cataloguing-in-Publication Data
Women and murder in early modern news pamphlets and broadside ballads, 1573–1697. – (The early modern Englishwoman : a facsimile library of essential works. Series III, Essential works for the study of early modern Women, Part 1 ; v. 7)
1.Murder in literature 2.Murder in mass media 3.Women murders – England – History – 17th century – Sources 4.Women murderers – England – History – 16th century – Sources 5.Murder – England – History – 17th century – Sources 6.Murder – England – History – 16th century – Sources 7.Pamphlets – England – 16th century 8.Pamphlets – England – 17th century 9.Broadsides – England – 15th and 16th centuries
I.Martin, Randall, 1958–
070.4'493641523'082

Library of Congress Cataloging-in-Publication Data
See page viii for complete CIP block

The image reproduced on the cover is the emblem from *A Collection of Emblemes*, Book 3, p. 178, by George Wither, 1635. *STC* 25900c. Reproduced by permission of the Folger Shakespeare Library, Washington DC.

ISBN 13: 978-0-7546-3115-6 (hbk)

CONTENTS

[Concerning Alice Davies]
The vnnaturall Wife (1628)
A warning for all desperate Women (1628)

[Concerning Alice Arden]
[*The*] *complaint and lamentation of Mistresse Arden of* [*Fav*]*ersham in Kent, who for the loue of one Mosbie, hired certaine Ruffians* [*and*] *Villaines most cruelly to murder her Husband* (*c.* 1633)

Henry Goodcole [concerning Elizabeth Evans, (Canberry Bess)]
Heavens Speedie Hue and Cry sent after Lust and Murther (1635)

[Concerning Elizabeth Evans, (Canberry Bess)]
Murder upon Murder, Committed by Thomas Sherwood, alias, Countrey Tom: and Elizabeth Evans, alias, Canbrye Besse (1635)

Henry Goodcole [concerning Alice Clarke]
The Adultresses Funerall Day: ... or The burning downe to ashes of Alice Clarke ... for the unnaturall poisoning of Fortune Clarke her Husband (1635)

[Concerning Susan Higges]
A true Relation of one Susan Higges (*c.* 1640?)

[Concerning Anne Hamton]
Murther, Murther. Or, A bloody Relation how Anne Hamton ... by poyson murthered her deare husband (1641)

[Concerning Elizabeth Lillyman]
A Compleat Narrative of the Tryal of Elizabeth Lillyman. Found Guilty of Petty Treason ... For the Barbarous and Bloody Murther of William Lillyman her late Husband (1675)
A Narrative Of the Proceedings at the Sessions-House in the Old-Bayly, ... And also an Account of the Tryal and Condemnation of Eliz. Lillyman, who killed her Husband, for which she was condemned to be Burned (1675)

[Concerning an unnamed wife]
Murder and Petty-Treason: Or, Bloody News from Southwark. Being A lamentable Relation of a barbarous Murder committed by a Wife upon the person of her Husband (1677)

[Concerning Sarah Elestone]
A Warning for Bad Wives: or, The Manner of the Burning of Sarah Elston (1678)

Sarah Elestone
The Last Speech and Confession of Sarah Elestone At the place of Execution: Who was Burned For Killing her Husband (1678)

[Concerning Margaret Osgood]
Great and Bloody News, From Farthing-Ally, In St. Thomas's Southwark, Or the True and Faithful Relatjo [sic] *Of a Horid and Barbarous Murther, Committed on the Body of Walter Osily* [sic], *by his own Wife* (1680)
Dreadful News from Southwark: or A true Account of the Most Horrid Murder committed By Margaret Osgood, On her Husband Walter Osgood a Hat-maker (1680)
The True Narrative of the Confession and Execution Of the Prisoners at Kingstone-upon-Thames, on Wednesday the 16th of this Instant March, 1681. Viz. Margaret Osgood Burnt for killing her Husband ... With ... more particular of the Confession and Burning of Margaret Osgood, of the Parish of St. Olives [sic] *Southwark, for the horrid Murther of her Husband, on the 21th* [sic] *of July last* (1680)

[Concerning Elizabeth Wigington]
The True Relation Of The Tryals At the Sessions of Oyer and Terminer ... As particularly of Elizabeth Wigenton [sic] *For Whipping a Girl to Death at Ratcliffe* (1681)

Library of Congress Cataloging-in-Publication Data
Women and murder in early modern news pamphlets and broadside ballads, 1573–1697 / selected and introduced by Randall Martin.
p. cm. – (The early modern Englishwoman. Series III, Essential works for the study of early modern women. Part 1; v. 7)
ISBN 0-7546-3115-X (alk. paper)
1. Women murderers – England – Early works to 1800. 2. Murder – England – Early works to 1800. 3. Trials (Murder) – England – Early works to 1800. I. Martin, Randall, 1958– II. Series.

HV6517.W66 2005
364.15'3'0820942–dc22

2004061135

PREFACE
BY THE GENERAL EDITORS

Until very recently, scholars of the early modern period have assumed that there were no Judith Shakespeares in early modern England. Much of the energy of the current generation of scholars has been devoted to constructing a history of early modern England that takes into account what women actually wrote, what women actually read, and what women actually did. In so doing, contemporary scholars have revised the traditional representation of early modern women as constructed both in their time and in ours. The study of early modern women has thus become one of the most important – indeed perhaps the most important – means for the rewriting of early modern history.

The Early Modern Englishwoman: A Facsimile Library of Essential Works is one of the developments of this energetic reappraisal of the period. As the names on our advisory board and our list of editors testify, it has been the beneficiary of scholarship in the field, and we hope it will also be an essential part of that scholarship's continuing momentum.

The Early Modern Englishwoman is designed to make available a comprehensive and focused collection of writings in English from 1500 to 1750, both by women and for and about them. The three series of *Printed Writings* (1500–1640, 1641–1700, and 1701–1750) provide a comprehensive if not entirely complete collection of the separately published writings by women. In reprinting these writings we intend to remedy one of the major obstacles to the advancement of feminist criticism of the early modern period, namely the limited availability of the very texts upon which the field is based. The volumes in the facsimile library reproduce carefully chosen copies of these texts, incorporating significant variants (usually in appendices). Each text is preceded by a short introduction providing an overview of the life and work of a writer along with a survey of important scholarship. These works, we strongly believe, deserve a large readership – of historians, literary critics, feminist critics, and non-specialist readers.

The Early Modern Englishwoman also includes separate facsimile series of *Essential Works for the Study of Early Modern Women* and of *Manuscript Writings*. These facsimile series are complemented by *The Early Modern Englishwoman 1500–1750: Contemporary Editions*. Also under our general editorship, this series includes both old-spelling and modernized editions of works by and about women and gender in early modern England.

New York City
2005

INTRODUCTORY NOTE

[The large number of short texts in this volume requires an introduction organised differently from those in other editions in this series. Rather than describing the writing and publication of each work sequentially, I have related selections to distinguishing features and developments of the murder pamphlet genre over the whole period and provided information about the printed texts (including STC *and Wing numbers) in the textual notes facing each selection. Similarly, because most of these ballads, pamphlets, and trial reports were published anonymously, biographical details of authorship are of less concern than their narrative content, social commentary, and contribution to the discursive construction of the early modern female murderer through their representational strategies and evolving legal and gender contexts. This introductory essay is followed by a list (arranged alphabetically) of the few authors who are identified in these pamphlets and about whom any information is known, and by a list of editorial considerations that have guided my selection of texts.]*

Murder Pamphlet writers, subjects, and readers

As voyeuristic and prurient as today's tabloid newspapers, early modern crime pamphlets and broadside ballads about women murderers tell of furtive love affairs and domestic poisonings, of battered wives who kill their abusive husbands, and of troubled mothers who murder their children. Despite the familiar recurrence of such stories, the early modern news pamphlet and trial report evolved into many different forms to serve a diverse range of reader interests, commercial markets, and social functions. On first acquaintance, many pamphlets leave an impression of shallow sensationalism yoked to idealised repentance, and for that reason modern critics and historians have often discounted their importance as culturally significant artifacts. The present selection of over forty texts is intended to encourage a reconsideration of these views.

Curiosity about the nation's most lurid murders was profitably fed by the relatively new, far-reaching technology of print, which served a rapidly expanding and increasingly competitive market. The news pamphlet was a commercially driven genre at the lowest end of the publishing trade. Most pamphlets sold for a penny or two, while broadside ballads went for a denier. ('Pamphlet' is a loose term referring to any short piece of writing, sold unbound; 'broadside' refers to the large single sheet on which ballads and later assize trial reports were printed for publication.) As texts, they are now usually classified as popular sub-literary ephemera. But their authors were often professional writers or clergymen, and their collective audience was broad, ranging from educated to semi-literate male and female readers. Certain longer accounts of murders, such as Arthur Golding's *A briefe discourse* (1573), Henry Goodcole's *Natures Cruell Step-Dames* (1637), and Roger L'Estrange's *A Hellish Murder* (1688), make a clear bid to interest readers in serious legal, theological, and social issues.

In most cases, however, the murder pamphlet's immediate appeal lay in the stories of bloody violence, illicit sex, and monstrous cruelty set in everyday houses, towns or cities. Juxtaposing the sensational with the commonplace heightened the shock-value of the murder and extended its impact beyond the local community. Published accounts from the 1570s onward created the first canon of notorious female homicides, beginning historically with Alice Arden. Her story is mentioned in *A View of sundry Examples* (1580) and *The Adultresses Funerall Day* (1635), and she is ventriloquised in *[The] complaint and lamentation of Mistresse Arden of Fav]ersham* (*c.* 1633). The festive associations and stylised melodic and rhythmic patterns of broadside ballads even gave some famous murderesses a measure of folk celebrity: e.g., Mrs. Page in Thomas Deloney, *The Lamentation* and *The Complaint of Mrs. Page* (*c.* 1591); Alice Davies in *The vnnaturall Wife* (1628) and *A warning for all desperate Women* (1628); and Susan Higges, in *A true Relation of one Susan Higges* (*c.* 1640). In other cases, broadside ballads fulfil their historical function as the forerunners of newspapers, relating conventionalised accounts of the latest crimes: *Anne Wallens Lamentation* (1616), for example, and *Murder upon Murder* (1635).

The pamphlet narrator's frequent indulgence in graphic horror was ostensibly justified by his (it was always his) edifying sentiments within a homiletic framework, and with biblical and Latin quotations and by pious exhortations to prayer and repentance. Serious crimes like murder were evidence of grave sin, whose public manifestations were widely decried as assaults on the social order. Writers earlier in the period use revelations of heinous crimes, while drawing on popular beliefs in the certainty of divine wrath and retribution, to illustrate the proverb 'murder will out': i.e., all-seeing Providence will always expose and revenge deadly crimes. Indirect agents such as inquisitive dogs or observant mute women are often credited as instruments of this process, as in *The Apprehension, Arraignement, and execution of Elizabeth Abbot* (1608) and Elizabeth James, *Three Bloodie Murders* (1613); so too are 'miraculous' accidents, such as the young girl who recover her speech after having her tongue cut out in *The Horrible Murther of a young Boy* (1606) and *The Most Crvel and Bloody Mvrther* (1606). Pamphlet writers likewise defend their activities with claims that publishing exemplary stories of murderers brought to justice performs a public service by warning fellow citizens and deterring future felons, e.g., *Sundrye strange and inhumaine Murthers* (1591) and Henry Goodcole's *Heaven. Speedie Hue and Cry sent after Lust and Murther* (1635). But as the seventeenth century wore on, and murders predictably continued, these rationales wore thin. Accounts of murder trials began to focus less on signs of divine outrage at crying sin and more on mundane human conflicts and problematic legal verdicts. After the Restoration, though some authors expressed scepticism about the purported deterrent value of publishing stories about crimes, publishers began regularly to issue summary reports of trial proceedings from county assizes, at which virtually all murders were tried, as routine commercial journalism (e.g. *A Narrative Of the Proceedings at the Sessions-House in the Old-Bayly, … And also an Account of the Tryal and Condemnation of Eliz. Lillyman, who killed her Husband, for which she was condemned to be Burned* [1675]; *The True Relation Of The Tryals At the Sessions of Oyer and Terminer … As particularly of Elizabeth Wigenton* [sic] *For Whipping a Girl to Death at Ratcliffe* [1681]).

Presenting the early modern female murderer in print

Given this gradual lapse in self-assurance about detecting providential control over human affairs and preventin future crime, it is interesting to observe the means by which pamphlets prior to the 1650s construct th inevitability of divine justice and natural law (the innate human desire to follow virtue and avoid evil). On common approach used by writers was to re-order events so as to give them causal coherence, and to plc stories in accordance with a familiar genre carrying readily understood moral meaning. Since most murder became explicable only after the main facts and motives were discovered, pamphlet writers never presente events exactly as they occurred, in a strictly factual sequence, but instead narrated them with the reconstructiv benefit of hindsight. Moreover because offenders had been arrested, tried, and in most cases had confesse before being executed – sometimes to the pamphlet writer himself – the knowledge gained from judici inquiries and the final verdict determined the viewpoint as well as the personal interests of authors interpretin a criminal's motives and piecing together the story-line. Also underpinning this process was the commonplac notion that one sin, unchecked, led inescapably to greater sins (e.g. William Perkins's highly popular an influential treatise, *A Golden Chain* [1592]). Narrators thus sought to confirm the inescapable reality c natural justice by linking the woman's degenerate character and criminal actions in a sequence of tragic event (e.g., *The Araignement & burning of Margaret Ferne-seede* [1608], *True Relation of the Birth, Parentage Education, Life and Conversation of Mrs. Margaret Martel* [1697]). In particular, the ghost-written confession by the condemned woman which often appeared at the end of these pamphlets caricatured her life as one c incremental sin and misconduct leading to disaster, followed by wonderful contrition after the guilty verdic (e.g., *A True Discourse. Of the practises of Elizabeth Caldwell* [1604] and Mrs Turner, *The Bloody downfall C Adultery. Murder, Ambition* [1615]). Puritan authors even tended to suggest that the murder was a kind c divine gift – a felix culpa – because it led to the woman's deep abjection and presumed salvation throug grace. In *Mistres Turners Repentance* (1615), the woman's tearful downfall – conventionally inscribing her as a daughter of Eve – was appropriated not only to exemplify Calvinist beliefs in deep-rooted human sin and unmeritable grace but also to bolster government authority in the aftermath of the Gunpowder plot (1605). The most common generic pattern imposed on these stories therefore takes the form of a conversion: ethical collapse, physical negation, and spiritual redemption. Writers such as Arthur Golding (*A briefe discourse*) and Henry Goodcole (*Heavens Speedie Hue and Cry*) explicitly attest that inconsistencies, facts deemed to be extraneous, and adverse public opinions which did not conform either to the official verdict or to the conversion model were routinely erased, suppressed, or rearranged to reduce the ambiguity of their impact. What is paramount in these cases is persuading readers of the story's moral truths, not presenting evidence for impartial evaluation. (See also Anne Hamton, *Murther, Murther* [1641].) Yet this imposition of an officially authorised or tendentiously moral perspective was never absolute. Even amongst the most dogmatic writers, perceptible gaps still remain between legal statutes, court judgements, and public opinion, as do traces of complex ethical perspectives or alternative interpretations of events and circumstances that the pamphlet writer, by virtue of his formal (though variable) commitment to narrating historical truth, feels obliged to record or glance at. Such slippage illustrates the institutional and social conflicts between official jurisprudence and moral equity which are an underlying theme in many of these pamphlets.

Certain accounts interweave this generically reordered and expurgated presentation with deliberately invented details intended to evoke particular value judgements and emotional responses from readers. The narrator's re-creation of first-person dialogue, for example in Anne Welles's *The trueth of the … murthering of Iohn Brewen* (1592), Annis Dell's *The Horrible Murther of a young Boy* (1608), and *A Compleat Narrative of the Tryal of Elizabeth Lillyman* (1675) is meant to sensationalise violent encounters and to elicit pity for victims. Authors fictionalise events to frame the murder-action as unquestionably wicked, to impugn the woman's character as deeply reprobate, and to wrest the significance of her trial and punishment in order to uphold established civil and judicial orders.

Traditional gender and class assumptions about women's proper social and domestic roles run through these pamphlets, as does a strong vein of commonplace misogyny. Only in a few cases do writers express direct sympathy for the condemned woman, or endorse mitigating factors which potentially challenge a court's judgement, as does, for example, Gilbert Dugdale's *A True Discourse* (1604). As murder pamphlets became conventionalised and subdivided into various kinds of conflict (viz., adulterous conspiracies, marital discord, religious disputes, urban crime, child murder), and as writers linked the latest killer to her notorious predecessors, they contributed to the construction of a new transhistorical gender identity: the murderous woman. Whereas homicides by men were typically attributed to a breakdown of rational control or a dereliction of proper male authority, the motives for women were nearly always related to unregulated sexuality and rebellion against patriarchal dominion. In terms of simple labelling, this means that the women in early murder pamphlets and ballads are routinely described as devils, beasts, and whores. If not actually prostitutes or bawds, as some women in these accounts may have been, middle- or working-class daughters, wives, and servants are treated as such and symbolically degraded to this status; for example, see Martha Scambler, *Deeds Against Natvre and Monsters by kinde* (1614). In conformity with the retorting dynamics of conversion, moreover, these caricatures sharpen the transformation back into meek subjection and proper womanhood, as happens in *Mrs Turners Farewell to all women* (1615).

Pamphlet writers also frequently stereotype individual women by assimilating catchphrases and character traits found in contemporary dramatic or literary representations of female murderers. For example, several accounts (Annis Dell, *The Most Crvell and Bloody Mvrther* [1608], *The Apprehension, Arraignement, and Execution of Elizabeth Abbot* [1608], and Elizabeth James, *Three Bloodie Murders* [1613]) allude to the symbolically inflected confrontation in Shakespeare's *Henry VI Part Three* in which Queen Margaret taunts the duke of York with a blood-stained napkin of his murdered son Rutland (1.4) and York passionately denounces her transgressions of natural female decency:

> She-wolf of France, but worse than wolves of France,
> Whose tongue more poisons than the adder's tooth,

How ill-beseeming is it in thy sex
To triumph like an Amazonian trull ....
O tiger's heart wrapped in a woman's hide ...
Women are soft, mild, pitiful, and flexible;
Thou stern, obdurate, flinty, rough, remorseless. (I.4.111–14, 137–42)

Early seventeenth-century writers echoed phrases from this well-known passage to encode violations c traditional gender boundaries and to universalise the otherwise personally distinguishing conflicts and motive of individual women. York's reference to poison, for example, related Margaret's outrages to a means of killin that became identified very closely with unruly early modern Englishwomen. Poisoning, long regarded i England as the most heinous form of murder, combined the devious and the extravagant in its betrayal c domestic trust, as with Anne Welles (1592), Elizabeth Caldwell (1604), Mrs Turner (1615), Alice Clar (1635), and Anne Hamton (1641). From a legal perspective, because it was deliberate and relatively slow t show itself, poison defined the woman offender's actions as calculated intent – unlike the hot-bloodedness b which male felons were sometimes excused and acquitted – and therefore beyond the scope of contemporar legal formulations of manslaughter or self-defence.

Changing textual representations and public attitudes

Notwithstanding these strategies designed to reduce women's crimes to simplistic scenarios of evil an redemption and to cut off debate about their relative guilt or innocence, many reports, especially later in th seventeenth century, were published in multiple versions presenting conflicting facts and interpretation Alternative accounts included here of Annis Dell (1606), Alice Davies (1628), Anne Greene (1651), Elizabet Lillyman (1675), Sarah Elston (1678), Margaret Osgood (1680), Elizabeth (or Leticia) Wigington (1681 Mary Hobry (1688), and Margaret Martel (1697) stimulated topical debates within these texts and occasionall beyond them. The discrepancies expose the commonplace prejudices and double standards of many contempora male authors. They also attest to increasing competition amongst publishers, who were often more concerne with getting a murder story out quickly than with checking its details for accuracy. Yet even in many of th single-version pamphlet accounts reproduced here, certain minor or marginal details bear witness to conteste explanations of events that resist legal and patriarchal hegemonies, thus breaking official or documenta silences about individual murderesses and their personal motives. Regardless of many writers' efforts destroy their female subjects' reputations (or 'credit') and to endorse circumstantial evidence of guilt ar hearsay (legal testimony which often carried greater weight than material facts in early modern trials-by-jury some women, such as Elizabeth Barnes (1637) and Elizabeth Lillyman (1675), refused to confess their crime Others, such as Margaret Ferneseede (1608), confessed to sinful lives in general but strenuously denied th murder of which they were accused. In two exceptional cases, Elizabeth Caldwell's *Letter from prison* Gilbert Dugdale's *A True Discourse* (1604) and *The Confession and Execution of Leticia Wigington* (1681), th defendants deny their guilt and reinterpret the crime in their own words.

Sometimes the contradictory or ambiguous perspectives in these pamphlets are attributable to agenci other than the writer or his female subject. In the Guildhall Library copy of *Murther, Murther* (1641), th variant names 'Katherine Web' and 'Mary Fusser' are substituted for Anne Hamton and her landlady Margar Harewood, names which appear in other copies. Because the pamphlet suggests that the women were love ('Ningles', A3^{v}) who conspired to poison Hamton's husband, the printer may have inserted the alternati names to shield the women's friends or relations from a same-sex scandal in addition to a murder.

Another source of semantic ambivalence is title page illustrations, in particular those showing women bei burnt at the stake, the penalty for petty treason (when a wife killed her husband). Burning became conspicuously gendered form of punishment in England after executions for heresy declined in the last half the sixteenth century, and occasional (i.e., infrequent, as recent historical research has shown) executions female witches continued. In terms of print culture, images of persons being burnt at the stake remain familiar from sectarian polemics and martyrologies, above all John Foxe's universally known *Actes a*

Monumentes (1563), which portrayed numerous women dying courageously in flames. One prominent victim was Cicely Ormes, executed at Norwich in 1557. Foxe reports her life, persecution, and burning in his 1570 edition and provides a matching woodcut. This image again appears on the title page of the 1592 pamphlet relating the murder of John Brewen by his wife, Anne Welles, and her lover John Parker (*The trueth of … the secret murthering of Iohn Brewen*). The duplication can be partly explained by the fact that printers commonly recycled images to illustrate the general or generic contents of a text. Nonetheless, for the many readers who knew Foxe's account of the Marian martyrs, what impression was made by the image of Ormes on a domestic murder pamphlet? As 'Anne Welles' she appears self-possessed and unfrightened. She looks directly at the viewer, perhaps proudly, perhaps a bit libidinously, hands raised in prayer. She appears virtually naked, wearing only a diaphanous shift that reveals the outline of her breasts. In Foxe, Ormes's nakedness presumably conveys her unselfconscious moral integrity and spiritual fearlessness. But in the murder pamphlet, it arguably becomes a sexualised sign of culpability, as do the suggestively phallic-shaped flames around her. Did the link between Ormes and the independent-minded Welles, who steadfastly refused to adopt her husband's name or to live in his house after he had bribed and blackmailed her into marriage, lend credibility to her dilemma or affect the readers' estimation of her actions?

Texts and images occasionally combine discursive and material afterlives to create complex public identities for female murderers. The title page woodcut of Henry Goodcole's *The Adultresses Funerall Day: In flaming, scorching, and consuming fire* (1635) shows an unidentified man (rather than the expected woman) burning at the stake, while his soul, depicted as a second visage, rises out of his body. Here the image of martyrdom connects incongruously with Goodcole's opening story of a battered wife who kills her husband after suffering life-threatening physical violence. These and other illustrations deviate from official accounts and verdicts and open spaces for sympathetic or dissenting contemporary readers (who presumably included women capable of evaluating these crimes independently) against the male narrator's perspective. In reading stories of wives who killed in self-defence, these readers might or might not recognise distant similarities to their own experiences of domineering or abusive spouses.

Sometimes, contradictory, mitigating, or compassionate viewpoints also arise out of the narrator's direct knowledge of and personal contact with his criminal charges. Henry Goodcole, the first English professional crime writer, substantially documents the complex reciprocity of these intersubjective relationships. Like other unnamed authors of these pamphlets, he was a clergyman who provided spiritual counsel to the condemned and prepared them to face death. But as Visitor of Newgate and Ludgate prisons he was also a paid officer of the justice system, participating in pre-trial examinations of the accused by magistrates, hearing testimony at assize trials, and extracting prison confessions from those who denied their crimes that would serve to vindicate court judgements. Despite this power imbalance between him and his charges, Goodcole's vindication of judicial authority was not myopic, nor was his authorial control and subordination absolute. He invested offenders' often confused and traumatised recollections with a degree of narrative stability and meaning. At the same time, mediating between the criminal law and the condemned created tensions, identifiable as specific rhetorical manipulations and palpable self-censorship. In comforting condemned women, Goodcole provided them with the conventionally moralising phrases of their gallows speeches, which they were expected to read to assembled spectators at public executions. While these speeches are co-written only in a very restricted sense, they nevertheless reveal visible intersections between the interests of a state official whose writing was a means of promoting his career, and the voices of his socially marginalised – yet often persistently defiant – subjects. (Besides Goodcole, see *The Araignement & burning of Margaret Ferne-seede* [1608], *The Last Speech and Confession of Sarah Elestone* [1678], and *The Confession and Execution of Leticia Wigington* [1681].) Wringing explanations out of the accused or condemned and writing their stories also sometimes generated a degree of identification with their motives, and this in turn created varying degrees of sympathy for their misfortunes. Occasionally it also prompted Goodcole and his fellow authors to step beyond their official roles and comment directly on the social and economic conditions behind a woman's actions. These contextualising perspectives tend to resist magisterial closure and to call into question patriarchal culture's regulation of female sexuality: viz. enforced marriage (Mrs Page, *Sundrye strange and inhumaine Murthers* [1591]); female servants seduced or victimised by masters or mistresses (*Three Bloodie Murders*

[1613], *Natures Cruell Step-Dames* [1637], Anne Greene, *Newes from the Dead* [1651], *The True Relation O* *The Tryals … of Elizabeth Wigenton* [1681]); and the severe limits on women's rights or options in dysfunctiona or violent marriages (*A Compleat Narrative of the Tryal of Elizabeth Lillyman* [1675] and Jane Lawson, *A Tru and Sad Relation Of Two Wicked and Bloody Murthers* [1680]).

Above all, many pamphlets later in the period such as *Murder and Petty-Treason* (1677), *A Warning for Ba Wives* (1678), and *Dreadful News from Southwark* (1680) raise the possibility of arguments for self-defence o manslaughter in the cases of battered wives who can see no alternative to killing their abusive husbands yet ar legally charged with murder. The most directly revealing document in this group is Roger L'Estrange's *Hellish Murder* (1688). L'Estrange presents depositions taken under oath but ultimately not used in the trial o Mary Hobry. The judge encouraged her to plead not guilty so that her own story could be heard, but, in a stat of extreme emotional despondency, she confessed to the murder. L'Estrange effectively mounts Hobry' defence and retries her case. Her personal testimony unfolds an appalling life of prolonged financial deprivatio and mental and physical violence culminating in what we would now call spousal rape. The horror of he husband's mistreatment equals and may be felt to surpass that of her killing. Pamphlets in this category attes to shifting social and judicial attitudes in the seventeenth-century towards wife abuse, changes that pamphle accounts helped to produce, by alluding to (but also sometimes contesting) popular support for batter women and public disapproval of judgements favouring their violent male partners. Whereas earlier in th period physical 'correction' by husbands was reported with little direct or implied criticism, and was partiall condoned in certain marital and legal advice books, by the last half of the seventeenth century writers tende to condemn violent husbands and were more inclined to see self-defending women as aggrieved victims rathe than as disobedient wives (though their punishment, if they were found guilty, remained the same).

Presenting the early-modern child murderer in print

Similar public controversy is visible in accounts of child murder and infanticide (presented in this volume as second grouping of selected texts). It arises in murder cases involving extreme differences in religion betwee spouses (Margaret Vincent, *A pittilesse Mother* [1616]), or the clandestine disposal of unwanted children b paying clients (Mrs Compton, *The Cruel Midwife* [1693]). Infanticide was legally defined by a 1624 statute a the concealment of the birth of a baby later found to be dead, and it reversed the common assumption c innocence before guilt was proved. In practice, the statute was meant to punish unmarried women who gav birth alone to hide their pregnancies, and hence without witnesses such as midwives who could later corroborat claims that the woman had miscarried or the child had been still-born. Prosecutions for infanticide peaked i the 1620s and 1630s and then fell off fairly rapidly, partly because communities did not wish to becom responsible for 'chargeable bastards' after the mother was hanged, and partly because of growing disapprov of the law itself. Women charged with either infanticide or murder could also evade the sentence by 'pleadin their bellies' – requesting stays of execution because of pregnancy. Requests were sometimes granted at onc by the presiding judge, but more often he ordered the convicted woman to be physically examined by juries c matrons: up to twelve local women who might know the accused or the circumstances of her life and action The matrons could open a path to informal clemency by confirming a pregnancy, since executions do not see usually to have been carried out after an imprisoned mother had borne a child. Public attitudes towards wome accused of killing their new-born children – often servant-girls made pregnant by male householders or the relations or women abandoned before marriage – were also decisively challenged by the widely discussed cas of Anne Greene (W. Burdet, *A Wonder of Wonders* [1651] and Richard Watkins, *Newes from the Dead* [1651] Greene caused a sensation among Oxford scientists by suddenly reviving, just as she was about to be dissecte in an anatomy, after she had been hanged for not revealing an early miscarriage (or, as the court had original judged following the 1624 statute, for concealing the murder of her prematurely born child). Her resuscitatio was widely understood as a sign of divine vindication, and it led pamphlets and other accounts to re-evalua the charge of murder, redefining the evidence, decriminalising her actions and character, and reconstructin Greene's identity as that of an unjustly victimised woman. The two pamphlets about her case, reproduce elow, also bring into focus the contested intersections of judicial power, criminal statute, and gender difference hat forensic and scientific procedures exercised on the dead bodies of early modern women (see also *Heavens Speedie Hue and Cry*). They likewise attest to a heightened awareness of physiological and psychological actors in later cases of child murder in which women suffer from severe depression, schizophrenia, and uicidal impulses (e.g., Jane Lawson, *A True and Sad Relation* [1680]).

uthors (in alphabetical order)

V. Burdet was an Oxford don who compiled an eye-witness report of Anne Greene's spectacular recovery fter she was tried and hanged for infanticide (*A Wonder of Wonders. Being A faithful Narrative and true Relation, of one Anne Green* [1651]). Nothing further is known about him. See also Richard Watkins below.

Thomas Deloney (*c*. 1560–1600) is described by contemporaries as a silk-weaver by trade, but if so he was n unusually educated one, since his first published writings were three Latin translations in 1583. As well as Protestant polemics against Catholics, he wrote a large number of news ballads on contemporary Elizabethan vents. These were collected in several volumes and reprinted throughout the seventeenth century. He is now est known for several volumes of prose fiction. Some of his stories are folkloric, while others celebrate the ard-working virtues and civic achievements of upwardly mobile artisans such as Simon Eyre, a shoemaker's pprentice who became Lord Mayor of London. Eyre's story appears in Deloney's *The Gentle Craft* (1597) and vas dramatised by Thomas Dekker in *The Shoemaker's Holiday* (1600). Another story-collection, *Thomas of Reading* (1600), includes an account of the murder of Thomas Cole by a tavern-keeper and his wife, raditionally seen as an analogue for *Macbeth*.

Most of Deloney's broadside ballads are now lost, but *The Lamentation of Mr. Pages Wife* and *The Complaint of Mrs. Page* (*c*. 1591, printed 1663–4) are surviving examples of his superior work in this highly tylised genre. They were printed side-by-side on the same broadside as a third ballad, *The Lamentation of George Strangwidge*, Ulalia Page's lover before her enforced marriage. But whereas this ballad contains few ersonal details and is conventionally sentimental, the other two, especially Mrs Page's *Lamentation*, vividly rticulate the subject's motives and anguish while constructing a damning indictment of her mercenary arents, who ignored her personal preferences and treated her as an exchange object. Deloney also focuses on ertain intimate domestic details that dramatise Ulalia's emotional revulsion for her apparently much older usband. The unusual intensity and greater realism of Deloney's ballad perhaps reflect the depth of public ympathy towards Ulalia's misfortunes and may hint at features that characterised Thomas Dekker and Ben onson's version of the story in their now lost play *Page of Plymouth* (performed 1599 by the Lord Admiral's Men).

About **Gilbert Dugdale** we know nothing beyond the information revealed in his two extant publications: a ympathetic and partially exonerating account of Elizabeth Caldwell, *A True Discourse. Of the practises of Elizabeth Caldwell … on the parson of Ma*[*ster*]*: Thomas Caldwell* (1604, reproduced below); and a flattering eport of James's coronation pageants written in the same year: *The Time Triumphant, Declaring in briefe, the riual of our Soueraigne liedge Lord, King Iames into England*. Dugdale describes himself in *A True Discourse* as a 'countryman of Chester', the same county where the Caldwells dwelt. His dedicatory epistle ddresses Lady Mary Cholmondeley (famously called the 'bold lady of Cheshire' by James) and twenty-seven ther members of the county gentry – virtually the entire administrative and judicial elite of Cheshire. Dugdale's dedication serves partly to recall the efforts made by Cholmondeley and others to appeal to James or clemency on Caldwell's behalf, an appeal that ultimately was unsuccessful. We learn most about Dugdale n a second epistle dedicated to Lady Mary Chandos and signed by Robert Armin. Armin was a writer of opular ballads and jestbooks as well as a famous comic actor who sometime after 1594 joined Lord Chandos's company as a player, later moving to the Chamberlain's Men, Shakespeare's company, in 1599–1600. (See Wiles, 136–44). In the epistle, Armin refers to himself as a former servant of Lord Chandos, and ince he further states that Dugdale was present throughout the time of Elizabeth Caldwell's imprisonment, rial, and execution. Dugdale may therefore have served as her chaplain. Because he shared in 'all her troubles, and for the better proofe that it was so', Armin explains that he has 'placed my kinsmans [i.e. Dugdale's name' to the pamphlet. His phrasing suggests they collaborated in writing the main murder story. But Armi also affirms that Caldwell's letter to her husband is 'of her owne indighting', and he suggests that her gentl upbringing and moving personal testimony make it unusually interesting in view of the striking contrast wit the public facts of the murder.

Arthur Golding (*c.* 1536–1605) is the author of the first English crime pamphlet, *A briefe discourse of th late murther of master George Saunders* (signed 'A.G.' in the 1573 edition reproduced below and 'Arthu Golding' in the otherwise identical 1577 edition), although he is better known for his influential translations c Ovid's *Metamorphoses* (1565) and Calvin's sermons. The stern tone and ideology of Calvinism are readil apparent in *A briefe discourse*, which strenuously rejects any moral relativism in recounting the domesti conflicts and intrigue that lead to Anne Saunders's murder of her husband. Because Golding attributes th causes of her crime to universal human sinfulness, by implication the pamphlet's author and readers ar fundamentally no better than she is; only the enforcement of stricter social and personal discipline preven them from falling into sinful crimes as heinous as hers. Golding thus appropriates Anne Saunders's misfortun to justify a public exhortation to moral vigilance while relying on his reputation as a translator of seriou literary works to invest his pronouncements with cultural authority. Although he alludes briefly to certai expressions of contemporary sympathy for Anne, he peremptorily dismisses any argument or informatio which might mitigate her actions or defend her innocence, instead heightening attention on her confession c guilt and abject repentance prior to execution. Besides establishing certain presentational features and soci attitudes that would become commonplace in popular murder narratives, his pamphlet serves as an apology fc state justice and government officials who became directly involved in the widely known case as a result c George Saunders's high-ranking social and family connections.

Henry Goodcole (1586–1641), a Londoner, was the first professional author to specialise in urban crim writing a half-dozen sensationalising pamphlets on several notorious murders (three of which are reproduce below: *Heavens Speedie Hue and Cry sent after Lust and Murther* [1635]; *The Adultresses Funerall Day: ... c The burning downe to ashes of Alice Clarke ... for the unnaturall poisoning of Fortune Clarke her Husban* [1635]; and *Natures Cruell Step-Dames ... Elizabeth Barnes and Anne Willis ... executed the 26. day of Apr 1637. at Tyburne, ... for the unnaturall murthering of their owne Children* [1637]). His best-known pamphlet, *Th wonderfull discouerie of Elizabeth Sawyer a Witch, late of Edmonton* (1621), provided a source for Dekker, For and Rowley's topical play *The Witch of Edmonton* in the same year. Goodcole was in a privileged position to wri such accounts because he was the first full-time Visitor (or chaplain) of Ludgate and Newgate prisons fro 1620–1641 and therefore heard stories and testimony of women murderers first-hand. His pamphlets embellis their accounts with quasi-forensic descriptions of physical details and locales and some striking illustration Together these heighten the realism and immediacy of the murderers' violence, partly to compete commercial with other published versions of the crimes (for example, a conventional ballad about Country Tom ar Canberry Bess, *Murder upon Murder* [1635, reproduced below]), and partly to heighten the visibility of h publications in bids for professional advancement from his employers, the Court of Aldermen of the City London. Overall, these ambitiously crafted features produce a fascinating multiplicity of discursive and leg viewpoints. Like those of Golding before him, Goodcole's pamphlets provided models for later authors ar journalists, and he established a professional precedent for the regularly published accounts of eighteent century Newgate chaplains. (Further discussion of Goodcole appears in the main introduction above.)

Roger L'Estrange (1616–1704) is the presumed author and compiler of *A Hellish Murder Committed by French Midwife, On the Body of her Husband* (1688), an unusually detailed and complex account of th genuinely shocking story of French émigrée Mary Hobry (or Aubrey). L'Estrange was an energetic To pamphleteer and journalist who was appointed 'surveyor' or licenser of the press after the Restoration ar who was knighted by James II in April 1685. He wrote a wide variety of popular and often ribald publication and he was a fluent translator of French, Spanish, and classical literature. In later life he translated comprehensive collection of Aesop's *Fables* (1692) as well as Josephus's *Works* (1702). His prose is memorab for its colloquial vigour and pugnacity, qualities that embolden the implied defence of Mary Hobry in *Hellish Murder*.

Anthony Munday (1560–1633) apprenticed as a London stationer but went on to became a minor actor for a time. In *A View of sundry Examples* (1580), he describes himself in a dedicatory epistle as a servant of the Earl of Oxford, in whose acting company he presumably played in occasional roles. Eventually he became better known as a prolific writer and translator, producing journeyman pieces in a wide variety of popular genres such as drama, civic pageantry, romance, and balladry. Jonson satirised what he considered to be Munday's miserable efforts in his portrait of 'Antonio Balladino' in *The Case is Altered* (1597). Munday followed Arthur Golding's precedent – albeit in a more journalistic style – by writing both *A View of sundry Examples*, a tritely moralising digest of 'all memorable murthers since the murther of Maister Saunders' (title page), and a report of the earthquake of 6 April 1580, about which Golding (again more seriously) had also written.

Of **T. Platte**, identified as the author at the end of *Anne Wallens Lamentation* (1616), we know nothing further.

Richard Watkins was another Oxford don who wrote an eye-witness account of Anne Greene's execution and recovery (*Newes from the Dead ... the miraculous deliverance of Anne Greene, Who being Executed ... afterwards revived* [1651]; see also W. Burdet above). Anthony à Wood confirms Watkins's profession with a handwritten annotation on his copy of the second edition (reproduced below) of *Newes from the Dead*: 'Mr Watkins. C[orpus]:C[hristi]:C[ollege]: Ox:[ford]' (Bodleian Library, shelfmark Wood 516 (7), lower-right corner of the title page). Otherwise, nothing is known about Watkins. Wood, however, mentions Greene's ordeal in his extensive diaries (*Life & Times*, ed. Llewelyn Powys [London, 1932], pp. 38–9), as do various other seventeenth-century commentators such as Plot, 197–99.

My selection of texts derives from a study of over 165 published accounts of early modern murders and serious felonies involving women as principals or accessories. The following considerations are reflected in my choices:

- I have concentrated on capital, non-clergyable crimes (i.e. not open to benefit of clergy to escape capital punishment) tried by assize courts and punishable by death: murder, robberies involving murder, and infant and child murder.
- Only accounts of real crimes are included, as well as ballads or broadside verses based on them containing at least a few historical details and which are not entirely fanciful, formulaic, or pedestrian.
- Selections cover a full range of literary forms deployed by early modern pamphlets and broadside ballads. They illustrate a variety of narrative voices and rhetorical constructions, which in many cases clearly reveal the interweaving of documentary and fictionalising narrative strategies.
- Because this is a facsimile volume, I have preferred texts that feature interesting woodcut illustrations.
- Accounts with named women criminals, substantial narratives, and material details (in both the physical and seventeenth-century legal sense) have been preferred. So too have been crimes represented by several different versions or accounts of a story which allow readers to make comparisons of content and form.
- My preference has also been for stories that open up the social contexts and gender relationships of their female subjects with as much information as possible. I have likewise chosen certain accounts that illustrate the legal procedures of early modern arrest, trial, and execution (Elizabeth Abbot 1608, Margaret Hobry 1688).

Further, I have included accounts that express or imply some degree of sympathy for the accused women; that deliberately or inadvertently introduce facts or circumstances mitigating or qualifying the motives for, or charges of, murder; that involve forensic medical procedures; and that construct or imply counter-narratives of self-defence or manslaughter.

References

Amussen, Susan Dwyer (1994), '"Being Stirred to Much Unquietness": Violence and Domestic Violence in Earl Modern England', *Journal of Women's History* 6 (2): 70–89

Baines, Barbara (1998), 'Effacing Rape in Early Modern Representations', *English Literary History* 65: 69–98

Bashar, Nazife (1983), 'Rape in England Between 1550 and 1700', *The Sexual Dynamics of History*, London: Londo Feminist History Group, 33–40

Beattie, J.M. (1975), 'The Criminality of Women in Eighteenth-Century England', *Journal of Social History* 8: 80–116

—— (1986), *Crime and the Courts in England 1660–1800*, Princeton: Princeton University Press

Bingham, Caroline (1971), 'Seventeenth-Century Attitudes Toward Deviant Sex', *Journal of Interdisciplinary History* 447–72

Brooks, Peter and Paul Gewirtz (eds.), (1996), *Law's Stories: Narrative and Rhetoric in the Law*, New Haven: Yal University Press

Butler, Judith (rev. edn 1999), *Gender Trouble: Feminism and the Subversion of Identity*, New York: Routledge

Chaytor, Miranda (1995), 'Husband(ry): Narratives of Rape in the Seventeenth Century', *Gender & History* 7.3: 372–407

Cioni, Maria L. (1985), *Women and Law in Elizabethan England, with Particular Reference to the Court of Chancer* New York: Garland Press

Clark, Sandra (1983), *The Elizabethan Pamphleteers: Popular Moralistic Pamphlets 1580–1640*, Rutherford, NJ: Fairleig Dickinson University Press

—— (2003), *Women and Crime in the Street Literature of Early Modern England*, New York: Palgrave Macmillan

Cockburn, J.S. (ed.) (1985), *Calendar of Assize Records: Home Circuit Indictments Elizabeth I and James I, Introductio* London: Her Majesty's Stationery Office

Davis, Natalie Zemon (1987), *Fiction in the Archives: Pardon Tales and Their Tellers in Sixteenth-Century Franc* Stanford: Stanford University Press

Dolan, Francis E. (1994), *Dangerous Familiars: Representations of Domestic Crime in England 1550–1700,* Ithac Cornell University Press

—— (1994), '"Gentlemen, I have one thing more to say": Women on Scaffolds in England, 1563–1680', *Moder Philology* 92.2: 157–78

Eden, Kathy (1986), *Poetic and Legal Fiction in the Aristotelian Tradition*, Princeton: Princeton University Press

E., T. (1632), *The Lawes Resolutions of Womens Rights: or, The Lawes Provision for Woemen*

Foucault, Michel (1978), *The History of Sexuality*, trans. Robert Hurley, Vol. 1. An Introduction, New York: Vintag Books

—— (1987), *The History of Sexuality*, trans. Robert Hurley, Vol. 2, The Use of Pleasure, New York, Vintage Books

Gaskill, Malcolm (1998), 'Reporting Murder: Fiction in the Archives', *Social History* 23.1: 1–30

—— (2000), *Crime and Mentalities in Early Modern England*, Cambridge: Cambridge University Press

Gowing, Laura (1996), *Domestic Dangers: Women, Words and Sex in Early Modern London*, Oxford: Clarendon Press

—— (1997), 'Secret Births and Infanticide in Seventeenth-Century England', *Past and Present* 156: 87–115.

Green, Thomas Andrew (1985), *Verdict According to Conscience: Perspectives on the English Criminal Jury, 1200–180* Chicago: University of Chicago Press

Herrup, Cynthia B. (1999), *A House in Gross Disorder: Sex, Law, and the 2nd Earl of Castlehaven*, New York: Oxfo University Press

Jackson, Mark (1996), *New-Born Child Murder: Women, Illegitimacy, and the Courts In Eighteenth-Century Englan* Manchester: Manchester University Press

Kellner, Hans (1989), *Language and Historical Representation: Getting the Story Crooked*, Madison: University Wisconsin Press

Lake, Peter (1993), 'Deeds Against Nature: Cheap Print, Protestantism, and Murder in Early Seventeenth-Centu England', in *Culture and Politics in Early Stuart England*, Kevin Sharpe and Peter Lake (eds), Basingstoke: Macmilla 257–83

Laqueur, Thomas W. (1989), 'Crowds, carnival and the state in English executions, 1604–1868', in *The First Moder Society*, A.L. Beier et al. (eds), Cambridge: Cambridge University Press, 305–55

Lawson, P.G. (1998), 'Patriarchy, Crime, and the Courts: The Criminality of Women in Late Tudor and Early Stua England', in *Criminal Justice in the Old World and the New*, Greg T. Smith, Allyson N. May, Simon Devereaux (eds Toronto: Centre of Criminology, 16–57

Lindley, David (1993), *The Trials of Frances Howard: Fact and Fiction at the Court of King James*, London and N Routledge

Linebaugh, Peter (1977), 'The Ordinary of Newgate and His *Account*', in *Crime in England 1550–1800*, J.S. Cockbu (ed.), Princeton: Princeton University Press

Luborsky, Ruth Samson (1987), 'Connections and Disconnections Between Images and Texts: the Case of Secular Tud Book Circulation, *Word & Image* 3 (1): 74–85

Marshburn, Joseph H. (1971), *Murder & Witchcraft in England, 1550–1640*, Norman: University of Oklahoma Press
McKenzie, Andrea (1998), 'Making Crime Pay: Motives, Marketing Strategies, and the Printed Literature of Crime in England', in *Criminal Justice in the Old World and the New*, Greg T. Smith, Allyson N. May, Simon Devereaux (eds), Toronto: Centre of Criminology, 235–69
Mendelson, Sara and Patricia Crawford (1998), *Women in Early Modern England 1550–1720*, Oxford: Oxford University Press
Plot, Robert (1677), *The Natural History of Oxfordshire, Being an Essay toward the Natural History of England*, Oxford
Roberts, Clayton (1996), *The Logic of Historical Explanation*, University Park, PA: Penn State University Press
Rollins, Hyder E. (1919), 'The Black-Letter Broadside Ballad', *PMLA* 34.2: 258–339
—— (1971), *A Pepysian Garland: Black-Letter Broadside Ballads of the Years 1595–1639*, Cambridge, MA: Harvard University Press
Rublack, Ulinka (1994), *The Crimes of Women in Early Modern Germany*, Oxford: Oxford University Press
Sawday, Jonathan (1996), *The Body Emblazoned: Dissection and the Human Body in Renaissance Culture*, London: Routledge
Sharpe, J.A. (1981), 'Domestic Homicide in Early Modern England', *Historical Journal* 24.1: 29–48
—— (1983), *Crime in Seventeenth-Century England: A County Study*, Cambridge: Cambridge University Press
—— (1985), '"Last Dying Speeches": Religion, Ideology and Public Executions in Seventeenth-Century England', *Past and Present* 107: 144–67
—— (1999), *Crime in Early Modern England 1550–1750*, Second edition, London: Longman
Somers, Margaret R. (1992), 'Narrativity, Narrative Identity and Social Action: Rethinking English Working-Class Formation', *Social Science History* 16.4: 591–630
Spufford, Margaret (1982), *Small Books and Pleasant Histories: Popular Fiction and Its Readership in Seventeenth-Century England*, Athens, GA: University of Georgia Press
Stachniewski, John (1991), *The Persecutory Imagination: English Puritanism and the Literature of Religious Despair*, Oxford: Oxford University Press
Stretton, Timothy (1998), *Women Waging Law in Elizabethan England*, Cambridge: Cambridge University Press
Travitsky, Betty S. (1990), 'Husband-Murder and Petty Treason in English Renaissance Tragedy', *Renaissance Drama* n.s. 21: 171–98
Walker, Garthine (1998), 'The Reading of Rape and Sexual Violence in Early Modern England', *Gender & History* 10.1: 1–25
Watt, Tessa (1990), 'Publisher, pedlar, pot-poet: The changing character of the broadside ballad, 1550–1640', *Spreading the Word: The distribution networks of print 1550–1850*, Winchester: St Paul's Bibliographies, 61–81
—— (1991), *Cheap Print and Popular Piety 1550–1640*, Cambridge: Cambridge University Press
White, R.S. (1996), *Natural Law in English Renaissance literature*, Cambridge: Cambridge University Press
Wiles, David (1987), *Shakespeare's Clown*, Cambridge: Cambridge University Press, 136–44
Wiltenburg, Joy (1992), *Disorderly Women and Female Power in the Street Literature of Early Modern England and Germany*, Charlottesville VA: University of Virginia Press

Acknowledgments

Securing reproductions of the large number of pamphlets in this volume as well as investigating the even larger pool of texts from which they are selected has made me more than usually indebted to the expertise and generosity of librarians and their institutions. I should like to thank the following people for their indispensable help: Aude Fitzsimons, the Pepys Library, Magdalene College, Cambridge; Geoffrey Groom, the Bodleian Library, Oxford; Susan Halpert, The Houghton Library, Harvard University; Christine Jack, Harriet Irving Library, University of New Brunswick; Adrian James, Society of Antiquaries of London; Susi Krasnoo, The Huntington Library; Ann Mar, The Huntington Library; Mona Noureldin, The Huntington Library; Sandra Powlette, The British Library; Monica Petraglia, the Newberry Library; Robert C. Ritchie, The Huntington Library; Michael Scott, the Folger Shakespeare Library; Stephen Tabor, The Huntington Library; David S. Zeidberg, The Huntington Library; Georgianna Ziegler, The Folger Shakespeare Library.

I wish also to thank the following libraries, besides those named above, for granting me permission to consult and reproduce material from their collections: Lambeth Palace Library, London; The Guildhall Library, London; Dr Williams's Library, London.

Research for this project was substantially supported by a grant from the Social Sciences and Humanitie Research Council of Canada. The Dean of Arts and the Vice-President, Academic, of the University of Ne Brunswick also generously underwrote part of the cost of microfilming texts.

I am very grateful to my colleagues Madeline Bassnett and Edith Snook for suggesting excellent improvemen to my introductory material and to Jennifer Bronson for proofreading it. My department's staff, Trac McDonald, Susan Miller, and Vera Zarowsky have helped me produce the volume with their usual cheerfu efficiency. And the series' general editors, Anne Lake Prescott and Betty S. Travitsky, have been steadfastl supportive throughout my work on this project and kindly offered me their knowledgeable advice an guidance.

RANDALL MARTI

A briefe discourse of the late murther of master George Saunders (*STC* 11985, signed A[rthur]. G[olding].) i reproduced with permission from the clear British Library copy (shelfmark C.40.a.36). The text-block measure 60 × 120 mm. The second edition (1577, *STC* 11986) is signed with the author's full name.

The following words are a transcription of the original:

A4v.23 cosentyng thereunto. Upon this confessiō he
B1r.24 she looked presently to lye downe) was
B1r.25 upon mistresse Druries

A briefe discourse of the late murther of master George Saunders, a worshipfull Citizen of London: and of the apprehension, arreignement, and execution of the principall and accessaries of the same:

(·:·)

G., A.
K

¶ *Imprinted at London by*
Henry Bynneman, dwelling in Knightriders *streete, at the signe of the Mermayde.*

ANNO. 1573.

FOrasmuche as the late murther of Master Saunders, Citizen and Merchant taylor of this Citie, ministreth great occasion of talk among al sorts of men, not only here in the Towne, but also farre abroade in the Countrie, and generally through the whole Realme: and the sequeles and accidents ensewing therevpon, breede muche diuersitie of reports & opinions, while some do iustly detest the horriblenesse of the vngratious facte, some lamente the greeuous losse of their deare friends, some reioyce at the commendable execution of vpright iustice, the godlye bewayle the vnmeasurable inclination of humane nature to extreame wickednesse, and therewith magnifie Gods infinite mercie in reuoking of forlorne sinners to finall repentance, many delight to heare and tell newes, without respect of the certentie of the truth, or regarde of dewe humanitie, euery man debating of the matter as occasion or affection leades him, and fewe folke turning the aduised consideration of Gods open iudgements, to the speedie reformation of their owne secrete faults: It is thought conuenient (gentle reader) to giue thee a playne declaration of the whole matter, according as the same is come to light by open triall of Iustice, and voluntarie confession of the parties, that thou mayst both knowe the truth to the satisfying of thy mind, & the auoyding of miscredite, and also vse the example to the amendment of thy life. Notwithstanding thou shalt not looke for a full discouerie of euery particuler bymatter appendant to the presente case, whiche mighte serue to feede the fond humor of such curious appetites as are more inquisitiue of other folkes offences than hastie to redresse their owne: for that were neyther expedient nor necessarie. And mens misdoings are to be prosecuted no further with open detestation, thã till the parties be eyther reclaymed by reasonable and godly perswasion, or punished by orderly and lawfull execution, according to the qualitie of their offence. When lawe hath once passed vpon them, and giuẽ them the wages of their wicked deserts: thẽ christian charitie willeth men eyther to burie the faults with the offendours in perpetual silence, or else so to speake of them, as the vices and not the parties them selues may seeme to be any more touched.

But hereof shall more be spoken (God

willing) in the winding up of this matter. Nowe I will set downe, first the marthering of master Saunders by George Brown, with Brownes apprehension, triall and execution: then the trial and execution of Anne Saunders, the wife of the sayd George Saunders, of Anne Drewrie widowe, and of Roger Clement, called among them trustye Roger, the seruant of the sayd Anne Drewrie: And lastlye a briefe rehearsall of certaine sayings and dealings of the parties conuicted, betwene the tyme of their apprehensions, and the tyme of their execution, whiche are not thinges proper and peculiar to the very bodie of the case, but yet incident, and therfore necessarie for the hearer, as wherby will appeare the verie originall cause and firste grounde of this ungodlye deede: And this rehearsall shall be shutte up and concluded with a shorte Admonition howe we ought to deale in this and al other suche cases.

The Tuisdaye in Easter weeke laste past (which was the xxiiij. day of March) the sayde George Browne receyuing secrete intelligence by letter from mistresse Drewrie, that master Saunders shoulde lodge the same nighte at the house of one Maister Barnes in Wolwich, and from thence go on foote to Saincte Marie Cray the nexte morning, met him by the way a little from Shooters hill, betwene seuen and eight of the clocke in the fore noone, and there slew both him, and also one John Beane the seruant of the said Master Barnes.

Assone as master Saunders felt himselfe to haue his deathes wounde (for hee was striken quite and cleane through at the first blowe,) he kneeled downe, and lifting vp his handes and eyes unto heauen, sayd, God haue mercie vpon mee, and forgiue me my sinnes, and thee to, (speaking to Browne, whome in deede he knewe not, whatsoeuer report hath beene made of former acquayntance betwixte them) and with that worde he gaue vp the Ghost. And Browne (as he himselfe confessed afterward) was forceably striken with suche a terrour and agonie of hart, as he wist not what to doo, but was at the poynt to haue fainted euen then and oftentimes else that day, and coulde brooke nother meate nor drinke that he receyued of all that day after. He was so abashed afterward at the sight of one of master Saunders little yong children, as he had much a doo to forbeare from swounding in the street, a notable example of the secret working of Gods terrible wrath in a giltie

and

and bloddie conscience. But M. Barnesis man hauing ten or eleuen deadly woundes, and being left for dead, did by Gods wonderfull prouidence reuyue againe, and creeping a great waye on all foure, (for hee could nother go nor stande) was founde by an old man and his mayden that went that way to seeke their kine, and conueyed to Wolwich, where he gaue euident tokens and markes of the murtherer: and so continewing still aliue till he had bin apprehended and brought vnto him, dyed the next Munday after. Immediatly, vpon the deede doing, Browne sente mistresse Drewrye worde thereof by trustie Roger, he himself repaired forthwith to the Court at Greenwich, and anone after him came thither the report of the murther also. Then departed he thence vnto London streightwayes, and came to the house of Mistresse Drewrie, howbeit he spake not personally with hir. But after conference had with him, by hir seruant Roger, she prouided him .xx. poundes the same day, for the which mistresse Drewry layde certaine plate of hir owne and of mistresse Saunders to gage.

And vpon the next day being Thursday morning (hauyng in the meane tyme had intelligence that Browne was soughte ler) they sent him fiue poundes more by the sayde Roger, and warned him to shifte for himselfe by flight, which thing he forslowed not to doe. Neuerthelesse the Lordes of the Queenes Maiesties Counsell, caused so speedie and narow searche to be made for hym in all places, that vpon the. 28. of the same moneth he was apprehended in a mans house of his own name at Rochester, by the Maior of the towne: and beeing broughte backe againe to the Courte, was examined by the Counsell, vnto whome he confessed the deede, as you haue hearde, and that he had oftentymes before pretended & soughte to do the same, by the instigation of the said widowe Drewrie, who (as he sayd) had promised to make a mariage betwéen him and mistresse Saunders, (whome he séemed to loue excessiuely,) the desire of whiche hope hasted him forwarde to dispatche the fact. Neuertheles he protested, (howbeit vntruly) ye mistres Saunders was not priuie nor consentyng thervnto. Vpon this confession he was arreigned at ye Kings Bench in Westminster Hal on friday ye xviij. of April, wher acknowledging himself guiltie, he was condemned as principall of the murther of master Saunders according to whiche sentence he was executed in Smithfield on monday

the

the .xx. of the same moneth, at which tyme (though vntruely, as she hir selfe confessed afterwarde) he laboured by all meanes, to cleare mistresse Saunders, of committing euill of hir bodie with him: and afterward was hanged vp in chaynes neere vnto the place where he had done the fact.

Thus much concerning the very case of the murther it selfe, and the punishment of the principall doer therof. As for the acknowledgement of the former wickednesse of his life, and the heartie repentance that he pretended for the same, euen to his very death; I deferre them to the laste parte of this matter, to which place those things do more peculiarly perteyne. In the meane time, mystresse Drevvrie and hir man being examined, and as well by their owne confessions, as by the falling out of the matter in consequence, and also by Brownes appeachment, thought culpable, were committed to warde. And anone after mistresse Saunders being deliuered of childe & churched (for at the time of hir husbands death she looked presently to lye downe) was vpon mistresse Drewries mans confession, and vpon other great likelyhoodes and presumptions likewise committed to warde, and on wednesday, the sixth of May, arreigned with mistresse Drewrie, at the Guilde hall, the effecte of whose seuerall inditements is this: That they had by a letter written, bene procurers of the sayde murther, and so accessaries before the fact: And knowing the murther done, had by money, and otherwise, relieued and bene ayding to the murtherer, and so accessaries also after the facte. Wherunto they both of them pleaded not giltie. And mistresse Saunders, notwithstanding the auouchement of mistresse Drewries man face to face, and the great probabilities of the euidence giuen in against hir by master Geffrey, the Queenes Maiesties Seriant, stoode so stoutly stil to the deniall of all things, (in which stoute deniall she continued also a certayne tyme after hir condemnation) that some were brought in a blinde beliefe, that either she was not giltie at al, or else had but brought hir selfe in danger of lawe through ignorance, and not through pretenced malice. Howbeit, forasmuche as bare deniall is no sufficient barre to discharge manyfest matter, and apparant euidence: they were both condemned as accessaries to master Saunders death, and executed in Smithfield the thirteenth of May, being the wednesday in the Whitsonweeke, at whiche time they

both

both of them confessed themselues guiltie of the facte, for which they were condemned, and with verye greate repentaunce and weakenesse, receyued the rewardes of their trespasse, in the presence of many personages of honor and worship, and of so great a number of people, as the like hathe not bene seene there togither in any mans remembraunce. For almoste the whole fielde, and all the way from Newgate, was as full of folke as coulde well stande one by another: and besides that, great companies were placed bothe in the chambers neere abouts (whose windowes & walles were in many places beaten downe to looke out at) and also vpon the gutters, sides, and toppes of the houses, and vpon the battlements and steeple of S. Bartholmewes.

Mistresse Drewries man was arreigned at Newgate on Friday the vij. of Maye, & being there condemned as accessarie, was executed with his mistresse, at the time and place aforesayd.

Thus haue ye heard the murthering of master Saunders, with the apprehension, arreignement, condemnation, and execution of the principall and of the accessaries to the same. Now let vs procede to the incidents that happed from the times of their apprehensions, to the time of their deathes, and so to the admonition, which is the conclusion and fruite of this whole matter.

Whereas it was determined that mistresse Saunders & mistresse Drewrie should haue suffered vpon the nexte saterday after their condemnation, whiche was Whitson euen: the matter was stayde till the wednesday in Whitson weeke, vpon these occasions ensuing. The booke of Maister Saunders accomptes and reckenings, wherevpon depended the knowledge of his whole state, was myssing. Certaine summes of money were sayde to be in the handes of parties vnknowne, the intelligence wherof was desyred and sought for to the behoofe of maister Saunders children. The parties condemned were to be reformed to Godwarde, and to be broughte to the willing confessing of the things for whiche they had bene iustly condemned, and whiche as yet they obstinatly concealed.

And besides al this, one Mell, a minister that had heretofore ben suspended from his Ministerie, accompanying mistresse Saunders, from hir condemnation to Newgate, and conferring with hir as it had bene to giue hir good counsell and comforte, was so blynded wyth hir solemne assenerations and protestations of innocencie, that notwithstanding he had heard hir inditement, with the exact and substantiall triall of hir case: yet notwithstanding, he perswaded himselfe that she was vtterly cleere, and thereuppon falling in loue with hir, dealte with mistresse Drewrie to take the whole guilt vpon hir selfe, vndertaking to sue for mistresse Saunders pardon. And so what by his terrifying of hir, with the horroure of mischarging and casting away of an innocent, what with his promising of certayne money to the mariage of hir daughter, and with other perswasions: she was so wholly wonne that way, that as wel before certaine personages of honour, as also before the Deane of Paules & others, she vtterly cleered mistresse Saunders of the facte, or of cōsent to the same, taking the whole blame thereof to hir selfe, and protesting to stande therin to the death, contrarie to hir former confession at the tyme of hir arreignement.

Mistresse Saunders also, after the laying of this platte, stoode so stoutely to hir tackling, that when the Deane of Paules gaue hir godly exhortation for the clearing of hir conscience, and for the recōciling of hir selfe vnto God, as the time and case most needefully required, (as other had done before) he could obtayne nothing at hir hande. By meanes whereof, he was fayne to leaue hir that time, which was the Friday, not without great griefe and indignation of mind to see hir stubborne unrepentauntnesse. In the meane while, the sayd Mell discouering his purpose and whole platforme to an honest Gentleman, whom he unskilfully toke to haue bin a welwiller to obtayne the pardon of mistresse Saunders, was partly by that meanes, and also by other follies of his owne, cut off from his enterprise. For when he came to sue for hir pardon, which thing he did with such outrage of doting affection, that he not only proffered summes of money, but also offered his owne body & life for the safety of the woman, whom he protested upon his conscience to be unguilty. The Lordes of the counsell knowing hir to be rightly condemned by good iustice, and being priuie to the state of the case before hand, and also finding him out by his owne unwise dealings (whereof among other one was, that he intended to marie hir) not only frustrated his desire, but also adiudged him to stande upon the pillorie, with apparant notes and significations of his lewde and folishe demeanour. According to the which award [illegible] he was set uppe a pillorie by the place of execution at the tyme of theyr suffering, with a paper pinned upon hys breast, wherein were written certain wordes in great Letters conteyning the effecte of his fact, to his open shame: *videlicet*, For practising to colour the detestable factes of George Saunders wife. Which was a very good lesson to teache all persons to refrayne frō any deuises or practises to deface or discredite the honorable proceedings of Counsellours, and publike & lawfull forme of trialles and iudgementes according to Iustice, or to hinder the beneficiall course of so good examples.

By this occasion Mistresse Sanders was utterly unprouided to die at that time, and therfore as well in respect of mercie, as for the considerations aforesaid, a further respite was giuen to them unwitting, and a repriue was sent by M. Mark Williams for a time if neede were. In the meane tyme, (that is to wit upon the saturday morning) the constant reporte goeth, that as certaine men came talking through Newgate, one happened to speake lowde of the gallowes that was set up, and of the greatnesse and strongnes of the same, saying it would hold them both and moe, the sounde of whiche wordes did so pierce into the watchfull

eares

eares of mistresse Saunders, who lay neare hand, that being striken to the heart with the horror of the present death which she looked for that day, she went immediatly to mistresse Drewrie, and telling hir that she knew certainely by the wordes which she had heard, that they should by all likelihode be executed that day, asked hir if she would stand to hir former promise. But mistresse Drewrie after better consideration of hir selfe, counselling hir to fall to playne and simple dealing: telling hir, that for hir owne parte she was fully determined not to dissemble any longer, nor to hazarde hir owne soule eternally for the safetie of an other bodies temporall life. Then Mistresse Saunders, who had determined to acknowledge nothing agaynst hir selfe, so long as she might bee in any hope of life, howbeit that she always purposed to utter the truth whensoever she should come to the instant of death, as she hir self confessed afterward: being striken both with feare and remorse, did by the aduise of master Cole, (who laboured verie earnestly with hir to bring hir to repentance, and was come to hir verye early that morning, because it was thought they shoulde haue bene executed presently) send for the Deane of Paules agayne, and

bewayling

bewayling hir former stubbarnes, declared vnto him and master Cole, master Charke, and master Yong, that shee had giuen hir consent and procurement to hir husbandes death, through vnlawfull luste and liking that she had to Brown, confessing hir sinfulnesse of life committed with him: and humbly submitting hirselfe to hir deserued punishment, besought them of spirituall comfort and councell, which thing they were glad to perceyue, and therevpon employed their trauell to do them good: and laboured very painfully to instruct them aright: for (God wote) they founde all the three prisoners very rawe and ignorant in all things perteyning to God & to their soule health, yea and euen in the very principles of the Christen religion. Neuerthelesse, through Gods good working with their labour, they recouered them out of Sathans kingdome vnto Christ, insomuch that besides their voluntary acknowledging of their late heinous fact, they also detested the former sinfulnesse of their life, and willingly yelded to the death which they had shunned, vttering such certaine tokens of their vnfayned repentance by all kinde of modestie & meekenesse, as no greater could be deuised. For Mistresse Saunders the same day sent for hir husbands brothers and their wiues and kinsfolke that were in the towne, whiche came vnto hir the day before hir death: in whose presence she kneeling mildely on hir knées, with aboundance of sorrowful teares, desired them of forgiuenesse for bereuing them of their deare brother and friende: whereunto maister Saunders the Lawyer in the name of them al answered, that as they were very sorie both for the losse of theyr friend, and also for hir heinous fault, so they heartily forgaue hir, and in token thereof knéeled downe altogyther, praying to GOD wyth hir and for hir, that hée also woulde remitte hir sinne.

Besides this pitiful submission, she also bewayled hir offence towardes hir owne kinred, whome she had stayned by hir trespas, and towardes the whole worlde, whom she had offended by hir crime, but especially hir children, whome she had not onely berefte bothe of father and mother, but also lefte them a coarsse and shame. Wherfore, after exhortation giuen to suche of them as were of any capacitie and discretion, that they shoulde feare God, and learne by hir fall to auoyde sinne: she gaue eche of those a booke of maister Bradfordes meditations, wherin she desired the foresayd thrée preachers thers to write some admonition as they thought good: Which done, she subscribed them with these wordes: Youre sorowfull mother Anne Saunders. And so blessing thē in the name of God & of our Saviour Jesus Christ, she sent thē away out of hir sorowfull sight, and gave hir selfe wholly to the settling of hir grieved heart to the quiet receiving of the bitter cup, which she dranke of the nexte day, as hath bene tolde before. Howbeit, without doubt, to hir everlasting comforte.

And mistresse Drewrie no lesse carefull of hir owne state, besides hir humble repentance in the prison, and hir earnest desiring of the people to pray for hir selfe, and the others with hir as they came towards execution, did upon the Carte not onely confesse hir giltinesse of the facte, as mistresse Saunders had don, but also with great lowlinesse and reverence first knéeling downe towards the Earle of Bedforde and other noble men that were on horssbacke on the East side of the stage, toke it upon hir death that whereas it had bin reported of hir that she had poysoned hir late husbande Master Drewrie, and dealt with witchcraft and sorcerie, and also appeached divers merchante mens wives of dissolute and unchast living,

she had done none of all those thinges, but
was vtterlie cleare bothe to God and
the worlde of all suche manner of dealing.
And then with like obeysance, turning hir
selfe to the Earle of Darbie, who was in a
chamber behinde hir, she protested vnto
him before God, that whereas she had bene
reported to haue bene the cause of separa-
tion betwixte him and my Lady his wyfe:
she neither procured nor consented to any
suche thing. But otherwise, wheras in the
time of hir seruice in his house, she had of-
fended him, in neglecting or contemning
hir duetie, she acknowledged hir fault, and
besoughte him for Gods sake to forgiue
hir: who very honorably, and euen with
teares accepted hir submission, and openly
protested him selfe to pray hartily to God
for hir.

Hir seruant also, hauing openly acknow-
ledged his offence, kneeled meekly downe,
praying seuerally with a preacher, as eche
of them had done at their first comming to
the place. Which done, they were all put in
a readinesse by the Executioner, and at one
instant (by drawing away the Cart wher-
on they stoode) were sent togither out of
this worlde vnto God.

And Browne also, a good while afore, during the time of his imprisonment, comming to a better minde than he had bene of in time paste, confessed that he had not heretofore frequented sermons, nor receiued the holy sacrament, nor vsed any calling vpon God priuate or publike, nor giuē him selfe to reading of holy Scripture, or any bookes of godlynesse: but had altogither followed the appetites and lustes of his sinfull flesh, euen with greedinesse and outragious contempt both of God and man. Neuerthelesse God was so good vnto him, and schooled him so well in that short time of imprisonment, as he cloased vp his life with a maruellous apparance of heartie repentance, constant trust in Gods mercy through Jesus Christ, and willingnesse to forsake this miserable worlde.

Nowe remayneth to shewe what is to be gathered of this terrible example, and how we oughte to apply the same to our owne behoofe. First I note with S. Paule, that when men regarde not to knowe God, or not to honour him when they know him: God giueth them ouer to their own lustes, so as they runne on from sinne to sinne, and from mischiefe to mischiefe, to do suche things as are shamefull and odious, euen in the sight of the worlde, to their owne vnauoidable perils. And when the measure of their iniquitie is filled vp, there is no way for them to escape the iustice of God, which they haue prouoked. Insomuche, that if they might eschue all bodily punishment: yet the very hell of their owne conscience would prosecute them, and the sting of their minde would be a continuall prison, torment, and torture to them, wheresoeuer they went. Agayne on the other side, we must marke the infinit greatnesse of Gods wisdome and mercy, who perceyuing the peruerse wilfulnesse of mans frowarde nature to sinning, suffreth men sometimes to runne so long vpon the bridle, till it seeme to themselues, that they may safely do what they liste, and to the worlde, that they be past recouerie vnto goodnesse: and yet in the end catching them in their chiefe pride, he rayseth them by their ouerthrow, amendeth them by their wickednesse, and reuiueth them by their death, in such wise blotting out the stayne of their former filthe, that their darknesse is turned into light, and their terrour to their comfort. Moreouer, when God bringeth such matters vpon the stage, vnto ye open face of the worlde: it is not to the intent that men should gaze and wonder at the persons, as by [illegible] an Owle, not that they should delight them selues & others with the fond & peraduenture sinister reporting of them, nor vpbrayd the whole stocke and kinred with the fault of the offenders: no surely, God meaneth no such thing. His purpose is, that the execution of his iudgements, should by the terrour of the outward sight of the examples, driue vs to the inward cōsideration of our selues. Beholde, wee bee all made of the same moulde, printed with the same stampe, and indued with the same nature that the offenders are. We be the impes of the olde Adam, and the venim of sinne whiche he receiued from the olde serpent, is shedde into vs all, and worketh effectually in vs all. Suche as the roote is, suche are the braunches, and the twiggs of a thorne or bramble can beare no grapes. That we stande, it is the benefite of Gods grace, and not the goodnesse of our nature, nor the strengths of oure owne will. That they are falne, it was of frayltie: wherfrom we be no more priuileged than they: and that shoulde we ouersoone perceiue by experience, if we wer left to our selues. He that looketh seuerely into other mennes faultes, is lightly blynd in his owne: and he that either vpbraydeth the repentant that hath receyued punishement.

parent, or reprocheth the kinred or offspring with the fault of the auncester or alye, how greate so euer the same hath ben: shewteth himselfe not to haue any remorse of his owne sinnes, nor to remember that he him selfe also is a man: but (which thyng he woulde little thinke) he fully matcheth the crime of the misdoer, if he do not surmount it by his presumptuousnesse.

When it was tolde oure Sauiour Christ that Pylate had mingled the bloud of certain men with their owne sacrifise, what aunswere made hee? Did hee detest the offenders? did he declame against their doings? Did he exaggerate the fault of the one, or the crueltie of the other? No. But framing and applying the example to the reformation of the hearer, suppose ye (sayd he) that those Galileans wer greater sinners than all the other Galileans, bycause they suffered such punishment? I tell you nay: but except ye repente, ye shall all likewise perish. Or think ye that those eighteene upon whom the toure in Silo fell, and slew them, were sinners aboue all y^t dwelt in Hierusalem? I tel you nay: but except ye repent, ye shall all perishe likewise. Let us applie this to our presente purpose. Were those whō we saw iustly executed in Smith
field.

held greater sinners than al other English people? were they greater sinners than all Londoners? Were they greater sinners thā all that loked upon them? No verily: but except their exāple leade us to repentance, we shall all of us come to as sore punishement in this worlde, or else to sorer in the worlde to come. Their faults came into the open Theater, & therefore semed the greater to our eyes, and surely they were great in dede: neyther are ours the lesse, bicause they lye hidden in the couert of oure hearte. God the searcher of all secrets seeth them, and if he list he can also discouer them. He hath shewed in some, what al of us deserue, to prouoke us al to repentance, that al of us myght haue mercie at his hand, and shewe mercie one to an other, & with one mouthe and one hearte glorifie his goodnesse. It is sayde by the Prophete Samuel, that disobedience is as the sinne of Witchcrafte. Lette euery of us loke into himselfe (but first lette him put on the spectacles of Gods lawe, and carie the lyghte of Gods worde with him) and he shall see suche a gulfe of disobedience in himselfe, as he maye well thinke there is none offender but himselfe. I say not this as a cloaker of offences, that white should not be called white, & blacke:

blacke: or as a patrone of misdoers, that
they shoulde not haue their deserued hyre:
but to represse our hastie iudgementes and
vncharitable speeches, that we myght both
detest wickednesse with perfect hatred, and
rue the persons with christē modestie: kno-
wing that with what measure we met vn-
to others, with the same shall it be moten
to vs agayne.

Finally, let al folkes both maried and vn-
maried, learne hereby to possesse and keepe
their vessell in honestie and cleannesse. For
if the knot betwene man and wife (whiche
ought to be inseparable) be once broken, it
is seldome or neuer knit again. And though
it be, yet is not the wound so throughly hea-
led, but there appeereth some skarre euer af-
ter. But if the sore rancle & fester inwardly
(as commonly it doth except the more grace
of God be) in the end it bursteth forth to the
destructiō or hurt of both parties, not light-
ly without great harme to others also be-
sides themselues, as we see by this example.
For when the body which was dedicated to
God to be his temple and the tabernacle of
his holy spirite, is become the sinke of sinne
and cage of vncleannesse the deuill ceasseth
not to driue the parties still headlong vnto
naughtinesse, till they be falne eyther into
open

open shame and daunger of temporall law: or into damnable destruction both of body soule, according as Salomon in his Prouerbes sayth, that the steps of a harlot leade downe vnto death, and hir feete perce euen vnto hell. Therefore good reader, so heare and reade this present example, as the same may turne to the bettering of thy state, and not to occasion of slaunder, nor to the hurt of thine owne conscience, nor to the offence of thy Christian brethren.

Farewell. A.G.

Anne Saunders confession as she spake it at the place of execution.

GOod people, I am come hither to die the deathe, whereunto I am adiudged, as worthely & as deseruedly as euer died any: I had a good husband, by whom I had manie children, with whom I liued in wealth, & might haue done stil, had not the deuill kindled in my hearte, first the hellish firebrand of vnlawfull lust, & afterward a murtherous intent to procure my saide husbande to be bereued of his life, which was also by my wicked meanes accomplished, as to the world is known. And as I woulde if he coulde heare me, if it might be, prostrate vpon the ground, at my husbands feete, aske mercy with plentiful teares of him, so that which I may & I oughte to doe, I aske mercye of God, I aske mercie of all men and women of the world, whō by my deede & example I haue offended: and especiallye I be-

bewaile my husbande, & aske mercie of my childrē whōe I haue beraued of so good a father, I aske mercy of his kindred and frendes whome I haue hurt, & of all my frends & kindred, of whom I am abashed and ashamed: and beyng of my selfe vnworthy of pittie, yet I besech them all, & you all, & all the whole worlde euen for gods sake, and for our sauiour Christs sake to forgiue me. And I thank God with my whole harte, he hathe not suffered me to haue the reigne and bridle of sinning gyuen me at my will, to the daunger of my eternall damnatiō, but that he hath founde out my sin, & brought me to punishment in this world, by his fatherly correctiō, to amend, to spare, and saue me in the world to come: & I beseche him graunte me his heauenly grace, that all who do behold or shall heare of my death, maye by the example therof be frayed from like sinning. And I besech you all to pray for me and with me.

The Prayer whiche was said by Anne Saunders at the place of execution, the copie wherof, she deliuered vnto the right honourable the Earle of Bedforde.

AS I doe confesse vvyth great sorrovv (O deare father) that I haue grieuously, and oftentimes sinned againste heauen and against thee, & am vnvvorthy to be called thy daughter, so (O deare Father) I acknovvledge thy mercy, thy grace and loue tovvards me, most vvretched sinner, offred me in my Lorde and sauiour Iesus Christe, in vvhom thou giuest me an hearte to repent. And by repentance hast put away my sinnes, and throvvne them into the bottome of the Sea, O deare Father encrease and continue this grace vntill the ende, and in the ende. I testifie this day (O Lord my God) thy loue, O Lorde, thy sauing health is life euerlasting, and ioy without end: and bicause thou hast touched my sinfull heart with the pleasure of my sinne, and with a de- of thy kingdome, O deare Father, f thy Christes sake, as I hope thou wilt, so I beseeche thee to finishe that good worke in me. Suffer me not, mercifull and louing Father, to be troubled with death when it layeth holde on me: nor with the loue of life, when it shalbe taken away. O Lorde, nowe as thou hast, so still lifte vp my soule as it were with an eagles wings vnto Heauen, there to beholde thee. Lorde into thy hands I commit my body, that it be not troubled in death, and my soule, that it see not damnation. Come Lorde Iesu, come assiste me with thy holy spirite, a weake womā in a strong battell, come Lord Iesu, come quickly saue thy handmaide that putteth hir trust in thee, behold me in Christ, receiue me in christ, in whose name I pray saying. Our Father. &c.

Anne Sāders dying to the world, and liuing to God.

After this she also said a godly Prayer out of the Seruice boke, which is vsed to be said at the hour of death

note of a certaine saying vvhich Master Saunders had lefte written with his owne hand in his studie.

Christe shalbe magnified in my body, whither it be thorough life or else death. For Christe is to me life, and death is to me aduauntage. These wordes were. M. Nowels Theame which he preached at the buriall of my brother Haddon vpon Thursday beyng ỹ xxv. day of Ianuarie *Anno. Do.1570. Anno. Reginæ Elizabeth.*13. Amōg other things which he preached, this saying of his is to be had alwayes in remembrance, that is, that we must all (when we come to pray) first accuse and cōdemne our selues for our sinnes committed against God before the seate of hys Iustice, and then after cleaue vnto him by faythe in the mercy and merites of our Sauioure and Redéemer Iesus Christ, whereby we are assured of eternall saluation.

A View of sundry Examples (*STC* 18281) is reproduced with permission from the clear Lambeth Palac Library copy. The text-block measures 60 × 125 mm.

The following words are a transcription of the original:

A2r.22	to your discretions construed
A2r.23	gathering these reports
A2r31	simple,
A3r.1	*Hercules* hearing the fine forged eloquence, of this
A3r.12	Vine the best Grapes:
A3r.21	should bee euer the more mooued
A3r.22	should refuse larger proffers
A3v.22	hazarding on your courtesyes
A3v.23	to your celemencies with the *Basoles*
A3v.24	*manos*)
B1v.17	Beholde, how the world is giuen to wickednesse,
B1v.18	for one disdayneth that his neyghbour should thriue by
B1v.19	him, another coueteth his neyghbours goodes vniustly
B2r.1	commendation and good report that followeth a godlie
B2r.2	and virtuous life.
C3r.26	what straunge births? and what alteration
C3r.27	of Nature haue wee seen? In Gelderland, a
C3r.28	Childe borne, of proportion very ougly with a long
C3r.29	bil and the belly like a Swan, feet with clawes, and

A VIEVV of ſundry Examples.

Reporting many ſtraunge *murthers, ſundry perſons periu-*red, Signes and tokens of Gods anger to-wards vs. What ſtraunge and mon-ſtrous Children haue of late beene borne:

And all memorable murthers ſince the murther of Maiſter *Saunders* by *George Brovvne*, to this preſent and bloody murther of *Abell Bourne* Hoſyer, who dwelled in Newgate Market. 1580.

Alſo a short diſcourſe of the late Earthquake the ſixt of Aprill. Gathered by A. M.

Honos alit Artes.

Imprinted at London for William Wright, and are to be ſold at the long ſhop, adioyning vnto S. Mildreds Church in the Poultrie.

9

A VIEW
of sundry Examples.

TO THE WORSHIPfull Maister *VVilliam Waters*, and *Maister* George Baker, *Gentlemen*, attendaunt on the Right Honourable, his singuler good Lord and Maister, the Earle of *Oxenford*.

A. M. vvisheth vvhat happines in this life is to be gained; and in the life to come, an immortall Crovvne of glorie.

THe Souldier *hauing* once ventured, and tryed the fauoring of Fortune, in bloody fight among his enemies (speeding well) hazardeth his hap the bolder the secod time. The Merchaunt making one lucky voyage: presumeth on the next, with greater affectiō. So I (worshipfull and my approoued freendes,) hauing once found freendly entertainement, to my booke receiued: am the more encouraged to present this also, referring the good meaning and freendly affection of the Author, to your discretions construed at leysure. I know that in gathering these reports, I shall offend the curious eares of some daintie deuisers: and I consider againe that the wise will allowe my labours to good end, so that pleasing your Woorships, and the mindes of other well disposed persons: I shall thinke my labours well bestowed, and my time not ill spent. *Cicero* I remember, reporteth, how there appeared vnto *Hercules*, two Maidens, the one attired base and simple, the other decked in sundry sutes of very gor-

Cicero. li. 1. Officio.

A.ii. gious

A proper discourse of the choyse of Hercules.

gious and gallant apparell; promising eche of them, such rewards as their habillitie might suffer them to bestowe: if according to their mindes he made his choyse. Fyrst quoth she so simply attired.

The simple maiden, named Vertue.

If thou choose me, consider what may fall.
thou in this life shalt be of wretched state:
And of account thou shalt be verie small,
But last of all, thou shalt proove fortunate.
Eternall ioy so much shall vauntage thee:
That thy good Fame then honored shalbe.

The braue Maiden, named Vaine Pleasure.

The other gallant Girle, shining like the Sunne, glistering in her golde, sweating in her silkes, braue in her beautye, comely in complexion, finely featured according to fancy, euery lim gallantly ioynted, and pounsed vp in her perfuming and odiferous smels, sayde.

Loe heere the golden promises that Vaine Pleasure maketh, to such as are easy to be intised.

If thou like me, and wilt me make thy wife,
So long as life within thee dooth remaine:
All vvorldly pompe with thee shalbe so rife,
That none but thou the golden dates shall gaine.
Thy riches shall aboundantlie exceede:
All thy desires shall graunted be with speede.

Thou in this world shalt be of rare renovvne,
and Glorie shall attendaunt on thee stand:
No labour shal once seeme to pul thee downe,
But thou shalt liue at ease vpon the Land.
Hovv saist thou novv? consider vvhat these be
Then goe to her, or els come vnto me.

Hercules.

Hercules hearing the fine forged eloquence of this delicate Dame; and how her offers were so good that he cared not for them: ran and embraced the simplest, which he found moste to his contentation. Heereby (woorshipfull) what is meant: I knowe you are not ignorant; the simplenesse of my capacitie, the meanesse of my learning, with the lack of eloquence, causeth my booke to sound nothing pleasaunt to the daintie eare.

But as the newest Vessels holde not the sweetest wine, the tallest tree not the pleasantest fruite, nor the biggest Vine the best Grapes: So perhaps the largest labours, containes not such Methode of matter: as a small volume may sufficiently vnfolde, nor the moste learned Preacher edifie not so much: as one that professeth lesse learning.

Hercules reposed greater creditin the simpler then in the brauer, and therefore he chose her, & therefore wee may heereby see that all is not golde that glistereth, nor all are not freends that are noted freendship.

Euen so some tymes may bee couched more promptnesse of wit, and more cunning conueyaunces vnder a plaine Countrey Cap: then perhaps vnder a Hat of Veluet. I speake not this, that your affection should bee euer the more moued to this simple gift, or that you should refuse larger proffers to prefer so meane a trifle: But this I may (vnder correction) boldely say, and also sufficiently discharge, that the quantitie and quallitie of good wyll, may as well be manifested in a sheete of Paper, as in a Booke of greater estimation. For surely if his affection be not to that man, on whom so euer he bestoweth so small a present: hee will not (you may be sure) commend to him the greater.

Munera sunt estimanda, non pretio suo, sed animo donantis.

So that by this you will iudge; that I make as much account of my sheete of Paper: as other doo of a larger volume. I aunswer, that if I looue my freend a little, and looue him long: it is better then looue him a great deale at the first, and neuer a whit after.

Loue me little, and loue me long.

Thinke not hereby (woorshipfull) that I enuye any way gainst writers of large and auncient volumes, for thereby I should condemne my selfe of meere folly, and displease a number that haue delight therin. Only this is my meaning, that this small Pamphlet. I offer with as free good will, as if I could present you with a bigger Booke, and that in this little labour, is contained as much affection, and as liberally bestowed: as any hee whatsoeuer that offreth a greater gift.

Luke. 2. 1.

The poore Widdowes mites pleased Christe better then the riches that the other offred. And the Cup of Whater presented to *Zerxes*, was as Princely receiued as a greater present: Then am not I in doubt, but that I shall like you with this little, & please you with this poore Pamphlet. If so it may chaunce: I haue my choise, and if it like you well, I haue my will. Thus hazarding on your courtesyes, and trusting to your clemencies: with the *Basiles wiues* I bid you farewell hartely.

Yours to commaund in
greater affaires, then he
minded to make his boast
Antony Munday.

TO THE COVRTEOVS company of Gentlemen, whose good *will and freendly affection is my* wished desire to obtayne, Greeting.

BVt that my want of learning, and eloquence to beautifye my stile withall, is so great a blemish to my bolde attempt: I should (courteous Gentlemen) thinke that this my booke would be gratefully accepted. But finding my self nothing acquainted with the one, and farre vnlike to gaine the other. I perswade my selfe, that I were better to shrowde in silence my simplicitie: then to let it passe beeing nothing woorthy. Yet finding my selfe so greatly bound in duty to your courtesyes so liberally bestowed, I thought (though I were vnhable to requite with the very vttermoste of my power) yet your courtesyes would accept of my good wil sygnifyed any way. And that though I am the simplest (yet synce mightie and puissant Emperours, haue vouchsaued to heare the meane stile of vnlearned Oratours) Gentilitie, adorned with clemencye (though they are vsually frequented

with

with the woorks of famous and worthy writers (they would (if it were but for pleasures sake) attend the homely note of a Countrey Coridon, and among the rest be content to heare so rude a Chaos as I. Thus leauing at large your courtesyes to conster my good intent, and to rewarde as shall like you best, praying for your continuall prosperitie: to God I commend ye.

Your affectioned freend
A. Munday, Seruaunt to the right
Honorable, the Earle of *Oxenford*.

¶ *To the Reader.*

GOod Reader suffise thee,
with this my good will:
Till I may deuise thee,
things woorthy of skill.
If thou doo content thee,
with this my poore wish:
Ere long shalbe sent thee,
a Delicate Dish.
Where thou shalt haue plentye,
fine toyes for thy pleasure:
Then seeme not too daintie,
but iudge this with measure.

A

A view of Examples, meete *to be peruſed of all faythfull* Chriſtians.

Iob. 14.

Man that is borne of a Woman hath but a ſhort tyme to lyue, and is full of miſerie, he commeth vp, and is cut downe like a flower, he flyeth as it were a ſhadowe.

WHereas we ſee (by perfect experience) that man is ſubiecte to many miſfortunes, multitudes of myſeries, yea, many and ſundrie miſchaunces, so that in this terreſtriall vale of myſerie, he bœing ſo fiercely aſſaulted by the miſcheuous motions, and ſharpe aſſaultes of his olde and auncient enimie: no ſuccour is lefte him, nor no comfort to cure him, but onely in heart and minde to flye to his ſwœte Sauiour and redéemer Jeſus Chriſte, to annimate him with continuall conſtancie, to vpholde him by his grace and mercie, and to arme him bodily with pure and ſincere fayth, which is able to confound al his vſurping enimies. For fayth is the victorie of this world, as wytneſſeth *Iohn* ſaying. And this is the victorie that ouercommeth the world, euen our fayth: vvho is it that ouercommeth the world: but he which beleeueth that Ieſus

Man ſubiect to many and ſundry miſeries.

His only hope in Chriſt Jeſus, which cõfoundeth all his foes

1. Ioh. 5. 4. 5.

Faith the onely weapon to vanquishe al the cares and troubles of this world.

Christe is the sonne of God. Then, since our fayth is the onelie weapon, wherewith we many wholy vanquish and subdue, all the ennormities of this lyfe, all the troubles, vexations, temptations, illusions, and all enemies whatsoever: let vs imbolden our selues vppon our Captaine Christe, let vs cast all our care on him: and he wyll goe to fielde with vs, he wyll shielde vs from our enmies, his mightie arme shall so protect vs: that all our foes shall runne on theyr owne confusion.

Psa.18.32. It is God that gyrdeth vs with strength of warre, and maketh our wayes perfect. Then mortall man, neuer boast so much of thy terrestriall strength, which is but a shadowe:

Psa.121.1. But cast vp thine eyes to heauen, from where commeth thy helpe: The helpe that is alway forceable, and wyll strike all thy enimies downe to the ground.

The world bent to all kinde of wickednes.

Beholde, howe the world is giuen to wickednesse, for one disdayneth that his neyghbour should thriue by him, another couteteth his neyghbours goodes vniustly, some one is bent to this vice, some to that. Some care not so they lyue in theyr iollitie and pleasure: who goeth to wracke, whome they murder, whome they spoyle, the proofe whereof is euident.

Example of George Browne, who murthered maister George Saunders.

NOt long since, one George Browne, a man of stature goodly and excellent: if lyfe and deedes thereto had beene equiualent. But as the auncient Adage is, goodly is he that goodly dooth, and comely is he that behaueth him selfe comely: so may it be witnessed in this man, who more respected a vaine pride and prodigall pleasure, which remayned in his person: then the commen-

commendation and good report that followeth a godlie and vertuous life.

But nowe a dayes, euerie couragious cutter, euerie Him swashbuckler, and euerie desperate Dick, that can stand to his tackling lustely, and behaue him selfe so quarrelously, that he is ashamed of all good and honest company: He is a gallant fellowe, a goodly man of his handes, and one I promise you, that as soone comes to Tyborne, as euer a one of them all. This is a vaine-glorious vertue (which some terme it) but it can be called no vertue, because it dependeth not vppon any goodnesse.

A blow to vaine vaunters.

A fellow worthy of commendation.

This George Browne (before named) addicted to the voluptuousnesse of this vaine world, to vnlawfull lyking, to runne at his lybertie in all kinde of lewde behauiour, murdred cruelly maister George Saunders, an honest, vertuous, and godly Cittizen, well knowne, of good name and fame, among his neyghbours well thought of, abroade and euery where, well esteemed, of wealth well stored, of credit well allowed, of lyuing Christianly disposed: and of those that knewe him, well beloued.

A report of maister Saunders.

This man beeing mette by this George Browne (who by the consent of maister Saunders wife, was appoynted to kyll him) after he perceyued what was his intent, and howe he sought to bathe his handes in his gyltles blood: fell to entreataunce, that pittie might take place in his bloody brest.

George Browne meeting him by S. Mary Cray.

But he a wretch, more desirous of his death: then wylling to his welfare, more mindfull of murther: then safegard of his soule, so bent to blindnesse; that he aspected not the light: stroke the stroke that returned his shame, dyd the deede that droue him to destiny, and fulfilled the fact, that in the end he found folly.

His diuelish intent & peruerse practises.

O minde most monstrous, O heart most hard, O intent

A hard heart that-could doo so cruell a deede. tent so yrksome, whome neyther preferment might perswade, rytches moue to regard, affection cause to respect, former frendship force to fancie, nor no vertue of the minde seeme to satisfie. Where was the bonds of loyaltie? where was the regard of honestie? where was the feare of the Almightie? where was the care of Christianitie? or where was the hope of eternall felicitie? and last, where was thy duty to God, thy Prince and Countrey? Alas, each of these seemed cleane vanquished in thee, they were smally regarded, yea, lyttle or none accompt made of. It is yet euidently seene in that common crew, that giue themselues to boasting and brauery, to swearing, fighting, quarrelling, and all such diuelish practises, but what sayth *Esai*. Shall the Axe boast it self against him that heweth therwith: or shall the Sawe make any bragging against him that ruleth it. That were euen lyke, as if the rod did exalt it self against him that beareth it, or as though the staffe should magnify it self (as who should say) it were no wood.

All feare of God cleane layd a side.

Esai.10.15.

Pro.17.1. And *Salomon* sayth. Make not thy boast of to morowe, for thou knowest not what a day may bring foorth.

The Prophet *Dauid* lykewise sayth. Howe long shall all wicked dooers speake so disdaynfully, and make such proude boasting. They smite downe thy people, O Lord, and trouble thine heritage. They murder the vviddow and the Straunger, and put the fatherlesse to death.

Psa.xc4.5.6

With many places more, that I might alleadge of the Scripture, of such as brag in their brauerie: and boast in their owne strength. But this example passed, may seeme somewhat to terrifie our stony hearts, to consider, through the misbehauiour of one man: Six lost theyr lyues, as it is euidently knowen to all men, for in Smithfeeld they payed the price of their lyues, for consenting to that odious fact.

Though the lewde life of one man, six lost theyr lyues.

It shall not be amisse in this place, to call to minde the wylfull periurie of certayne persons ; whose wicked lyues, at their death were perfectly wytnessed. Examples of periury.

Example of widdowe Barnes, in Cornhyll in London. 1574.

Let vs remember the widdow Barnes, béeing an auncient Woman, and dwelling in Cornhyll in London, who frequented much swearing, & neither friendly rebuking, godly instructions, nor diuine perswasions could turne her heart from this wicked and detestable exercise, but thereby laboured to defeat an Orphant of her right : the Diuell who droue her to such cruell abuse, caused her to cast her selfe out at her windowe into the streete, and there brake her neck.

She threw her self into the streete, and brake her neck.

Example of Arthur Myller, at Hackney, in. 1573.

One Arthur Miller, lykewise dwelling at Hackney, a very lewde talker, a common blasphemer & swearer, in the tyme of his sicknesse, casting all Christianlike care from him, and all feare of God and his Lawes: vehemently cryed out, the Diuell, the Diuell, yet felt he the omnipotency of Gods power, as himselfe confessed: but for grace he could not pray, the cause whereof was knowen to himselfe, but he would not utter it to any. And so kissing oftentymes his hand, wherein he sayd he held the Diuell, and calling alwayes for helpe to the Diuell: this wretched lyfe he ended most miserably.

Example of one Berry who cut his owne throate in the Counter in the Poultry. 1575.

In the Counter in the Poultry in London, also there was one Berry, who in some one cause had wylfully periured him selfe, and beeing brought therefore to the prison, to sustayne what punishment thereto was due: he despayring of Gods mercie, and giuing him selfe to the Diuells temptations, cruellie cut his owne throte.

Example of Anne Aueries, that bought the Towe. 1575. Febru. 11.

ANne Aueries, likewise a widdowe, who dwelled in Duck Lane without Aldersgate, comming to the house of one Richard Williamson in Woodstreete, whose Wife vsed to dresse Flax and Towe, she tooke vp there sixpennie of Towe, and departed without paying therefore, when she was required eyther to send the Towe againe, or to pay money therefore: by and by she rapt out two or three terrible oathes, that she had payde for it, and beeing come back to the shoppe, she desired vengeance at Gods handes, that she might presently sincke where she stoode, if she payde not the money before she went out of the shoppe. Gods iudgement so iust, seeing her vniust

Gods iust iudgement fell on this wicked person.

dealing, presently accorded thervnto, and before the face of all the standers by, she was immediatly stroke to the earth, not able to rise without help, nor yet to blaspheme the name of God as she had done: but holding out her left hand, wherein she held thirteene pence, which she

A notable & straunge example to terrify all wicked and cruell blasphemers.

should before haue payed for the Towe withall, and her mouth beeing put to such a vyle office, that from thence issued that which should haue discended at the lower partes. So was she caried from thence, where she was fayne to lye in a stynking stable, and few dayes after yeelded her life.

Example of Father Lea. 1577.

FAther Lea, a man almost of foure score yeeres, in Foster Lane in London, meeting with the party against

whome

whome he had periured him selfe: held up his handes, desiring him to forgiue him, for that he had falsly forsworn himselfe against him. The man replyed, that the offence against him might be easily forgiuen: but the offence against God was ten tymes more. So after in a whyle, this Father Lea, with a rusty knife, rypped his owne belly, and griped his guts with his owne handes, and so ended his life the. xxi. of Ianuary, 1579. He rypped his owne belly.

Lo deere Christians, what examples we can fetch of our selues, what neede we to looke after other Countryes: these we know to be true, and we cannot deny it: but alas, how long shall we remaine in this wickednes, when we heare God himself say.

If a soule sinne and trespasse against the Lord, and deny vnto his neighbour, that which was taken him to keepe, or that was put in his handes, or doth violent robbery, or wrong vnto his neighbour. Leuit. 6. 2.

Or if he haue found that which was lost, and denieth it, and sweareth falsely vpon whatsoeuer thing it be that a man dooth, and sinneth therin. 3.

If he so sinned and trespassed: he shall restore again that he tooke violently away, or the wrong which he did, or that which was deliuered him to keep, or the lost thing which he found. 4.

And all that about which he hath sworne falsely: he shal restore it againe in the whole sum, and shall adde the fift part more therto, and giue it vnto him, to whome it apertayneth, the same day that he offreth for his trespasse. 5.

Thou shalt not sweare by my name falsely; neither shalt thou defile the name of thy God: I am the Lord. Leui. 19. 12.

The wise and famous Salomon, lykewise sayth. Let not thy mouth be accustomed with swearing, for in it are many falles, let not the naming of God be continually in thy mouth. Eccl. 29. 9.

For like as a seruaunt that is much beaten, can not be without some sore: euen so, whatsoeuer he be that sweareth 10.

reth and nameth God , shall not be cleane purged from sinne.

11. A man that vseth much swearing , shalbe filled with wickednes,and the plague shal neuer go from his house,if he beguyle his brother: his faulte shalbe vpon him, if he knowledge not his sinne:he maketh a double offence,and if he sweare in vaine: he shall not be found righteous,for his house shalbe full of plagues.

12. The words of the swearer bringeth death (God graunt that it be not found in the house of *Iacob*) but they that feare God,will eschew all such,and lye not weltring in sin.

13. Vse not thy mouth to vnhonest and filthy talking: for in it is the word of sinne.

15. The man that is accustomed with the wordes of blasphemy: wyl neuer be reformed all the dayes of his lyfe.

Zach.5.2. *Zacharias* the Prophet also sayth Behold a flying book, of twenty cubits long, and ten cubits broade.

3. This is the curse that goeth forth ouer the vvhole earth, for all theeues shalbe iudged according to this book.

4. And I will bring it foorth (sayth the Lord of hostes) so that it shall enter into the house of the theefe, and into the house of him that falsly sweareth by my name, and shal remayne in the middest of his house, and consume it,with the tymber and stones therof.

Leui.24.15. And further lyst what God sayth. And thou shalt speak vnto the chyldren of Israel,saying. Who soeuer curseth his God: shall beare his sinne.

16. And he that blasphemeth the name of the Lord:let him be slayne, and all the multitude shall stone him to death: vvhether he be borne in the Land,or a Straunger, vvhen he blasphemeth the name of the Lord,let him be slayne.

Thus deerely beloued, are we warned by the sacred Scripture, to take heede and to be cyrcumspect in our dealyngs, not for euerie tryfling thing, to rappe out othes, for therein we hyghlie offend the Maiestie of God.

Example

Example of Paule Green that slevv Maister Temple.

NOw wil I returne to my former matter again, as touching murder, which is a hainous and abhominable offence in the sight of God and man. I must not forget the committed crime of Paule Green, who desperatly slew Maister Thomas Temple neer to the Royall exchaunge in London, the which Maister Temple was a sober, wise and discreet Gentleman, one of godly liuing, and taking a house to saue him self from the vnsatiable malice of this Paul Grẽe, could not so appease his ire, for he thrust ouer the stall at him, & at length gaue him that hee long looked for. But what became therof? hee for his paines condemned by law and iustice: ended his despetat dayes at Tiburn.

The author returneth to his former matter.

Paul Green hanged at Tiburn.

Example of the tvvo Sheriffes that hung them selues at Glocester, 1579.

IT is commonly reported and is in euery mans mouth, how this last yeere at Gloocester two men in yeers ancient, supposed to be very godly liuers and were called to the bearing authoritie in the Citie, as to wit, bothe of them hath been Sheriffes, yet for want of firme & faithful trust in God, they bothe hanged them selues.

Example of Iohn Morgan vvho slevv Maister Turberuile in Somerset shire. 1580.

LIkewise in Sommersetshire, one Iohn Morgan by common reporte a lewd and wicked liuer, and giuen to swearing, roysting, and all wickednes abounding in him, slew his Brother in law Maister Turberdile a Gentlemā of godly life, very sober, wise and discreet, whose wife lying in Childbedde, yet arose and went to haue law and iustice pronounced on that cruel malefactor. So at Chard before the Lord chief Iustice, hee was condemned and suffered death for his offence. 1580.

Example of Richard Tod that murdered Mistresse Skinner at Saint Katherins. 1580.

THen let vs rehearse the bloody parte of Richard Tod who murdered and cruelly massacred an auncient and honest woman dwelling at Saint Katherins named Mistres Skinner, a woman of godly dispositiō of life inferiour to few, for friendly neighbourhod beloued of all, in yeeres wel passed, of credit wel accounted, & of mony and riches sufficiently instored, to whome this bloody Butcher, came with his entrenching knife and for the minde hee bare to her money, more then good will to her welth: caused her to forsake this earthly life.

Hee first led to the place & brought back and executed at Tibourn.

Hee being apprehended for the same, condemned by the law, and adiudged to dye: was led to the place where he committed this murderous offence, the which beeing found not so conuenient: was reduced back, and in the after none was executed at Tibourn the xxix. of March.

Example of Marmeduke Glouer vvho slevv Sergeant Grace. 1580.

And

AND should I séem to be oblivious of the great and gréeuous offence of Marmeduke Glouer, who béeing arrested by Sergeant Grace: drew out his weapon, and there presently murdered him: nay sure his crime is to be accounted, a moste vile and hainous offence, in that hée resisted wherof duty he should haue obeyed, and more better had it béen for him, for then had he saued bothe his life and his owne. But following his owne will and cruel intent: made her become a widowe, who might els haue liued longer in ioy with her mate & husband. So likewise (as blood requireth blood) hée was executed in publique view in Cheapside on a Jibbit the xxvij. of March. 1580. *Glouer executed in Cheapside.*

Example of a Maid that buried her Childe quick.

A Maid also, who had abused her body with vnchaste liuing, and béeing deliuered of a swéet and tender Infant; casting all motherly and naturall affection from her: buryed the same aliue. What hardned hart had shée, to play so vile a parte to the frute of her owne body? alas it causeth to relent eche Christian hart that heareth therof. First to consider how wickedly shée violated the commaundements of our God, wheras by his owne mouth hée hath pronounced, Thou shalt not commit Adultrie. Then what wicked Wretches are wée, which abuse our bodies with voluptuous pleasures, with carnall delights, with wicked inuentions, and with sin out of measure, yet not contented therwith, but to dispoyle ye frute of our owne bodyes, to hide our sin to the world: to run hedlong *Exod. 20.*

to the Deuil, yet can wee not so hide our sinne, but God seeth it, and no wilful murther wil hee suffer unreuealed, though wee collour it for a time, though wee think it clean out of remembrance, and that the brunt is gon and past: yet wil hee cause the very fowles of the Aire to bewray it, our owne Consciences shall cause us open it, our lookes wil bewray us, our deeds wil deceiue us, so that wee shall need no more euidences then our owne selues.

God wil not suffer wilful murder to be concceled.

Acts. 15. 20.

(Saint Paule saith) vvee vvrite unto them that they abstaine them selues from fornication, euery sinne that a man doeth, is vvithout his body: but hee that committeth fornication: sinneth against his ovvne body: Let euery Christian be mindefull, that his body is the Temple of the Lord, and ought not to be defiled, but be kept pure and holy, euen that our bodies may be a quick sacrifice to GOD.

1. Cor. 6. 18.

An Example of the Gentlevvoman that kild her maid at S. Giles in the feeld.

AT Saint Giles in the feeld also, dwelt a Gentle woman named Mistres Amy Harison (alias) Midleton, who was a very wicked liuer, an uniust dealer, a bewrayer of fortunes, and one who was wholely inclined to vice abandoning vertue. This womã had a goodchilde of hers in the house w her, whom shee kept to doo such necessary busines about the house as was commaunded her by her Mistres, or as her yeers might sufficiently reach unto, but sometime was constrained to more, so that ofte her unhabilitie caused her to be whipt, beaten, tyranically

nically tormented, and very Iewishly intreated, sometime with big cudgels, sometime with a girth, so that from the crown of the hed, to the soles of the feet, was left no member unmartired. At length the Girle dyed by such excesse of correction, and shee therfore suffered death against her owne house, for an example to all Mistresses and Dames, how they misuse their Servants in such unmerciful māner. A woman void of all reason.

These Examples witnessed apparant in our eyes may warne us how wee lead such carcles liues, for feare of displeasing the Almightie, to hasten his anger upon us and so utterly to reiect us.

Examples of blasing Starres, and other Accidents.

WEe haue had manyfolde motions, sundrye signes, yea & exceeding examples of his wrath, and displeasure, by commets and blasing starz as lately hath béen séen ouer this Citie of London, as also great flames and flashing of fire issuing out of the North parts in the Ellement.

Likewise two great Tides in one houre contrary to Nature. Besides this there hath béen séen straunge Flyes, which on their wings bare the example of Gods iustice. two great Tides strange Flyes.

Example of the Childe in Gelderland.

AND furthermore what monsterous shapes: what straunge births and what alteration of Nature haue wée séen? In Gelderland, a Childe borne of proportion very ougly with a long bil and the belly like a Swan, feet with clawes, and as sone as it was borne ran vnder the bed.

Example of the Childe in Italy. In Italy also, of an anciẽt woman was borne a deformed Creature, the which spake many words, as the book in print doth witnes, which was printed by Thomas East.

Example of the Childe in Dutchland at Lutsolof. Likewise at Lutsolof in Dutchland was a straunge and monsterous Childe borne, which in one hãd had a rod, in the other a sword, which demaũded if the warres of men were not as yet fully finished, and cryed to make peace, and that the time should come that one should say to an other. Oh Brother why art thou not dead: with other words moste straunge as the printed book doth witnes.

The other Childe with two heds. Also with the same Childe there was an other, who had two heds, the one side of the body all black and wept abundantly, bothe borne of one woman, the Fathers name Baltus Maler, and the Mother Katherin Peeters.

A childe borne at Manchester. Then look héer into England, at Manchester, a Childe borne without euer a hed, yet sone after was the Mother deliuered of a goodly and swéet Infant.

A childe borne at Aberwick in Noth. At Aberwick also in Northumberland, a Child was borne hauing two heds in perfect proportion, and the eares like a horsse.

A mõstero⁹ Childe now in London. At this present in London is to be séen a Man childe very monstero⁹, all these are examples now of late dayes.

Example at Praga in Bohemia.

We hear also of the fearful tempest that was at Praga in Bohemia, wheras on the twentie fiue of of January. 1579. at two of the clock in the after none that the people durst not shew them selues in the streets. Thre steeples of Churches were blowen down, brusing about nineteen houses, and six persons slain therby. At euening again there was a maruelous thunder wherin fel hail stones ꝑ that weighed the quantity of 3. quarters of a pound, and therafter fel such an earthquake, during for the space of half an hower that the houses did shake very wounderfully. Example of an Earthquake.

At twelue a clock at night was perfectly viewed a black cloude wherin were plainly escried a mans two armes and hands naturally, the right hand holding a sword, the other a bowle which poured forth blood, therby was perceiued a peece of ground with corne standing theron, and therby lay a sickle and a great voice heard but nothing seen, which said. Wo, wo to the Earth, and to the Inhabitants therof, for hee commeth that is to come, and all People shall see him. This voice caused great terror through al the town, that the Infants shriked sucking at their Mothers brests, and women were then deliuered of Children. Signes in the Element. An other Signe. A voice heard but nothing seē. Great feare through all the Citie.

A VVoman of lix. yeers deliuered of three Children.

Aboue the rest, a Woman of lx. yeeres olde, named Margaret, her husband called John Bobroth the Clark of the Town. This woman for the space of xxv. weeks was diseased and no help could be had, but through this present accident shee was deliuered of three Children, their mouthes

replenished

A Woman of lix. yeers deliuered of Children. replenished with teeth as Children of three yeeres olde, the first borne spake saying.

The wordes of the first, the second and the third. *The day appointed vvhich no man can shun.*

The second said. *VVhere shall vvee finde liuing to bury the dead?*

The third said. *VVhere shall vve finde corne to satisfie the hungrie?*

Example of one in VVorcestershire vvho slevv his Brother and buryed him vnder the hearth of his Chimney.

Ihs returneth to murder. I Am sure that it is not yet out of remembraunce, nor men are not so forgetful to let slip so soone ẏ murder committed in Worcester, where as one vnnaturally killed his owne Brother, and when hee had doon, to couer his fact withall, buried the dead corps vnder the hearth of his chimney, a moste monsterous and bloody parte, far passing the committed offence of Cain who slew his Brother Abel.

Example of Thomas Hil at Feuersam, vvho kild his ovvne Mother.

AT Feuersam there dwelled one Thomas Hil, who in the house wt him had his owne Mother an olde woman, whome hee regarded but very small, & vsed her like an vngrateful Childe which made her to seek meanes to departe thence, and to goe to her other Sonne who dwelled at Canterbury, which when hee perceiued: thought to defeat her of her purpose, & one night in her bed murdered

dered her, sending word to his brother that she was dead, and so buried her before he came. This man béeing one who loued her déerly, & come to his brothers, his hart throbbed, and desired for to satisfie his minde that the dead corps might be taken vp, when it was taken vp, they saw nothing wherof shée dyed; neither her flesh abated with sicknes nor any sore wherby they should say it was the plague. So this Murderer was brought before her, and presently in the sight of all the standers by, it bled bothe at the nose and at the mouth, wherupon hée was accused, and hée did presently confesse it.

The dead Corps take vp and serched, and he brought before it, it presently bled.

Then was hée presently sent to Prison, wherin hée dispairing of Gods mercy, and giuing him self wholely to the Deuils temptations: with v points of his hose hung him self on an olde hedlesse naile in the Prison.

He hung hi self with v. points.

Example of Quernby vvho kild his Mother.

WE haue to remember how Edward Quernbie in Nottingham shire playd the like butcherly parte, for hée for the goodwil hée had to his Mothers riches cruelly & vnnaturally murdered her.

Margaret Dorington vvho killed Alice Fox.

LIkewise at Westminster how Margaret Dorrington a woman of a wicked and naughty life murdered Alice Fox thrusting a knife vp vnder her clothes, wherfore shée suffered death not long after.

Example of one hanged in chaines at miles end.

THere was one also who in the gardens at miles end had murdered a man, who therfore suffered death there, and was afterward häged vp in chains.

Example of the VVoman that kild her 2. Children.

AT Kilborne also neer London there was a woman who with a peece of a billet brayned her two Children, the summe wherof is at large described in a book imprinted. The Woman dyed in Newgate.

The murder of Abel Bourn Hosier beeing found by the brick killes, slain the xv. of April last.

A Virginal maker that cãe to look Rauens quils found thẽ mã slain

A Man whose facultie in profession is a maker of Virginalls going to the Brick kiles at the ẏ vpper end of Golding lane to seek Rauẽs fethers, which hee putteth to some vse in his handy craft: by chaunce espyed there lying in a deep trench or gutter, a man murdered, which when hee saw fearing least some suspition should be taken of him: went & bewrayed it presently. So the Cunstable with other men wel appointed there watched ẏ dead corps all that night. On the next day (beeing Saturday) among the egresse and regresse of people that came to see him: were many that were wel acquainted wͭ him, as a yung woman to whome hee should haue been maryed the Tuesday following, his kinsman, his Apprentice and other toward the euening.

The Coroner came thither and impanceled a quest of inquiry.

When the Coroner had paneled his inquest of inquiry, to serch and seek ẏ causes of this mans death whether

whether hée murdered him self wilfully, or slain by some chaunce, or els murdered by mées vilany.

There came before him thrée that gaue euidence the one his Apprentise, the other a very fréend of his dwelling in Bridewel, and the third one Sadler that dwelleth in Theames stréet. Thrée Euidences that were present there.

The Coroner willing to finde out this matter so suddainly chaunced: desired them to say what they could of the matter.

First (quoth hée) who dwelled in Bridewel named Dauis my fréend Abel Bourn that is slain was acquainted with one Hodgesses wife, whose husbād dwelled at the end of Saint Nicholas shambles, a Hosier by occupation, now lying in the hole in the Counter in Woodstréet, a very naughty woman in liuing, whose company hée vnhonestly vsed, bothe in his prentiship, and til the time that hée was slain the more to his greater gréef, hauing thus long vsed her company, and now drawing to honest liuing to match him self with an honest Maiden, which he should haue don on Tuesday next, at Christmas last gaue to this Hogges wife ten Angels to leaue his company and not to frequent him any more, but neuerthelesse shée did stil, (saying thus) thou wilt now be maried wilt thou? yea answered this Abel Bourn, I mean so God willing. Wilt þu so indéed? truely shée that maryeth thée shall haue but little ioy of thée, for look in what estate I haue had thée all this while: so wil I haue thée stil, for I wil haue thy purse and body at my commaundement and plesure. Dauis first telleth what hee knoweth of the matter. Hodggesse wifes woords and Abels.

Abel hearing this, on the Sunday before hée was slain, hée went to a Tailers where certain apparel of this Hodges wife was at making, and brought it away with him, comming to her where Abel fetcheth from the Tailers her apparel.

shée lay in the same morning, bidding her to come and fetch her apparel, and so shée went with him, and hée entring into a house with her, caused the Constable to serue a warrant on her, and so sent her to Bridewel, where shée said, if euer I come forth again: I wil haue him hewed as small as flesh to the pot, this hée said to this Dauis, euen as hée tolde before the quest.

Hodgesse his wife set to Bridewel.

Her woords in Bridwel.

Then Sadler hée began and said, Abel Bourne, thus tolde mée, that hée walking by the mount at ỹ vpper end of Aldersgatestréet was met by one who said vnto him, if thou séeme to vse Hodges wife in this order and doo not set her frée, the next time I méet thée I wil kil thée. This hée tolde him euen as hée said before the quest.

Sadler saith what he knowes.

One met Abel at the mount and threatned him.

While they were thus in talking, at last came a Woman by, who was suspected of the matter, and information giuen to the Coroner presently sent after her to bring her back again, shée hauing taken a garden, and they fain to climbe ouer the pale, so at the last brought her out and led her to the Coroner, her wench béeing by said, I tolde my Dame of this before, that shée should beware, so the wench was taken also.

Cranes wife comming by suspected, she entred into a Garden.

Her wenches woords.

When shée was come before the Coroner hée examined her if shée knew the said Abel, shée answered that shée knew him wel, and shée saw him not since Tuesday, on which day there was a fray in ỹ féelds and shée ran to sée it, where shée chaunced to se Abel with swoord and dagger vnder his arme, shée demaunded of him why hée went so weaponed, hée answered that hée was threatned to be slain, (quoth shée) then you were best to kéep your house and not to go so abrode. At the length hée went home with her

Shee saw Abel in the feeld on Sunday.

Abel goes to her house with her.

her to her house which was in Toys rents, & there hee poured out on the table about thirtie pound in golde, and at last sent for a pot of beer and drank wt her, but hee had no great lust to drink, and so shee said hee went his way.

Then afterward they led her to see the Corps, of the dead man, where shee seemed to be very sorowful for his death in their sight. But her house being serched, there was found what I knowe not, & the wench saith that shee fecht a great deale of water and washt the rushes, and so strawed fresh rushes on them. So shee and her husband and other more is in Newgate, and on wednesday after they were brought to Finsbury, & there was one Wood examined, beeing greatly suspected of the matter, & as it is iudged he wil be found to be doer of the deed, for the same day as ẏ man is said to be slain: hee can make no direct answere how hee spent that day, nor where hee lay that night, for the Coroner demaunded of him what hee professed, and hee answered ẏ hee had a trade a thing wherby hee lived. What is that (quoth the Coroner?) Sir (quoth hee) I am a Servingman and I professe to be a Faulkconer, I ment to go over sea now to buy hawkes for divers Gentlemen, whome doo you serve quoth the Coroner? I did serve such a one (quoth hee) at Christmas last, my Father is wel knowen to be an honest mā, hee dwelleth heerby at Newington green So to divers questions that were put unto him hee answered very evil favouredly, and was sent to prison again til weddensday next. Thus have you heard as much as yet may be gathered, when I understād more, I wil make you pertakers therof (God willing) I pray God trueth may come to light.

One Wood examined at Finsbury.

Wood answereth the Coroner of what trade hee was.

The manner hovv the said Abel Bourne vvas found slain, in a trench by the Brick killes.

This man thus cruelly murdered, had his owne cloke lying under him, straight was hee laid upon his back, the one of his legges straight out the other bending up a little, bare headed, in a lether Jerkin, his hose & doublet, his owne dagger thrust through his left iaw, comming out at the crown of his hed, six other wounds beside, all in his neck, the very least of them his mortall wound. And in this order was hee there found.

Example of the Earthquake at London the 6. of April.

Lastly call to minde the greeuous and suddain Earthquake hapning heer in London, the 6. of April, at 6. of the clock at night, which caused such a mazement through the whole Citie: that it is wunderful to be tolde.

¶ The great Bel of Westminster tolled of it self, Whitehall shook: the Gentlemen of the Temple cāe running forth with their knives in their hands being then at supper, a peece of the Temple Church fel down, Stones fel of from Paules Church, and at Christes Church in the Sermon while, a stone fel & and brayned Thomas Gray Apprentise to one Iohn Spurling Shoomaker dwelling without Aldersgate, an other stone also stroke Mabel Everite his fellow seruāt in ỳ same house, & she lived foure daies after

and

and then dyed. Diuers Chimnies in the Citie, parte of them fel down. At the play houses the people cāe running forth sapprised with great astonishment.

¶ A peece of Sutton Church in Kent fel down, the Earthquake beeing there in those partes heard and felt three seuerall times. A peece of Douer Castel fel down, and parte of the Castel wall fel into the sea. The Ships quaked and trembled as the houses on the drye land, and the waters were greatly out of temper. Out of England it was also felt, at Callis also it was so vehement that parte of the Staple house fel down, & likewise some of the law or town house was ouerthrowen.

In Brabant, as Antwerp, Zeland, Middleborough Flushing, S. Thomas in Artoys, Deep, Flaunders, Dunkerk, Barborough, Grauelin, Bridges, & Gaūt, it was felt also very forcible. No dout deer Brethe-ren this was a token of the indignation of our God against our wicked liuing, wherin so highly wee offend his diuine Maiestie. Let vs remember three of the fairest Cities in Asia sunk for sinne. Constanstinople had a twelue mōthes earthquake. Many places for sinne haue been greeuously punished, as Sodom and Gomorra, Ierusalem, Niniuie, and many other places. Let vs remember that it shalbe better for Corazaine & Bethzaida at the dred ful day of Iudgement then for Tire and Sidon.

These Examples are for our sins.

Mathew. 11. 21.

Let vs lift vp our harts cheerfully vnto God our saluation, be sory for our former offences, & from the very bottōe of our harts inwardly lament thē.

Let vs turn to the Father of all mercy saying. O Father wee haue sinned against heauē & against thee, we are no more woorthy to be called thy Children. So wil the Lord of his fatherly mercy forgiue our sinnes and make vs pertakers of his kingdome which God graunt vs for his sonnes sake. Amen.

Luke. xv.

Sundrye strange and inhumaine Murthers (*STC* 18286.5.) is reproduced with permission from the uniqu
Lambeth Palace Library copy. The text-block measures 75 × 105 mm.

The following words are a transcription of the original:

B1r.1	coming on whē
B1r.24	tolde the maisters of the parrishe
B1r.25	seen, wherevpon they came to behold
B1r.26	perceiued was but
B1v.1	who being examined before a Justice, confessed that the

Sundrye ſtrange and inhumaine Murthers, lately committed.

The firſt of a Father that hired a man to kill three of his children neere to Aſhford in Kent:

he ſecond of maſter Page of Plymoth, murthered by the conſent of his owne wife: with the ſtrange diſcouerie of ſundrie other murthers.

Wherein is deſcribed the odiouſneſſe of murther, with the vengeance which God inſli-cteth on murtherers.

Printed at London by Thomas Scarlet. 1591.

A declaration of the monſtrous crueltie of a Father that hired one to murther three of his owne children.

THE heauie ſentence that almightie God pronounced vppon the paricide Caine, when hee ſaide, Thou art curſed from the earth, that hath opened her mouth to receiue thy brothers bloud from thy hand, Ge.4. ſheweth how odious murther is in his ſight. It therfore behoueth euerie one to haue a ſpecial care what actions wee commit, not ſeeking to murther thoſe that haue in ſome ſorte offended vs, but to leaue, as wee ought, the reuenge of all wrongs vnto the Lord: for we may be aſſured we cannot deale colourablie with God, as Pilate thought to haue done when he pronounced ſentence againſt his own conſcience, for hee hauing at the importunate ſute of the Iewes pronouned death vpon our ſauiour Chriſt, thought to haue waſhed awaie the facte with the waſhing of his handes and his proteſtation, in ſaying I am innocent of the bloude of this iuſt perſon, Whereby indeed he could not cleere himſelfe, but according to the ſaying of Eraſmus, In murther the conſenter is as euill as the deed dooer. So Pilats conſcience made him guiltie of Chriſtes death, for which the wrath of God still followed him: for after that time Pilate in executing his office did nothing but that which was iniustice. And beeing thereof accused in Rome, he was by the Emperour Caligula bannished, and went to Lions, the place (as some saie) of his birth, through griefe of which disgrace, by the sufferance of God, he desperately slew himselfe, that hee might die by the hand of the most wickedst person that liued. God sayd vnto Caine, The voice of thy brothers bloud crieth vnto me out of ẏ ground. And Plutarch dooth describe many straunge discoueries of murthers, among which hee sayth, that a monstrous sonne slew his owne father, the act being so much against nature, as no man suspected this gracelesse childe for the same, and yet in his owne conscience hee sawe millions of accusers standing before him, & readie (as he thought) to attach him for the same, insomuch as vpon a daie sitting in a Tauerne with a companion of his, he sodainly thrust his swoorde vp into the chimney, and cried out, saying, Ah you villaine swallowes, quoth hee, leaue your babling and exclayming that I slew my father, or I will doe by you as I did by him. His companion hearing this his voluntarie accusation, secretly bewrayed the matter to the magistrate, whereby the vngracious sonne was soone apprehended, and executed according to his demerites.

Horrour and feare allwayes accompanieth the murtherer, his owne conscience is to him a thousand witnesses, hee standeth in dreade of euerie bush, beast and birde, he imagineth that euery thing discouereth his euill, and many times it falleth out, that the silly creatures of the earth detecteth him.

Oh what a straunge and vnlooked for discouerie was this, yet nothing strange considering the horrour of the filthie fact. God seldome or neuer leaueth murther vnpunished, nor will the marke of murther goe forth of the murtherers weapon, neither can murther bee kept so close, but that by one meanes or other the Lord will compel the murtherer to discouer and laie open the truth vnto the worlde, as by this lamentable accident following manifestlie appeareth.

IN the Towne or Parish of Warborne, within foure miles of Ashford market, being within the Countie of Kent, dwelled one Lincolne, the vnnaturall father of foure vnfortunate children. This man being about fiftie yeeres of age was a widower, and therefore became a sutor to a widow not farre from thence, who beeing of some reasonable wealth, refused to marrie with him, in respect of his great charge of children. Wherat, as it seemeth, the deuill entered so farre into his minde, that he cast many wayes in his thought how to make them awaie, and returning home sate downe in great heauinesse by the fire side. Whereupon he hauing a married man that wrought with him in his house, demanded of him why hee was so pensiue, who requiring him also to sit downe by the fire, tolde him that he could not be merrie. Why (sayd hee) howe comes it that you marrie not some honest woman to comfort you, considering you haue wherewithall to keepe her. Oh sayde he (fetching a great sigh) there is none wyll haue me, in respect of my great charge of children, but, sayd he, if I could make them awaie by anie meanes, I coulde marrie with a rich widowe. And thereuppon (as it was since confessed) none being present but themselues, the sayd Lincolne perswaded this labouring man to perfourme his request, and to take this matter in hand, so should he haue fortie shillings in money and a good cowe for his paines. But the poore man notwithstanding he seemed at the first vnwilling, yet as he was pore, so hee was couetous, and the hope of the money and the cowe so wrought in his thought, that forgetting God and all godlynes, in the ende without anie greate delaie he consented to the fact, and the rather hee was induced thereunto, for that this vnnaturall Father promised, that when the murther was committed, not to pursue or make after him for the same, and that if hee

 were

were compelled thereunto, yet woulde he deale in such sort, that he would let fall his sute, rather than to take his oath, to saie he was the murtherer. Thus concluding betweene themselues, the daie came wherin the wicked act was performed, which was vpon a saterdaie in Nouember last, on which morning, the Father and all his children with the murtherer broke their fast at home together. That done, olde Lincolne prepared himselfe to goe to Ashford market, which he did, taking his eldest sonne with him and the murtherer, they departed towards Ashforde: but in the waie the murtherer returned home againe to the thrꝫ innocent children, whome he speedily murthered, knocking them on the heads with a hatchet, and cutting all their throates. The father the better to colour his vnnaturall consenting to the death of his owne children, bought thrꝫe paire of new shoes for them, whom he knew shoulde bee murthered before hee came home, and sent his eldest sonne home before, beeing about fiftꝫne yeeres olde, who could not get in at the doors which was barred on the inner side, & sꝫing hee heard none of the children stirring, staide there vntill his father came, who seeing no light, nor hearing of the children, contrarie to his vsuall custome, (yet might haue gone in on the backe side) came to his next neighbours house, and prayed that some bodie would goe home with him to see what had happened. In conclusion hꝫ came home with companie, who were eie witnesses of this tragicall spectacle, for hauing entered the house, they found murthered two pretie boyes and a girle: which grieuous and vnexpected sight made the beholders to stand amazed, neuerthelesse the harde hearted Father made no signe of sorrowe for them, neither woulde he sꝫke meanes to pursue the murtherer, which by the reporte of his neighbours sꝫmed to bee his man, who onelie was sꝫne about the house after his departure and none else. But this wretched man commended him to bee a verie honest fellow, and therefore supposed his eldest sonne to bee the author of this murther, and vpon him woulde willinglie haue imposed the same.

The

The next daie following the Father woulde seeke no meanes to burie the children, nor that the crowner should view them, but suffered them most vnnaturallie to lie aboue the ground for the space of thrée daies, vntill a Gentlewoman named mistres West came and reproued him of his vnnaturall dealings towardes them, which done, hee digged a hole in the house about two foote déepe, and layde them in it, but by reason of springs in the ground, the water issued into the pit, and therby soaked the childrens woundes and bodie, and made them verie cléere and white. Within fiue dayes after the Crowner came thether, béeing procured thereunto, and founde the children couered with a lyttle earth and a boord ouer them, whome he caused to bee taken vp. This was the eight daie after the murther was committed, in which time the murtherer was apprehended and accused thereof, but he vtterly denied the fact. But beeing brought before the dead bodies of the children, the Father being there also, the woundes began to bléede afresh, which when the Crowner sawe, hee commanded the partie apprehended to looke vpon the children, which hee did, and called them by their names, whereuppon, behold the wonderfull workes of God, for the fact beeing still denied, the bodies of the children, which seemed white like vnto soaked flesh laid in water, sodainly receiued their former coulour of bloude, and had such a liuely countenance flushing in theyr faces, as if they had béene liuing creatures lying asléepe, which in déede blushed on the murtherers. when they wanted grace to blush and bée ashamed of theyr owne wickednesse. Which wonderfull miracle caused the murtherer there present not onely to confesse and acknowledge himselfe giltie of that damnable déede, but also to accuse the Father of the children as principal procurer of their vntimely deaths. Whereupon they were both sent prisoners to Canterbury, where they remained vntill the last Assizes holden at Senocke in Kent eightéene miles from London, where they were araigned and condemned to die for the same, so that vpon the seauen and twentith daie of Februarie last past

they

they were both executed neere to Ashford, where the father of the children confessed himself giltie of ÿ murther, hauing before denied it euen till the houre of death. Whereby appeareth that his owne conscience was ouercharged with this foule and odious offence, and therfore would not suffer it to be concealed.

Thus may you see how murtherers are ouertaken, and their actions opened by themselues, yea if there were no body to accuse the murtherer, the murthered coarse wold giue euidence against him. It hath bene a meane appointed by the Lord to discerne the murtherer, that when hee approched, the dead carkasse would at some issue or other bleede: many haue by this miraculous worke of the Lord bene discouered, when the proofe hath bene onely bare suspition. This example insuing is much to that purpose.

There was not long since at Uppingham in Rutlandeshire, a shoomaker that had murthered a yong man, who was buried, and the murtherer litle suspected for the same: neuertheles vpon bare suspition hee was apprehended, and the dead coarse digged vp againe , before whome this shoomaker was brought, vppon whose approche the murthered coarse not only bled, but with one of his eies standing wide open, he stared vpon the shoomaker that murthered him. The standers by wonderfully amazed thereat, remoued the shomaker, and presently the eie closed vp, and being brought againe, the coarse with his eie wide open, stared vppon him as before, as who wold saie, this is the murtherer, stay him, my bloud asketh for vengeance. I haue here published this matter vpon such due proofe as cannot be reproued, it is not yet long since the murtherer was executed at Dukam in the foresayd Countie. An example of great terrour to such as delight in bloud. But what may examples preuaile where grace and the feare of God is wanting, as appeareth by the sequele.

Of late there was dwelling in Salisburie a young damsell named Alice Shepheard, who being with childe, and yet neuer maried, wold sweare when she was charged therwith

that

that it was most vntrue: but the time comming on that she should be deliuered, she was constrained to reueale the trueth to her Mother and Grandmother, who presently fetched a Mydwife, making none other acquainted therwith, neither did she after her comming stay very long, before this maid was deliuered of a man childe, whose neck they presently broke, and secretly buried it in the Churchyard, thinking therby to escape worldlye punishment: not fearing the wrath of God for their wilfull murder, nor considering that he saw the secrets of their harts, nor that he would not suffer innocent blood shed to goe vnpunished. But now see the will and wonderfull work of almighty God to reueale this most wicked act. It happened a dog came ouer the place where the childe lay buried, and hauing found the sent of the fleshe, he neuer rested vntill he had with his feete scraped it vp out of the ground: leauing it bare aboue the earth, whereby it seemeth that they buried it but very shallowe, and was fearfull to be espied, least the fact should thereby be discouered. Now when the dog had laide it open to the eye of eche passenger, it happened that one Hugh Mawdes of Salisbury comming by, chaunced to spye the same, and was greatly amazed to see so greeuous a sight, who presently went and tolde the maisters of the parrishe what he had seen, whervpon they came to behold this greeuous sight, which they perceiued was but new born, and therfore concluded that it was the childe of some strumpet, and that she had murdered it, and then buried it in that shallowe place, which doon, it was conuayed into our Lady church in Salisbury, where all the cheefe of the towne came in and gaue their censures for finding out the vnnaturall mother and murderer therof.

Among whom mistris Shepheards daughter was nominated and greatly suspected for the same: notwithstanding, vpon this bare suspition, the suspected person with her Mother, Grandmother and Midwife was sent for, who being examined before a Iustice, confessed that the said childe was still borne, and that therfore they priuily buried it in that sort; wherupon the Iustice caused them to be sworne vpon a booke that they had said nothing but the trueth, which they seuerally did. But heer God shewed a miracle before them all, for they hauing taken their othes before the Iustice, they were discharged and sent away, not meaning to deale any further therin.

But the Midwife being touched in conscience with her othe which she had then newe taken, going forth of the Iustices doores, suddenly fetcht a great sigh and said: Oh what a wicked woman am I to sweare that ẏ childe was still borne, when in troth it was borne aliue: which words being ouer hard by one of the Iustices seruants, they were all called in againe: where they were charged with the murdering of the said childe, which after a faint deniall, they generally confessed. Then were they committed to prison until the last assises, where they receiued the doome of iudgement by death, which of duetye they had deserued for so wicked a deede. Thus we see that although God suffer the murderer to escape for a time, yet doth he followe them with so sharpe reuenge, as either they desperatlye slay themselues, or reape such shame as the worlde may be satisfied, that God hath dealt iustlye with them.

FINIS.

A true

A true discourse of a cruel and inhumaine murder, committed vpon M. Padge of Plymouth, the 11. day of February last, 1591. by the consent of his owne wife, and sundry other.

IN the Towne of Testock 10. miles or therabouts from Plimouth, there dwelled one M. Glanfeeld, a man of as good wealth and account, as any occupier in that Cuntrie. This M. Glanfeeld fauoured a yong man named George Strangwich, who was of such great credit with him, that he turned ouer al his wares, shop and dealings into his handes: and tooke so good liking of him being a proper yong man, that it was supposed he should haue had his daughter in mariage, and the rather for that he had learned the full perfection & knowledge of his trade in London, in the seruice of a worshipfull Citizen called M. Powell in Bred-street, and grew so painfull, and seemed so good a husband as the said M. Glanfeelds Daughter did wholye resolue that the saide Strangwidge should be her husband and no other: whereto in troth her parentes neuer did condescend. But Sathan who is the author of euill, crept so farre into the dealinges of these persons, that he procured the parents to mislike of Strangwidge, and to perswade their Daughter to refraine his companye, shewing her that they had found out a more meeter match for her, and mocioned vnto hir that it was their pleasures shee should marrye one M. Padge of Plimouth, who was a widdower, and one of the cheefest inhabitants of that towne, and by reason that the sayde M. Glanfeeld did mean to abide at Plimouth, he thought it a more sufficient matche to marrye her in Plimouth, where she might be hard by him, then to marrye her to Strangwidge who dwelt farre from him: In the end such was the successe, that although she had setled her affection altogither vpon Strangwidge, yet through the perswasion of her freendes though sore against her will, she was married to M. Padge of Plimouth, notwithstanding that she had protested neuer to loue ẏ man with her hart, nor neuer to remoue her affection setled vpon the saide Stranguidge, which she perfourmed as the sequell maketh manifest: for this mistris Padge had accesse to Stranguidge, and he to her at his comming to Plimoth: wherby the diuell so wrought in the harts of them both, that they practised daye and night how to bring her husband to his end. And therupon the said mistris Padge as appeereth since by her own confession, did within ẏ space of one yeere and lesse, attempt sundry times to poison her husband, for it was not full a yeere, but that she had procured him to be murthered, as you shal hear immediatly.

But God who preserueth many persons from such perils and dangers, defended stil ẏ said M. Padge from the secret snares & practises of present death, which his wife had laid for him, yet not without great hurt vnto his body, for still the poison wanted force to kil him, so wonderfully did almighty God worke for him, yet was he compelled to vomit blood and much corruption, which doubtles in the end would haue killed him, and that shortlye. But to prosecute and that with great speed to perfourm this wicked & inhumain act, the saide mistris Padge and Strangwidge omitted no opportunitie: they wanted no meanes nor freends to performe it for their mony, wherof they had good store, and more then they knewe how to imploy, except it had beene to better vses: for she on the one side practised with one of her seruants named Robert Priddis, whom as she thought nothing would more sooner make him pretend the murdering of his maister thē siluer and gold, wherwith she so corrupted him, with promise of seauenscore pounds more, that he solemnly vndertook and vowed to performe the task to her contentment.

On the other side Strangwidg hired one Tom Stone to be an actor in this tragicall action, and promised him a great summe of mony for perfourming the same, who by

a solemne

a solemne vow had graunted the effecting therof, though to the hazard of his own life.

These two instruments wickedly prepared themselues to effect this desperate and villanous déed vpon the 11. of February being wednesday, on which night following ẏ act was committed, but it is to be remembred that this mistris Padge lay not then with her husband, by reason of the vntimely birth of a child wherof she was newly deliuered, the same being dead borne: vpon which cause, she then kept her chamber, hauing before sworn ẏ she would neuer beare child of his getting ẏ should prosper: which argued a most vngodlye minde in the woman, for in that sort she had béen the death of two of her own children.

About ten of the clock at night M. Padge being in his bed slumbring, could not happen vpon a sound sléepe, and lyung musing to him selfe, Tom Stone came softlye and knocked at ẏ doore, wherupon Priddis his companion did let him in, who was made priuie to this déed, and by reson that mistris Padge gaue thē straight charge to dispatche it that night whatsoeuer came of it, they drew towardes the bed, intending immediatly to go about it, M. Padge being not a sléep as is afor said, asked who came in, wherat Priddis leapt vpon his maister being in his bed, who roused himself and got out vpon his féete, & had béen hard enough for his man, but that Stone flew vpon him being naked, and suddenlye tripped him, so that he fell to the ground: wherupon both of them fell vpon him, and tooke the kercher from his head, and knitting the same about his neck, they immediatly stifled him: And as it appéereth euen in ẏ anguish of death, the said M. Padge greatly laboured to pul ẏ kercher from about his neck, by reason of the marks & scratches which he had made with his nailes vpon his throat, but therwͭ he could not preuaile, for they would not let slip their hold vntil he was full dead. This don, they laid him ouerthwart ẏ bed, and against the bed side broke his neck, and when they sawe he was surelye dead, they stretched him and layde him in his bed again,

 spreading

spreading the clothes in ordinary sort; as though no such act had beene attempted, but that he had died on Gods hand.

Wherupon Pridis immediatly went to Mistris Pages Chamber and tolde her that all was dispatcht: and about one hower after he came againe to his Mistris chamber doore and called alowd, mistresse quoth he, let some body looke into my Maisters chamber, me thinkes I heare him grone, with that she called her maide, who was not priuie to any thing, and bad her light a Candle, whereupon she slipt on her petticote and went thether likewise, sending her maid first into the chamber, where she her selfe stoode at the doore, as one whose conscience would not permit her to come and beholde the detestable deed which she had procured.

The maid simply felt on her Maisters face, and found him colde and stiffe and so tolde her mistresse, wherat she bad the maide to warme a cloth and wrap it about his feete, which she did, and when she felte his legges, they were as colde as claye: wherat she cried out saying, her maister was dead.

Wherupon her mistris got her to bed, and caused her man Pridis to goe call her Father M. Glanfeeld, then dwelling at Plimouth, and sent for one of her husbands sisters likewise, willing her to make haste if euer she would see her brother aliue, for he was taken with the disease called the Pull as they tearme it in that Country: these persons being sent for, they came immediatly, wher at mistris Padge arose, & in counterfeit mãner sounded, whereby there was no suspition a long time concerning any murder persourmed vpon him, vntill mistris Harris his sister spied bloud about his bosome, which he had with his nailes procured by scratching for the Kercher when it was about his throate: then they moued his head, and found his neck broken, & on both his knees the skin was beaten off, by striuing with them to saue his life.

Mistris

Mistris Harris heerevpon perceiuing how hee was made away, went to the Maior and the worshipfull of the towne, desiring them of Iustice, and intreated them to come and beholde this lamentable spectackle, which they immediatlye persourmed, and by searching him, found that he was murdered the same night.

Vpon this the Maior committed Priddis to prison, who being examined, did impeach Tom Stone, shewing that he was a thæfe actor in the same: this Thomas Stone was married vpon the next daye after the murther was committed, and being in the midst of his iollety, suddenly he was attached and committed to prison, to beare his fellow company.

Thus did the Lord vnfold this wretched déed, whereby immediatly the said mistris Padge was attached vpon the murther: & examined before Sir Fruncis Drake Knight, with the Maior and other maiestrates of Plimouth, who denied not the same, but said she had rather dye with Strangwidge, then to liue with Padge.

At the same time also the said George Strangwidge was newly come to Plimouth, being very heauy & doubtfull, by reason he had giuen consent to the saide murder: who being then in company wt some of London, was apprehended, and called before the Iustices for the same, wherupon at his comming before them, he confessed the truety of all: and offered to proue that he had written a Letter to Plimouth before his comming thether, that at any hand they should not perfourme the act: neuertheles M. Padge was murdered before the comming of this Letter, and therefore he was sent to prison with the rest vnto Excester: & at the assises holden this last Lent, the said Gorge Stranguidge, Mistris Padge, Priddis, and Tom Stone, were condemned and adiudged to dye for the saide fact, and were all executed accordinglye vpon Satterdaye béeing the twentith day of Februarye last, 1591.

other

Other strange things seene at that time.

VPon the same night & thrée nights after, there was séen an vgly thing formed like a Beare, whose eyes were as it had béen fier, bearing about him a linnen cloth representing the instruement wherewith the saide M. Padge was murdered.

Also in Plimouth the same wéeke in the presence of sundry honest persons, was visibly séene a Rauen, which did alight vpon the head of a Ships mast, sunk at the end of the towne: this Rauen standing vpon the top of the maine mast, did with her talents pluck vp certaine rope yarnes that hung downe from the head of the mast, and fastned them about her necke, and often turnde them about her neck with all her force, which done, she plunged her selfe right down, clapping her wings close to her body, and neuer left vntill she had hanged her self.

Now the ship was all this while a ground, lying with her sterne to the shore, and suddainly the said ship turned her selfe round, and brought her stem where earste her sterne did lye, all which are strange, yet is the same so true, as it cannot be disproued, being iustified by those that saw the same.

The Lord blesse vs, and giue all other grace to bee warned by these examples and inhumaine actions before recited: that we may auoid the danger of shedding of innocent blood, and feare the iudgement of God which continually followeth wilfull murderers. Eternal God preserue this little Iland, blesse the Quéenes Maiestie, and her honourable counsell, turn thy wrath awaye from vs O Lord, and poure downe thy blessinges vpon her highnes, that she our Moyses, maye long liue to holde vp the Tables of the Law in her gratious handes, and that we may séeke continually to please her in such due sort, as she may haue no iust cause to throw them down, which God graunt for his mercie sake. Amen.

FINIS.

The Lamentation of Mr. Pages Wife (Wing D955E) is reproduced with permission from the unique Harvar College Library copy, which includes *The Complaint of Mrs. Page* (see next item) on the same broadsid sheet. The text-block measures 240 × 170 mm. The title of another edition (*STC* 6557.2, Wing D955D p 1663–5), reads '*against their will*'.

The Lamentation of Mr. *Pages* Wife of *Plimouth*:

Who being enforced to wed against their wills did consent to his Murder for the love of *George Strangwidge*, for which fact they suffered death at *Barstable* in *Devonshire*.

The tune is, Fortune my Foe.

UNhappy she whom fortune hath forlorne,
Despis'd of grace that proffered grace did scorn,
My lawless love, hath luckless wrought my woe
My discontent, content did overthrow.

My loathed life too late I do lament,
My woful deed in heart I do repent,
A wife I was that wilful went awry,
And for that fault am here prepar'd to die.

In blomy years my Fathers greedy mind,
Against my will a match for me did find:
Great wealth there was, yea gold and silver store,
But yet my heart had chosen one before.

Mine eyes dislik't my Fathers liking quite,
My heart did loath my Parents fond delight,
My greedy mind and fancy told to me,
That with his age my youth could not agree.

On knees I crav'd they would not me constrain,
With tears I cry'd their purpose to restrain,
With sighs and sobs I did them often move
I might not wed whereas I could not love.

But all in vain my speeches still I spent,
My Mothers will my wishes did prevent;
Though wealthy Page possest my outward part,
George Strangwidge still was lodged in my heart.

I wedded was, and wrapped all in woe,
Great discontent within my heart did grow:
I loath'd to live, yet liv'd in deadly strife,
Because perforce I was made Pages wife.

My chosen eyes could not his sight abide,
My tender youth did scorn his aged side,
Scant could I taste the meat whereon I fed,
My legs did loath to lodge within his bed.

Cause knew I none, that should despise him so,
That such disdain within my heart did grow,
Save onely this that fancy did me move,
And told me still George Strangwidge was my love.

But here began my downfall and decay,
In mind I mus'd to make him straight away,
I that became his discontented Wife,
Contented was he should be rid of life.

Methinks the heavens cries vengeance for my fact,
Methinks the world condemns my monstrous act,
Methinks within my Conscience tells me true,
That for that deed Hell fire is my due.

My pensive soul doth sorrow for my sin,
For which offence my soul doth bleed within,
But mercy Lord, for mercy still I cry,
Save thou my soul, and let my body die.

Well could I wish that Page enjoyd his life;
So that he had some other to his wife,
But never could I wish of low or high,
A longer life then see sweet Strangwidge die.

O woe is me that had no greater grace,
To stay till he had run out natures race;
My deed I rue, but more I do repent,
That to the same my Strangwidge gave consent.

You Parents fond that greedy minded be,
And seek to graft upon the golden tree,
Consider well, and rightful Judges be,
And give your doom twixt Parents love and me.

I was their Child and bound for to obey,
Yet not to love, where I no love could lay;
I married was in much and endless strife,
But faith before had made me Strangwidge wife.

O wretched world! whom cankered rust doth blind,
And cursed men who bear a greedy mind;
And hapless I whom parents did force so,
To end my dayes in sorrow shame and woe.

You Devonshire Dames, and courteous Cornwal Knights
That here are come to visit woeful Wights,
Regard my grief, and mark my woeful end,
But to your children be a better friend.

And thou my dear which for my fault must die,
Be not afraid the force of death to try;
Like as we liv'd and lov'd together true,
So both at once lets bid the world adieu.

Ulalia thy friend doth take her last farewell,
Whose soul with thine in heaven doth ever dwell;
Sweet Saviour Christ do thou my soul receive,
The world I do withal my heart forgive.

And Parents now whose greedy mind do show,
Your hearts desire, and inward heavy woe:
Mourn you no more, for hope my heart doth tell,
Ere day be done, that I shall be full well,

And Plimouth proud I bid thee now farewel,
Take heed you wives, let not your hands rebel:
And farewel life, wherein such sorrow showes,
And welcome death that doth my Corps enclose.

And now sweet Lord forgive me my misdeeds,
Repentance cries for soul that inward bleeds:
My soul and body I commend to thee,
That with thy blood from death redeemed me.

Lord bless our King with long and happy life,
And send true peace betwixt each man and wife,
And give all parents wisdome to foresee,
The match is mar'd where minds do not agree.

The Complaint of Mrs. Page (Wing C5613A) is reproduced with permission from the unique Harvard College Library copy. The text-block measures 240 × 70 mm.

The Lamentation of George Strangwidge, who for the consenting to the death of Mr. Page of Plimouth, suffered death at Barstable.

The man that sighs and sorrows for his sin,
The corps which care and wo hath wrapped in
In doleful sort records her Swan-like Song,
That waits for death and loaths to live so long.

O Glanfield cause of my committed crime,
So wed in wealth as birds in bush of lime,
What cause hadst thou to bear such wicked spight
Against my Love and eke my hearts delight.

I would to God thy wisdome had been more,
Or that I had not entred in thy door;
Or that thou had a kinder father been
Unto thy Child, whose years are yet but green.

The match unmeet which thou didst make,
When aged Page thy daughter whom did take,
Well may'st thou rue with tears that cannot dry,
Which is the cause that four of us must die.

Ulalia more bright then Summers Sun,
Whose beauty had for ever my love won,
My soul more sobs to think of thy disgrace,
Then to behold my own untimely race.

The deed late done in heart I do repent.
But that I lov'd I cannot it relent:
Thy seemly sight was ever sweet to me,
Would God my death would thy excuser be.

It was for me alas thou didst the same,
On me by right they ought to lay the blame:
My worthless love hath brought my life in scorn,
Now woe is me that ever I was born.

Farewel my Love whose Royal heart was seen,
Wouldest thou hadst not half so constant been:
Farewel my Love the pride of Plimouth town,
Farwel the flower whose beauty is cut down.

For twenty years great was the cost I know,
Thy unkind father did on thee bestow:
Yet afterwards so sower did fortune lower;
He lost his joy and Child within an hour.

My wrong and woe to God I do commit,
Who was the cause of matching them unfit:
And yet my guilt I cannot so excuse,
We gave consent his life for to abuse.

Wretch that I am that my consent did give,
Had I deny'd Vlalia still should live:
Blind fancy said do not this suit deny,
Live thou in bliss, or else in sorrow die.

O Lord forgive this cruel deed of mine,
Upon my soul let beams of mercy shine:
In justice Lord do thou no vengeance take,
Forgive us both, For Iesus Christ his sake.

The Complaint of Mrs. Page for causing her Husband to be murdered for the love of Strangwidge, who were executed together.

If ever woe did touch a womans heart,
Or grief did gall for sin the outward part,
My conscience then and heavy heart within,
Can witness well the sorrow for my sin,

When years were young my father forc'd me wed
Against my will where fancy were not fed,
I was content his pleasure to obey,
Although my heart was link'd another way.

Great were the gifts they proffered in my sight,
With wealth they thought to win me with delight,
But gold nor gifts could not my mind remove,
For I was link'd whereas I could not love,

Methought his sight was loathsome to my eye,
My heart did grudge against him inwardly,
This discontent did cause my deadly strife,
And with this wealth did cause a grievous life.

My constant love was on young Strangwidge set,
And woe to him that did our welfare let:
His love so deep a root in me did take,
I would have gone a begging for his sake,

Wronged he was through fond desire of gain,
Wronged he was even through my parents plain;
If faith and troth a perfect pledge might be,
I had been wife unto no man but he.

Eternal God forgive my Fathers deed,
And grant all Maidens may take better heed,
If I had been but constant to my friend,
I had not matcht to make so bad an end.

But wanting grace I sought my own decay,
And was the cause to make my friend away,
And he on whom my earthly joyes did lye,
Through my amisse a shameful death must die.

Farwel sweet George alwaies my loving friend;
Needs must I laud and love thee to the end:
And albeit that Page possest thy due,
In sight of God thou wast my Husband true.

My watry eyes unto the Heavens I bend,
Craving of Christ his mercy to extend,
My blody deed do me O Lord forgive,
And let my soul within thy Kingdom live.

Farwel false world and Friend that Fickle be,
All wives farwel, example take by me,
Let not the Devil to murder you intice,
Seek to escape such foul and filthy vice.

And now O Christ to thee I yield my breath,
Strengthen my Faith in bitter pangs of death:
Forgive my faults and folly I thee pray,
And with thy blood wash thou my sins away.

Printed for F. Coles, T. Vere, W. Gilbertson, and J. Wright.

The trueth of the most wicked and secret murthering of Iohn Brewen (*STC* 15095) is reproduced wit
permission from the unique copy at Lambeth Palace Library. The text-block measures 95 × 150 mm.

The following words are a transcription of the original:

5.22 whatsoeuer else he listed
5.35 You see (quoth she) in what case I am
5.36 suffer mee not
5.37 pointing marke for others, and a shame among my niegh-
6.1 was nothing moued therewith, but churlishly answered, she
6.2 so minded
6.3 twice aduised how I did wed with
6.21 Alderman Haward
6.37 and he will not leaue so vilde a thing vnpunished.

The trueth of the most wicked and secret *murthering of Iohn Brewen, Goldsmith of* London, committed by his owne wife, through the prouocation of one Iohn Parker *whom she loued: for which fact she was burned,* and he hanged in Smithfield, on wednesday, the 28 of Iune, 1592. two yeares after the murther was committed.

Imprinted at London for Iohn Kid, and are to be sold by Edward White, dwelling at the little North doore of Paules, at the signe of the Gun. 1592.

Tho Kydde

The murder of Iohn Brewen Goldsmith of London, who through the entisement of Iohn Parker, was poysoned of his owne wife in eating a measse of Sugersops.

HOw hatefull a thing the sinne of murder hath béene before the sight of the eternall God, the holy Scriptures doe manifest, yet from the beginning we may euidently see how busie the diuell hath beene to prouoke men thereunto, in so much that when there was but two brethren liuing in the world, the onelye sonnes of the first man Adam; hée prouoked the one most vnnaturally to murther the other. And albeit there was none in the world to accuse Caine for so fowle a fact, so that in his owne conceit hee might haue walked securely and without blame, yet the blood of the iust Abel cried most shrill in the eares of the righteous God for vengeance & reuenge on the murderer. The Lord therefore ordayned a Lawe that the cruel & vniust blood-sheader should haue his blood iustly shed again: of which law, although no man is ignorant, and that we sée it put in execution daylie before our eyes, yet doth the Diuell so worke in the hearts of a number, that without respect either of the feare of God, or extreame punishment in this world they doe notwithstanding committe most haynous and grieuous offences to the great hazard of their soules, and the destructions of their bodies on earth, onely through Sathans suggestions, as by this example following may euidently be proued.

There was of late dwelling in London a proper yong woman named Anne Welles, which for her fauour and comely personage, as also in regard of her good behauiour and other commendable qualities, was beloued of diuers young men, especially of two Goldsmithes, which were Batchelers, of good friends, and well estéemed for fine workmanship in their trade: The one of them was called Iohn Brewen, and the other Iohn Parker, who although hee was better beloued, yet least deserued it (as the sequell hereafter will shewe) But as the truest louers are commonly least regarded, and the plaine meaning man most scorned of vndiscreete maidens, so came it to passe by Brewen, who notwithstanding his long and earnest suite, the gifts and fauours which she receiued was still disdained and cast off, albeit he had the good will & fauour of al her friends & kinsfolk: but no man was so high in her books as Parker: he had her fauours whosoeuer had her frowns: he sate and smiled, when others sobbed, and tryumphant in the tears of the dispossessed. It came to passe that this nice maiden had vpon a promise betweene them, receaued of Brewen both golde and iewels, which he willingly bestowed vpon her, esteeming her the mistris and commaundres of his life, but when he saw his suite despised, and his goodwill nothing regarded, and seeing no hope of her good will and fauour, he determined, that seeing his suite tooke no effect; to demaund his golde and iewels againe. And vpon a time comming vnto her, requested that he might haue his gifts againe, to whom disdainfully she made answere that he should stay for it: and the young man hauing been thus driuen off longer than hee thought good of, made no more adoe but arested her for the iewels.

The stout damsel that had neuer before been in the like daunger, was so astonished & dismayed, that she concluded on condition he would let his Action fal, & not to think euer the worse of her afterward, to marrie him by a certain day, & to make him her husbād: And this before good witnes she vowed to performe. Brewen was hereof very ioyfull and released his prisoner on his owne perill being not a little glad of his good successe. And thereupon so soone as might be, made preparation for their mariage, albeit it proued the worst bargain that euer he made in his life. Now when Parker vnderstoode of this thing, he was most grieuously vexed, and as one hauing deepe intrest to the possession of her person, stormed most outragiously, and with bitter speeches so taunted and checkt her, that she repented the promised she made to Brewen, although she could not any way amend it, neuerthelesse it kindled such a hatred in her heart against her new made choyce, that at length it turned to Brewens death & destruction. And this accursed Parker although he was not as then in estate to marrie (notwithstanding he ere then had lien with her and gotten her with child) & would neuer let her rest, but continually vrged her to make him away by one meanes or other. Diuers and sundry times had they talke together of that matter, and although she often refused to work his death, yet at

length

length the grace of GOD being taken from her, she consented by his direction to poyson Brewen: after which deede done Parker, promised to marrie her so soone as possibly he could.

Now she had not been maried to Brewen aboue three dayes whē she put in practise to poyson him. And although the honest young man loued hir tenderly, yet had she conceiued such deadly hatred against him, that she lay not with him after the first night of her mariage, neither could she abide to be called after his name but still to be termed Anne Welles as she was before: And to excuse her from his bed, she sayd she had vowed neuer to lie by him more till he had gotten her a better house. And the more to shadow her trecherie & to shew the discontent she had of his dwelling she lodged neuer a night but the first in his house, but prouided her a lodging neere to the place where this graceles Parker dwelt. By this meanes the villaine had free accesse to practise with her about the murther, who was so importunate and hastie to haue it done that the wednesday after she was married she wickedly went to effect it, euen according as Parker had before giuen direction: which was in this sorte. The varlet had bought a strong deadly poyson, whose working was to make speedy haste to the heart, without any swelling of the body or other signe of outward confection. This poyson the wicked woman secretly caried with her to her husbands house, with a mery pleasaunt countenance, and very kindly shee asked her husband how he did, giuing him the good morrow in most courteous manner, and asked if he would haue that colde morning, a measse of suger soppes, (for it was the weeke before shrouetide) I mary with a good will wife (quoth he) and I take it verie kindly that you will doe so much for me, alas husband (quoth she) if I could not find in my heart to doe so small a matter for you (especially being so lately married) you might iustly iudge me vnkinde, And therwithall went to make ready his last meat, the thing being done, shee powred out a measse for him, and strewed secretly therein part of the poyson, and hauing set the porringer downe beside her, while she put the posnet on the fire againe, with her rising vp from the fire, her coat cast downe that measse which for her husband she had prepared, out alas quoth she, I haue spilt a measse of as good sugar sops as euer I made in my life. Why, quoth her husband, is there no more? Yes, quoth she, that there is, two, as good as they or I will make them as good; but it greeues me that any good thing should so unluckily be cast away. What woman quoth he? vex not at the matter, your ill lucke goe with them: mary Amen, quoth she, speaking God knowes with a wicked thought, though the well meaning man thought on no euill.

But I pray you John (said she) shall I intreate you to fetch mee a penny worth of red herrings, for I haue an earnest desire to eate some, that I will quoth he with a good will. This sly shift she deuised to haue his absence, that she might the better performe hir wicked intent, and by the time he came againe she had made ready a messe of suger sops for him, one for her selfe, and another for a little boye which she brought with her, but her husbands she had poysoned as before: when he was come, she gaue her husband his messe, and she and the childe fell also to eating of theirs. Within a pretty while after hee had eaten his, hee began to ware very ill about the stomack, feeling also a grieuous griping of his inward partes, wherupon he tould his wife he felt himselfe not well, how so quoth she you were well before you went forth, were you not? yes indeed was I said he, then he demaunded if she were well, she answered I: so likewise said the childe. Ah quoth her husband, now I feele my selfe sicke at the very heart: and immediatlie after he began to vomet exceedingly, with such straines as if his lungs would burst in peeces, then he requested her to haue him to bed, neuer mystrusting the trecherie wrought against him. Now when it drew somewhat late, she tould her husband she must needs goe home to her lodging, and when he requested her to stay with him, she said she could not nor would not: And so unnaturally left the poysoned man all alone that whole night longe, without either comfort or companie. All that night was he extreame sicke, worse and worse, neuer ceasing vomiting til his intralles were all shrunke and broken within him (as is since supposed.) The next morning she came to him againe, hauing been once or twice sent for, but made little semblance of sorrow, and when he quibd her with unkindnes, for not staying with him one night, she asked him if he would haue her forsworne, did I not quoth she sweare I would not stay in the house one night, till you had gotten another: well Anne quoth hee, stay with mee now, for I am not long to continue in this world, now God forbid quoth she) and with that she made a shewe of great heauines and sorrow,

and

and then made him a caudle with suger and other spices, and so on the thursday, immediatly after he had eaten it he dyed, & on the Friday he was buried. No person as then suspecting any manner of euill done to him by his wife, but esteemed her a very honest woman, although through her youth, she knew not as then how to behaue her selfe to her husband so kindely as she ought, which they imputed to her ignorance, rather then to any mallice conceaued against her husband. Now you shall vnderstand that within a small space after her husband was dead, she was knowne with child, and safely deliuered: euery neighbour thinking it had béen her husbands, although she since confessed it was not, but that child liued not long but dyed.

The murder lying thus vnespyed, who was so lusty as Parker with the Widdow, being a continuall resorter to her house, whose welcome was answerable to his desier. And so bould in the end he grew with her, that she durst not denie him any thing he requested, and became so ielious, that had shée lookt but merely vpon a man, she should haue knowne the price thereof, and haue bought her merement déerely. And yet was he not married vnto her, yea to such slauerie and subiection did he bring her, that she must runne or goe wheresoeuer he pleased to appoint her, held hee vp but his finger at any time, if she denied him either money or whatsoeuer else he listed to request, he would so haule and pull her, as was pittie to behold, yea and threaten to stabbe and thrust her through with his dagger, did she not as he would haue her in all things, so that he had her at commandement whensoeuer hée would, and yet could shée scant please him with her diligence. In this miserable case hée kept her vnmarried for the space of two yeares after her husband was dead, at length he got her with child againe, which when the woman knew, she was carefull for the sauing of her credit to kéepe it vnspied so long as she could, in so much that she would not goe forth of her dores for feare her neighbours should perceaue her great bellie. In the meane space Parker comming vnto her, she was vpon one day aboue the rest most earnest with him to marrie her. You sée (quoth shée) in what case I am, and if you wil not for your owne credit, yet for my credits sake marrie me, and suffer mée not to be a poynting marke for others, and a shame among my neighbours. The varlet hearing the great mone shee made vnto him was

was nothing moved therewith, but churlishly answered, shee should not appoint him when to marrie, but if I were so minded (quoth he) I would be twice aduised how I did wed with such a strumpet as thy selfe, and then reuiled her most shamefully: whereunto shee answered shee had neuer been strumpet but for him, and wo worth thee (quoth she) that euer I knewe thee, it is thou and no man else that can triumph in my spoyle, and yet now thou refusest to make amends for thy fault: my loue to thee thou hast sufficiently tried, although I neuer found any by thee. Out arrant queane (quoth he) thou wouldst marry me to the end thou mightest poyson me as thou didst thy husband, but for that cause I meane to keepe me as long out of thy fingers as I can, and accurst be I if I trust thee or hazard my life in thy hands: why thou arrant beast (quoth shee) what did I then, which thou didst not prouoke me to doo, if my husband were poysoned, thou knowest (shameles as thou art) it had neuer been done but for thee, thou gauest me the poyson, and after thy direction I did minister it vnto him, and woe is mee, it was for thy sake I did so cursed a deede. These speeches thus spoken betweene them in vehemencie of spirite, was ouer heard of some that reuealed it to the maiestrates, whereupon the woman was carried before Alderman Haward to be examined, & the man before Iustice Younge, who stoode in the denial thereof very stoutly, neither would the woman confesse any thing, till in the ende shee was made to beleeue that Parker had bewrayed the matter, whereupon she cōfessed the fact in order, as I haue declared. Then was she carried into the countrey to be deliuered of her childe, and after brought back to prison. And then shee and Parker were both araigned and condemned for the murder at the sessions hall nere Newgate, and the woman had iudgement to be burned in Smythfield, and the man to bee hanged in the same place before her eyes. This was accordingly performed, and they were executed on Wednesday last, being the 28. of Iune 1592. two yeares and a halfe after the murder was committed. The Lord giue all men grace by their example to shunne the hatefull sinne of murder, for be it kept neuer so close and done neuer so secret, yet at length the Lorde will bring it out, for blood is an vnceassant crier in the eares of the Lord and he will not leaue so vilde a thing vnpunished.

FINIS.

A True Discourse. Of the practises of Elizabeth Caldwell (*STC* 7293) is reproduced with permission from th clear Huntington Library copy. The text-block measures 108 × 195 mm.

The following words are a transcription of the original:

B2v.1	many liue, one or two pickt out by the hand of God, must
B2v.2	thousands in feare
B2v.3	worldes terror
C3r.1	raunce must not excuse you, for the Prophet saith
C3r.10	as our Saviour saith, *he that dispiseth you, dis-*
C3r.11	*piseth me,*
C3r.14	loue one another saith our Saviour
C3r.18	if euer we desired to be partakers of
C3r.19	spirituall Saboth in heauen, whereof ours on
C3v.1	words, as concerne of voca-
C31.4	assured he is a iealous
C3v.5	and will visite sinners, and one seed of his
C3v.6	shall not be lost
C3v.8	willingly indeuour
C3v.9	the condemnation of those who wilfully oppose
C3v.10	to pro-
C3v.17	since taken
C3v.18	execute his vengance a-
C3v.19	disobedient wretches
C3v.31	he deferre the Sessions, yet they will come,
C3v.32	he haue Leaden feete, yet hath he Iron
C4r.1	hands, though the fier light not vppon *Sodome* all
C4r.2	came. Doe not therefore
C4r.5	shal be cut
C4r.6	be stoned
C4r.9	if we wilfully persist
C4v.1	sed are the people that are in such a case,
C4v.3	nether be you
C4v.5	runne on, the more you set on the score
C4v.32	*Your poor wife*

A True Discourse Of the practises of *Elizabeth Caldwell*, Ma: *Ieffrey Bownd*, *Isabell Hall* widdow, and *George Fernely*, on the parson of Ma: *Thomas Caldwell*, in the County of Chester, to haue murdered and poysoned him, with diuers others.

Together with her manner of godly life during her imprisonment, her arrainement and execution, with *Isabell Hall* widdow; As also a briefe relation of Ma. *Ieffrey Bownd*, who was the Assise before prest to death.

Lastly, a most excellent exhortorie Letter, written by her own selfe out of the prison to her husband, to cause him to fall into consideration of his sinnes, &c. Seruing likewise for the vse of euery good Christian. Beeing executed the 18. of Iune. 1603.

VVritten by one then present as witnes, their owne Country-man, *Gilbert Dugdale*.

(·.·)

AT LONDON,
Printed by Iames Roberts for Iohn Busbie, and are to be sold at his shop vnder Saint Peters Church in Cornewell. 1604.

To the right vertuous, the Ladie *Marie Cholmsly*, & the right worshipfull these Knights; Sir *Tho: Houlcroft*, Sir *Iohn Sauadge* of Egerton, Sir *Iohn Egerton*, Sir *Peter VVarborton*, Sir *Rowland Stanly*, Sir *Vrian Leigh*, Sir *Tho: Aston*, Sir *Thomas Smith*, Sir *Tho: Sauadge*, Sir *George Leister*, Sir *VVilliam Damport*, Sir *Tho: Stanly*, Sir *George Booth*, Sir *Henry Bunberry*, Sir *Hukin Beeston*, Sir *Richard Wilbrome*, Sir *Richard Brooke*, Sir *Richard Egerton*, Ma. *Peter Warborton* Esquire, Ma. *Thomas Wilbrom* Esquire, Ma. *Thomas Brooke* Esquire, Master *Richard Granesnor* Esquire, Ma. *Hugh Calmelie* Esquire, Ma. *Robert Cholmsly*, Esquire, Ma. *Ralfe Egerton* of Ridly, Esquire, Ma: *Thomas Marburie* Esquire, Ma. *Richard Brerton* of Wetten-hall, Esquire, and all the rest, as well Knights as Gentlemen then at the Assiles present, the true witnesses of this following historie: your kind poore Countryman *Gilbert Dugdale*, engaged to you all in debt and dutie, committeth this dicourse with true and due commends: with continuall prayers for your good healths, and succesfull fortunes.

MOst indered and right vertuous Ladie, and you the rest of the right VVorshipfull these kinde *Cheshiere* Knights; After my long beeing at *Chester*, in the time of this reported trouble. I in my mellancholie walkes bethought me of the strange inuasion of Sathan, lately on the persons of *Elizabeth Caldwell*, and her bloody louer *Iefferie Bownd*, together with that vntimely actor *Isabell Hall* widdow, howe that vglie fiende (euer mans fatall opposite) had made practise, but I hope not purchase, of theyr corruptible liues, & brought them to the last steppe of mortall miserie. And then reuoluing with my selfe, the great goodnes of God, in calling sinners to repentance, and withall, admiring his gifts in the penitent, I could no lesse then write my harts trouble, as well to pertake the world with my meditation, as to make them vvonder at this *Cheshiere* chaunce; and thereby to plant or to engrafe a kinde of feare by this way of example, howe murder should heereafter beare any braine in sensible creatures, considering how the very stones shal bewray the inward thoughts of massaker. All these considered, when I had coted this wonder, thinking how incredulous our Nation is in things true, and how vncertaine they are to beleeue fopperies fayned, I could no lesse for the certaintie heereof, but call you to witnesse of the proofe, because sith such an example was preferd vnto vs, that others, not eye witnes therevnto, might the rather assure themselues of the same. First, I knowing your generall griefes for the fall of so good a Gentlewoman, and when no remedy could be, to comfort such a godly soule, aswell in her time of imprisonment as at the houre of her death, my owne occasions also for that time considered, and beeing your true and naturall Countryman, I could doe no lesse but ostend my dutious loue to you all in this kinde, desiring you to accept my poore mite, onely considering this, the poore mans plenty is prayer to regrate your worthy loues, & as truly as I liue, that shall be no niggard; for that night wherein I lie me downe, and pray not for you all, let my rest be broad-waking slumbers, and my quiet, waking dreames; and that will be punishment more then I would enioy for so regardlesse a good as I so late and so happily receaued. True it is that diuers reports passed vp and downe the streets of Loudon as touching this act of murder, but how scandelously, as fiue murdred, three murdred by the meanes of six persons, which your VVorships know is false, only three murdered one; marry the intent was to him that now liues. Therefore being an eare-witnes to this false alarum, it made me more diligent in the setting foorth the truth, whereby GOD in his power might be knowne, sathan in his meaning no doubt ouerthrowne, and the worlds idle fabling by a contrary meaning knowne. For as it was, it was, and no otherwise, and thus it was, as your presences both at the examination, arraignement, and execution can iustifie; and how odious it is to heare any truth rackt by slaundering tongues, iudge or imagine; onely this, pardon my boldnes, witnes the right, accept my good will in the publishing; and so I commit you to Gods protection.

Your poore Countryman, euer yours, *Gilbert Dugdale.*

The practise of *Elizabeth Caldwell*, against the life of her owne husband.

I purpose God willing to discribe in briefe, the life and death of Elizabeth Caldwell, late wife of Thomas Caldwell in the countie of Chester, and daughter to one Maister Duncalffe of the sayd countie; A gentleman of very good sort, who fatherly and carefully trained vp his daughter from her infancie, she being framed and adorned withall the gifts that nature could challenge, and wanting no good education, did in her tender infant yeares bestowe her in marriage; to the said Thomas Caldwell, giuing her a good dower to her better preferring in the sayd marriage; with a yearely newety of ten pounds, to extend to her said husband, and his heires for euer: and as the like matches doe not often proue well, so this Caldwell being young, and not experienced in the world, gaue his minde to trauell, and see forraine countries, which tended rather to his losse then profit, as also to the great discontentment of his wife, and other his friends, leauing her often times verie bare, without prouision of such meanes as was fitting for her, ẏ by these courses hee did withdrawe her affection from him, so ẏ in the continuance of his absence; a young man, named Iefferey Bownd, a neighbour vnto the said Elizabeth Caldwell, and she as I sayd before, inioying all the excellent gifts of nature, set his affections abroch, and being a man of good wealth, spared neither cost nor industrie both by himselfe & others,

to

to withdrawe her to his unlawfull desire, and omittnig no opportunitie in this sute; though she along time withstood their allurements, insomuch that hee feede an old woman named Isabell Hall, late wife of Iohn Hall, and preferred as an instrument to worke her to an unlawfull reformation, so that in processe of time, with many earnest perswasions, they wone this silly soule, to their will; and hauing so done, the sayd Bownds insatiable desire could not bee so satisfied, but perswaded her of himselfe, and also by the sayd Isabell Hall, to yeelde her consent by some meanes to murder her sayd husband, the which she was though drawne to the other, yet very unwilling to agrée unto that. But by many and often assaults and incouragements, their perswasions did worke with her, and tooke effect; the which being obtained, then were they as busie as before, deuising which way, to set their deuillish and most hellish practises aworke, preferring many deuises for the accomplishment thereof. And shee often times entring into consideration with her selfe, what a damnable part it was, first to abuse her husbands bed, and then in seeking to depriue him of his life, was greatly tormented in her conscience, and diuers times, earnestlie intreated them to surcease in this practise, laying before them the great and heauie punishments, prouided for such offenders both in this world, and in the world to come: but their harts being so deeply possest by that filthy enimy to all goodnes, that there was nothing to them more odious then such perswasions, still perseuered in there former wicked inuensions, and drew her to associate them in this villany, laying many plots for the performing of it, amongst which Isabell Hall as she was verie expert in such like actions, beeing an ancient motherly woman, and to all mens iudgements in her outward habite, was farre from harboring such a thought, yet as I was about to say, she aduised Bownd to giue to a brother of hers, namely, George Fernley, fiue pounds, & she would perswade him, that he should use some meanes to murder Caldwell, the which Bownd agreed unto, being that to him all her motions

tions were medicines, and for that her house was the place, that Bownd and Elizabeth Caldwell did resort for there meeting place; and he hauing an intent to further this matter, caused this Fernley to be sent for, and conferred with him: and hee being a man slenderly furnished with meanes, agreed to this there motion, affirming, that he would delay no time till hee had effected their desire, though in my conscience hee pretended nothing lesse, but onely to sooth them with faire words, for lucre of the money, made a showe to Bownd as if he were verie diligent about the execution thereof, but still was preuented, in so much that Bownd entered into a great rage with the poore fellow, and swore most terribly, if hee did not dispatch his busines withall expedition, he would lay him by the heeles for his fiue pounds.

Notwithstanding, hee made delaies so many, that the old fox, I meane Halls wife deuised with her selfe of another course, & willed Bownd to buy some Ratsbane, and she would minister it in Oaten-cakes for that she knewe Caldwell much affected them, and they being made, his wife should giue them vnto him, and so procure his speedy dispatch. Which deuise he verie willingly consented vnto, and vsed no delay in the matter, but presently repaired to a towne in Cheshiere called Knutsforth; there bought the poyson, and brought it to Elizabeth Caldwell, and wished her to send it to Isabell Hall with all speede, whereuppon she receiued it, and instantly vppon the receite thereof, Halls wife sent her maide to Elizabeth, and willed her to send the spice she spoke to her for: so the maide innocently went as her dame commanded her, and receiued the poyson, and brought it to the sayd Isabell Hall her dame, who presently did take it, and minister it, (as I sayd before) in oaten cakes: the which being done, she sent them to Elizabeth Caldwell, where she and her husband did soiourne; whereuppon, being in the euening, she layd them in her chamber with her: In the morning next ensuing, Caldwell as his accustomed manner was, rose verie earlie,

 and

and his wife still keeping her bed, he spied the cakes lie in the windowe, and demaunded of her if he might take any of them, she answered, yea, all if he would, and thereupon he tooke some three or foure of them, and went into the house, and called for some butter to eate them with, the which was brought him.

But let me tell you by the way, so soone as he was departed the chamber with the cakes, feare draue such a terror to her hart as she lay in bed, as she euen trembled with remorse of conscience, yet wanted she power to call to him to refraine them, insomuch as he himselfe did not onely eate of them, but the most part of the folkes in the house, children and all, yet God bestowed his blessing so bountifully on them, as they were all preserued from daunger, sauing one little girle which could not so wel disgest them, which was a neighbours child of sixt or seauen yeares old, and comming in by chance for fier: to the which maister Caldwell gaue a peece of a cake, and she eate it, and by reason she had beene long before visited with sicknes, she went home and died presently, while the rest by way of vomit were saued. But that which maistar Caldwell did vomit vp againe, two doggs and a cat did eate, and they died presently also. Whether vppon the force of that poyson or no the childe died I cannot say, but well I knowe, they were all three brought within the compasse of murder for the death of it, and were all executed at Chester for the same fact, as you shall heareafter vnderstand.

Upon the death of this child, Elizabeth Caldwell was apprehended, and brought before three Justices of the peace; namely, Sir John Sauage, Sir Thomas Aston, and maister Brooke of Norton, where before them she truly confessed all their practises and proceedings from the beginning, euen till that day. Upon which confession, Bownd and Isabell Hall were apprehended, and brought before the same Justices, and examined as touching the murder, and they very stoutly denied all, affirming that

they

they were not guiltie to any such action, although her confession in her Examination did manifest against them, being layd to their charge: all which would not mooue them to acknowledge their fault, the deuill hauing so great a commaund ouer them. Notwithstanding, they were all committed to the Castell of Chester, there to remaine without Baill or Maineprise, till they should be deliuered by due course of Lawe, according to the tenure of warrants directed in such a case.

So the Assise approching within few dayes after theyr commitment, their causes and tryall for that time was reiourned, till the next great Assises holden there. And whether it was by speciall meanes of Bownd made to the Judge, or for that Elizabeth Caldwell was with childe, I cannot truly say, but there they continued from that time, beeing a senight after Easter, till Michelmas following: during which time they were not admitted one to speake to another. And for Elizabeth Caldwell, from her first entrance into prison, till the time of her death, there was neuer heard by any, so much as an idle word to procéede out of her mouth, neither did shée omit any time, during her imprisonment, in seruing of GOD, and séeking pardon for her sinnes, with great zeale and industrie, continually meditating on the Bible, excluding her selfe from all companie, sauing such as might yéelde her spirituall comforts, as learned Diuines, and such, the faithfull seruaunts of God. There was many of all sorts resorted to sée her, as no fewer some daies then thrée hundred persons: and such as she thought were viciously giuen, shee gaue them good admonitions, wishing that her fall might be an example vnto them.

Thus the deceitfull deuill, who hath sometime permission from GOD to attempt the very righteous, (as Iob) was now an instrument to her sorrow, but her feeling faith the more increased, and no doubt to her comfort, though in our eyes terrible: for indéede so it ought, béeing sent from God as an example to thousands. For where so many like, one or two pickt out by the hand of God, must serue as an example to the rest, to keepe thousands in feare of Gods wrath, and the worlds terror. But see her constancie. All the time of her imprisonment, she vsed all possible meanes, both of herselfe, and by those good members that did visit her, to conuert all the rest of the prisoners, which good worke begunne in her did take good effect, for she sent some dayes a dozen Letters to seuerall Preachers to be resolued as touching her fayth, and the want of a sound resolution that G O D had pardoned her offences. Where the Lady Mary Cholmsly of Cholmsly amongst others, together with the comfortable reliefe of one Maister John Battie, (no doubt both Gods Children) so relieued, as want neuer grieued her conscience, but that shee continued in zeale, without griefe of the worldes offences both in soule and body: nay, not onely her, but also to the rest of the prisoners. For note, that death neuer feared or daunted her, but onely fearing shee was not fully purged from her sinnes, till at the end, as by her words at her execution appeareth.

This foresaide Maister Battie well deserues a due remembrance for his clemencie and charitie shewed to that distressed and deceased poore soule, by whose good meanes, which in meere compassion by him extended, did not onely receiue comforts for her bodily releefe, but also great satisfaction for her soule, hee oft imployed such industry to the Learned, both to repare vnto her themselues, as likewise daily in sending vnto her good and learned instructions: Surely, he deserues to be registred in the harts of all well disposed persons, and his demerits (no doubt) will finde restitution at the handes of him, who is the Pay-Maister for all such charitable deserts.

It is also to be noted, that after these three aforenamed persons had remained in prison all the whole Summer, at Michelmas then ensuing the Assises were holden, and Elizabeth Caldwell had her triall, where shee openly before the Judges, and the rest of the Worshipfull Audience, acknowknowledged her offence: for the which shee first demaunded pardon at the hands of God, then of her husband, lastly of all the world: and desiring, as it was euer her prayer, that she might be as a Looking-glasse to all that eyther did see or heare of her fall, that by her they might see into theyr owne frailnes, and the infirmities which are subiect to the flesh. And hauing, as I said, acknowledged her guiltines, was condemned. And by reason shee was not then deliuered of child, still repriued: and at ẏ same Assise Bownd was indited: and whether by euill counsell giuen him, or for his owne obstinacie, I cannot truly report, but he would not answer to the Articles obiected against him, nor refer his cause to GOD and the Country, but stoode mute, though the Iudges very earnestly moued him to put his cause to triall: all which would not perswade him, and therefore, according to the Law, he was adiudged to be prest, receiuing his iudgement on the Saturday, to be executed on Munday following. And for Isabell Hall, her matter that Assise was not called in question, which yeelded her such incouragement, that shee was altogether regardlesse of the good of her soule.

But Bownd, euer before he perceiued how hee should speede, pleaded to euery one whom he had any communion with, of his innocencie, till he saw no hope of life: then hee, before two or three Preachers, and others, did manifest the whole truth, and affirmed that flesh and blood was not able to endure the often assaults that Elizabeth Caldwell had of him, and Isabell Hall: and vppon the Munday about nine of the clocke, was prest: where to euery mans iudgement there present, hee made a very penitent end, beeing hartily sorrowfull for his offences, and very deuoutly craued pardon of GOD and all the world, and so died (I trust) the true seruaunt of Iesus Christ.

Then that night next after his death, Elizabeth Caldwell was deliuered of a boy, which child is yet as I take it, still liuing with another boy she had before her imprisonment, the which are at the keeping of Caldwell their father, and as it was generally reported, hee made sute to the Iudge to procure a warrant to haue his wife executed, within a certaine time after her deliuerie; but how true it was that he made such meanes, I cannot truly affirme, but sure I am, a warrant was granted and sent the keeper for to haue her executed, within 13 daies or thereabouts after she was deliuered, the which was conuented by reason the Cunstable of the castle, did mistake the deliuerie of the warrant to the Sheriffe till the date was out. Though she a senight before the time, had prepared her selfe, only to receiue the mercy of God, and terror of death, yet it pleased God otherwise a while to prolong her daies; which time giuen her, she did not vainely spend, but imploy her vttermost indeuors to obtaine mercie, and forgiuenes in such rare sort, as if I should discribe the perticulers thereof, it would not only be endlesse, and tedious, but I doubt, to the hearers and readers, it would be though incredable, for in her might be seene the true image of a penitent sinner, as the like hath not often in these daies beene seene, God showing his glory so aboundantlie, working her penitency, as to me, and many more, was most admirable. For if she espied in any one, of what calling or degree soeuer, that they wilfully or carelesly abused Gods holy ordinaunces, shee would reproue them for it, and curtiously intreate them to amend such and such abuses; though some disdained she should seeme so to doe, in regard of her owne former offence, though indeede none might better doe it then shee, hauing smarted euen at her soule for her sinnes. This is the frailnes of our flesh, we only disdaine not our afflicted bretheren, but also there good admonitions: God of his mercy I beseech him giue vs grace, that we may see into our fickle estates, and receiue willingly any reproofe that may tend to the good of our poore soules.

So by this meanes, as I showed you before, this Elizabeth Caldwell was still detained in prison till the next Assise following, at what time Isabell Hall was indited, as

an

an actor in this murder, and found guilty by the Jurie, condemned, and executed. And Elizabeth Caldwell also receiued the death of execution at the same instant, though my Lady Cholmsley very worshipfull and louingly made earnest sute, unto the Judge for her repriue till the Assise following: ẏ which by no meanes would be granted. And she seeing her sute would not take effect, being very sorrowfull, like a kind Ladie, went unto Elizabeth Caldwell her selfe, and showed her she could not therein preuaile for her.

Indeede my Lady and others had an intent, if they could haue got her repriue, to haue used meanes to the King for a petition, but seeing it would not be, Elizabeth dutifully yeelded thanks unto her Ladiship; and said shée was very well content to receiue the death ordained for her. My Lady departed, and she practising her former exercises, I meane prayer, untill such time as the Keeper came and told her the Shrieffe was come to the Glouersstone, to receiue her and the rest of the prisoners appointed for death: and she very chéerefully aunswered, I trust in my God I am ready, and farewell to the Lawe, too long haue I béene in thy subiection: & so departing the castell, taking leaue with euery one, and from hence to the place of execution, she some times sung Psalmes, and used other godly meditations, as was thought fitting for her, by those Diuines and godly Preachers, which accompanied her euen to her death.

A Letter written by *Elizabeth Caldwell* to her Husband, during the time of her imprisonment.

(∴)

ALthough the greatnes of my offence deserues neither pittie nor regarde, yet giue leaue vnto your poore sorrowfull wife to speake vnto you what out of her owne wofull experience, with aboundance of griefe and teares, she hath learned in the Schoole of affliction, it is the last fauour that I shall euer beg at your hands, and the last office that euer I shall performe vnto you. And therfore deere Husband, if you haue, any hope or desire, to bee partaker of the ioyes of heauen, let my speeches finde acceptance, and doe not slighly esteeme what I write vnto you, but reade these lines againe, and againe, and lay them vp in your hart, where I beseech Almightie God they may take deepe roote, and impression. For my witnesse is in heauen, that my harts desire and earnest prayer to GOD is, that your soule may be saued. And if the losse of my blood, or life, or to endure any torments that the world can inflict vpon me, might procure your true conuersion, I should esteeme it purchased at an easie rate: but sith none can haue saluation without true Reformation, both inward, and outward, amendement, in changing the affection, words, and works,

works, from euill to good, which till you feele in your soule & conscience to be effectually wrought, you haue not repented, defer not time, but call to God for grace of true Repentance, which may be found euen in this accepted time, when the doores of Gods mercy are open, that so he may haue mercie on you, least he giue you ouer to hardnesse of hart, that you cannot repent: and so you knocke with the foolish virgins, when the date of Gods mercies are out, and then nothing but woe, woe, and vengeance: therefore the longer you deferre, the harder it will be for you to repent: and delayes are most dangerous, for what know you how suddenlie, death may strike you, and then, as the tree falls, so it lies, that is, as you die, so shall you haue, if in true repentance, ioy, if in your sinnes, sorrow. Therefore saith *Salomon*, All that thy hand shall finde to doe, doe it withall thy power, for there is neither worke, nor knowledge, inuention, nor wisedome in the graue whether thou goest.

O husband, be not deceiued with the world, & thinke that it is in your power to repent when you will, or that to say a fewe prayers from the mouth outward a little before death, or to cry God mercie for fashion sake, is true repentance. No, no, not euerie one that saith Lord, Lord, shall enter into the kingdome of heauen, but he that doth the will of my Father which is in heauen, saith our Sauiour, Late repentance is sildome true, & true repentance is not so easie a matter to come by, as the word doth iudge. Doe not presume on it, and so runne on in your sinfull course of life, & thinke to repent when

 you

you list, you can not doe it; for repentance is the rare gift of GOD, which is giuen but to a verie fewe, euen to those that seeke it, with many teares, and verie earnestlie with feruent prayers. None can better speake of it, for none better knoweth it then my selfe, my sorrowfull hart hath smarted for it, and my soule hath beene sick to the gates of hell, and of death to finde it: and to haue it, is more precious then all the world, therefore cease not to pray day and night with the prophet, Turne thou vs vnto thee, ô Lord, and we shall be turned, and with *Ephraim*, conuert thou mee, ô Lord, and I shall bee conuerted: for except you be conuerted, you shall not enter into the kingdome of heauen.

And because none can be conuerted, nor come vnto Christ except the Father drawe him, neuer leaue to solicite the Father of mercy to create a new hart, and renewe a right spirit within you, and call to remembrance the desolutenesse of your life, I speake it not to lay any thing to your charge, for I doe loue you more deerely, then I doe my selfe, but remember in what a case you haue liued, howe poore you haue many times left me, how long you haue beene absent from mee, all which aduantage the deuill tooke to subuert mee. And to further his purpose, he set his hellish instruments a work, euen the practise of wicked people, who continuallie wrought vpon my weaknes, my pouertie, and your absence, vntill they made me yeeld to conspire with them the destruction of your bodie, by a violent & suddaine death; which God in his great mercy preuented, and on the knees of my hart, in the abun-

dance

dance of his compassion, I beseech him to forgiue vs all, & wash our soules in the blood of his Christ, and to open the eyes of your vnderstanding, that you may see by my example, which the prouidence of God, for some secrete cause best knowne to him selfe, hath appointed to come to passe. How weake and wretched wee are, and how vnable to stand of our selues, when it shall please him to take his grace from vs, and to leaue vs to our selues. Therefore good husband, as you tender the welfare of your soule, goe no further on in your sinfull race, but turne vnto the Lord, & so shall you saue your soule aliue. If you continue in your abhominations, and shut your eares against the worde of Exhortation, you cannot haue any hope of saluation, for the booke of God is full of iudgements against wilfull sinners, and mercie is to them that repent & turne:

Therefore I beseech you vse no delay, deferre no time, but presently bee acquainted with the Scriptures, for they will leade you to eternall life: make hast, euen before your hands part with this paper to search therein, that so you may truly vnderstand the wretched estate, & condition of those, who following the lusts of there eyes, wallow in all sensualitie, and so heape vp vengance against the day of wrath: euen heauie Iudgments, no lesse then condemnation both of soule and body. As *Salomon* saith, *Reioyce O young man in thy youth, & let thy hart cheare thee, in the daies of thy youth, and walke in the waies of thy hart, and in the sight of thine eyes, but knowe that for all things God will bring thee to Iudgement*. Remember he spared not the Angells when they sinned, but cast them downe into hell; nor of the old world but eight onely escaped; the rest were drowned in their sinnes because they would not be warned. *Baltasar*, sayth *Daniell*, expounding the fearefull vision of the hands writing, when hee was banqueting with his Concubines, thou art wayed in the Ballance, and are found light.

These and many more are written for our admonition, vppon whom the ends of the world are come, search for them, and I pray God you may be warned by them, and that you may seeke the Lord now while hee may bee found, and call vppon him while he is neere. Behold now the day of saluation, euen now, when he in mercy offereth himselfe vnto vs, by preaching of his word, receiue not these graces in vaine, but redeeme your time, and runne vnto the house of God, and there in the great congregation, power foorth your plaint, with obedience heare the word of God, and indeuour to practise what you heare in your conuersation, for the doores onely shall bee iustified at the last day, the word must iudge vs, in this life it worketh effect, for which it was sent: it either conuerts or hardens, it is the sauour of life, vnto life, or of death, vnto death, it is offered to all: to those that imbrace it, it brings life, to those that will not be reformed by it, it brings death, to those that loue and desire it, it is the quicking spirit, to those that refuse it, it is the killing Letter, it is no speciall argument of God his fauour vnto any, vnlesse they feele the power thereof working reformation in them, then it is the power of his spirit, the pledge of his blessing. Ignoraunce much must not excuse you, for the Prophet saith; my people languish for want of knowledge, and knowledge without practise, leaues al men without excuse, for hee that knoweth his masters will, and doth it not, shall be beaten with many stripes: therefore make more conscience of the word of God, then you haue done, and loue his Messengers, the Preachers that brings that glad tidings, for to loue them is to loue Christ, and to hate them, is to hate Christ, as our Sauiour saith, *he that dispiseth you, dispiseth me*, and it is hard to kick against the prick. And loue the children of God that professe Christ Iesus; for hereby shall men knowne, that you are my Disciples, if you loue one another saith our Sauiour. And for the Saboth day, bee yee assured, that the Lord of heauen, hath not in vaine chosen it to himselfe, commaunding vs to Sanctifie it vnto his holy name; no, no, if euer we desird to be partakers of the spirituall Saboth in heauen, whereof ours on earth is but a tipe, and a figure, then must we striue to keepe the same Saboth on earth as much as in vs lyes, which the Saints keepe in heauen: they are at rest from those labours that mortality is subiect vnto, and vncessantly sing prayses vnto the Lamb; so should we rest that day from the labours of our calling, and spend the whole day in hearing of the word preached, praysing the Lord publickly in the great congregation, priuatly at home with our families, preferring such other holy exercises, as may tend to the glory of God, the comfort of our soules, & the good of others, which we are bound to performe so straightly, as that we may not that day, be

 alowed

alowed to speake such words, as concerne of vocations, And how soeuer it please the world, to thinke of the great God of Heauen; and of the sanctifying of the Saboths, yet be you assured he is a iealous God; and will visite sinners; and lose seede of his word, shall not be lost, but he will be glorified by it either in the saluation of those, who in a good conscience willingly indeuour to sanctifie them, or in the condemnation of those, who wilfully oppose themselues against his blessed ordinances, to prophane them: which is one of the crying sinnes of this land, wherewith the whole Kingdome is infected: and if there were not some fewe to stand in the gap, for whose sake the Lord doth spare the rest, it had not beene possible, we should so long haue escaped his heauy iudgements.

O deere husband, the Lord hath long since taken his sword in his hand, to execute his vengeance against all disobedient wretches, who turne the Saboth of the Lord, into a day of wantonnes, liberty, and licentiousnes, and although in his great mercy he doth yet forbeare to proceede to iudgement, as it were in great mercy, waiting our repentance, yet there will suddainely come a day of reckoning, all together: and the wicked make the patience of our God an occasion to commit sinne, and prophanes, yet let them knowe, the Lord will take vengance of his aduersaries, and reserue wrath for his enemies, and though hee be slowe to anger, yet is he great in power, and will not surely cleare the wicked: though he deferre the Sessions, yet they will come, and though he haue Leaden feete, yet hath he Iron hands, bands; though the fier light not vpon *Sodome* all the euening, yet it came on. Doe not therefore prouoke the Lord any longer by your prophanes, for he is strong, readie to punnish, and hath promised, that the person that dispiseth his words, shalbe cut of. Did hee not commaunde a man to be stoned to death, for gathering a fewe stickes on the Saboth day, and is hee not still the same God? yes certaine, his arme is not shortned if we wilfully persist in our disobedience.

Sixe market dayes hee hath giuen vs, to prouide vs necessaries for our bodies, and but one hath hee chosen for himselfe to be a day of holines, which is the market day for the soule, wherein wee should prouide vs of comforts for the whole weeke. The excellencie and woorth of this day is vnspeakable to those that sanctifie it. It is the badge and liuerie whereby they are knowne to bee the seruaunts of God: to those that prophane it, in spending the day in worldly pleasures, drunkennes & filthinesse, it is the certaine badge and liuerie, whereby they are knowne to be the seruants of the deuill, according to the sayings of the Apostle; *knowe you not that to whomsoeuer ye giue your selues as seruaunts to obey, his seruants yee are, to whom yea obey, whether it be of sinne vnto death, or of obedience vnto righteousnes.*

If my people will sanctifie my Saboth, saith the Lord, it shall be a signe betweene me and them, that they may knowe that I ame the Lord there God; and blessed are they who haue the Lord for their God. So that to those that prophane the Saboth, the Lord is not their God, but the deuill: and cur-

sed

seehere the people that are in such a case, therefore deere husband, deferre no time, put not of from day, to day, to turne vnto the Lord, neither be you deceiued; for God is not mocked, the longer you runne on, the more you set on the score, and such as you sowe, such shall you reape: for the Lord hath sayd, Hee that heareth my words, and doth blesse himselfe in hart, saying, I shall haue peace, although I walke according to the stubbernes of my hart, thus adding drunkennes to thirst, the Lord will not bee mercifull vnto him, but the wrath of the Lord, & his iealosie, shall smooke against that man; and euery curse that is written in this booke shall light vppon him, and the Lord shall put out his name from vnder heauen. but vnto them that repent, the Lord hath sayd, when the wicked turneth away from his wickednes, that he hath committed, and doth that which is lawfull and right; hee shall saue his soule aliue. You see the iudgements of God are begunne alreadie in your house, happie shall you be if you make a holy vse of them, otherwise heauier may be expected, especially, if you persist. In his mercy he hath spared you, and doth yet waite for your repentance, doe not you abuse his patience any longer, lest thereby you prouoke him to proceede to execution against you, but imbrace his mercy which is yet offered vnto you: for which, that you may so do, I shall not cease, to pray whilst I liue; to him who onely is able to effect it, euen the Lord of heauen, who send vs ioyfull meeting at the day of our Resurrection.

Your poore wife
Elizabeth Caldwell.

The words of Elizabeth Caldwell at the time of her death.

FIrst she desired, that the Lord would giue a blessing vnto the speeches that she deliuered, if they might tend to the conuerting of many of the hearers, and also she sayd, that the word of God did not giue her any priuiledge, and authority to sinne, but that it was her owne filthy flesh, the illusions of the deuill, and those hellish instruments which he set on worke: yet notwithstanding, she euer had a detestation to those sinnes that she liued in, but she affirmed that she wanted grace to auoyd them, therefore as she had giuen a great scandall to the word of God, by professing, and not practising the same, euen so she desired the great mercy of God, to forgiue her that sinne, acknowledging that she stoode to presumptiously vpon her owne conceite, and [illegible] vowing and swearing, that she would neuer [illegible] such things, but suddainly fell into the like againe.

Therefore she gaue Saint Paules admonition vnto euery one, Let him that thinketh he stands, take heede of a present fall: likewise she exhorted all to the diligent obseruation of the Saboth day, saying, that it was the chiefe and

D. capitall

capitall sinnes was, the neglect thereof, and although the world did recon and esteeme it a small matter, yet she knewe it to be one of her greatest sinnes, wishing all people in the feare of God, to make a reuerent account of the Lords glorious Saboth, she complained much of adultery, and said it was that filthy sinne which was the cause of her death, and was perswaded in her conscience, that her afflictions was rather for that, then any murder shee euer committed: notwithstanding, shee yeelded her selfe culpable in concealing of it, manifesting that in regard of her sinnes, and iniquities, she deserued a thousand deaths, praying most earnestly vnto God, that her selfe might be a warning and example vnto all there present, wishing them most earnestly to serue the Lord, of what degree soeuer they were, if they were neuer so poore, but were forst to craue there liuing from doore to doore, which done, then were they happy creatures.

Then againe, she admonished all to keepe the Saboth, to goe to the church, and heare the word of God preached, for that was the only truth, and able to saue their soules. But as touching Papistrie, she euer hated it, knowing it contrary and flatly opposite against the truth of the great God of heauen, and his holy word, praying for the confution and desolution of the great whore of Babilon, but most deuoutly and sencerely, praying for the currant passage of the Gospell of Christ Jesus throughout the whole world, to the conuerting of thousands, desiring that the very stones of the streete might set foorth the glory of God: and withall, most religiously she prayed for the Kings most excellent Maiestie, and sayd she might call him her King while shee liued, that his sacred & royall Person, might be a bright shining lampe of Gods glory in the aduancement of the Gospell of Christ, and the ouerthrowe of poperie & superstition, in these his Kingdomes and dominions. Then made knowne that she could teach as the Preachers, for they taught as they found it in the word, and she was able to speake from a feeling hart, ve-

ry

ry confidently affirming, that her sinnes were the greatest reason of the dulnes and hardnes of her hart, and the seperation of Gods mercies from her: and therefore she carefully aduised all to beware of sinne, because it was hatefull and odious in the sight of God, and all reasonable creatures.

Concerning repentance, shee spake thus, that it was not in the power of man to repent when hee list, but the only gift of God, protesting before the Lord of heauen and earth, that during the time of her imprisonment, being a full yeare and a quarter, she had sought the Lord with many bitter teares, with broken and contrite hart, to see if his Maiestie would be intreated, and yet she found not such assurance as she desired: but auouched what she did, was done in simplicity of hart, whatsoeuer the world did other was censure. Moreouer, saying that in the mercies and merites of Christ Iesus, shee hoped her sinnes were pardoned, and sayd I belieue Lord, helpe my vnbeliefe. Also she sayd, that in the time of her imprisonment, the Lord had beene very gracious and mercifull vnto her, for many the faithfull ministers, and deere seruants of Iesus Christ, had recourse vnto her, by whose meanes she had recouered great comfoorth, praysing the Lord for the same: yet notwithstanding, the world most iniuriously did deride, scofe, and mock them, which was most wicked and abhominable: saying, that if there were fortie and two children deuoured for mocking the Prophet Eliza, what then shall befall of them that doe blaspheme the name of the great God of heauen, prophane his holy Saboth, speake euill of his word, and abuse his faithfull Ministers. Therefore she desired all to turne from their sinnes, and to turne to the Lord by true and vnfained repentance, praysing very earnestly for her husbands conuersion, and that her two children might haue the feare of God before their eyes, and that the glory of God might appeare in the conuersion of prisoners, though it were with the losse of her owne life, so infinite was her zeale.

Then shee prayed the Lord, that hee would pardon all her grieuous and heynous sinnes in the bloodshed of Christ Jesus, beseeching him to clense her from her secret sinnes: praying that she might be a Doore-keeper in the house of God, and receiue the meanest place of glory. Then said shee, that if the great and tall Ceaders of the Church of God haue fallen, as David, Salomon, and Manasses, how then coulde shee stand, beeing but a bramble, and weake wretched woman. Therefore shee exhorted euery one to depend onely vpon the Lord, and not to stand vpon theyr owne strength as shee had done. And greatly then desiring all the people to pray vnto GOD for her, shee called for her Prayer booke, reading and praying zealouslie and deuoutly to Almighty GOD, with her eyes lift vp towards heauen; which done, shee requested that they would sing a Psalme, reading it her selfe, & singing with a good spirit, that afterwards she vttered that shee felt the mercies of GOD, and her soule was much comforted: and hoped, that in the blood of Christ Jesus her sinnes were pardoned: and saide shee coulde not amend that which was past: but was most hartily sorrowfull for her former sinnes: saying, that if shee shoulde liue yet many yeeres, her desire would be in seruing the Lord: therefore she desired him vpon the knees of her hart, that hee would respect the will for the deede, and accept her poore desires: saying, O suffer me yet once to recouer my strength, before I goe hence and be seene no more. Praying likewise for all those that ministred comforts vnto her in her misery and distresses, that the Lord would blesse them, and continue them faithfull vnto the end.

Then forgiuing, and asking forgiuenes of all, making her selfe ready, saying her bodily death did not dismay her, concluding with these her last words, Lord Jesus receiue my spirit: and so she left this miserable world, and dyed the true seruaunt of Jesus Christ, the xviij. day of June, 1603.

¶ Nowe yet againe remember our old beldame afore-named, that vncharitable creature Isabell Hall, widdow, béeing the onely instrument of this timelesse action: who standing on the Ladder, and ready to suffer for her fact, did notwithstanding very stoutly denie euery thing that had béene done in theyr late procéedings, nay and abiurd it, had not Elizabeth Caldwell with affirmation of all inserted her confession in that behalfe: Who with an easie repentance to the worlds eye, ended her life. Whereby may be séene how strong the deuill in some actions is, that shée by whose instigation all was done, both in the adulterie and murder, would so impudently deny euery particuler, notwithstanding the triall of the cause both manifested by Judge and Jurie. But thus we sée the boldnes of sinne, and the coldnesse of the truth, till God in mercie makes plaine the truth of the one, and the wonder of the other. All which tending to the example of others, may moue vs to liuely repentance, which not doone, saluation cannot come, but truly effected, bréedes both the comfort of the soule and body. To which comfort, God in mercy bring vs for his sonne Jesus Christ his sake.

FINIS.

To the right honourable, and his singuler good Lady, the Lady *Mary Chandois*, R. A. wisheth health and euerlasting happinesse.

MY honourable and very good Lady, considering my dutie to your kind Ladiship, & remembring the vertues of your prepared minde, I could doe no lesse but dedicate this strange worke to your view, being both matter of moment and truth. And to the whole world it may seeme strange, that a Gentlewoman so vvell brought vp in Gods feare, so well married, so vertuous euer, so suddainly wrought to this act of murder; that when your Ladiship doth read aswell the Letter as the Booke, of her owne indighting, you will the more wonder that her vertues coulde so aptly tast the follies of vice and villanie. But so it was, and for the better proofe that it was so, I haue placed my kinsmans name to it, who was present at all her troubles, at her comming to prison, her beeing in prison, and her going out of prison to execution. That those Gentlemen to whom he dedicates his worke witnessed, may also be pertakers in that kind, for the proofe thereof, that your Ladiship & the

the world so satisfied, may admire the deede, and hold it as strange as it is true.

We haue many giddie pated Poets, that coulde haue published this Report with more eloquence, but truth in plaine attire is the easier knowne: let fixion maske in Kendall greene. It is my qualitie, to adde to the truth, truth, and not leasings to lyes. Your good Honor knowes *Pincks* poore hart, who in all my seruices to your Late deceased kind Lord, neuer sauoured of flatterie, or fixion: and therefore am now the bolder to present to your vertues, the view of this late truth, desiring you to so thinke of it, that you may be an honourable mourner at these obsequies, and you shall no more doe, then manie more haue doone. So with my tendered dutie, my true ensuing storie, and my euer wishing well, I do humbly commit your Ladiship to the prison of heauen, wherein is perfect freedome,

Your Ladiships euer,
in duty and seruice,
Robert Armin.

The Araignement & burning of Margaret Ferne-seede (*STC* 10826) is reproduced with permission from th unique copy at The British Library (shelfmark C.21.b.5). The text-block measures 78 × 140 mm.

THE Araignement & burning of *Margaret Ferne-seede*,

for the Murther of her late Husband *Anthony Ferne-seede, found deade in* Peckham Field neere Lambeth, hauing once before attempted to poyson him with broth, being executed in S. Georges-field the last of Februarie.
1608

LONDON
Printed for *Henry Gosson*, and are to be solde at the Signe of the Sunne in Pater-noster-rowe.
1608

THE

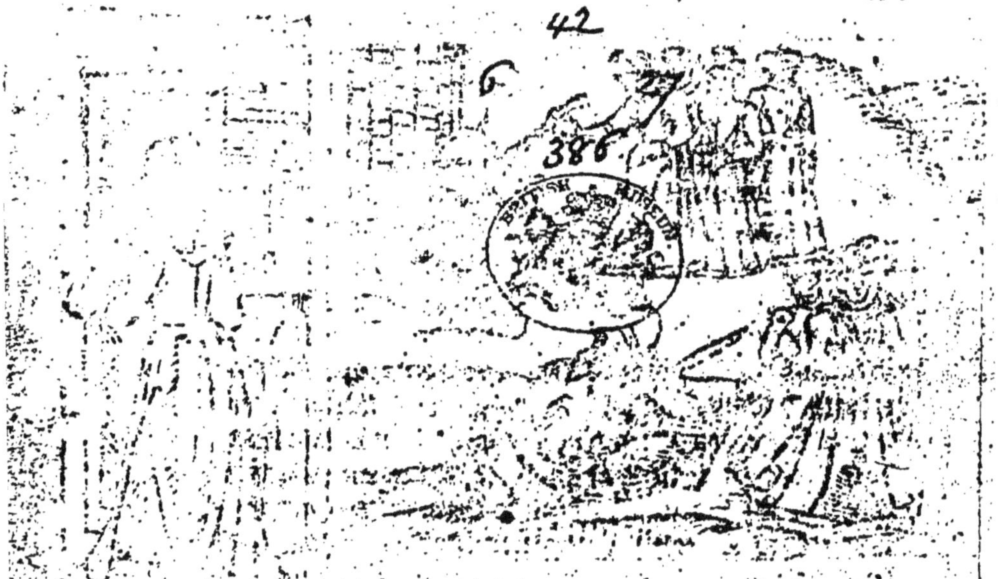

LONDON

THE Burning of Margaret Ferne-ſeede.

THe groſeſt part of folly, and the moſt repugnant, euen vnto our owne naturall reaſon, is to thinke that our hidden abhominations can be concealed from the eie of the Almightie, or that hee ſeeing our bloodie and crying ſinnes, will not either reueale them before his Miniſters of publique iuſtice, or in his beſt pleaſ'd time, power downe ſome vengeance for ſuch preſumptuous and rebellious offences. Oh! the miracles in theſe Reuelations are ſuch, and ſo infinite, that the thought of man or his wiſdome is but meere weakeneſſe, going about to comprehend ſuch vnſpeakeable iudgements: & of this wee haue before our eyes a moſt notable exāple in this wretched woman, of whome my preſent diſcourſe intreateth, named Margaret Ferne-ſeede, a womā that euen from her time of knowledge (if the generall report of the world, according to the old adage may be taken for an Oracle) was giuen to all the looſeneſſe & lewdneſſe of life, which either vnlawfull luſt, or abhominable proſtitution could violently caſt vpon her, with the greatest infamie, yea, and with such a publique and irrespectiue vnchastitie, that neither beeing chaste nor caute, she regarded not either into what eare the loathsomnesse of her life was sounded, or into what bed of lust her lascivious bodie was transported: in this more then beastiall lasciuiousnes, hauing consumed the first part of her youth, finding both the corruption of her blood to check the former heate of her lust, and the too generall vglinesse of her prostitution, to breed a loath in her ordinarie customers, being then confirmed in some more strength of yeares, tooke a house neare vnto the Iron-gate of the Tower, where she kept a most abhominable and vilde brothell house, poysoning many young women with that same wherewith her owne body long before was filthilie bebotched. From this house at the Iron-gate, she was married vnto one Anthony Ferne-seede a Taylor, dwelling in Ducke-lane, but keeping a shop vppon Adle-hill neare Carter-lane. This Anthony was amongst his neighbours, reputed to be both sober and of verie good conuersation.

Now it hapned that some few moneths agoe in the fieldes of Peckham neare London, there was found a man slaine hauing his throate cut, a knife in his hand, golde rings vppon his fingars, and fortie shillings in money in his pursse, his woundes of so long continuace that it was not onely corrupted, but there was also Maggots, or suchlike filthie wormes ingendered therein, which gaue testimony to the beholders, that he had not slaine himselfe in that place, as well because the place was free from such a spectacle the day before, as also that such corruption could not proceede from a present slaughter. Againe, what the person slaine was no man knewe, both because his phisnomie was altered in his death, and because his acquaintance was little or none in those partes about Peckham: in the end, searching his pockets, and other parts of his apparaile, amongst other notes and reckonings, they found an

Inden-

Indenture wherein a certaine youth, which did serue him was bound vnto him: this Indenture gaue them knowledge both of his name, and of the place of his dwelling, whereupon, certaine discreete persons of Peckham, sent to London to Ducke-lane, and inquiring for the house of one Anthony Ferne-seede, deliuered to his wife the disaster and mischance which had befallen her husband, which her hardened heart receiued, not as a message of sorrow, neither did she grudging of an afflicted countenance giue her remembrance, but as if she had beene the report of some ordinarie or vulgar newes, she imbraced it with an irrespectiue neglect and carelesnes, & demaunded instantly (before the messenger could tell her how he dyed) whether his throate were cut, or that he had cut his owne throate, as either knowing or prophesying how he died, yet to obserue a customarie fashion, or (as the prouerbe is) to carrie a candle before ỹ deuil, she prepares herselfe & her seruant, in all haste to go to Peckham to behold her husband: in ỹ way as she went, it was her chance to meete with one of her husbands antient acquaintance, who feeling that in charitie which she ought to haue felt in nature, began to complaine her misfortune, telling her she had lost a most honest & good husband: she whome the deuill now would not suffer to dissemble, (though his greatest art be in dissimulation) told him her feare was, she should not heare so well of him: he wondring at her vngodly carelesnesse, let her passe, when presently she met another of her acquaintance, who with like charitie to the former began to pittie her griefes, (though griefe was neuer further from her heart) and to wish her those comforts which are fit for affliction; but she as carelesse as before, gaue him (by the neglect of her words) true testimonie how far sorrow was from her heart, which when he noted, he said, why mistris Ferne-seede, is ỹ losse of a good

husband

husband so slightly to be regarded: for mine owne part, had such a mischance falne to my fortune, I should ers this haue wept out mine eyes with true sorrow: but she quickely made him answere, tut sir, mine eyes are ill already and I must now preserue them to mend my cloathes, not to mourne for a husband: after that, in her going, the winde blowing the dust in her face, she takes her skarffe & wiped her eyes, & said she should scarce know her husband when she saw him: these curtizan like speeches made her acquaintãce leaue her, & wished her more grace, so she & her boy came where the bodie was, where more for awe of the Magistrate then any terror she felt, she made many sower faces, but the drinesse of her braine would suffer no moisture to descend into her eyes: many questions were asked her, to which she answered with such constancie, that no suspition could be grounded against her: then was her boy taken and examined, who deliuered the abhomination of her life, and that since her mariage with his maister, she had liued in all disquietnes, rage, and distemperature, often threatning his life and contriuing plots for his destruction: that she had euer since her mariage, in most publique and notorious maner, maintained a yong man, with whom (in his beleif) she had often committed adultrie: that the same young mã since his maisters losse was fled he knew not whether, and that his mistris had euen then before the message of his maisters death, sould all his goods (as he supposed) to fly also after him whom she loued: all these speeches were not only seconded, but almost approued by some of her neighbors, which liued neare vnto her, insomuch that she was the second time taken

into

into a more strict examination, wherein albeit she would not denie any of her generall assertions; yet touching the death of her husband, that she [illegible] & renoun-ced the fact or practise thereof to be hers; with such a shamelesse constancie, that [illegible] amazement in-to all that heard her: in the end by the authoritie of Justice she was committed to the [illegible] prison in Southwarke: during the time of which imprisonment, till her time of tryall, thinking to out face truth with boldnesse, and sin with impudence, she continued still in her exa-minations taken before severall Justices in her former denials, and whereas the dread of imprison-ment laid uppon others, is received as a gentle correcti-on, whereby to looke into themselves, it was to her ra-ther the bellowes of indignation then a temperate pa-tience: rather a [illegible] of revenge, then a cooler of [illegible], & rather a provoker to evill then a perswader to goodnesse, for she was seldome found to bee in charitie with any of her fellow prisoners, nor at any time in quiet with her selfe, rather a provoker than an appeaser of dissentions, [illegible] unthankfull to all them that [illegible] her late home the prison, as shee was to people of honest conversation, having deserved the name of a Bawd) while she lived abroad,

In this uncivill order, spending her houres, the time of tryall comming on, when such offenders were to appeare before the earthly Judge, to answere for their lives past, amongst many others, this Margaret Ferne-seed was one and at the assizes last, according to the or-der of law, she was indighted, & arraigned, the purpose of which inditement, was to have practised the murther of her late husband Anthony Ferne-seede, who as be-fore was found dead in Peckham field nere Lambeth:

to the inditement she pleaded not guiltie , putting her cause to God and the Countrie , which were a credible Iurie paniled, and had there made their personall appearance for that purpose: then were these severall witnesses produced against her, namely of the incontinentnes of her life past, her attempt to poyson her husband before this murther, as also to prepare broth for him, and put powder in it, her slight regard of him in his life, and her carelesse sorrow for him after death: with other circumstances, as the flight of the fellowe whome she had lived long in adulterie with all, her present sale of her goods uppon her husbands murther, as it may be iustly thought, with purpose to flie after him: on which lawfull evidence, she was cōuicted, & after iudgement given her to be burned: and from thence she was conveyed backe to the White Lyon, till the time appointed for her execution.

How

How Margaret Ferne-seede spent her time in prison, from Satterday, the day of her conuiction, till Munday the last of Februarie, when in S. Georges fieldes she was executed.

Being come backe to the prison, on the first night she disposed her selfe according to her auncient habit, being as it were so rooted, and accustomed to euill, that as euen death it selfe had not power to make her forget it, and endeauour a better course: but being at the same time in the prison with her, three Gentlemen who likewise were condemned, and who, though the course of their liues had not taught them to liue well: yet the care of their soules remembred them to dye well. These Gentlemen hauing heard how ill her life past had bene, and that her countenance was as resolute, they perswaded the keeper that they might haue her company, partly to instruct her, but especially y she might see them, & by the reformation of their liues she might learne to amend her owne, and as they did, to prepare her selfe fit for death: whose perswasion and wholsome counsells of their owne, with comfortable promises of our mercifull Sauiour Jesus Christ to them that will stedfastly beleeue in him, and by unfained repentance make way for their saluation, as also with threatning her with the terrible Judgements of Hell, which are prepared for them that perish through lacke of grace, they so wrought in her, she was at last perswaded to make a confession of her former life past, and to repent her of the same. The forme of which was in this manner.

The Burning.

The Confession and repentance of Margaret Ferneseed, after her condemnation in the White Lyon.

TO prepare the reader for this confession of hers, know that I was credibly satisfied, that when the heat of her fury was past, (to which she was much subiect unto) she a womā wel spoken, of faire deliuerāce, and good perswasion: and so to her confession.

To excuse my selfe O Lord before thee, who knowes the conspiracies of our thoughtes euen to the utmost of our actions, (how euer so priuat or publikely committed,) were folly, or to iustifie my selfe were sinne, since no flesh can appeare pure in thy sight: I here therfore, with prostrate knees, & deiected eyes, as unworthie to looke up unto thy diuine Maiestie, with a contrite hearte and penitent soule, also here voluntarily confesse, I am the greatest of sinners, which haue deserued thy wrath and indignation: In this good manner she proceeded, and withall satisfied all that came, & desired to haue priuate conference with her, of the whole course of her life, that in her youth, euen from the age of aptnesse, she had bene a prostitute, whore but growing into desabled yeares, to please the loose desires of such customers, she after turned bawde, a course of life more hatefull in tempting and seducing youth, then the other in committing sinne: the one makes but spoile and rapine of her selfe, and the other of a multitude, for (quoth shee) I my selfe haue had ten seuerall women retaining to my house for that purpose: some were mens wiues, which repaired thither both by appointment, and at conuenient houres, when their husbands might least suspect or haue knowledge of their absence: and these women did

I first tempte to their fall, some, by perswading them they were not beloued of their husbands, especially if I could at any time haue note of any breach or discontent betweene them: others, that their husbands maintained them not sufficiently to expresse their beauty, and according to their owne desarts: of these, the hauing brought my purpose to effect, & that I knew they had offended, I made this booty that they were as fearefull to offend mee, as their husbands should haue knowledge of their offences: and these allowed mee a weekly pention for comming to my house, and durst not at all times but finde opportunitie to come whensoeuer my selfe or such loose friendes, whome either they had bene familiar withall, or now desired to be acquainted with them, should send for any of them, to supply my house, and make spoile of yong maides who were sent out of the countrie by their friends, here with hope to aduance themselues: I went weekly to the Carriers, where if the maide liked mee, I so wrought with the Carrier that shee seldome left mee till I had brought her to be as bad as I purposed, which effected, euery one of them I compelled to giue mee ten shillings a week out of their gettings: hauing as I said seldome lesse then ten whose bodies and soules I kept in this bondage: Besides I confesse I was a continuall receiuer of theft stollen but in all this, as it was badly got, so was it wors consumed for nothing of it did prospere with me, whereby (quoth she) I acknowledge I haue deserued death, and in the highest degree; but for this which I am condemned, Heauen that knoweth best the secrets of our hearts, knowes I am innocent.

But who knowes not that in euill, there is a like impudence to deny, as there is a forwardnesse to act: in which

which we will leaue here whom the law hath found guilty, and hauing thus truly related her owne confession, wee proceed to the manner of execution.

First onely touching the euidence of two Sailers, giuen to the Iurie at her arraignment: Among other circumstances that was auailablest to condemne her, this was one and the chiefest: during the time while she kept a bad house about the Iron-gate by Tower-ditch, there happned a couple of Bargemen to come to reuell at her house with such Guestes as she kept to entertaine lose customers, and hauing spent the whole day in large ryot and much expence, ẏ night being late, for that time they made their lodging there, they beeing a bed, it happned that night (which was seldome) her husband came to make his lodging there also, and being chambered with his wife, but a wall betweene where these Bargemen lay, they could expresslie heare them euerie word that passed betweene them, the effect of which: was, the reprouing of her for her bad life, his perswading her to amendment, which she not willing to listen unto fell a scoulding at him, and so left both his bed and chamber some time passing.

At last Maister Fernesecde heard these Barge-men cough, & wondring to haue strangers lodged in his house (for it was not common to his knowledge) arose out of his bed, and demanded of them what they were: who asked of him also wherefore hee questioned them: mary (quoth hee) for if you be honest men, and haue a care either of your bodies or soules, auoide this house as you would doe poison, least it be the undoing of you all, they seeing him of a comely personage: and that his wordes tended to some purpose, demanded of him what he was that gaue them such wholesome counsell: I am (quoth he) the maister of this house (if (if I had my right) but I am bard of the possession and commande thereof, by a deuilish woman, who makes a Stewes of it to exercise her sinnefull practises: so with some other admonishment left the roome, when these Barge-men tolde mistris Ferneseed what they had heard of her husband, to which she replyed: hāg him slaue and villaine: I will before God bee reuenged of him (nay ere long) by one meanes or other, so worke, that I will bee rid of him, which making good in the iudgement of the Iudge, to gather with her life & prac-tises, she as aforesaid was condemned.

On Munday being the last of February, she had notice giuen her, that in the after-noone she must suffer death, and a Preacher commended vnto her to instruct her for her soules health, who laboured much with her for the confession of the fact, which she still obstinately denied, but made great showe of repen-tance for her life past, so that about two of the clocke in the after-noone she was stripped of her ordinary wea-ring apparell, and vppon her owne smocke put a kirtle of Canuasse pitched cleane through, ouer which she did weare a white sheet, and so was by the keeper deliuered to the Shreue, one each hand a woman leading her, and the Preacher going before her. Being come to the place of execution, both before and after her fastning to the Stake, with godly exhortations her admonished her that now in that minute she would confesse that fact for which she was now ready to suffer, which she denying, the reeds were planted aboute, vnto which fier being giuen she was presently dead.

FINIS.

The Apprehension, Arraignement, and execution of Elizabeth Abbot (*STC* 23) is reproduced with permission from a Harvard College Library photostat of the now destroyed British Library copy, the only one known previously to exist. The text-block of the photostat measures 104 × 148 mm.

The following words are a transcription of the original:

A2r.5 loue yeelde dislike
A2r.12 not to touch
A2r.13 who as they
A3r.4 mishap
A3r.16 as skilfull
C2v.1 prison she was conueied to be the place
C2v.3 for her to play her last prize vppon,
C2v.32 the life of a cōdemned creature & deserue

THE APPREHENSION, ARraignement, and execution of Elizabeth Abbot, *alias Cebrooke, for a cruell and horrible murther,* committed on the body of Mistris *Killingworth* in S. Creechurch Parish neere Aldgate in London.

THe calamity of this age wherein we liue, and the cruelty of vs, who professe our selues Christians one to another, who in stead of pity, pay oppression: who in stead of charity render cruelty: who for loue yeelde dislike: and who for mercy pay these manifold offences: as slaunders, thefts, and murthers euen to the liues of those, who receiued them to their armes of hospitality; hath made me find time to set pen to this discourse.

There liued not long since in Crœchurch parish nere Aldgate in London, a widow, called Mistris Killingworth, the reputation of whose life I meane not to touch, since mens tongs are like an instrument made of many strings; who as they are many in number, so are they as seuerally different in sound, some high, some meane, some base, all speaking according to the pleasure of the musitiã who hath them in tuning; so in the conditions of men, there is none how euer their liues be infinite in euils, but haue some who report in their praises, nor none how euer their maners be worthy & gratious (deseruing record euen in the noblest Chronicle) but find slanderers, who are busie in their reproch. But for this Mist. Killingworth, it is said, she had bin the wife of three husbands, and now contented her selfe to liue widdowed by the death of the last: what hir life and obedience had beene towards all of them, during the time of her marriage, I rather leaue to opinion & the generall report of her neighbours, then giue it to the report of my pen: only touching one infirmity which she had; (especially now toward her latter time) since it is both a generall disease that raignes in our age, and was an excuse to her murtherer euen in the instant of her tragedy; may liue as an example to this present world and succeeding times, and is so proper for my discourse: I intreat thee Reader to take this for my excuse; in the handling of it I am no way willing to bite the dead, but giue it to him as a medicine for himselfe.

This Mistris Killingworth hath beene often times knowne to come home to her house, hauing abroad so abused her body in drinke (a disease most abominable in women, since it is so detestable in men) that shee hath beene found by her neighbours wallowing unseemely on the ground in her owne soyle (a habit common amongst drunkards) and a custome that should be only proper to swine and not to people of honest conuersation, her neighbours then (especially the women whom for womanhood sake it most concerned to be a helpe to her infirmity) haue come often thither, (after notice giuen them) either by seeing her come home, or by hearing her groane, while she lay in such extremities, here raised her and seene her lodged in her bed, and so leauing her haue not knowne her stirring abroad the next day.

Heere is especiall note to be taken, that shee kept no seruant at all, although reputed to bee of a reasonable and sufficient substance; and the reason was, that both during the time of her mariage and the continuance of her widowhood shee was so sharpe in blowes, and pinching in victuals, that few at first could & at last none would tarry with her.

But to our purpose. Mistris Killingworth hauing béen thus often times found and so often times comforted by her neighbors that they brought her to her bed, to ẏ which she had not power to bring her selfe, they at their going from her, vsed to shut the doore, and throw in the key, (thinking as indéede it was,) the best security for her selfe, and the goods she possest, and so left her to take her full sléepe, awake and arise at her owne pleasure, sometimes they sawe her not the next

Day

day, no nor the next day following, when at other times, she was knowne to bee as painfull in her busines (her trade being a Sempster, as any woman of the best seeming sincerity could be.

But it is commonly seene, there is seldome a mishap, which succeedeth not another, so is it rare to see one sinne, which begetteth not a successor: and so in Mistris Killingworth, for after shee was awake from her drowsines, when shee should haue had reason to commend, and haue bin thankfull for the loue of her neighbours, she taught her selfe a kind of peruersnes to condemne them, first by reporting of them, that they were more busie then needfull, next, that they came to prie into her rather then to comfort her, and last, which was most hateful, of al that vnder pretence of comming to do her good, they were vnfriendly theeues and pilfered away that shee had. This vnthankefulnes of hers, in requitall of the paines bestowed vpon her friendly neighbours, so animated their opinions against her, that after notice taken of her ingratitude, they from thence left her, as [illegible]full Physitians do their franticke patients, who not being able to gouerne them, either by doctrine or perswasion, giue them ouer wholly to their liues destruction or to their owne cure, & euen so did these neighbours this mistris Killingworth: for now some of them, especially of the better sort, scorning to be thus abused, others repining to bee thus neglected, and in breefe all disdayning that their former loue and labour had no more regard, but to be answered with her reproch, they from thence (when the same occasion was offered them) left her to bee her owne helpe, and which after proued to be her vntimely destruction. Here reader I aduise thee to take note, that if in reading this, thy conscience tell thee, thou art toucht with the same sin, (for I haue heard it multiplies in England) or if thou knowest any of thy familiar acquaintance, stubborne in the same offence, perswade them, and reforme thy selfe, lest that Mistris Killingworths, be but like a flash of lightning sent from her, who foretels thunder, when the bolt and stroke thereof may hit vpon thee.

But to the murther. Mi. Killingworth hauing thus continued in disdain with some, & dislike with others, yet through their modesty so cōcealed, yͭ it caried no general knowledg, either to her especial friends, or those whom shee wrought unto, with their silence & hir perseuerance, much time past, when it happened about the middest of January last, one Elizabeth Abbot, alias Cebrooke came to haue entertainement and be lodged in hir house; the manner of hir acquaintance with hir, is as yet by this Elizabeth Abbots confession unknowne, and by the others suddaine death preuented; but thus much for certaine is. the very day before hir death, it was hir chance to come to a citizens house in Cornehil, where being kindly welcome, the Mistris & she fell into some friendly conference together; in which hauing past some time, upon the suddaine Mistris Killingworth start up, offring hastily to take hir leaue of hir, making the reason of hir so suddaine departure this: am not I a good huswife, quoth she, to stay heere so long, hauing a stranger lodged in my house? who I haue more reason to suspect then trust, for in my conscience, quoth shee, I thinke she be with child, notwithstanding, I take such delight in hir pretty odde country talking, that hauing no body but my selfe, she seemes much comfort to me; then the citizens wife demanded of hir, how she durst, or why she was so unwise to entertaine a stranger to lodge with hir, the world being so bad, and the condition of people so uncertaine? whereunto she replied: that she trusted hir the rather, for that she was commended unto hir by an especiall friend, whose name and the streete he dwelt in, she then told; but from thence to this Abbots triall this, citizens wife could by no meanes bring hir selfe to remember it: besides quoth Mistris Killingworth, she hath often told me she hath a husband, who is a taylor now working in the strand, who though I haue not yet seen, she promises me, wil one of these dayes bring him home, and we shall be merry together. So with this & such other conference leaue being taken betweene them, they parted.

Being thus gone home from this citizens wife on Tuesday the twentieth of January, on the morrow following shee sent this lodger of hers, to another citizens wife in Cornehill being one of her workemistresses, to send her some stockes for bands which she had to make for her, the which by a token she brought from mistris Killingworth were deliuered hir; and no especiall note she tooke of hir, but giuing more regard to the token shee brought, then hir presence, dispacht hir with hir message, onely being examined after the death of mistris Killingworth,

Killingworth what shee could tell for hir discouery, it was a little to describe hir fauour, but made good mistres Killingworths words before, which was, that she spoke broad and somewhat northernely. But this wensday night comming on when this hir horrid intent, tooke fatall execution, one mistris Sutton keeping a victualling house at the next doore, from which Mist. Killingworth was accustomed to fetch hir ordinary prouision of bread and drinke, the maister and the mistris that night supping abroad, at one of their friends houses, it is testified by their seruant, that there was that night fecht from hir, by this Abbot to mistris Killingworths house, more store of bread and beere then had ordinarily bin, and more then might well suffice to content them being but two, for one meales satisfaction, whereby shee ghest, there was at that time some extraordinarie prouision in mistris Killingworths house, and that some strangers or friends of hirs did that night sup with hir, so indeuoring painefully about hir busines, it past from hir without further thought of it, onely by this Abbots comming often for drinke, shee had time to take especiall note whereby to know hir, more then any other had; yet going from rome to rome about hir busines, about tenne of the clocke, shee reports that shee heard mistris Killingworth complaine, as if shee had beene sicke, when hir maister and mistris comming home presently vpon her hearing of this, shee tould them what she had heard, and that she supposed mistris Killingworth was not well, which they perceiuing to be her old sicknes, and knowing as before, hir vnkindnesse to those had vsed her kindly, answered they knew it was but her old desease, she would be wel againe to morrow, and so went to their rest, some two chambers from hir house, so the maid bringing hir maister and mistres to bed, and going to hir one lodging, which was the next wall to mistris Killingworths, while shee was making hir vnready heard some mouing of stooles in the next chamber, and so being wearied with the former dayes labour, soone fell a sleepe.

About twelue a clocke a Duch-mans maide ouer the way right against her house, heard her giue a great groane, and at last spake out thus: O Lord shal I die thus and neuer a neighbor come at me: wherupon the maide opening the casement, call'd to hir, and asked hir how she did, when this Abbot came to the window, (before which was

hung

hung a thicke cloth, so as the maid could not see into the house for it, where at other times the casements were so neere and opposit one to the other, that any of that dutchmans house could haue euidently perceiued what she had done within) and answered, that God helpe hir, Mistris Killingworth was not well, it was but hir old disease, shee would most carefully looke to hir, & she doubted not but she would bee well againe when shee had slept, so the honest seruant praying God to comfort hir, was satisfied, and for that time heard no more of it.

Heere Reader mayest thou approue the wonderfull iudgements of God, who giues to euery offence his due punishment, and makes our sinnes like fire the which consumes it selfe in his owne glory: drunkennes was hir sinne, drunkennes was hir punishment: the neglect of hir neighbours was hir sinne, and their neglect toward hir for that sinne, was an excuse to hir murtherer and a furtherer to hir death: for had she beene thankefull to them for their paines to hir, and not answered their kindenes with despight and slander, they at this time as before when they heard shee was ill, and supposed it to be but hir old distemperature, had come in to be hir comfort, had apprehended hir murtherer, and no doubt had preuented hir death, but by these helpes the diuell preuailed: hir sinne by hir owne course was punished: and I pray you suppose that she is murthered.

On thursday morning then, about foure of the clocke, a chare-woman came to washing to the dutch mans house ouer the way, saw a light in Mistris Killingworths window, but saw no body stirring, and so went to hir worke: at fiue of the clocke the maid of the alehouse being likewise vp, and about hir busines, and heard hir low window neere the streete let downe, and hir doore open and shutte, but misdoubted nothing. Thursday wholly passing, and through hir custome, which they had knowne hir vse before, they suspected nothing till Friday morning, when wondring that they could neither see hir nor this same Abbot stirring, whom, though a stranger, they knew she lodged in hir house; they began now somewhat to mistrust of hir welfare, and demaunded one of the other when they saw hir, when all the circumstances as before were recited, of the store of drinke which was fetcht at Mistris Suttons house, of Mistris Suttons maide, hearing hir not well, and of the dutch mans seruant, who heard hir say, Lord, shall I

die

die thus and neuer a neighbour that I haue come at me? as also of this Abbots answere, and the cloth hanging before the window, which vntill that time, she had neuer beene accustomed to haue so, they began now to suspect more fearefully some danger had happened to her: so sending for the Constable and Officers ere they would attempt any thing themselues, they first knockt very forcibly, but finding no body to answere them, they determined to breake open the doore, but afterwards it was otherwaies agreed thus: that one should goe fetch a ladder, by the helpe of which one climing vp to the window, they might haue knowledge whether shee were in the chamber or no, and if not there, to giue them instructions below, in what manner the chamber was left, the which effected, they might perceiue the bed turned downe as she had lately come out of it, and on the ground: and a foots space before the chimney some store of water to haue been spilt, which was after coniectured to be with the quenching of the mantle-tree, which by the violence of the fire which had beene made, was burnt euen to the brickes, whereupon the Constable sent the Beadle of the ward for the Aldermans Deputy, and with other neighbours got in, and made search all ouer the house for her, but missing her, found all hir apparell, child-bed-linnen, with the best & lightest of hir goods (which hir neighbours knew her to be well stored withal carried away, & nothing left but heauy lumber, which was too ponderous for carriage, yet continued carefully searching in euery place, at last a neighbour looking on the ashes in the chimney, found certaine small bones which they put into a boxe: & carried them to my Lord Maiors, who presently vpon view of them sent for a Surgeon, who forthwith satisfied his honour they were the bones of some man or woman which had bin burned: but ere the Aldermans deputy left the house, making further search after they had taken vp the bones, they found behind certaine brickes which were raised vp to guard the backe of the Chimney, a locke of her haire tide in her hairelace, and her stay which went vnder her chinne pinde to it, whereby it was straight coniectured, she was first made drunke, a vice shee was properly inclined vnto by disposition, then strangled in her bed, the coverleds of which were found folded downe, then brought and set vpright in the chimney, there burnt, and so to be consumed to ashes, the windowes also shut in with a cloth; whereby the steame and savor which the body would cast, might ascend forth thorow the funnell of the chimney. O diuellish and not hard of practise! But this aboue the rest was most strange: that so great and vehement fire which was able to consume the whole body to ashes, had not power to consume that locke of haire, haire lace and chin band, the which was falne from her head, and was defended but with two or three brickes, but that it should be preserued: that by the colour her neighbours might witnesse it was shee which was burnt; and so as it befittes every Christian to take warning by her ruine, and for Charities sake to make diligent search for the apprehension of the murtherer: which in this maner was effected.

The Lord Maior and Justices of this City, like prouident Captaines ouer this peacefull common-wealth, and that such an vnheard of murther might not escape vnreuenged, where the thirstines of the Deuill was not satisfied in shedding blood, but must after sacrifice the body of the dead (who now had neither power to complaine nor knowledge to accuse) to the fury of consuming fire, caused diligent enquiry to be made every way, to haue this worse then woluish woman apprehended: much search was made, and all diligence vsed, but the subtill policy of hir maister the Deuill, whom she still continued to serue, as thinking hir yet not villenous enough to be his one, keept hir so priuate now for the contriuing of after actions, that no search could take hold of her. But the reports of this murther being here about London in every tongue, & the cruelty therof sounding in every eare; it happened that the bayliffe of Burnt wood in Essex comming vp to London with certaine prisoners did lye at the three Nunnes without Aldgate, and hearing of this murther, for there was litle other talke had thereabouts, and that a woman was held in suspition for it, as also her person and apparrell discribed

to

to him, bethought himselfe that to his iudgement, such a like woman hee had lately seene about their towne of Burnt-wood; which suspition of his being giuen to the right honourable the Lord Maior, expedition was made for her apprehension, which Ministers comming thither found that such a like woman had beene there, but gone from thence, after whom pursuit being made euery way shee was at the last apprehended at Grauesend, and by the beadle of Aldgate ward who had authoritie from the Lord Maior to that purpose, she was brought vp to London, where such was the desire of all eyes to see her, that their eyes might beare witnesse if women could bring forth a woman so detestable, as she was, being carryed through the streets, the people that came to behold her were infinite, some cursing her all reuiling her, and the most desirous to haue had her presently torne to peeces as a creature not worthy to continue to her triall; which doubtles the ruder sort (who are like a tempest violent but not lasting,) would haue done, had not the care and many labours of the officers withstoode their violence.

But such was the care and prouidence of our worthy Iustices, who on slight presumptions take not away life, that by sending seuerally for all parties who had seene the suspected murther of mistris Killingworth, and aduisedly taken their iudgements whether she were the woman or not, it soone appeared to their grauities, that in this sort wherein this wretch was suspected shee was innocent; although they found her, by her owne examination to be a woman of loose life and base condition: yet such was their noble minds & worthinesse in this case, that, since she had falne into this imprisonment & publike disgrace, for the cause which she was not guiltie of, they had resolued of their charitable beneuolence to haue giuen her in requitall a peece of monie, and so haue conducted her to the place where she was borne. But see the wonderfull workes of God, that the beginning of one sinne should be the reuealing of another: and this Cities care in looking for a murderer, doth now discouer a fellon, and help an honest man of the white Friers to his goods againe, of which by this woman he was robbed,

bed, partly undone thereby, but utterly helplesse of the recouerie of them.

For the great and chiefest cause which made this Baliefe of Burnt-wood suspect this former apprehended to be mistris Killingworths murtherer was a gowne which he had knowne her to sell, and by all description like a gowne of mistris Killingworth; which the neighbours missing in the search repeated this Abbot had carried from mistris Killingworths house, which gowne being brought to London for the neighbours to see, and thereby to haue beene a witnesse against her that if shee had not beene a principall, yet shee might haue proued a party, if the gowne, as it did not, had proued hers, and iust as the Lord Maior was ordering mony to haue discharged her and so haue sent unto her friends, the poore man who before was robd came to the sight of the gowne, knew it to be his wiues, upon which robbery being examined shee confest the fact, and the sessions following had her tryall at New-gate, condemned for fellonie, but repreeued by the fauour of the bench, and rests there in prison at the mercy of the King.

Them that shall read these testimonies then, and find how strangely God of his infinite iustice, brings offenses to light and the offenders to shame, and finds his owne conscience toucht with this or the like guilt, me thinks he should say to himselfe, O God I will be no more a sinner, for I see no sinne is acceptable unto thee, and what auaileth it us to commit our actions in darkenesse, since the pichiest night is to thee all one with the purest day? But to our discourse.

This Elizabeth Abbot hauing thus long continued wandring up and downe light enough in all things but in a burthened conscience, and thinking that so long time had worne her selfe free from all suspition, shee came with her husband neere unto a little Towne in Surrey two miles wide of None-such: Where lurking afraid in the out part of the towne till night, they came with intent to haue robd the house of a good honest yeoman, and so farre had furthered their purpose, they had broken downe

downe the peece of a wall for entrance, with the noyse of which the good man being awaked misdoubting no lesse, then what indeed was in action, he caught up a pich-forke, as the best weapon which was next him and out of dores he flew, which the theefe hearing, made his heels his best manhood & took himselfe to running, the countrey man after him: but what with the extreame darknesse of the night, and the honest man wisely not thrusting himselfe too farre in daunger, the theefe escapt, and the countrey man came backe againe, who at his returne he found his dogge, which in deed was a part of his waking at the first, as busie and as eager now as before the theefe whom he pursued was fled, for while the countrey man was chasing this Abbots husband, and she thinking to make the advantage of his absence an escape for her another way, the dogge winding her never left chasing her, till from the fury of the masty, & for her one safety, she was faine to leape down into a sawpit, where the curre kept her at full bay till his maister returned, who hearing his dogge continue his former barking, & he suspecting there had beene no more theeves but the one which was fled, at least confident that theeves seldome stay when they heare any body stirring, he began to rate his dogge and earnestly to call him in: but all the checking, commanding, or flattering he could use, could not drawe the dogge, who was so gentle to him before, that hee would come to his hand, leave his office he had tooke upon him of a Gayler or let goe his prisoner, which the countrey man wondring at, tooke courage to himselfe, and adventured to draw neere him, whom he found still beating about the sawpit, and wondring what the event would be, he thrust his pich-forke downe two or three times in severall places, and at the last it lighted upon this Abbots shoulder, when he perceiving that his forke had grounded upon somewhat that yeelded to it, hee cald aloud, who is there, who is there, but no body making answere hee thrust in his forke hard againe, and pierst her in the arme somwhat below her shoulder, wherewith shee was constrained to cry, when he presently calling for help shee was taken out of the pit, and the next morning, this

happening

happening on Satterday night she was carried to the neerest Iustice, being Sir Edward Sanders to be examined: where wee will leaue her, and shew the wonders of God in reuealing this murder by returning towards London.

In Creechurch Parish neere the place where Mistris Killingworth was murthered, dwels a substantiall woman, and of honest conuersation, called Mistris Cox, who the same satterday that this Abbot intended to haue done this robbery in the night, went from London of purpose to be merry with a brother of hers an Inne keeper neere None-such in Surrey, where beeing lodged on satterday night, and vp to make her selfe ready on sunday morning, shee perceiued diuers men with forches and staues, shee calling to her brother, demanded of him what the matter was: why sister, quoth hee, nothing but a scuruy queane, she is carrying before a Iustice this morning for attempting to rob an honest man one of our neighbors last night, whereupon she intreated him that at her comming backe he would be a meanes shee might see her and speake with her, which hee promised, as also that hee would be a meanes to intreat his neighbours and the Constable to bring her into his house, that then shee might see her, and talke with her without disturbance: and because, quoth Mistris Coxes brother, I will not faile but be as good as my word, I will goe heare her examination my selfe, and bring both her and my neighbours this way by my perswasion, lest they should carry her to the Iayle before they come backe: which promise of his he performed.

Thus this Elizabeth Abbot hauing béene examined before Sir Edward Sanders, touching her life and liuing, of which she could make no honest account, among other questions he demanded of her: what the man was which was with her in this pretended robbery: to whom she answered, he was her husband, and a taylor: then beeing willed to discouer where hee was, nay, shee replyed suddainely; if hee bée escaped, why then I care not, all's then well, and if you hang me now, I care not. So for this attempt, which it is thought would haue beene to little purpose

pose to haue taken her life, shee was by vertue of Sir Edwards Mittimus commanded prisoner to the white Lyon in Southwarke: and by the way they tooke Mistris Coxes brothers house to drinke in: where being set in a roome together, Mistris Cox mildely began to aske her, how shee beeing a woman could bee so hardy to attempt to breake open a house, to robbe and vndoe an honest country-man, that liues faithfully by his labour? hearing which, this Abbot replied: why, as I did before with my handes; and were it to doe I could as resolutely attempt it againe: vpon which impudent answere, Mistris Cox fixing her eye more earnestly vpon her, began now to conceiue in her selfe that she had seene her some where, but could by no meanes call to mind where, and thereupon demanded of her in this manner: woman, if I mistake not, I haue seene you some where in London; where, she answered, it might be so in the Strand perhaps: no, quoth Mistris Cox, about Aldgate if I be not deceiued: when, she suddainely replied: (heere note the power of the Diuell, that would make her owne tongue betray her into that mischiefe of which no man had suspition of her) O I sound your meaning: you goe about to intrap mee about the woman that was burnt by Aldgate, but you are deceiued in that in faith, as they that did it were deceiued of their expectation: why of what were they deceiued, quoth Mistris Cox? why, quoth shee, I tell you, of their expectation, they lookt for much and had little, she was a good old gentlewoman, and she had beene a proper young gentlewoman: but if you thinke to insnare or intrappe mee you are deceiued: whereupon, quoth Mistris Cox and other who stood by: surely you were much interessed in the villany, that knew so well what profitte they made by their murther, and what manner of person the murthered was, and can so readily deliuer it: when shee answered scornefully; Lord, how people may be deceiued, for I tell you, I heard it of a woman at Luttruge some three or foure mile off, and about three or foure dayes since: where being againe demanded, what woman she was that told her so, and not beeing able to render a direct an-

swere,

swere: Mistris Cox intreated of the Constable that hee would be a meanes to the Justice she might be sent to be examined at London, for, quoth shee, though I for my part am no way able to accuse her, yet I feare me she will proue guilty in the murther of Mistris Killingworth: which request of yours, quoth the Constable, you shall not neede further to looke after, for I haue here Sir Edward Sanders warrant to commit her prisoner to the white Lyon in South-warke. Where, reader, I pray thee suppose that shee is imprisoned, and that Mistris Cox hath made knowen to all the neighbours of Mistris Killingworth what hath happened, the neighbours to my Lord Maior and the Recorder; and on the Monday morning diuers of them repaire to her, to the white Lyon: Before whose comming thither, and indeed as soone as shee was Chambred her selfe, shee straight laboured with an old woman there, called widdow Barthelmew, to change peticotes with her, offering to doe it without profit, though by the iudgement of any man, hers by the double in value exceeded the old womans, which she giuing notice to the keepers of, they by no meanes would permit her to shift her clothes, of which purpose of hers, finding her selfe intercepted, she ript off all the lace that was about her cote and bestowed it, she would neuer confesse where: the purpose of all which was indeed to disguise her selfe as much as might be, for she heard that diuers were comming to see her about Mistris Killingworths murther: but Munday morning being come many of the neighbours, as Mistris Cox, Mistris Sutton, Mistris Suttons maid, with seuerall others came to see her, as also the maid that deliuered the stocks for bands in Cornhill; but it was so ordered that against their cōming she was placed amongst other women, to try if they who had seene her before in the time of Mistris Killingworth could select her from the rest: both which Mistris Suttons maid and the Semsters maid in Cornhill as soone as euer they came into the roome chose her from the rest, crying, this is shee; where on the contrey being shewed the former woman single, they as firmely approued it was not she.

On

On the selfe same Munday, when this testimonie was taken at the White-lyon by the parties aforesaide, and they approued that this was that shee creature (for a woman she was in nothing but in showe) that gaue this fearefull testimonie to the world, of mistres Killing-worths death. the right Honorable ẏ Lord Maior, with that most worthie Gentleman sir Henry Mountegue Recorder of London, accompained with the Worshipfull Shriues, and Maister Justice Dale, sat in the Court vppou Saint Margets-hill, commonly called the Marshals Court: vpon especial busines for the King, which by their wisdoms dispached, and by their foreknowledge ofthe apprehension of this Elizabeth Abbot, they sent for the prisoner, who by the Gaoler of the White-lyō was brought before them, and the witnesses examined, who approued her to be the woman, but herselfe being questioned, most impudenlty (as there is no sinne without impudence) vtterly denide to haue any knowledge with mistres Killingworth, or any acquaintāce in the fault: when the Justice sending her downe, and once againe examining the witnesses charging them, by the care they had of their owne soules, to be well aduised, that what they did infer was for truth, they most constantly appreued their former euidence.

But it happened that mistres Sutton was now belowe, while the other were in question aboue, and she of her selfe as other ẏ were present, did demaūd of her seueral questions, wishing her since the fact was done, and that by euidence it was so apparant she was guilty of it, that she would not now heap sinne on sinne by the denying of it, but rather cleare her owne conscience, prepare herselfe for repentance, make her selfe fit for Heauen, and satisfie the world, when she continuing obstinatly amongst other motions that were then made vnto her, mistris Sutten asked her if she had not a husbād: she answeare yes, is he not a Tailor (saies mistresse Sutten) I graunt he is (said the prisoner) did hee not work in the Strand? yes, and did not you tell mistresse Killing-worth so much (quoth mistresse Sutten) I confesse I did answered the murtheresse, which confession of hers, she instantly would haue calde in, but though the Diuell bee the father of lyes, yet in these cases he is often ẏ author of truth, for he hastens to haue his owne with him, for now he makes her owne tongue speake her owne truth, & thought afterward to deny it againe, yet stood there by her besides mistris Sutten a Chirurgian in this Towne, vertuous and substantiall, as also an honest Stationer, who besides mistresse Sutten gaue testimony to my Lord Maior, Maister Recorder and the rest, of what she had spoken, and that her owne tongue hath aproued the same words that mistresse Killing-worth the day before her death had deliuered to the Cittizens wife in Cornwell, the approbation was so strong, that she was remoued from the White-lyon in Southwarke, to the common gaole of Newgate in London, where though she was sent for diuers times before sir Henry Mountegue for further examination, she remained there til her time of trial.

Which trial of hers being on Friday the eight of Aprill, shee was arraigned and indighted by the

name

of Elizabeth Abbot late of London spinster, for practising a murther against the body of mistresse Killing-worth late of London widow: to which inditement, she pleaded not guilty, and put her selfe uppon tryall of God and her Country, for the proofe of which, the aforesaide evidence was produced, namely mistresse Killing-worths conference with the Citizens wife, which she her selfe there in person approoved her wordes to mistresse Coxe, and the confession of her owne tongue by mistresse Sutten, others which made good also that she was the woman mistresse Killing-worth spoke of: then the personall approovances of mistresse Suttens maide and others, who directly tooke their oathes she was the woman y fetcht drink from her mistresses house, and the other that it was she and no other fetcht the flocks for bands in her mistresse shop, all which though she denied, it pleased that most Worthy Judge Sir Edward Cooke, Lord cheefe Justice of the common pleas, somewhat in this forme, to explaine to the Jury, first that hee had compared mistresse Killing-worths wordes with the Cittizens wives in Cornwel, and the Cittizens wives evidence with the prisoners owne confession to mistresse Sutten, and found them all three not to differ in one sillable, then what can be more plainer that she is the party, when she her selfe speakes the same words mistresse Killing-worth spoke, againe, that Algate was no sooner named in the Country to her by mistresse Cox, but she straight breakes out, as (if suspecting that every shaking leafe were one to discover her) had so over charged her guilty conscience, that she must now breake out: oh

 you

you go about to intrap mee, about the Gentlewomans death ỳ was burnt by Algate: further, ỳ she did reply, that they which did it, mist of their purpose, and being demaunded who should tel her so, she answered idly a woman of Luttry, but neither knowes her name nor what she was: then if this were all, what could be more suspicious? but you of the Jury, heere is further euidence to satisfie you, though if but this in my conscience in this case I thinke it sufficient, that here are seuerall witnesses aboue two or three, who say vppon their othes directly she is the woman, not such as sweare rashly or indiscreetly, but say as first these h[illegible] from many other women, and as if God himselfe would giue vs cause to put trust in their othes, sent another woman before, who was hainously suspected for the fact, whom they refused to be she, and indeed was proued after by other testimony it was not: and as if by their othes, though she was hidden in darkenesse, he would bring her once to her deserued shame. When my Lord leauing the Jury to their discretions, Sir Henry Mountegue vrges, that besides all this, hauing bene seuerall times examined where she had liued, and had bestowed her selfe from a yeare after, to a quarter, nay from a quarter to a very moneth, nay from a moneth to a day before she came to mistresse Killingworth, she could giue account of all but till then: ỳ which beside her confession vnder her owne hand, was approued by maister Hicock, Clarke of New-gate, when my Lord Cheife Justice, rising from his seate againe, gaue Sir Henry Mountegue a worthy commendations for his industry and labor in this case,

protesting

professing that since he was acquainted inӱ state of such busines, he neuer heard examinatiõs better gathered, a course better shifted, nor a murther strõglier discouered: so the Jury brought together, she was by verdit of ӱt twelue returned guilty, and the next day being Satterday she receiued her sentence.

Betwixt which time and her death, though the proceedings against her were so Just, the euidence so plaine, and her tryall so gratious, that she had leaue to speake in her one defence, euen what she would, & where it is not ordinariey seene, she was called into ӱ inner conrt, euen to ӱ barre where ӱ foreman of the iurie stood, that my lords and the whole conrt might plainely heere what she could speake, in her owne excuse, which was nothing but obstinacie the ground of all euill. I can not yet with silence passe ouer, the care which our moste honourable Magistrates, tooke of her soule, labouring by all meanes to haue her make it plaine by confession, which was so cleere by euidence, which shal for euer from hence stop scandalls tongue for speaking against their gouerment and deserued such a Chronicle of a brasse to record their vprightnes the Justice of their actions, which ages shold not weare out, nor death deface, but should liue as an example to men, while to the world was left any posteritie. First then, that they sent into the prisõ vnto her a reuerend & graue Doctor of diuinitie, who with such strong instances, beat against the dores of her harte, that had they not beene made of harder then marble they had had power to haue broke them open: for marble yeeldes sometimes, she not all.

 From

From prison she was conueied to the place of execution, where before her eyes she saw a high erected gibbet, for her to play her last prize vpon, where both the Shrieues being, they themselues began of their owne charitable disposition, to perswade her, yet to disburthen her conscience, shewd her how neere her death she was, pointed to her towards the house where Mistris Killingworth dwelt, and bad her let the sight of that where shee had committed so foule a fact, be a remembrance to haue her clense her soule & causd her vpon her knees then in the Cart to offer her praiers to god, that he would be pleasd to open her harte, and make her fit for him in this her houre of death: which praiers as they directed her, she saide, but still (oh grieuous obstinacy) shee persisted in her deniall of being any way guiltie of the fact, acquainted with the house, or knowne to Mistris Killingworth, which confidence of hers so mooued the Shrieues, that one of the rode presently to satisfie my Lord Maior how she stil perseuerd pleading her innocency, while the other caused her to be loosed out of the Cart, & conueied her into Cree-Church, ouer against the place where she suffered, and thither sent for all those who gaue euidence against her: first charging them now vpon the loue they bare to their owne soules, to view her well, whether she were the woman or no, or whether vpon better consideration had since by any words of hers they did but yet thinke they had mistooke themselues, It could be any way no impeachment to them but would reioyce the world, saue the life of a condemned creature, & deserue their great commendation: when they all againe testified

as

as they did hope for blisse in heauen, and by the help of heauen comfort on earth, this is the woman fetchd the drink, this is the womā fetcht the flocks for the bands lay at Mistris Killingworths, fetcht coales, and lighted a candle (with all their testimonies as before) when presently they turnd to her & vrged her now vpon that she heard, yet to cleere her conscience and to assure her selfe that with going with a charg'd soule, and smotherd sinnes to her graue, there was no help to be lookd for of her, but from aboue, and that she wold yet tell whither shee knew Mistris Killingworth, or if she shamed to open that sinne, that shee would but discouer who was pertaker with her in the roberie ẏ he might be found, or what manner of man he was, and promised her recompēce that he should haue no hurt, neither of which by all the perswasiōs that might be, could she be once brought to confesse: by which it is euident, the deuill whom she serued, had fully hardned her heart, & she that would die vnpurging her soule of one sinne, it is to plaine she was guiltie of the other. So she was presently brought from the church againe, and there suffered Execution.

FINIS

Three Bloodie Murders (*STC* 18287) is reproduced with permission from the clear and uncropped Bodleia Library copy (shelfmark Wood 365 [4]). The text-block measures 87 × 155 mm.

The following words are a transcription of the original:

C1v.1 to let her stay a little
C1v.2 and she
C3v.1 to come within any reasonable distance
C3v.9 fowre dayes

Three Bloodie Murders:

The first, committed by *Francis Cartwright* vpon *William Storre*, M[r.] of Art, Minister and Preacher at *Market Raisin* in the countie of *Lincolne*.

The Second, committed by *Elizabeth Iames*, on the body of her Mayde, in the Parish of *Egham* in *Surrie*: who was condemned for the same fact at Saint Margarets hill in Southwark, the 2. of Iuly 1613. and lieth in the White Lion till her deliuerie: discouered by a dombe Mayde, and a Dogge.

The Third, committed vpon a Stranger, very lately, neere *High-gate* foure miles from *London*: very strangely found out by a Dogge also, the 2. of Iuly. 1613.

Imprinted at London for *Iohn Trundle*, dwelling in Barbican 1613.

The cruell Murder of a yong Maiden,

committed by Elizabeth Iames, *of the Parish of Egham* in *Surrey*, most strangely reuealed by a *dogge, and a dumb-woman, for which bloody fact (being with child) she lyeth con*demn'd in the VVhite Lyon in *Southwarke.*

All the life of a wise-man, is a meditation of death : *Aug.*

HOw happy are those men that are so truly wise? for this serious meditation of death, is a sure shield of defence, against the multitude of most grieuous, and dangerous temptations, that in this world, men are subiect vnto. Out of such a diuine meditation spake S. Hierome these words: Whether I eate or drink, or whatsoeuer I doe, methinkes I heare alwaies sounding in mine eares, *surgite mortui, &c.* Arise you dead, and come to iudgement. O happy, thrice happy is that man, that this most blessed meditation of death and iudgement, prepares and makes ready (in the multitude of the mercies of Christ Iesus) for death and iudgement? But how this sweet meditation is neglected, and the meditation of mischiefe respected, and practiced, is by the many cruell, bloody and damnable ends of it, almost euery day, and in euery place laid open vnto vs. And among others, let vs look with wet eyes, and heauy hearts, vpon the cruelty of Elizabeth Iames, a Keepers wife of the Parish of Egham in Surrey, which was thus.

It chaunced that a young Mayden, going to seeke a seruice, came to the house of this woman, and desired her pitty, either to take her in, and entertain her as a seruant, or there, as a Boorder

C to

to let her stay a little time; till shee might (thereabout) heare of a seruice, and she would willingly content her sufficiently, both for her boord, and house-roome: this woman seeing the Maide, to be a pretty young wench, and handsomely apparreled; but especially minding tho profitable promise she made her, with an outward shew of pious compassion, & pitty, took her into her house; where, for a time, sho so kindly and louingly vsed her, that the poor harmlesse Mayden thought her selfe very happy, that it was her chance to find out so good and vertuous a woman. But as tis commonly said; They that know least mischiefe, mistrust least; and so consequently, are soonest deceiued. Tis apparent betweene these two, for this deceitfull woman, when shee perceiu'd the Mayd had some store of mony, by little, and little, some at one time, and some at an other, she nere left borrowing of her, till shee had left no more to lend her; and not onely thus deceiued her of her money, but her cloathes also: when this poore Mayden had, many times, patiently demaunded them, and could not get them, shee was forst to complaine to her Master, who, till then, knew nothing of his wiues cosenage, and hard vsage of her: He pittying the Maydens plaint, and very (honestly) willing that shee should haue her owne, spoke some-what sharpely to his wife about them, and forced her to returne vnto her, that mony and apparell, that she so deceitfully had taken from her. Whereupon, much strife arose betweene this wicked woman, and her honest well-meaning husband: but of this good that he intended, much more euill succeeded; for the next day her husband beeing gone forth, about his ordinary businesses, as looking to his grounds, and such like: this cruell woman, being empty of all grace, (as wee haue before sayd) no thought of death and iudgement, no loue to heauen, nor feare of hell in her bosome, most mercilesly dragg'd this silly mayden, by the haire of her head, into an inner Roome, where hauing her at that aduantage she looked for, shee drew her knife, and told her that now shee would be soundly reuenged vpon her for the hard words, and blowes, that she had receiued from her husband, vpon the complaint that she had made against her.

The poore Mayden, seeing there was no hope of life, but in mercy, vpon her knees, with her hands heau'd vp, her eyes dropping

ping, and such pittifull greaning, as would haue extorted pitty from a Pagan, entreated that she would not kil her, and told her, that all that she had (if she would be so mercifull) should bee hers, and that she would presently bee gone, without speaking any word to any creature, of the mischiefe, she intended against her.

But neither her promises, prayers, teares, groanes, nor any other pitty-mouing action, that past from her, could turne that more then Tiger-hearted woman, from that bloody purpose: for presently she began her butcherie at the throate of this poore Mayden; which when she had so cruelly cut, (her hands reaking in the blood of it) with a hatchet that she had ready for the purpose, shee cut off her head: then by the diuell prompted still, to the very vtmost of this most horrid impiety, she cut her poore wounded body into many small peeces, some of which she burnt, some broild, and some in the dead time of night, she buried in her garden.

Her husband at his returne, when he mist the maiden, thought nothing, but that his wife had giuen her her due (as hee commanded) and turn'd her away. A day or two after, he was purposed to go digge that bed in his garden, vnder which his wife had buried the bloody pieces of that poore maidens body: but she perceiuing his purpose, desired him of all loue, that he would not stirre that bed, nor in any sort meddle with it, because she had bestowed great labor and cost in seedes, that she had but newly sowen in it: he thinking of no such mischiefe, as she fear'd would be discouered, did not goe as he purposed, but forbore it, as she requested.

Thus, for a time, this bloody murther lay concealed, though to reueale it a poore dumb woman, that saw the cruelty acted, many times, and to many persons, by her signes, and dumb shewes, so well as she could did labour her best to bewray it. But from all her signes, as pulling her selfe by the haire, drawing her hand ore her throate, stabbing her selfe (as it were) vpon the breast, wringing her hands; weeping or any thing that she could doe, they could not gather any thing, that they knew how to make any matter of.

But here see the certainty of the sacred word of the Almighty; which sayes, that he that smites a man that he die, shall die for it, *Exod.* 21. See here (I say) the goodnesse of this omnipotent God, that sees sinne, hates sinne, and wil punish sinne: When this dumb woman sufficiently expressed her meaning, to make them understand her, a hungry dogge senting about for prey, in the garden of this bloody murdresse, sented out the peices of that poore Maiden, that she had there buried, and then neuer left scraping vp the earth, til he found the head of her, which (by the haire of it) he carried in his teeth, and there before the honest Keeper, Goodman Iames, the bloody harted woman his wife, and other of his Neighbors that were with him laid it down: vpon the sight of this, they were all very much amased, the innocent persons at the strangenesse of it, and the murdresse with her feare. Then againe, this poore dumb woman, made signes to resolue them absolutely of the murder, in which she tooke vp the head, and pointing to the murdresse, shew'd how she cut it off. Then wafting them with her hand to haue them follow her, she went into the garden, and there pointed to the bed, that the poore murdered maide was hid in. Her husband seeing this, presently call'd to mind, his wiues forbidding him to dig in it, and the excuse that she made to preuent him, and by these circumstances began to haue setled thoughts of the cruelty of his wife, in the murdering of this Maiden, and presently digg'd a little deeper, and found other small pieces of her. The Neighbours likewise, by all these and other guilty signes they saw in her, (which did as it were in a plaine confession bewray her) did presently apprehend her as a Murdresse, when being carried before a Iustice, she was sent vp to the white Lyon in Southwarke, where long she lay not, ere at S. Margets hill, she was arraign'd, and sentenced to her deserued death: but because there is

with

with child, her execution is put off, till after her deliuery. From this sinne and all other, good Lord deliuer vs.

But now, tho this little be too much, I must speake somewhat more of this bloody sin, but briefly, because yet the cruell actor, or actors, cannot be found, or heard of.

VPon Friday last, being the second day of Iuly, a maid going a milking, neere Finchly, and with her a young man, her fellow seruant, hauing a mastiffe dogge with him: This dogge, while they were about their businesse, strayd from them, senting vp and downe, to finde somewhat to feed on, and going thus too and fro (not farre from the place where they were) in a by field, neere Newgate lane, he found the slaughtered body of a man, vpon which the dogge staide feeding. After a little time, the young man missing him, whistled and called about for him; and by and by the dogge leapt ore a hedge out of the field, and came to him, and being come presently hee retired to the dead body againe. The young man marueiling to see him so hastily and greedily go backe againe, followed him, and being come to the place, found him feeding very earnestly vpon a leg of that dead body, all which he had almost eaten (for which, the young man presently after fearing, that hauing had a taste of humane flesh, he would be rauenous after it stil, and so prey vpon children, hanged him.) But (as I was saying): this young man and the maid seeing this lamentable spectacle, ran presently vp to the Towne and told it, which was no sooner spoke, but many both men and women came downe to see him, but amongst them all, there was not any that knew him.

The body it seemed had lyen long in that place, before it was thus found out, for the haire was falne from the head of it, and lay thereby in a cloth that had been bound about it, the eyes pickt cleane out of their places, and (as some say) the empty holes, were fill'd vp with the dung of birds, and some other such like filthinesse: his body stunke so insufferably, that no man almost could endure to some within any reasonable distance of it. In the wounds that were to be seene upon his body, was to bee seene, the most inhumane, bloody, and ineffable cruelty, of that, or those Caius, those marble hearted villaines that there had kill'd him, for he had three or fowre thrusts, quite through his body, neere the heart, his nose was cut off, and his cheekes were slit, and crost so lamentably, that it was euen a terror almost to behold him.

Thus, fowre dayes (after he was remou'd from the priuate place, where he was found) did he ly open, neere the high way, to the view of all passengers, to find if any amongst the multitude, that came to see him could know him. But, whether by reason his face, was so grieuously disfigured with cuts, or otherwise, I know not, but there hath not beene any yet heard of, that could either tell his name, or the place of his dwelling.

But by whomsoeuer murdered, or wheresoeuer hee dwelt, he now lies there buried in the high way, neare the place where hee was murdered, and found: and till the Murderers can be found here is al that can be spoken of him; what they are, and where they are God knowes, and will (no doubt) at his good wil and pleasure reueale them. For, howsoeuer they doe yet ly hidden from the eyes of men, from the all-seeing eye of the almighty God, they do not: but that's a thing we too seldome thinke on. For as a reuerend Doctor sayes concerning this: If we could alwaies haue in minde these three things, viz. that there is an eye aboue vs, that sees all wee do, an eare that heares all we say, and a booke, in which all our words and deeds are written, we should neuer sin, (meaning capitally).

This Almighty God, that sees all, heares all; and knowes all, giue vs all grace to meditate of those things, and labour in these things, that make to his honor, and glory, and the happinesse of our soules, with him in his blessed kingdome, euerlastingly, Amen.

FINIS.

The Bloody downfall Of Adultery. Murder, Ambition (*STC* 18919.3) is reproduced with permission from th clear Huntington Library copy. The text-block measures 90 × 144 mm.

The following words are a transcription of the original:

B1v.12 offend not he the law
B1v.13 possession of another

SIR THOMAS OVERBURY

The Bloody downfall

Of { *Adultery.* *Murder,* *Ambition,* }

At the end of which are added *Westons*, and Mistris *Turners* last Teares, shed for the *Murder of Sir* Thomas Ouerbury *poysoned in the* Tower; who for the fact, suffered deserued *execution at Tiburne the* 14. *of* Nouember last. 1615.

Mercy Sweet Jesus.

Printed at London for *R. H.* and are to be sold at his shop at the Cardinalls Hat without Newgate.

The Bloody downfall of Adultery, Murder, and Ambition, preſented in a black ſeane of Gods iuſt *Judgements in reuenge of the Inocent* blood lately ſhed in this Kingdome.

LOoking lately into the cuſtomes of this age, & coniecturing the inward affections of men, I gather that the world is the houſe of confuſion, and the inhabitants thereof ſet vpon miſchiefe, for the ſeauen Cappitall ſins are growne to ſuch a cuſtome, that our eies want no alurements to bewitch, our eares no perſwayſions to ſeduce, nor our ſences no ſubtlety to affect: Which ſeazing on the hearts of men, haue brought fourth many pernitious children, to the hurt of Nature, ſome like centaures, begotten of clouds: as *Ambition*, ſome like Serpents nurriſhed in dunghils, as *Senſuallity*, ſome like Vapors, rayſed vp to be conſumed as *Flattery*, and ſuch like, generally all dangerous and full of trouble: therefore is it (in the ſence of man) moſt fitting to haue the painting taken off from theſe foule faces, the couers pulled off from theſe cups of Poyſon, and the couert of this bed of Serpents ripped vp, that we may diſcerne what hath long time bene hidden cunningly.

The firſt that preſents himſelfe vpon our ſtage; will wee call *Ambition*, catching at nothing but Starres, climing onely for Greatneſſe, this is hee, that cunningly can inuent ſtrattagems to his owne ouer throw, giuing Pens occation to wright Tragedies, if hee riſe from obſcurity, (as many haue done) hee laboreth to be skilfull in those things, which are most pleasing to the greater Sort, and tollerable among the commons: His study is for prayse, and not for vertue: His lookes like *Mansolus* toumbe, faire and comly without, but within, nothing but rotten bones, and corrupt practisses, his aparrell increaseth with his Fortune, and as worldly affaires direct him, so suteth hee both fashions and affections, in his studdy hee affecteth singularity, and is proud in being author of a new stratagem: if hee chance to come into the eie of the World, hee then creepes into the fauour of some great Peersonage, in feeding whose humors (to relieue his wants) makes intrusion into some heritage, and matcheth not according to his birth, but to the increase of his fortune, and by that meanes, by hooke or crooke, hee atayneth to some place in the Court: Then begins hee with guifts to winne hearts, by fayned humillity to a voyd hatred,

by

by offices of friendſhip, to bind his e-qualls, by cunning inſinuations to worke his ſuperiours, by which meanes hee is held to be worthely a Stateſman: being growne to this ſteppe higher, the authority likes him not, without the ſtile, wherein if any croſſe him, looke for poy-ſon in his cuppe, or conſpiracy in his walkes, yea ſo peſtilent is his nature, that (like fire raked vp in embers) hee neuer ſheweth but to conſume, both himſelfe and others: if hee perceaue any that by ripe Iudgment conceiteth his courſes, with him hee ioyneth, as if hee ſought his onely protection vnder the wing of his Glory, but the very truth is, hee hath no other intent but this, to clip the wings of his renowne for feare, hee flie beyond him, if the nature of the Noble-man whom hee enuieth be gentle, hee bringeth him in feare, either of his ſer-uants in his houſehold, or his familliars that loue his honour, or elſe ſome miſ-

like

like bewixt his Prince and him , ſworne and confirmed by flatteries and intelligences, till the noble looſeth either his land, authoitie, or place, and hee attaine both his ſtile and promotion : yet plaie hee neuer ſo cunningly, ſuch vncertaine honours beget daily dangers , and makes him carelesſe of his ſoules proſperitie : For then there entreth into his mind a delightfull ſinne called curioſity, by which to make him more able in other miſchiefes, hee giues intertainment to witches and charmers , and conſorts him-ſelfe with nouell mongers , and ſtrange inuenters of banquets, to ſet luſt on fire, and that can deuiſe confections to beſot youth with luxury, that for an irefull man can worke ſtrange reuenges, for a fearefull , a ſtrong tower to keepe him in : to be excellent at poyſons, to kill lingringly, like the *Italian* : But againe to our purpoſe, to the *Ambitius* man there is commonly belonging a ruſtick troup, of Flaterers, Bauds, Adulterers, Soothers, and ſuch like, that hating al vertue makes ſin ſeeme pleaſing, which workes in the flexable heart ſuch a ſweet deſire of forbidden pleaſures, that it euen ſurfets and growes ſicke, with exceſſe, Luſt and Adultery I meane, which I diſcribe in this maner, it is the moſt inſolent of all things, it troubles the mind and taketh away the empire of liberty, it confounds memory, kills prouidence, and treads downe good councel: offends not he the law, that takes poſſeſſion of another mans free hold, and makes a common of his neighboures incloſure, Adulterers I ſay haue no ſpirits to goodnes, nor will they be by any councell moued to godlines, for their felicity is in the ſurfets of the fleſh, and the pleaſures thereof bring nothing but too deare repentance, the Adulterer ſpights him moſt that examines his proceedings, and plots his ouerthrow that doth but touch

his

his infirmities, Oh! what an enemy is it to Vertue, the onely wrake of wealth, and plaine high way to pouerty. The Adulterer is so blinded in heart, and so hardened withall, that hee can hardly looke vp towards Heauen to behold Gods iust iudgements: yea so iust and sure they are, that in all ages this vile sinne hath beene seuerely punished, as by the example of *Iudas*, iustice on *Thamar*, *Dauids* Adultery with *Vrias* Wife, punished in his Sonne *Absolon*, thousands of men died in the fields of Moab for this fault, threescore thousand of the children of Israell were put to the sword for the rauishing onely a Leuits Wife, of all sins it is in nature the most odious, and brings with it the greatest shame vnto mankind: it is a sinne that hath made the Earthe drunke with blood, to the confusion of many Townes and Cities, Sodome and Gomorah were consumed with fire for

Incest and Adultery: Troy a proud City made a plow-land for the same sinne: It was the onely adulteries of the French that caused a massaker of fourescore thousand, by the ringing of one bell: Let not the Strumpits eye, saies one of the sages of Greece, shine vpon the countenance of young men, least with the Basaliske, it pearce vnto the death: for her malice is as lightning, and more raging then the she Beare, vpon her attends malitious hatred, whose felicity is onely to reioyce at the harmes of others, giuing more affliction to them that are most troubled with affliction, where if any offend her, she admitts no reconciliation, but liues as a partiall Iudge in her owne cause, if she heares the aduancement of vertue then growes she pensiue, & if she want credit amongst the mighty then falls shee working with the meaner sort, shee smiles not vppon any man but

but to be tray him, nor giue him countenance but to vndoe him, nor contriue, any stratagems without Murder, nor dwels by any neighbour but to hurt him; and if shee be but crossed in her will, shee euer frets her selfe away in anger, and after in Hate and Malice becomes infamous, for her loue is a minet, but her spight euerlasting, her hand being once dipt in mischiefe, shee neuer walks abroad but in suspition, fearing to bee accused by Vertue, and still liues in dread of her good Fortune, yet by nature is shee such, that shee hath courage enough to aduenture on any sinne, an Ambitious woman shewes her selfe to bee a troublesome disturber of the world, powerfull to make smale things great, and great, monstrous, enuy by nature is greeued at the Prosperity of others, hee enuyeth the Great in that hee cannot Equall them, hee enuieth the weake, dreading they ſhould compare themſelues with him: hee enuyeth his Equalls becauſe they ſhould not become his Companions: in Kingdomes, Common-Wealths, Princes Courtes and Ambitious mens Houſes he is ſtill working, no Man hunteth after Honor but hee affronts him, onely the miſerable man hee enuies not, becauſe (beeing kept in Priſon) hee feares not his riſings, yet hath hee a ſcorne ouer him: Machiuell knowing the venome of this vice, gaue his ſonne this laſt and not leaſt inſtruction: that hee ſhould not bee enuious, but to doe (ſaith hee) ſuch deeds that others may enuy thee, for to bee enuied is the token of good deſert, but to be enuious the ſigne of a fooliſh nature, which verefies the ſaying of *Marcus Tullius* the Orator, that the moſt floriſhing fortune is moſt enuied at: But now to bee more familiar in my Diſcourſe, where Ambition,

Ambition, Adultery, Pride, Enuy, Malice, and ſuch like Capitall Sinnes haue ſet in foote, there cannot choſe but follow Mnrder and confuſion, and where the foundation is ſayd with blood, there can bee a building but of ſmall continuance; but where Honors haue a true beginning, a ground of vertue ſpringing vp by noble deſerts, continued by Wiſedome and maintayned with Care, there cannot chooſe but follow a fruitfull harueſt, and a plentifull Winter: contrariwiſe to obtaine ſodaine Honors begets Pride and Vaine-glory, Pride and Vaine-glory are the cheriſhers of Enuy and Mallice, Enuy and Mallice the Nurſes of Bloodſhed and Murder, in which whoſoeuer dippeth but the tippe of his finger, giues to his Soule a ſcarlet ſtaine, which neuer can bee cleared vntill the diſſolution of the Body, and then well

a.e

are they that can wash it away with the true teares of repentance.

Brittle is that greatnes that fadeth in a moment, and vaine the ioy that is vnwisely lost, hee that hath a sodaine rise and can wisely stand, is a most happy Worldling, but he that forgets himselfe on the Pinacle of prosperity is besotted with arrogancy: therefore let him that hunts for honors in Princes Courts, wander in an euen passage, for dangerous are the proceedings and busines of a Statesman, take this for an example: suppose that a yong man from the lowest ebbe of worldly chance haue the aduancement of greatnes laid vppon his shoulders, will it not for a time seeme a heauy burthen, and a great trouble to his new transformed fortunes? will not the pride of his heart swell to a full Sea; euen ready to burst ouer the bankes of his Honour-giuer? Then rightly may the Picture

of

of Ingratitude bee imprinted in his fore-front; playing the Viper to his high fortunes first beginner.

Beeing thus intituled with State Offices, hath he not many soothers in sinne, personages of base condition attending him, hemming him round with perswasions of selfe conceit, which for a need will venture their liues to gaine him the commands of his will: what becomes of such follies, but a sorrowfull repentance, and no recouery. All you that haue your hearts pierced with sad considerations, take this for a remembrance of greefe, that is: That when a Woman of noble Parentage, placed on the mountaine of smiling chance, hauing the dignity of Greatnesse shining on her fore-head, should humble her selfe to base conditions, giuing her whole mind to malicious hatred, secret consents of iniquity, selfe-will and wicked proceedings, neuer pacified till the end of damned performances. Oh was not this Woman created for a deep sorrow to her Aliance, a great greefe vnto her Country, and a foule staine vnto her owne reputation? Is it not also a lamentable example, for a Gentleman of good birth and calling, placed in dignity, in high office and charge for his Country, to giue way by consent to a bloody stratagem, and for feare of the displeasures of Greatnes intangles himselfe in the snares of reproch? will not this also be a continuall remembrance to his posterity, and a barre of disgrace branding the coat Armes of his house, to haue the common course of iustice passe vppon him in the eye of the multitude. Is it not also great pitty that for want of grace some of a seruile (yet an obseruing condition) should from the golden meane of low estate wait at the elbow of Greatnes, and bring fuell to their fire of iniquity ty, wherein at the length they themſelues are likewiſe conſumed. Oh, wherefore ſhould ſimplicity thus blind vp their eyes of vnderſtanding, to bee thus the inſtruments of ſuch dangerous drifts, that aymes at nothing but grudge & mallice? if with *Solons* ſaying, they had ſealed vp their hearts, *Remember the end*, this had neuer beene: then how are they led away with amiſſe, that hauing the guifts of art and experience, the ſecrets of the ſimples of Phiſick, ordained by God for mans good vſe, ſhould by the Diuell and them be conuerted thus to malignant purpoſes, if the feare of God had ſhined in their hearts, it would haue been a light to haue led them from all thoſe darke practiſes, which hath now ſpotted the foreheads of their reputations with the marks of black infamy, ſhame cannot chooſe but be the reward of ſuch enterpriſers, that for the fauors of Greatnes, will dip their hands

In the blood of Innocents, and euen as it were worke against nature: Oh more then sauage minded Creatures, in the very deepenesse of your blacke and bloody immaginations, (imboldened by whomsoeuer) this might haue been your *Memento*, in which I conclude, that strange and wonderfull are Gods iudgements, that in these fore-passed stratagems haue shined in great glory, say you then, that blood innocently shed, is layd vp in Heauens Treasury, not one droppe of it can bee lost, but lent out to Vsury: water poured forth, sinkes downe quietly into the earth, but blood spilt on the ground, sprinkles vp to the Firmament, Murder is wide mouthed, and will not let GOD rest till hee grant reuenge, not onely the blood of the slaughtered, but the soule of the Innocent assending to his throne, crying out and exclaiming for Iustice, which (the Lord bee prayfed) praysed) hath beene, and will bee carefully followed by the learned and worthy Magistrates of this Kingdome, whom the Lord God prosper and protect in all their proceedings, to which let all true hearts say.

Amen,

FINIS.

Mistris Turners *Teares, for* the Murder of Sir *Thomas Ouerbury* who was poysoned in the Towre of London.

1

IF euer Teares fell from a Wretches eyes,
I am that Creature: waues on waues do rise,
So fast, and swel so high they drowne my soule,
In her owne Crimes as numberlesse as foule.

2

Oh had my Cradle beene my sodaine Graue,
In Peace my Soule had slept, which is a slaue
Now both to sinne and shame: I had not then
Been of God hated and so scornd of Men

3

Vnhappy was the Wombe that lent me breath,
Would it had bin the *Charnell-house* of Death,
Had I bin stifled there, then had my flight
To Heau'n bin like a Doues, with wings more (white.

4

O would to God the Day when I was borne,
Had from the Calender of time beene torne,
Where now it stands accursed, and does beare
The marke of a most fatall Character.

5

Many a Widdow reading there my name,
Will curse it, and the leafe that holds the same,
Children as yet vnborne, comming to spell,
Will take it for a Furies name in Hell.

6

And casting by the Booke no more will reade,
But onely learne to heape vppon my head
VVishes of mischeefe though in Graue I lye,
For to confound mee euerlastingly.

7 But

7

But leauing this, let my sad Story tell,
Both from what height I fall, & how I fell: (state
That though time present does not mone my
Yet times to come may pitty my hard fate.

8

My birth was faire, my bringing vp was good,
My dayes were golden in my widdow-hood,
And might haue been so still, but climbers hye,
Beyond their reach must downe, and so doe I.

9

Plenty and I at board together sate,
I fed with *Diues* dranke in ritchest plate:
VVore ritch attires, tasted all worldly pleasure,
But ne're had care to hoord vp heau'nly treasure

10

VVith *Eue* I might haue liu'd in Paradice,
But that a Serpent did my Soule intice
To touch forbidden fruit, which relish'd well
In chewing, but be[ing] downe it smelt of Hell.

11

Twas not one onely Apple to deuoure,
For which I long'd: my hunger gap'd at more,
At a whole tree I look'd: it was a Tree, (see.
Me thought the goodliest mortall eyes could

12

This Tree I climb'd, and as I pluckt it grew,
Still freſh and freſh, the boughs were euer new;
The branches euer greene, buſhy and faire,
It ſeem'd the Darling both of ſunne and ayre.

13

But when my Soule lookt vp with open eyes,
I ſaw the top-bough brauing euen the ſkies:
VVhen the root ſtuck in Hell, where looking in
I knew it then to be the tree of ſinne.

14

And though my Conſcience told me I ſhould
If that I leand to: nothing could appall (fall,
My ſetled reſolution, I would on,
Though ſtill before me ſtood damnation.

15

From this I pluckt the guilded fruit of pride,
Like Queen apples they ſhew'd, for euery ſide
VVas ruddy and alluring, but (what truſt (duſt.
Is in vaine earth) being to which they turne to

16 (well,

From this I ſuckt Enchantments which drunke
And luſcious ſweet, yet prou'd the milke of hell,
Hence did I gather poyſonous drugges to kill
Such as withſtood my friends, or croſt my wil.

17 Luſt

17

Luſt often lay within my widdowed ſheetes,
And taught me how to taſt vnbidden ſweetes,
And that toward hell I might go one ſtep furder
The laſt and worſt I went into was murder.

18

O crying ſinne, which ſmothered nere ſo deep,
In caues, which ſilent night her ſelfe does keep,
Bound vp in darknes, like the ſteeme of Hell
which none can peirce, yet the black deed to tell.

19

Euen graues of dead men rotten long agoe
VVill open wide: Vengeance walks often ſlow
To our weak ſight, but when to Strike it ſtands,
On Heau'ns high Tower, it hath a 1000 hands.

20

Th' Almighties Arrowes, fly both ſure & ſtrong
And where they hit great Oakes fall all along,
No hidden mark but ſtands within his eie (flie.
And that he cleaues, when forth his wrath does

21

VVitneſſe my ſelfe and others, who defying,
The buſieſt ſearching Sunbeam from diſcrying:
VVhere Villany lay lurking, wrapd in cloudes,
ſo ſafe we thought as dead men in their ſhrouds

22

When to Mans Sence twas as impoſible,
Mountaines to moue, as find a tongue durſt tel
Our buried plots, See they are rent and torne,
By Gods leaſt finger; and we left in Scorne.

23

Our maskes pluckd off our faces now appeare,
Such as they are indeed, not as they were,
Plaine on our browes are our close miſchiefes
Who moſt did hide, now moſt diſcouer it. (writ

24 (now.

The Wolues are caught in ſnares; the ſhepherd
Knows that a Lamb was ſlain, by whom & how,
The blood of whom by cruell friend ſo ſpilt,
Flowes like a Sea, yet waſhes off no guilt.

25

If any aske mee, why I was ſo led,
And why ſo neere to hell I ventured,
I was bewitch'd, for what I did behold,
Was a moſt bitter *Pill*, but wrap'd in gold.

26

That liquoriſh baite intic'd me take it downe,
As wholeſome Phiſick, but (with ſhae) tis known
No poiſon can ſo ſoone deſtroy the *Soule*,
The out-ſide glorious, but the inſide foule.

27 (deſt
O Gold! thou glittering diuell that confoun-
The Richeſt, Faireſt, Strongeſt, wiſeſt, Soundeſt,
Would God, as He to Indians is vnknowne,
That ſo their Droſſy God were theirs Alone.

28

Soules would not tumble then ſo faſt to Hell,
Nor of my Fall ſhould I this Story tell,
Terror to Soule and Body, had not heauen,
To Sinnes more high and horrid, pardon giuen.

29

Pardon of thee (ſweet *Ieſus*) then I craue,
What thou haſt Bought and Payd for deerely
Men let me beg forgiuenes from you too, (Saue
Becauſe I did more then my Sex ſhould doe.

30

And you of Modeſt dames that beare the note,
And my black Name quite from your tables
As I am loſt, ſo let my fault I craue, (blot,
And write Obliuion on my wretched Graue.

31

You Fathers whom of Children I bereaue,
You Children whom of Parents I deceaue,
You Wiues whom Husband les my Guilt does
Forgiue me All: of All this Leaue I take. (make,

32

Heauen frownes to looke vpon me and my Sin,
Earth trembles that by her I fed haue bin:
My very breath poysons the Aire abont me,
Hell onely is within me, and without me.

33

Yet in despite of Hell, from Heauen comes
Mercy I see holding a glorious Crown, (down,
Of immortality ouer my faint head,
Iesus in that and thee I'me Comforted.

34 (grim,

Strengthen my weake heart, Death is fearefull
One finger of thy Hand can vanquish him,
Giue to my fleeting Soule a prosperous gaile;
That I to Blest Ierusalem may Saile.

FINIS.

A Prayer made by Mistris *Turner*, the night *before her Suffering Death.*

VVIth *Mary Magdalene*, I kneele. (O *Iesus*) at thy feete, which I wash with the teares of a penitentiall bleeding heart, dry them vp againe with the Sighes of my afflicted Soule, O my sweet Sauiour what pretious bloud didst thou pay in ransome to fetch my Soule out of euerlasting Death and Hell: And how (for a golden bribe) haue I sold that loue of thine, and my owne Saluation? I am vndone for euer, for since I could speake the Name of God, or his blessed Sonne, I did neuer speake or doe any thing that was worthy of Heauen. What haue I not beene, that in the world is Euell, and what is now in me, that I dare call Good? My youth was Licentious, my Age wicked, my Latter daies offensiue and odious to God and Man. Yet notwithstanding (Heauenly Father) Since my Repentant Soule comes crying to Thee for Mercy, as before my Sinnes cryed to Heauen for Vengeance: bow downe I beseech thee thine eare: dry vp my Sorrowes with thy beames of Grace. I haue not knowne thee, nor neuer reguarded thy Sacred word, yet (O Lord) shut me not out of Heauen, because it is a broken, wounded, and oppressed heart that knocketh at thy gates of Pitty. Let not my name be blotted out of thy booke of Life, but set the Seale on my forehead, that I may be knowne to be one of Thine. I desire not to liue in this World (of which I am weary, as that is of me) but onely in thy Kingdome: to the intent I may change my bloody garments, for a roabe of Immortality: Comfort me in my Combat of Death, take dispaire from mine eies, set an Angell to guard me, Help me, Strengthen mee, Hasten me to my home, and let that dwelling be with thee for euer and euer, I come deere Redeemer, I come, into thy blessed Hands I commend my Spirit.

Westons

Master VVestons Teares, for the Murder of Sir Thomas Ouerbury who was poysoned in the Towre of London.

GOD of my Soule and Body, haue mercy vpon mee: the one I haue cast way by my folly, & the other is likely to perish in thy Fury, vnlesse, in thy great mercy thou Saue it. My Sinnes are deepe Seas to drowne mee; I am swallowed vp in the bottomles Gulph of my owne transgressions. With *Caine* I haue beene a Murderer, and with *Iudas* a Betrayer of the Innocent. My body is a Slaue to Sathan, and my wretched Soule is deuowred vp by Hell. Black haue bin my thoughts, and blacker, are my deeds. I haue beene the Diuells instrument, and am now become the Scorne of Men, a Serpent vpon earth, and an Out-cast from Heauen. What therefore can become of me (miserable Catiffe;) if I looke vp to my Redeemer, to him I am an Arch Traitor, if upon Earth, it is drowned with Blood of my shedding, if into Hell, there I see my Conscience, burning in the Brimstone lake. God of my Soule and Body haue mercy therefore vpon mee, Saue me, O saue me, or else I perish for euer, I die for euer in the world to come, vnlesse (sweet Lord) thou catchest my repentant Soule in thine Armes; O saue mee, saue me, saue me.

FINIS.

Readers you that are desirous to see the Reward of, the Adulterer and the Adulteresse, paid by Gods own hand: there is a little Table, called the Spectacles, *where you may Read them more at Large.*

Mistris Turners Farewell to all women (*STC* 24341.5) is reproduced with permission from the unique copy a
the Society of Antiquaries. The text-block measures 360 × 450 mm.

Mistris Turners Farewell to all women.

Angell (turn'd Diuell) Pride:
by thee I fell
When heere on earth I dwelt
too'th pit of Hell:
Yet spite of all thy Poysons,
I am faire
Now in Gods eyes,
Women by me Beware.

Mistris Turner.

Lady Pride.

Mistris Turner.

1 THou, of all sinnes the first, of all, the highest,
Because thou fell'st from Heauen before Mans fall,
Who, (when to Happines thou wert the nighest,)
In enuy of the best of all, lost all.
2 Wo worth that whorish face of thine, which tempted
Me to more Hells then thou hast vaine attires,
For which my spotted Soule, is not exempted
(With out Gods mercy) from eternall fires.
3 Shee-Diuell, (destroyer both of man and Woman,
That with thy sorcerous Drugges didst catch my Soule:
To the last Barre Tribunall, thee I summon,
Where I shall stand all white, thou black and foule.
4 Washd are my spots away by *Christs* red passion,
For I am there whence headlong thou wert throwne:
And now I glory in triumphant fashion,
That thou art there whether I should haue gone:
From Heauen thou fellst to Hell, and I being drownd
In Sinnes, got vp and now in Heauen sit Crownd.

Lady Pride.

1 THou, of all Woemen worst of all, the basest,
Who (when I am of Sinnes the worst and proudest,
And throwne from Heauen me in thy bosome placest;
And what thy heart lou'd best, now rail'st at loudest.
2 'Tis not thy hate of Pride, makes thee to cry
Wo worth my Whorish Face, but tis because
Thy Pride hath caught her fall, and thou must dye,
And frighted art with Hels deuouring Iawes.
3 Enough it is for me that I haue made thee
Drunke with my cup: nor care I though thou boast
That from eternall fires Gods mercy staid thee;
For say thy soule be sau'd, thy bodyes lost.
4 As for thy yellowed Ruffes, phantastick Tires,
Paintings, and Poysonings (now by thee abhorred)
I laugh to see thee wrap them vp in fires,
For Pride hath more to bewitch many a Forehead.
And though thy soule should climbe the highest Sphere,
Ile pluck downe thousands that shall nere come there.

Printed for Iohn Trundle.

Mistres Turners Repentance (*STC* 3720) is reproduced with permission from the unique copy at the Society of Antiquaries. The text-block measures 305 × 480 mm.

Miſtres

Turners Repentance,

Who, about the poyſoning of that Ho:

Knight Sir THOMAS OVERBVRY, VVas executed

the fourteenth day of Nouember, laſt.

TO ſtay the venome of Ill ſpeaking breath
Kills, men aliue, & makes them liue in death
By his il-ſounding Language; this poore ſcrowle,
My Chriſtian loue, to a Repentant ſoule
Sends to the view of all; that all may ſee,
That did not ſee her, all the ſignes that bee
Soule-ſauing greifes bewrayers: how her hands,
(While ſhe with heauy ſuſpiration ſtandes)
To Heauen are raiſed: how her eyes are bent
The way of Angells; fixt, as then ſhe meant,
(With Egle-ſight) that Glory to behold
Eye neuer ſaw; Eare heard, nor Tongue hath told.
H[o]w humbly-lowe, in her deuotious prayer
Sh[e] bends her knee, eſcaped from the ſnare,
Of [H]ells temptation. Heare her like wiſe ſpeake:
While her Repentant ſorrow ſtriues to breake
Her very heart ſtrings; when her tongue bewrayes
The many miſcheifes, of thoſe many dayes
She had bin ſlau'd to Sathan. Heere ſaid ſhee,
Are many come, a wretched thing to ſee,
Take her deſerued Death: may my ſad end
Teach euery bad beholder, how to mend
All ill (in cogitation) 'fore it growes
To that foule act, our frailty ouerthrowes.
Dehorting ſtill, from thoſe beloued ſinnes,
Are boſome Traytors; baites: by which Hell winnes
Increaſe to his blacke Kingdome. But in cheiſe,
From thoſe, whoſe ſad remembrance, were her greiſe
In that laſt houre of life: luſt, gawdy pride,
And wanton painted pleaſures, whoſe ſtrong Tide,
Had borne her ſo from goodneſſe. And in ſumme,
(For ſinne, with her, to this account did come)
All, all is vaine; and this vaine World can ſhowe
Nothing that's good, but what from Heauen doth flowe.
Then, lifting vp her fingers to her eye,
And feeling thoſe faire Fountaines to be drye,
From which had runne ſo large a flood of teares:
Alas (ſaid ſhe) heere little Grace appeares.
And ſome (I feare me) that beholde this face,
Will iudge this want of teares, my want of Grace:
But good, good People doe not, my heart's ſore,
And I haue wept ſo much, I can no more.
With that, freſh teares vpon the ſuddaine fall,
Extorting water, from the eyes of all
That ſtood to ſee, and heare her: from the deepe
Of greiſe, ſhe weepes, to thinke ſhe could not weepe.
And through thoſe teares, from her ſuſpitious thought,
(Knowing, men knew ſhe had much miſcheiſe wrought)
She thus breaks out: When Death hath cloſ'd mine eyes
And that my Body, colde, and ſenceleſſe lyes,
My ſpotted Soule, will be imagin'd ſtraight,
To ſinke to Hell, vnder my ſinnes ſad weight.
But, Heauen hath ſeal'd, to my afflicted breſt
My ſinnes forgiueneſſe, and my ſoule poſſeſt
With full aſſurance, of that endleſſe Good
Is purchaſd onely by my Sauiours blood.
I know (ſaid ſhe) that *She* that with her teares,
Waſht *Ieſus* feete, and wip't them with her heires,
Was, like my ſelfe a Sinner; yet her ſinne,
Did *Mercy* wipe (as it had neuer bin)
From foorth the booke of *Iuſtice*: this I know,
And know that God, that did that mercy ſhow
Hath ſhowen the like to me, for in my heart,
I feele Heau'ns pleaſure, dreadleſſe of *H*ells ſmart.
Then wiſtly looking, on that fatall place,
Where Life muſt leaue her, and pale Death imbrace
Her [illegible] cold Body, as that *Death* to dye
Did more then Deaths grim viſage, fright her eye;
From ſuch conceit (diſturbant to her minde)
That * man, (in Death, the way of Life to finde,) ** Doct:*
Did then direct her; with Religious care,
Doth thus recall her: You muſt now forbeare
To place a thought, on Earth, or earthly things;
And onely that, Cœleſtiall comfort brings
Fixe heart and eye on: Now, ſhould you tranſcend
The troublous view, of this reproachfull end;
Regarding no diſgraces. On a Tree
Dyed our Redeemer; hee that dyed for thee,
And all Repentant Sinners. For the way,
It makes no matter (greatly) how we pay
This debt of Life, ſo Heauen aſſurance giue,
That then we dye, a better life to liue.
Fire, Water, Torture, any way: 'tis well
To goe to Heau'n, eu'n by the Gates of Hell.
From theſe ſweete wordes, her weakeneſſe did receiue
Such Heauenly comfort, ſhe prepares to leaue
The Bodyes burthen (and her Soule releaſe,
From that ſad Priſon, to *Eternall* Peace)
With cheerfull freeneſſe. No man knowes the breſt;
But this, her Language, to the Life expreſt,
In this bleſt manner: Let not any heere,
That notes me pale, and quaking, thinke 'tis feare
To ſee my Deathſ-man: Or to meete with *Death*
That now attends me, for the minutes breath
Is yet within me. No, 'tis no ſuch thing,
This little paine, nere-ending pleaſures bring
And therefore I embrace it. This pale cheeke,
Sighes, palſy-quaking, faintnes and the like,
Are the effects of Griefe; a hearty woe,
That makes me heart-leſſe: to the beſt I knowe.
As if ſhe thus had ſaid: *Theſe Embleames are,*
Of Peters ſorrow; not of *Caynes* diſpaire.
To that, ſhee adds this comfort; Lord my God
So dearely welcome to me, is this Rod,
That (ſtead of harſh repining) I giue praiſe,
And humble thankes, that through ſo many dayes
Of Soule-poluting miſcheife, 'twas thy will,
I liue to taſte it. In the prime of Ill,
Had ſodaine ſickneſſe, or ſome other croſſe,
(When droſſe was Gold, and golden vertue Droſſe)
Bereau'd me life, 'I had then moſt wretched bin,
And vnrepented, periſht in my ſinne.
Then, with a Mothers tender loue, and care,
She calls to minde her Children; and her Prayer
Directs to Heau'n; deſiring, thence deſcend
Thoſe *Holy* bleſſings, might their Soules defend
'Gainſt *Hels* ſuggeſtions; that, (as ſhe had done)
They neuer might, in graceleſſe courſes runne.
And (now) to make her penitence, more cleare,
That *Image*-worſhip, that her breaſt once bare
A heart *Deuote* to; ſhee in death denide,
And *Rome*, and Romes fowle *Hereſie* defide.
Praies, Heau'ns beſt bleſſings, on our Royall King
Might ſtill be ſhewr'd; and a continuall Spring,
Of Peace, Content, and happy dayes remaine,
With him, with his, and all his right maintaine.

Thus ſhe, in life, was ſo extreamly nought
As if one Act, or ſound Religious thought
Remain'd not in her; in her end appear'd
A bleſt Repentant; as if Heau'n had clear'd
Her ſpotted Soule, and, in his ſecret will,
Then made *All Good*, that was *Before all Ill.*
What God will doe, he can: with this I reſt:
'T becomes a Chriſtian, ſpeake, and hope the beſt.

FINIS. *T. B.*

Printed at London, for *Henry Goſſon*, and *John White*. 1615.

Anne Wallens Lamentation (*STC* 19997) is reproduced with permission from the unique copy at the Pepys Library, Magdalene College, Cambridge. The text-block measures 110 × 135 mm.

Anne VVallens Lamentation,

For the Murthering of her husband *John Wallen* a Turner in Cow-lane neere Smithfield; done by his owne wife, on satterday the 22 of Iune. 1616. who was burnt in Smithfield the first of Iuly following.

To the tune of Fortune my foe.

GReat God that sees al things that here are don
Keeping thy Court with thy celestiall Son;
Heere her complaint that hath so sore offended,
Forgiue my fact before my life is ended.

Ah me the shame vnto all women kinde,
To harbour such a thought within my minde:
That now hath made me to the world a scorne,
And makes me curse the time that I was borne.

O would to God my mothers haples wombe,
Before my birth had beene my happy tombe:
Or would to God when first I did take breath,
That I had suffered any painefull death.

If euer dyed a true repentant soule,
Then I am she, whose deedes are blacke and foule:
Then take heed wiues be to your husbands kinde,
And beare this lesson truely in your minde,

Let not your tongues oresway true reasons bounds,
Which in your rage your vtmost rancour sounds:
A woman that is wise should seldome speake,
Unlesse discreetly she her words repeat

Oh would that I had thought of this before,
Which now to thinke on makes my heart full sore:
Then should I not haue done this deed so foule,
The which hath stained my immortall soule.

Tis not to dye that thus doth cause me grieue,
I am more willing far to die then liue;
But tis for blood which mounteth to the skies,
And to the Lord reuenge, reuenge, it cries.

My dearest husband did I wound to death,
And was the cause he lost his sweetest breath,
But yet I trust his soule in heauen doth dwell,
And mine without Gods mercy sinkes to hell.

In London neere to smithfield did I dwell,
And mongst my neighbours was beloued well:
Till that the Deuill wrought me this same spight,
That all their loues are turnd to hatred quight.

Iohn Wallen was my louing husbands name,
Which long hath liu'd in London in good fame.
His trade a Turner, as was knowne full well,
My name An Wallen, dolefull tale to tell.

Anne wallens Lamentation,

Or the second part of the murther of one *John Wallen* a Turner in Cow-lane neere Smithfield; done by his owne wife, on satetday the 22 of June 1616. who was burnt in Smithfield the first of July following.

To the tune of Fortune my foe.

My husband hauing béene about the towne,
And comming home, he on his bed lay down:
To rest himselfe, which when I did espie,
I fell to rayling most outragiously.

I cald him Rogue, and slaue, and all to naught,
Repeating the worst language might be thought
Thou drunken knaue I said, and arrant sot,
Thy minde is set on nothing but the pot.

Swéet heart he said I pray thée hold thy tongue,
And if thou dost not, I shall shall doe thée wrong,
At which, straight way I grew in worser rage,
That he by no meanes could my tongue asswage.

He then arose and stroke me on the eare,
I did at him begin to curse and sweare:
Then presently one of his toles I got,
And on his body gaue a wicked stroake

Amongst his intrailes I this Chissell threw,
Where as his Caule came out, for which I rue,
What hast thou don, I prethée looke quoth he,
Thou hast thy wish, for thou hast killed me.

When this was done the neighbours they ran in,
And to his bed they streight conueyed him:
Where he was drest and liu'd till morne next day,
Yet he forgaue me and for me did pray.

No sooner was his breath from body fled,
But unto Newgate straight way they me led:
Where I did lie untill the Sizes came,
Which was before I there thrée daies had laine.

Mother in lawe, forgiue me I you pray,
For I haue made your onely childe away,
Euen all you had; my selfe made husbandlesse,
My life and all, cause I did so transgresse.

He nere did wrong to any in his life,
But he too much was wronged by his wife;
Then wiues be warn'd, example take by me.
Heauens graunt no more that such a one may be.

My iudgement then it was pronounced plaine,
Because my dearest husband I had slaine:
In burning flames of fire I should fry,
Receiue my soule swéet Jesus now I die.

T: Platte.

FINIS.

Printed for *Henry Gosson*, and are to be solde at his shop on London bridge.

The vnnaturall Wife (*STC* 6366) is reproduced with permission from the unique copy at the Pepys Library, Magdalene College, Cambridge. The text-block measures 80 × 140 mm.

The vnnaturall Wife:

Or,

The lamentable Murther of one goodman *Dauis*, Locke-Smith in Tutle-ſtreete, who was ſtabbed to death by his Wife, on the 29. of *Iune*, 1628. For which fact, She was Araigned, Condemned, and Adiudged, to be Burnt to Death in *Smithfield*, the 12. *Iuly* 1628.

To the tune of Bragandary.

IF woefull obiects may excite,
  the minde to ruth and pittie,
Then here is one will thee affright
  in Weſtminſters faire Citie:
A ſtrange inhumane Murther there,
To God, and Man as doth appeare:
    oh murther,
    moſt inhumane,
To ſpill my Husbands blood.

But God that rules the hoſt of Heauen,
  did giue me ore to ſinne,
And to vild wrath my minde was giuen,
  which long I liued in;
But now too late I doe repent,
And for the ſame my heart doth rent:
    oh murther,
    moſt inhumane,
To ſpill my Husbands blood.

Let all curſt Wiues by me take heed,
  how they doe, doe the like,
Cauſe not thy Husband for to bleed,
  nor lift thy hand to ſtrike;
Leſt like to me, you burne in fire,
Becauſe of cruell rage and ire:
    oh murther,
    moſt inhumane,
To ſpill my Husbands blood.

A Locke-Smith late in Weſtminſter,
  my Husband was by trade,
And well he liued by his Art,
  though oft I him vpbraide;
And often times would chide and brawle,
And many ill names would him call:
    oh murther,
    moſt inhumane,
To ſpill my Husbands blood.

The ſecond part.

I And my Husband foorth had bin,
at Supper at that time,
When as I did commit that ſin,
which was a bloody crime;
And comming home he then did craue,
A Shilling of me for to haue:
oh murther,
moſt inhumane,
To ſpill my Husbands blood.

I vow'd he ſhould no Money get,
and I my vow did keepe,
Which then did cauſe him for to fret,
but now it makes me weepe;
And then in ſtriuing for the ſame,
I drew my knife vnto my ſhame:
oh murther,
moſt inhumane,
To ſpill my Husbands blood.

Moſt deſperately I ſtab'd him then,
with this my fatall knife,
Which is a warning to Women,
to take their Husbands life;
Then out of doores I ſtreight did runne,
And ſayd that I was quite vndon,
oh murther,
moſt inhumane,
To ſpill my Husbands blood.

My Husband I did ſay was ſlaine,
amongſt my Neighbours there,
And to my houſe they ſtraite way came,
being poſſeſt with feare;
And then they found him on the floore,
Starke dead all weltring in his goore,
oh murther,
moſt inhumane,
To ſpill my Husbands blood.

Printed at London for M. T. Widdow.

To the ſame Tune.

Life faine I would haue fetcht againe,
but now it was too late,
I did repent I him had ſlaine,
in this my heauie ſtate;
The Conſtable did beare me then
Vnto a Iuſtice with his men:
oh murther, &c.

Then Iuſtice me to Newgate ſent,
vntill the Seſsions came,
For this ſame foule and bloody fact,
to anſwere for the ſame;
When at the Barre I did appeare,
The Iury found me guiltie there:
oh murther, &c.

The Iudge gaue ſentence thus on me,
that backe I ſhould returne
To Newgate, and then at a Stake,
my bones and fleſh ſhould burne
To aſhes, in the winde to flie,
Vpon the Earth, and in the Skie.
oh murther, &c.

Vpon the twelfth of Iuely now,
I on a Hurdle plac't,
Vnto my Execution drawne,
by weeping eyes I paſt;
And there in Smith-field at a Stake,
My lateſt breath I there did take:
oh murther, &c.

And being chayned to the Stake,
both Reedes and Faggots then
Cloſe to my Body there was ſet,
with Pitch, Tarre, and Rozen,
Then to the heauenly Lord I prayd,
That he would be my ſtrength and ayde.
oh murther,
moſt inhumane,
To ſpill my husbands blood.

Let me a warning be to Wiues,
that are of haſty kinde,
Lord grant that all may mend their liues
and beare my death in minde,
And let me be the laſt I pray,
That ere may dye by ſuch like way.
Oh Father
for thy Sonnes ſake,
Forgiue my ſinnes for aye.

FINIS.

A warning for all desperate Women (*STC* 6367) is reproduced with permission from the unique copy at th
Pepys Library, Magdalene College, Cambridge. The text-block measures 110 × 130.5 mm.

A warning for all desperate VVomen.

By the example of *Alice Dauis* who for killing of her husband was burned in Smithfield the 12 of Iuly 1628. to the terror of all the beholders. To the tune of the Ladies fall.

VNto the world to make my moane,
I know it is a folly,
Because that I haue spent my time,
which haue beene free and iolly,
But to the Lord which rules aboue,
I doe for mercy crie,
To grant me pardon for the crime,
for which on earth I dye.

Hells fiery flames prepared are,
for those that liue in sinne,
And now on earth I tast of some,
but as a pricke of pin,
To those which shall hereafter be,
without Gods mercy great,
Who once more calls vs to account,
on his Tribunall Seate.

Then hasty haire-braind wiues take heed,
of me a warning take,
Least like to me in coole of blood,
you burnt be at a stake;
The woman which heere last did dye,
and was consum'd with fire,
Puts me in minde, but all to late,
for death I doe require.

But to the story now I come,
which to you Ile relate,
Because that I haue liu'd like some,
in good repute and state,
In Westminster we liued there,
well knowne by many friends,
Which little thought that each of vs,
should haue come to such ends.

A Smith my husband was by trade,
as many well doe know,
And diuers merry dayes we had,
not feeling cause of woe,
Abroad together we had bin,
and home at length we came,
But then I did that fatall deede,
which brings me to this shame.

He askt what monies I had left,
and some he needes would haue,
But I a penny would not giue,
though he did seeme to craue,
But words betwixt vs then did passe
as words to harsh I gaue,
And as the Diuell would as then,
I did both sweare and raue.

The second Part, To the same tune.

AND then I tooke a little knife,
and stab'd him in the heart.
Whose Soule from Body instantly,
my bloody hand did part,
But cursed hand, and fatall knife
and wicked was that houre,
When as my God did giue me ore
vnto his hellish power.

The deede no sooner I had don,
But out of doores I ran,
And to the neighbours I did cry,
I kil'd had my good man,
Who straight-way flockt vnto my house,
to see that bloody sight,
Which when they did behold with griefe,
it did them much affright.

Then hands vpon me there was lay'd,
And I to Prison sent,
Where as I lay perplext in woe,
and did that deede repent,
When Sizes came I was arraign'd,
by Jury iust and true,
I was found guilty of the fact,
for which I haue my due.

The Iury hauing cast me then,
to iudgment then I came,
Which was a terrour to my heart,
and to my friends a shame,
To thinke vpon my husbands death,
and of my wretched life,
Betwixt my Spirit and my flesh,
did cause a cruell strife.

But then the Iudge me sentence gaue
to goe from whence I came,
From thence vnto a stake be bound
to burne in fiers flame,
Untill my flesh and bones consum'd,
to ashes in that place,
Which was a heauie sentence then,
is on so voyd of grace.

And on the twelfth of July now,
I on a sledge was laid,
To Smithfield with a guard of men
I streight way was conueyd,
Where I was tyed to a stake,
with Reedes was round beset,
And Faggots, Pitch, and other things
which they for me did get.

Now great Iehouah I thee pray,
my bloudy sinnes forgiue,
For on this earth most wretched I
vnworthy am to liue.
Christ Iesus vnto thee I pray,
and vnto thee I cry,
Thou with thy blood wilt wash my sinnes
away, which heere must dye.

Good wiues and bad, example take,
at this my cursed fall,
And Maidens that shall husbands haue,
I warning am to all:
Your Husbands are your Lords & heads,
you ought them to obey,
Grant loue betwixt each man and wife,
vnto the Lord I pray.

God and the world forgiue my sinnes,
which are so vile and foule,
Sweete Iesus now I come to thee,
O Lord receiue my Soule.
Then to the Reedes they fire did put,
which flamd vp to the skye,
And then she shriek'd most pittifully,
before that she did dye.

The Lord preserue our King & Queene,
and all good Subiects blesse,
And Grant the Gospell true and free,
amongst vs may encrease.
Betwixt each husband and each wife,
send loue and amitie,
And grant that I may be the last,
that such a death did dye.

FINIS.

Printed for F. Coules.

[*The*] *complaint and lamentation of Mistresse Arden of* [*Fav*]*ersham in Kent* (*STC* 732) is reproduced wi
permission from the unique British Library copy (shelfmark Rox.III.156). The text-block measures 248 × 38
mm.

complaint and lamentation of Miſtreſſe *Arden* of ...rſham in *Kent*, who for the loue of one *Mosbie*, hired certaine Ruffians ...d Villaines moſt cruelly to murder her Husband; with the fatall end of her and her Aſſociats.

To the tune of, *Fortune my Foe*.

Ay me, vile wretch, that euer I was borne,
Making my ſelfe vnto the world a ſcorne:
And to my friends and kindred all a ſhame,
Blotting their blood by my vnhappy name.

Unto a Gentleman of wealth and fame,
(One Maſter Arden, he was call'd by name)
I wedded was with ioy and great content,
Liuing at Feuerſham in famous Kent.

In loue we liu'd, and great tranquility,
Untill I came in Mosbies company,
Whoſe ſugred tongue, good ſhape, and louely looke,
Soone won my heart, and Ardens loue forſooke.

And liuing thus in foule adultery,
Bred in my husband cauſe of iealouſie,
And leſt the world our actions ſhould bewray,
We did conſent to take his life away.

To London faire my Husband was to ride,
But ere he went I poyſon did prouide,
Got of a Painter which I promiſed
That Mosbies ſiſter Suſan he ſhould wed.

Into his Broth I then did put the ſame,
He lik't it not when to the boord it came,
Saying, There's ſomething in it is not ſo good,
At which inrag'd, I flung it on the ground.

Yet ere he went, his man I did coniure,
Ere they came home, to make his Maſter ſure,
And murder him, and for his faith and paine,
Suſan, and ſtore of gold that he ſhould gaine.

Yet I miſdoubting Michaels conſtancy,
Knowing a Neighbour that was dwelling by,
Which, to my husband bore no great good will,
Sought to incenſe him his deare blood to ſpill.

His name was Greene; O Maſter Green (quoth I)
My husband to you hath done iniury,
For which I ſorry am with all my heart,
And how he wrongeth me I will impart.

He keepes abroad moſt wicked company,
With whores and queanes, and bad ſociety;
When he comes home, he beats me ſides and head,
Would I were with that one of vs were dead.

And now to London he is rid to roare,
I would that I might neuer ſee him more:
Greene then incenſt, did vow to be my friend,
And of his life he ſoone would make an end.

O Maſter Greene, ſaid I, the dangers great,
You muſt be circumſpect to doe this feat;
To act the deed your ſelfe there is no need,
But hire ſome villaines, they will doe the deed.

Ten pounds Ile giue them to attempt this thing,
And twenty more when certaine newes they bring,
That he is dead, beſides Ile be your friend,
In honeſt curteſie till life doth end.

Greene vow'd to doe it; then away he went,
And met two Villaines, that did vſe in Kent
To rob and murder vpon Shooters hill,
The one call'd Shakebag, t'other nam'd Black Will.

Two ſuch like Villaines Hell did neuer hatch,
For twenty Angels they made vp the match,
And forty more when they had done the deed,
Which made them ſweare, they'd do it with al ſpeed

Then vp to London preſently they hye,
Where Maſter Arden in Pauls Church they ſpy,
And waiting for his comming forth that night,
By a ſtrange chance of him they then loſt ſight.

For where theſe Villaines ſtood & made their ſtop
A Prentice he was ſhutting vp his ſhop,
The window falling, light on Blacke-Wills head,
And broke it ſoundly, that apace it bled.

Where ſtraight he made a brabble and a coyle,
And my ſweet Arden he paſt by the while;
They miſſing him, another plot did lay,
And meeting Michael, thus to him they ſay:

Thou knowſt that we muſt packe thy Maſter hence
Therefore conſent and further our pretence,
At night when as your Maſter goes to bed,
Leaue ope the doores, he ſhall be murthered.

And ſo he did, yet Arden could not ſleepe,
Strange dreames and viſions in his ſenſes creepe,
He dreamt the doores were ope, & Villaines came,
To murder him, and twas the very ſame.

The second part. To the same tune.

HE rose and shut the doore, his man [illegible],
which cunningly he [illegible],
I was so sleepy, that I did forget
To locke the doores, I pray you pardon it.

Next day these Ruffians met this man againe,
Who the whole story to them did explaine,
My master will in towne no longer stay,
To morrow you may meete him on the way.

Next day his businesse being finished,
He did take horse, and homeward then he rid,
And as he rid, it was his hap as then,
To overtake Lord Cheiney and his men.

With salutations they each other greete.
I am full glad your Honour for to meet,
Arden did say: then did the Lord reply,
Sir, I am glad of your good company.

And being that we homeward are to ride,
I have a sute that must not be denide,
That at my house youle sup, and lodge also,
To Feversham this night you must not goe.

Then Arden answered with this courteous speech,
Your Honours pardon now I doe beseech,
I made a vow, if God did give me life,
To sup and lodge with Alice my loving wife.

Well, said my Lord, your oath hath got the day,
To morrow come and dine with me, I pray.
Ile wait upon your Honour then (said he)
And safe he went amongst this company.

On Raymon-Downe, as they did passe this way,
Black-will, and Shakebag they in ambush lay,
But durst not touch him, cause of the great traine
That my Lord had: thus were they crost againe.

With horrid oathes these Ruffians gan to sweare,
They stampe and curst, and tore their lockes of haire
Saying, some Angell surely him did keepe.
Yet vow'd to murther him ere they did sleepe.

Now all this while my husband was away,
Mosby and I did revell night and day;
And Susan, which my waiting maiden was,
My Loves owne sister, knew how all did passe.

But when I saw my Arden was not dead,
I welcom'd him, but with a heavy head:
To bed he went, and slept secure from harmes,
But I did with my Mosby in my armes.

Yet ere he slept, he told me he must goe
To dinner to my Lords, hee'd have it so;
And that same night Blacke-will did send me word,
What lucke bad fortune did to them afford.

I sent him word, that he next day would dine
At the Lord Cheinies, and would rise betime,
And on the way their purpose might fulfill,
Well, Ile reward you, when that you him kill.

Next morne betimes, before the breake of day,
To take him napping then they take their way;
But such a mist and fog there did arise,
They could not see although they had their eyes.

Thus Arden scap'd these villaines there,
And yet they heard his horse goe by that way,
I thinke (said Will) some Spirit is his friend,
Come life or death, I vow to see his end.

Then to my house they strait did take their way,
Telling me how they missed of their pray;
Then presently, we did together gree,
At night at home that he should murdered be.

Mosby and I, and all, our plot thus lay,
That he at Tables should with Arden play,
Black-will, and Sakebag they themselves should hide
Untill that Mosby he a watchword cride.

The word was this whereon we did agree,
Now (Master Arden) I have taken ye:
Woe to that word, and woe unto us all,
Which bred confusion and our sudden fall.

When he came home, most welcome him I made,
And Iudas like I kist whom I betraide,
Mosby and he together went to play,
For I on purpose did the tables lay.

And as they plaid, the word was straightway spoke,
Blacke-Will and Sakebag out the corner broke,
And with a Towell backwards pul'd him downe,
which made me think they now my ioyes did crowne

With swords and knives they stab'd him to the heart
Mosby and I did likewise act our part,
And then his body straight we did convey
Behind the Abbey in the field he lay.

And then by Iustice we were straight condemn'd,
Each of us came unto a shamefull end,
For God our secret dealings soone did spy,
And brought to light our shamefull villany.

Thus have you heard of Ardens tragedy,
It rests to shew you how the rest did dye:
His wife at Canterbury she was burn'd,
And all her flesh and bones to ashes turn'd.

Mosby and his faire Sister, they were brought
To London for the trespasse they had wrought,
In Smithfield on a gibbet they did die.
A iust reward for all their villanie,

Michael and Bradshaw, which a Goldsmith was,
That knew of letters which from them did passe,
At Feversham were hanged both in chaines,
And well rewarded for their faithfull paines.

The painter fled none knowes how he did speed,
Sakebag in Southwarke he to death did bleed,
For as he thought to scape and run away,
He suddenly was murdered in a fray.

In Kent at Osbridge, Greene did suffer death,
Hang'd on a gibbet he did lose his breath:
Blacke-Will at Flushing on a stage did burne,
Thus each one came unto his end by turne.

And thus my story I conclude and end,
Praying the Lord that he his grace will send
Upon us all, and keepe us all from ill,
Amen say all, if't be thy blessed will.

Printed at London for C. W.

FINIS.

Heavens Speedie Hue and Cry sent after Lust and Murther (second edn.; *STC* 12010.5) is reproduced wit permission from the unique British Library copy (shelfmark C.27.c.17). The text-block measures 130 × 22 mm. The second edition differs from the first (*STC* 12010, Huntington Library only) in having a revise woodcut image on the recto of the first leaf (A1). Its title page includes a new subsection ('Also some ne Additions ... death'). This refers to the sections on C1^{v}–C2^{r} ('A briefe observation ... the Kings Roya prerogative') and the last two pages of the final leaf (C4), '*The* Habeas corpus'. The layout and type of som sections have been reset, though without any substantive changes in wording from the first edition. The secon edition, B4^{r}, omits a depiction of the murder-weapon which appears vertically down the right margin of C2^{r} i the first edition (and which in both editions appears horizontally across the bottom of the opening image o A1^{r}, and down the left margin of first edition B4^{v}, and second edition B2^{v}). The catchword 'A True' on A erroneously refers to the page that originally followed in the first edition (B1^{r}). The second edition also omi Goodcole's closing affirmation immediately before '*FINIS*' on the last page (C4^{v}) of the first edition:

> There is nothing contayned in this Booke concer-
> ning this *Murder*, but that I know to bee truth:
> and therefore may lawfully be printed.
> *April* 23. 1635.
>
> *Hen. Goodcole.*

The Bodelian Library copy (*STC* 12010.3, shelfmark Ashmole 739 [1]) is a transitional edition between th first and the second. It lacks the first-leaf (A1) woodcut image and '*The* Habeas Corpus' on the final leaf (C4 of the second edition.

The following words are a transcription of the original:

A2v.34 a blessing unto his good
A2v.35 I was thy true
A2v.36 mortality
A3v.4 listes
A4v.1 The narration of the manner
A4v.24 space of 4. yeares
B2v.28 fell to rifling
B2v.29 strip (all humanity laying
B4r.3 Night repaire
B4v.18 a serious asseve-
B4v.22 day, to beware of
B4v.25 blind-fold … by such
B4v.30 eiaculations
C1r.1 his Sinnes, most hartely implored
C1r.4 the word Mercy
C1r.6 owne mouth
C1r.13 these speeches
C1r.15 haynous
C1r.20 exercises
C4r.1 The Habeas corpus, or Remove of Countrey
C4r.2 Tom into the Countrey
C44.3 Good Reader, to the precedent
C4r.4 succeeding true
C4r.7 confusion
C4r.8 Sceleton … Gristles
C4r.20 insolent act

HEAVENS SPEEDIE

Hue and Cry sent after *Lust* and *Murther*.

Manifested upon the suddaine apprehending of *Thomas Shearwood*, and *Elizabeth Evans*, whose manner of *Lives*, *Death*, and free *Confessions*, are heere *expressed*.

Also some new Additions, concerning the man that was tide to the Gibbet, with a discovery of those places where such kind of lude people haunt and resort unto, and by what signes and tokens you may discover them: disclosed by this *Sherwood* a little before his death.

Who were Executed the one upon the 14. and the other on the 17. of this Moneth of *April* 1635. neere to the place where the facts were committed, and he now hangeth in chaines at *Ring-Crosse*.

Written by *H. G.* their daily Visiter, at the *time of their Imprisonment, and severall dayes of Execution.*

Published by Authority.

LONDON.
Printed by *M.* and *I. Okes*, dwelling in *Well-yard* in little St. *Bartholmews*, neare unto the *Lame Hospitall* gate, 1635.

IF one smite another with an Instrument of Iron, that hee Dye, hee is a *Murderer*, and the *Murderer* shall dye the Death. Or if hee smite him with an hand-weapon of wood whereby hee may be slayne, if hee dye, hee is a *Murderer*, and the Murderer shall dye the Death. *Numb*. 35. *v*. 16.

Countrey-Tom. *Canberry Besse.*

he forme of the instrument of wood and iron that he used to hurt with.

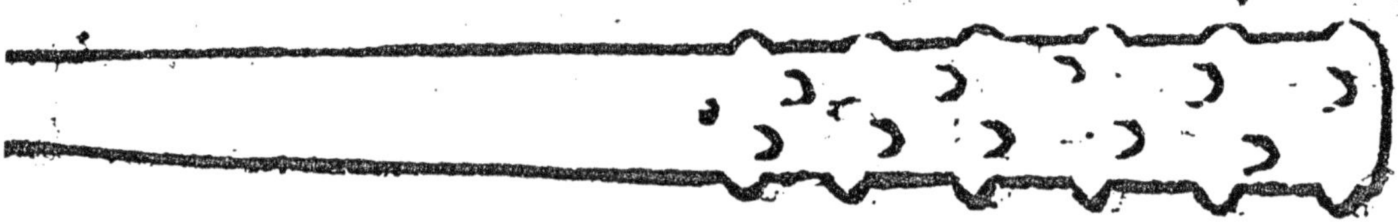

The Preface.

I Have resumed my Pen which I resolved in this Nature for ever to be silent: But the Common good, and preservation of my Countries welfare, incites me unto this officious service. As one that standeth Centinell in the Night unto whom Fidelity and Trust is reposed, and the safety of the whole Army dependeth: (Even so am I) to discover the private and suddaine approaching of the Enemies. Like a Watchman to observe all commers in and out, into the Gates of the City, to unvaile pernicious passengers, which dayes and nights uncessantly passe through the Streets, and in the secret corners of the same privily lurke, and watch an opportunity to cozen, rob, and murther. I presume not to instruct the prudent and wise, that were absurde and ridiculous: But the Levell of my intention is to make the vulgar Ignorants so wise, as to walke warily and circumspectly; which plaine path they may knowingly see, and discerne by this sequent discovery of such notorious offenders, that live upon the spoyles of such Passengers, and Travellers resorting up unto London upon their necessary affaires. A new kind of invented wickednesse, and fearefull mischiefe, but I hope by Gods mercy, and the late exemplary Justice, strangled in the birth, is the Narration of Country Tom, and Besse of Canberry, so termed by those of their base disposition. A woman, Oh shame unto her modest tender Sexe! to become a setter, or set on such a brazen face, that upon a man unknowne unto her, shee seazeth in the open Streets, and with her deceitfull smiles, and salutes, so inchants, and inceptivates, and leads him unto slaughter. Like a decoy Ducke, shee is alone going abroad, but not alone returning, associated with multitudes homeward: The bargaine shee strikes up, and goeth before, to a secret appointed place, upon whom unawares, to the seduced person, attendeth a mercilesse strong Theefe, and most barbarous cruell Murtherer, that at once strikes and slayes: of whose cunning practices, secret snares, and subtil wiles I labour to give all people a light and true insight; God Almighty give it a blessing unto his good pleasure and thy benefit, unto whom I am thy true professed friend during the time of my mortality. H. G.

Certaine pregnant inducements, out of the Holy Scripture againſt murder and Man-ſlaughter.

THe firſt is, the direct words of Gods Commandements, thou ſhalt not kill. Exod. 20.

WHo ſo ſheddeth mans blood, by man ſhall his blood be ſhed. For in the image of God hath hee made Man. Gen. 9. 6.

HE alſo that killeth any Man, he ſhall ſurely bee put to Death. Leviticus 24. 17

YEE are of your Father the Divell, and the luſts of your father you will doe: He hath been a Murderer from the beginning, &c. Ioh. 8

IF any kill with the ſword, hee muſt bee killed by the ſword: Here is the patience and the faith of the Saints.

And therefore,

LEt all bitterneſſe, and anger, wrath, and evill ſpeaking be put away from you, with all maliciouſneſſe.

A True

THE EXAMINATION AND Confession of *Thomas Sherwood*, and *Elizabeth Evans*.

BEFORE I enter into the lists of the ensuing Relation, there are of these two most miserable Catifes, remarkeable Observations in their severall lives: (lives did I say?) to say so I doe grosly mistake; for although they were living, yet then dead they were in most foule and abhominable sins, and clamorous crimes, that sent hot pursuit after them at all times, and in all places without intermission, to sweepe them from off the face of the earth.

The Observations.

Note. 1. First, what a viperous brood of Sinnes were ingendred, conceived, and brought forth by these Monsters Male and Female: what a Chaine of sins is heere linked, and twisted one to each other.

2. Secondly, the Stygmaticall marke that *Heaven* did set upon them both in their two severall names.

1. First, Idlenesse the indulgent Mother, cannot she is so indigent of her selfe, be able to give bread, or cloathing to her pampered and poysoned little ones in youth with Sloth, but like a curst Step-mother sends them out of doores, to seeke bread in desolate places.

The Originall of all vices. 2. Secondly, Sloth or Idlenesse scornes to worke, especially with the hands, for that is not gentilelike: yet worke they see they must for necessities sake, & and a master they have at hand, (the Devill) that safely as they suppose, setteth them on worke.

3. Thirdly, from Sloth springeth forbidden Theft.

4. Fourth

4. Fourthly, frō Theft springeth beastly Lust.
5. Fiftly; from filthy Lust they lanch out into the deepe, to Blood-shed and Murder.
6. Finally, thus by degrees they finish their destruction, and the full Cup of Gods heavy wrath and displeasure, forcibly they drinke up.

2. *Observation.*

On both their Names, behold what a Brand is set on them by *Heaven*: high scorne and derision, perishing before they perished, forgotten before they were dead: For by the Names of *Countrey-Tom*, and *Canberry-Besse*, they were knowne unto the World: The honest Stocke, and Parents from which they descended, forgetting, and denying. *Scripture* saith, *The memoriall of the wicked shal perish: Let him be wiped out of the Booke of Remembrance, and that, because his minde was not to doe good.* Thus with them.

No feare
No thought
No care
No love
} of God.

And therefore for them,
No memory,
No losse,
No place of Buriall, &c.
No mourning, to say, Alas my Brother, or alas my Sister.

The

The narration of the manner of the course of their lives.

AS they confessed, their Names were *Thomas Sherwood*, and *Elizabeth Evans*, the one borne in *Stafford-shire*, there brought up by his Parents, a laborious Husbandman: The other borne in *Shropshire*, of a very good parentage descended, who carefully for her good education, and future preferment, sent her up unto *London*, to some friends, who setled her in a good service, as shee confessed at her Death: But unfortunately it happened, that shee grew acquainted with a young man in *London*, who tempted her unto folly, and by that ungodly act her suddain ruine insued.

By reason of such her folly, her Friends failed, and frowned on her: Oh unnaturall blemish! thus to forsake, cast off, and forget their owne deare flesh, all meanes of livelyhood failing, her left thus destitute, and out of all, credit, friends, money, apparrell, and service: A base loose course of life shee resolves on, and therein as shee freely confessed, continued the space of 4. yeares, untill at last shee unhappily happened to get into familiarity, and acquaintance with this *Countrey-Tom*, otherwise *Thomas Sherwood*; with whom shee constantly accompanied day and

and night for the terme of a yeare, or there abouts. And having obtained such a mate fit for his owne humour and inclination, secretly these two combin'd, resolv'd, and put in practice their new invented mysterie of Iniquity, as followeth.

Whensoever they went forth out of their Lodgings, they severed not themselves, but kept within sight one of another alwayes, both hunting for one prey; and frequenting and watching such places, and houses, for persons fitted for their occasion, and to make use of.

The places they resorted unto,
1 To Play-houses.
2 To Tavernes.
3 To Innes.
4 To Ale-houses.
5 To the open Streetes.
6 To the Fields.

If by chance they did meete with one that had beene that day too busie with the Pot, such an one was fish for their Net: then the brazen-face Strumpet presently claimes acquaintance, that she knew him of long time, whose face she never saw before; and so farther into familiar discourse, and complements they proceed, that further courtesies are desired, and promised in some secret place, to passe betweene them. This new guest, and acquaintance thus taken up in the way by her, away she hastens with her prize, and carries him unto the Chambers of death: As witnesse the Murthering by such her slights, these Gentlemen of great Note, and good quality, Eminent in place and substance, Master *Rowland Holt* a Merchant, and Cittizen of *London*, whom they murthered in *Clarkenwell* fields, in *January* last past: Likewise Master *Thomas Claxton* Gentleman, a Lieutenant, in *Grayes Inne-fields*, the first of this instant *April*, 1635. Also to another Gentleman, whom they robbed of his Cloake and Hat, by name Master *Michael Lowe*, at the pitch of the Hill going downe to *Hockley Hole* in *Clarkenwell* Parish, at which place they gave him his Deaths wound, and had not ayde upon his out-cry hastily come upon them, they had without doubt slaine him; but within one quarter of a yeare afterwards Master *Michael Lowe* dyed of the same wound in his Head then by *Countrey Tom*, so forcibly strooke, that Master *Low* did then very narrowly escape bleeding to death.

The free Confession of Thomas Sherwood, after the time of his apprehending.

TWo Moneths, and two Weekes were compleatly expired, before it could bee knowne

knowne what barbarous hand had acted that acinorous Fact on the body of Master *Rowland Holt* found dead, and with blowes very much bruised.

This Hound of Hell, that did this cruell murther, flesht thus, greedily seeketh for more *Mans* flesh, and thirsteth afresh after more blood. He thought, that in that little space *God*, and the *People* had forgotten Mr. *Holts* blood, as himselfe had; who securely againe starts out, and he with his constant mischievous Companion, to their damnable former resolutions in all Impieties, putteth on the habit, that now to kill a man, (tush) it is not worth the talking of, or taking of notice as so it may be conjectured of them; who in so short a space, to the first murder added the second, the places both of them being with in the sight of each other, which might deterre them from such their unnaturall and ungodly intention and determination, from the shedding of more innocent blood.

Upon *Wednesday* at Night, in *Easter* weeke last past, 1635. about the houre of *Nine*, these two inhumane Creatures did meete about the Kings Gate which is by *Blomesberry*, a proper costly apparrelled Gentleman, Master *Thomas Claxton*, a Souldier, and Lieutenant, who that day and time that this Monster of her Sexe interchanged discourse, and with familiar complements (oh lamentable to ſpeake) had drunke to much, as theſe two vild wretches confeſſed.

The form of his weapon which lay ſecretly in his breeches.

Words paſt betwixt Maſter *Claxton* and that Harlot *Beſſe* of *Canberry*, together theſe two goe, but who followed them both, the poore Gentleman was altogether ignorant, and little ſuſpected; After them both *Countrey Tom* haſteneth, with a ſhort Trunchin, or Baſtinado under his cloake, and findes companying together his Harlot with Maſter *Claxton*, whom ſhe had treacherouſly trayned into *Grayes Inne* fields, a ſtones caſt wide from the High-way, where what they did, I ſo charitably am opinionated of the deceaſed Gentleman, that to their ſlanderous calumniations, and traducings concerning him, I give not the leaſt credence. For thoſe to beleeve, whoſe hands were ſo foully ſtained with blood, their breath unworthy to blaſt the good name, or brand the good that the world conceived of the reputation of ſuch a Gentleman as Mr. *Claxton* was. Inhumanely with a ſhort Trunchin of Iron which *Sherwood* carried under his cloake by his bloody polluted hands, with this weapon he inſtantly deprived maſter *Claxton* of life, and after that done, they both fell to rifling the pockets, and uncivilly ſtrip, (all humanity laying a ſide) the body bare and naked, and in that

manner

manner left it and so fled away.

When he had recollected his distracted thoughts and throbbing hard heart, within two houres after, (as he sayd) shee return'd unto the place, to behold that sad spectacle of master *Claxtons* slaughtered body, who (as he said) was not slaine out-right, for he heard him sleepe and snore, and that he had turned himselfe on his Belly after he left him; and had not the winde taken his wounds, he might very well have beene recovered unto health. But perceiving life was extinct in him, flight is become the chiefest comfort, and refuge: Shee flyeth to her old acquainted lodging, at St. *Giles* in the fields, and he taketh his course another way.

The Morning ensuing, betimes hee dispatcheth a speedy messenger unto his Copartner in mischiefe, appointing his matchlesse Mate to meete with him forthwith in *Moore-fields*, which according unto his appointment, she did at the place, and time by him prefixed. And observe how thither hee commeth with his understanding so infatuated by the irefull Judge of *Heaven*, that with the apparrell he commeth on his backe that morning, of the Gentlemans whom he slew the Night before, and waite was layd for such fashioned apparrell, which he wore, and profered to sell in *Houndsditch* so inconsiderately, suddainly was apprehended. Preparation he was making to travell downe into the Country: For he bought a new Peticoate for her that dearely earned it: and he profered unto Sale the Apparrell which hee never bought, nor paid for; to put himselfe into money likewise, to beare both their charges for their intended journey.

But as, *Equity* and *Justice* commanded, they both

together were apprehended, and by the Authority of Magistracy presently sent unto *Newgate*, unto whom thither an industrious, judicious, and discreet Gentleman Master *Long*, a Commissioner of the Peace, in the County of *Middlesex*, frequently resorted, and tooke there their severall Examinations so carefully, punctually, and truely, that both the Malefactors out of their owne mouthes, against themselves confessed the same, totally iust: I touch here but briefly upon them; for I intended not at all omention much of their confessions, for feare my brevity should wrong, or intrench upon his prudent discussion and politicke insinuations into them, by which forcibly he discovered all their Villanies, and made the truth apparant.

There was a great Rumour spread, that this *Sherwood* had slaine divers persons else, besides Mr. *Claxton*, and Mr. *Holt*, as the woman at *Lambeth*, that was slaine in her house the last Winter, a Child also; for which two were executed, all these are but flying Tales. To give therefore the *World* satisfaction, I have here set downe his free and voluntary confession of such persons he slew, which he confirmed at his Death: besides many great Robberies he was guilty of, whereof master *Long* hath his free confession.

The day of his conviction, I heard it in the *Sessions yard* reported, that *Sherwood* had slaine a Gentleman master *Michael Low*, whose Father was sometimes *Lord Maior* of *London*, and himselfe of late collated into the place of Secondary in the Counter of *Woodstreete*.

I was entreated by master *Lowes* friends to be instant with *Sherwood*, to discover if he could, the person

son that robbed and wounded him. His Answer concerning that unto me, was thus; that he knew the parties that did it, and if I would at Night repaire unto to him, he would really make them knowne unto me.

Hereupon I addressed my selfe unto master *Long*, and acquainted him what I had done, and that as I suspected by my discourse with *Sherwood*, that hee could not be guiltlesse of the Robbing of master *Low*. That very Evening although late, master *Long* went to *Sherwood* to *Newgate*, where there as at his death, he sayd, hee with *Elizabeth Evans* Robbed master *Lowe* of his Hat and Cloake by the Lady *Hattons* wall about *Michaelmas* Terme last; and further said, hee thought that the wounds hee then gave him in his Head with this Instrument, or the like, was the cause of his death; which generally is so voted, because he died within a quarter of a yeare with an Impostumation in his Head, the wound being cured, but inwardly rankl'd and festred. For money, he said, hee tooke none at all from him; for that day a little before he had delivered up all his money unto his Servant.

Freely he confessed the muthering of Master *Rowland Holt* in *Clarkenwell* fields: The murthering of Master *Thomas Claxton* in *Grayes Inne* fields, and robbing and wounding of Master *Michael Lowe* by the Lady *Hattons* wall; Besides, guilty of many Notorious Felonies and Robberies, committed in *Middlesex*, to a great number. Further, discovering many base persons of his condition, and the dispersed places of secret harbouring such unprofitable obnoxious members unto a State and Common-wealth.

At

At the place of his Execution, and what he there said, the Relation.

THere was no profite at all in his life time to his Countrie, but in his Discoverie and Death, I hope some use, and good service unto the Countrie may redound. His associates, I hope, shall be banished, which he hath branded, and with them, their Receivers and Harbourers. His Death and hanging up now in chaines, an example to deterre others not so to offend, which I pray God give such a Blessing to all the people. *Amen*

Being brought unto the place of his Death, *he there minded nothing else, but how to dye, desiring of the people that they would not presse him unto further confessions, to debarre his* Soule *of better meditations, but to rest satisfied with his confessions, which he had made unto Master* Long *and my selfe, and nothing else but truth conteined in them, confirmed by a serious asseveration proceeding then out of his mouth. This done hee turned himselfe towards the people, speaking unto them, and praying for them very hartily; withall admonishing all that did see him that day, to beware of* Whores, for they were the worst Company in the World, *wishing all to beware by his fall, and not to bee seduced, or blind-fold led, as hee was by such bewitching Creatures, to irrevocable ruine. In the* Posture *of his* Body, *hee expressed true* Humility, *for all the time of Prayer, he prayed kneeling. In his Prayers unto* God, *he expressed an unexpected fervency by these words, and short eiaculations unto* Heavens *mercy seat, sensibly feeling the heavy Burden of his*

his Sinnes, most hartily implored, at the hands of Almighty God, *his mercy and forgivenesse for them.* *I will doe him this right, to expresse the Ardency of his* Soule, *when the word Mercy was uttered: this Ejaculation from his owne mouth proceeded, the hearing of the word* Mercy, *was sweet and savory unto his sorrowfull* Soule, *for in the great anguish of* Soule *he prayed, and onely relyed saying thus:* O Lord my sinnes are so haynous, great and many, if thy Mercy helpe me not, what will become hereafter of my poore Soule. *To that I flye unto, and onely trust thy mercy did save the whole World of sinners, and Lord I hope my great sins cannot exceed thy great mercies. After these speeches hee returnes with Hearty requests unto* God *to forgive him his haynous sinnes: Hee beseeched all the People that were there present, all to forgive him, whom he had offended, and to ioyne with him in harty prayes unto the* Almighty *in his behalfe, to forgive him, and to receive his* Soule *to mercy.*

After these holy exercises accomplished, the first part of the 51. Psalme *was sung, and after that by his request was sung the* Lamentation of a sinner. *That ended, I asked him if hee was willing to dye, to which hee made answere, most welcome death was unto him; for all the while he lived, his life was as a kinde of Hell unto him, and most uncomfortable. But his death he ioyfully embraced, and mortall life cheerfully did surrender up, and sent his soule out of his Body flying, calling on the name of the Lord Iesus to receive him. And all the people speaking to God for him, likewise with their lowd voyces, and strong acclamations,* Lord Jesu *take mercy on him, sweete* Jesu *forgive his sinnes, and save his* Soule.

Hereendeth the Narration of Thomas Sherwood, who now hangeth in Chaines at Battle-bridge, neare Pancras Church.

A briefe observation for all persons, both in *City and Countrey, to know lewd tempting persons lurking in the Streets and High-wayes, by these tokens following.*

FIrst, if they be Cheaters, looke if they bee not Gentile-like cloathed: then if they intice you to play at Cards or Dice for a Pot of Beere, or Pint of Wine, beware of such, and if by such tricks you chance to be deluded, take notice of that house.

Secondly, if a Woman in the day time complements with you, and sends after you, a messenger to say, that one would speake with you, beware of such.

Thirdly, take heed of such as boldly stand at their doores to intice you, or say, some Friend is in their houses that would speake with you: that is a true token of some ensuing mischiefe, to picke your pocket, and to bring you unto an Harlot.

Fourthly, if any Women meete you late in the evening, to aske of you what time of the Night it is, then watch over your purse and person, that your pocket be not pick't.

Fifthly, if a Woman come unto you alone, with inticing faire promises of Curtezan courtesies, to meete you in the Fields, or some other private remote places, remember the case of Mr. *Claxton*, and Mr. *Holt*.

Sixtly, remember the Suburbian places, where these abhominable Creatures attend their prey, by day and night.

This hath beene often confessed by these who have used the same course, and dyed for some of these facts.

An

An intimation of ſuch places, in, and about the City of *London*, that *Harlots* watch their opportunities to ſurpriſe men, confeſſed by this Malefactor.

First, at *Weſt Smithfield* within the Railes, and *Duck-lane end*.

Second, and thirdly, by the Tavernes in *Smithfield*, and Cookes ſhops in Pye-corner, and Cloath-faire, a great harbor for ſuch.

Fourthly, by *Smithfield* Pond, and ſheepe-pens.

Fiftly, by the little conduit in *Cheapſide* in the evening

Sixtly, St. *Antholins* Church when the ſhops are ſhut up.

Seventh, and laſtly, remember *London-bridge*, over which you muſt neceſſarily travell into the Southerne parts: Beware you goe not by Night with a cloak-bag, but in your hand, nor behind you on horſbacke, leſt you be iuſtled againſt the wall by a cutpurſe in the habite of a Gentleman and ſo loſe it: Beware likewiſe of your Hat and Purſe in a fray ſtirred up purpoſely in the ſtreete, to allure people into concuſſions, in plaine to ſpeake, Pick-pockets deceite, and coſenage. In *Middl.* towards *Pancras Church*, in the fields: At *Cow-croſſe* towards the Butchers, at *Bloomesberry* in St. *Giles* in the fields, beware of ſuch like offenders; and ſo much of my advertiſment unto all paſſengers comming in, and going out of the Suburbs of the City of *London*.

Likewiſe at this Seſſions, there were executed for coyning of Six-pences, and Shillings, two *French-men* and an *Engliſhman*, who were drawne and hanged for that fact of Treaſon; a iuſt reward for ſuch wicked perſons, that uſurpe the Kings Royall prerogative.

Now to the particular Narration of *Elizabeth Evans* the impious Fellow-mate of *Thomas Sherwood*.

Concerning her, I have very little matter offered to dilate; I found this Sherwood *and her so different in their severall confessions unto me, that I wonderfully admired, that two alwaies unseparable in such prosecutions of evill, should be so contradictory one unto each other. But I easily reconciled the doubt, in the particular observation in their two severall manners of dying.*

A Woman she was that died, for whose weake and timerous Sexe sake, something must bee allowed tollerable: Yet something I found to me worthy of note, at the time of her confession, a perfect hate, and exclamation against all Theeves, which caused her destruction. And furthermore in signe of such her detestation, of such unholy courses, proceeded from her mouth a most serious request unto all then present, especially advising all poore simple women to marry an honest man, though but a Ragge-gatherer, rather then a lewd man or a Theefe, rendring the reason of such her earnest admonition, because an honest man may make an evill woman turne from her evill waies, but it was hard for an evill man, to make a wicked woman good; with divers other admonitions to the wonder of the standers by, considering what a life shee had lived in.

Concerning what shee said at the place of *Execution*.

ONe thing shee here expressed very remarkable, concerning her old Companion in Mischiefe, *Thomas Shearwood*; who on Candlemas day last pressed amongst the Jurers, at the *Christopher* Taverne in Turnmill Street *alias* Turnebull Street to view the dead Corps of Master *Rowland Holt*, by him murthered, *Sherwoods* Nose immediatly gushed out with such issues of blood, that he feared thereby to be discovered, and returning unto her said, I have suffered such a thing this day about Master *Holt*, wee must of necessity, leave of this course of life.

I found her with the feares of Death very much perplexed and amazed, distractively casting her eyes here, and there, at last shee espies the high Elmes neere which place Master *Claxton* was slaine, and fetcht a deepe sigh and said, would to God I had never seene that place. I found both *Shearwoods*, and her Confession to agree both in the Murthering of Master *Holt*, Master *Claxton*, and Master *Low*, onely they differred, in the stripping of Master *Claxton*; for *Shearwood* in the receiving of the blessed Body and Blood of Jesus Christ with her, then affirmed to her face, that she helped him, for to take Master *Claxtons* cloathes off, she there confidently, denyed the same, and confirmed at her Death, whereunto as also unto other base aspersions on the dead, I give no credence, thus of her who died very penitent, and after her execution was conveied to Barber Surgions Hal for a *Skeleton* having her bones reserved in a perfect forme of her body which is to be seene, and now remaines in the aforesaid Hall; of whom I hope, God did take mercy.

A generall

A generall Admonition.

DEare Countrey men, what I have heere done, is intended for a generall good, Cautionary for all.

1. Parents. 2. Children.
3. Masters. 4. Servants.

1 Parents, cast not off your Children, neither leave them to shift in the wilde world in their Youth, knowing how subiect Youth is unto temptation, and to be seduced in the times of necessitie, and extreame want.

2 Children, obey your earthly Parents: unto such as obey, God hath promised his two-fold blessing: first, Life temporall: Secondly, Life eternall.

3 Masters terrestriall, be good to your earthly Servants, knowing yee have all one Master, which is *Christ* in Heaven, that shall one day judge you for the good and evill yee have done.

4 Servants, obey your earthly Masters, and the Masters authority is knowne by obedience to their Commandments: Whosoever resisteth, receiveth the greater condemnation.

One thing more I will commend unto you, the modesty of a milke-woman, in finding him naked, covereth him with her approne.

CONCLUSION.

Thy God feare to offend,
To him doe dayly pray,
He will thee send an happy end,
And live with him for aye.

The

The Habeas corpus, or Remove of Countrey Tom from the Countrey.

GOod *Reader*, to the precedent, give leave to adde these succeeding true Relations; Since the execution of the horrid and unheard of paire of Murderers, the Coy-duck, or divellish allurer to sinne and confusion, was dissected, and her dryed Carkase or Sceleton of Bones and Gristles is reserv'd, in proportion to be seene in *Barber Surgeons Hall*.

As for the dismall accomplisher of her damned plots, hee was hang'd in Chaines neere *Pancras* Church, being a iust reward for his vile attempts.

One thing of note I here speake of; Two Gentlemen comming early in a Morning that way, were astonished at a sad obiect, committed by a company of villaines: Oh pitty! still running on to more mischiefe, having such a fearefull spectacle before their eyes as *Countrey Tom*, which should rather have frighted and hindred them from doing this bold and insolent act upon a Butcher comming that way, though late; who said only thus, that it was no matter if all such rogues were serv'd so, which words when these lurking villaines heard, presently seized on him, and tooke his cloathes, and bound him naked to the Gibbet with a gagge in his mouth, bidding him watch the Coarse: but as this poore man said, he lost no money; because he had a little before bestowed it other wayes; and thus he was hamper'd by a cursed crue, who lurked there-abouts for their prey.

But

[illegible]
the adjoyning Inhabitants much dammified and an-
noyed by his hanging there, [illegible]
the same. And indeed the chiefest cause, was the
spoile and depopulating the growing fields there a-
bouts, stript of all fences, and the grasse troden
downe, and made levell by the infinite confluence of
all sexes from all parts, which caused the Farmers
and those that tooke grounds, to petition to the
King and Councell for redresse, who ou[illegible]
and compassion, graciously granted the *Habeas cor-
pus*, and remove of the said murdering Moor;
which (to avoid confusion of Spectators) they per-
formed in the Night, carrying the hated spectacle
to the place assigned for it, to the King crosse be-
yond *Islington*: where those that are not yet satisfi-
ed, may see *Country Tom* got farther into the Coun-
trey.

Thrice remov'd, first to *Grayes-Inne-fields*, next
neere *Pancras*, last, to *King-crosse*, to parallell his
base inhumane Murders in divers distinct places.

———— *Nec enim lex justior ulla,*
Quam necis artifices arte perire sua.

Sceletos, quasi cadaver assicatum, est ossium corporis humani invicem cohærentium universarum universa compactio.

FINIS.

Murder upon Murder (*STC* 22431) is reproduced with permission from the unique copy at the Bodleian Library (shelfmark Wood 401 [129]). The text-block measures 180 × 265 mm.

Rowl. Holt merchant of London A. 1654 =

Tho: Holt serj. at Law =

Joh. Holt recorder of Lond. 1686.

Murder upon Murder,

Committed by *Thomas Sherwood*, alias, *Countrey Tom*: and *Elizabeth Evans*, alias, *Canbrye Besse*: The first upon M. *Loe*, The 2. of M. *George Holt* of *Windzor*, whom inhumanely they kild neare *Islington* on the 22. day of January 1635. The last upon M. *Thomas Claxton* of *London*, whom mercilesly they murdered upon the second day of Aprill last past, neare unto Lambs Conduit on the backside of Holborne, with many other robberies and mischiefes by them committed from time to time since Midsomer last past, now revealed and confest by them, and now according to Judgement he is hangd neare to Lambs Conduit, this 14 of Aprill, 1635. to the terror of all such offenders.

To the tune of Bragandary downe, &c.

All Christians all unto my song,
'twill move your hearts to pitty,
hat bloody murders have beene done,
late about the City:
e daily see the brood of Cain,
mongst us ever will remaine.
urder, lust and murder,
the foule sinke of sin.

re's scarce a moneth within the yeare,
t murders vile are done,
Son, the Father murdereth,
: Father kills the Son,
t man and man there's such debate,
ch in the end brings mortall hate.
rder, &c.

The mother loseth her owne life,
cause she her child doth kill,
nd some men in their drunkennesse,
r deare friends blood doth spill,
any more, through greedy gaine,
rother hath the brother slaine.
rder, &c.

the story now in hand,
truth I will declare,
God leaves man unto himselfe,
athan then beware,
doth Sherwood truely finde,
o murder bent his mind.
r, &c.

A man of honest parentage,
traind up to husbandry,
But weary of that honest life,
to London he did hye:
Where to his dismall wofull Fate,
He chose a Queane for his copesmate.
O murder, &c.

One Canbery Besse in Turnball-street,
on him did cast an eye,
And prayd him to give her some drinke,
as he was passing by:
O too too soone he gave consent,
And for the same doth now repent.
O murder, &c.

For by alluring tempting bates,
she sotted so his minde,
That unto any villany,
fierce Sherwood was inclind,
His corne all spent he must have more,
For to content his filthy (Whore)
O murder, &c.

Much mischiefe then by them was done
in and about the City,
But still they scape unpunished,
(not knowne) more was the pitty,
To deadly sinnes they then did fall,
Not onely robbe but murder all.
O murder, lust and murder,
is the foule sinke of sin.

The first was Master William Loe,
a Gentleman of note,
And cruell Sherwood laid him low
with an inhumane stroke:
Nor birth nor blood they did regard,
Yet death for blood is their reward.
O murder, &c.

One Master Holt of Winsor towne,
a Norwich Factor he,
Walking abroad to take the ayre,
felt next their buchery,
For Sherwood with a fatall blow,
This goodman kill'd, his quean will se,
O murder, &c.

His cloak, hat, ruffe, from him they tooke
eleven groats also,
And were about his cloathes to stripe,
his shirt, shooes, hose thereto,
But being scard, away they flye,
he hath confest this villany.
O murder, &c.

A vile loose life they still run on,
regarding not their end.
Their hearts still bent to cruelty,
not minding to amend:
They cannot see Sathan the devill,
That drags them unto all this evill.
O murder, lust and murder,
is the foule sinke of sin.

The ſecond part To the ſame tune.

A W

For being fluſht with humane blood,
  they thirſted ſtill for more,
The more from God O man thou runſt
  the greater is thy ſcore:
Like rauening wolues they pry & watch,
How they the innocent may catch.
O murder, luſt and murder,
  is the foule ſinke of ſin.

The laſt that fell into their hands,
  was Maſter Claxton he,
A Gentleman of good deſcent,
  and well belou'd truely,
Who walkt vnarm'd by breake of day,
In holborne fields they did him ſlay.
O murder, &c.

A ſcarlet coate from him they tooke,
  new ſuit from top to toe,
His bootes, hat, ſhirt they tooke from him
  much money eke alſo,
And left him in the fields ſo wide
So fled away and not diſcride.
O murder, &c,

But marke the goodneſſe of the Lord,
  on the ſucceeding day,
That Sherwood with his trull did think
  beyond ſea take their way,
In Hounſdich were together tane,
Selling the coat in the ſame lane.
O murder, &c.

With the new ſuit vpon his back,
  and all things elſe beſide,
The queane the hat of Maſter Holt,
  which they had murdered,

So vnto Newgate were they ſent,
Confeſt all this, and doe repent.
O murder, &c.

Wiſhing all men when as they walke
  to haue a ſpeciall care,
And not to go vnarm'd, or late,
  but ſword or truncheon weare,
Had they done ſo Sherwood doth ſay,
He had not ventred them to ſlay.
O murder. &c.

Within three quarters of a yeare,
  theſe murders they haue done,
And maim'd and ſpoiled many a one,
  by their confeſſion:
Such deadly blowes he did them giue,
Twas ſtrange that after they ſhould liue
O murder, &c.

For theſe bad facts he now doth dye,
  iuſt iudgement for his meede,
All ſuch ill liuers grant they may,
  no worſe nor better ſpeed,
So ſhall England from crying ſinne,
Be euer freed, Gods mercy winne.
For murder luſt and murder,
  is the foule ſinke of ſinne.

F I N I S.

Printed at London for *T. Langley*,
and are to be ſold by *Thomas Lambert*
in Smithfield, neare to the Hoſpitall
gate.

The Adultresses Funerall Day (*STC* 12009) is reproduced with permission from the unique copy at th Harvard College Library. The text-block of the copy measures 95 × 150 mm.

The following words are a transcription of the original:

B2r.1	May, Anno 1635.
B2r.24	Clarke
B3r.1	unto Vxbridge forthwith
B3r.2	of Mercury
B3r.3	unto her Hus-
B4r.1	Raro antecedentum scelestum deseruit poena pede claudo.
B4r.2	Effectus prior, sensus stupifaciendo: by
B4r.3	absolutely taking away
B4r.33	what a haynous sinne

The Adultresses Funerall Day:

In flaming, scorching, and consuming fire:

OR

The burning downe to ashes of *Alice Clarke* late of *Vxbridge* in the County of *Middlesex*, in *West-smithfield*, on *Wensday* the 20. of *May*, 1635. for the unnaturall poisoning of *Fortune Clarke* her Husband.

A breviary of whose Confession taken from her owne mouth, is here unto annexed: As also what she sayd at the place of her Execution.

By her daily Visiter H. G. *in life and death. And now published by Authority and Commaund.*

LONDON

Printed by *N.* and *I. Okes*, dwelling in *Well-yard* in little St. *Bartholmews*, neare unto the *Lame Hospitall* gate, 1635.

MVRDER VPON MVRDER:

OR,

THE OLD WAY OF POYSONING NEWLY REVIVED.

In the remarkeable Act of *Alice Clarke*, performed upon her Husband *Fortune Clarke*, by her, poysoned on *Ascension day* last past: For which being arraigned, convicted, and condemned, shee suffer'd by *Fire* in *West-Smithfield*, upon Wednesday in *Whitson-weeke*, being the 20. day of *May*, 1635. *with the last words shee delivered at the time and place of her Execution.*

GReat and stupendious are the workes and wonders of the God Almighty, who onely searcheth the hearts and reines, and therefore perspicuously knoweth the very thoughts and strength of man: For bee his vaine apprehensions never so cunning to contrive, his policy to conceale, or his boldnesse to out-face any nefarious act committed, yet his unsounded and incomprehensible Wisedome, which can be no way circumscribed, is able at all times, and upon all occasions, as well to publish, as punish it in the open eye of the world, of which, as well those times past, as these present, have, and doe afford us remarkeable Examples: I will begin with the Sinne, before I proceed to the Fact.

A Murderer, the *Latines* call *Homicida*, from *homo* and *cædo*, id est, *Hominem occidere*, To kill a man: Now who the father of murder is, you may read in the *Gospell* of St. *Iohn* Chap. 8. Verſ. 44. where our bleſſed Saviour ſpeaking to the Phariſees, ſaith, *Yee are of your father the Devill, and the luſts of your father yee will doe: He hath beene a murderer from the beginning, &c.* For the puniſhment thereof, read *Gen.* 9. verſ. 5. *For ſurely I will require your blood wherein your lives are, at the hand of every beaſt will I require it; and at the hand of man, even at the hand of a mans brother, will I require the the life of man: Who ſo ſheddeth mans blood, by man ſhall his blood be ſhed: for in the image of God hath hee made man, &c.* And *Numb.* 35. 31. *Moreover, you ſhall take no recompence for the life of the murderer, which is worthy to dye, for he ſhall be put to death.* That, for the puniſhment. Now for the execrableneſſe of the Sin: We find in *Gen.* 4. 11. God ſpeaking to *Caine*, after the ſlaughter of his Brother *Abel*, after this manner, *Now therefore thou art curſed from the Earth, which hath opened her mouth to Receive thy brothers blood from thine hand:* As alſo *Deutronomy* 27. 24. *Curſed be hee that ſmiteth his neighbour ſecretly: And all the people ſhall ſay, ſo be it.*

If this monſtrous ſinne be ſo heynous in the ſight of God, betwixt neighbour and neighbour, or if committed by one ſtranger upon another, how much more horrid appeareth it in his eyes; when the husband and Wife, who in the matrimoniall Contract, are no more too, but one fleſh, ſhall barbarouſly and treacherouſly inſidiate one anothers life. According to that verſe of the Poet:

Vivitur ex rapto, non hoſpes ab hoſpite tutus,
Non ſocer a genero, fratrum quoque gratia rara eſt:

Imminet

Imminet exitio vir coniugis, illa mariti:
Lurida terribiles miscent aconita noverci,
Filius ante diem patrios inquirit in annos, &c.
which I have late read thus paraphras'd,
All live on spoile, the guest is not secure
In his Hosts house, nor is the Father sure
Protected by the Sonne: even brothers iarre,
True love and friendship is amongst them rare.
The husband doth insidiate the wife,
And she againe seekes to subplant his life:
The rough-brow'd Step-dame her yong step-son hugs,
Tempering for him (meane time) mortiferous drugs:
The Sonne after the Fathers yeares enquires,
And long before the day, his death desires, &c.

Such were the passages of those times there amongst the Heathens, when Christianity was not knowne, but that they should be so familiar and conversant with us, is the more to be pittied and lamented.

In the flourishing State of *Rome*, there were many temperers of poyson, and these were call'd *Venifice*, which word wee apply too, and conferre upon, Effacination, Sorcery, and Witchcraft: Concerning which the Civill Lawes of the Empire thus speake, *In institut. Iur. in fine in lege Cornelia*, in the Cornelian Law, *Et venifeci capite damnantur, qui artibus odiosis tam veneno, quàm susurris magicis homines occiderint, vel mala medecamenta publice vendiderint*, that is, Let those be held guilty of capitall offence, who by odious and abhorrid Arts, as well by poyson, as by magicke spells and wisperings, shall kill any man: In which State are likewise included all such, who shall publickly sell any evill Confections: From which Canon we may ground three severall sorts of delinquents in this kind, which passe under the name of *Veni-*

ficium:

veneficium: the first Poysoners, the second Sorcerers, or Witches, the third these Apothecaries or *Empricks*, who shall vend any mortiffarous drugs, knowing that by them any man or womans life, may bee insidiated, and in this case now in hand, though the seller (as he hath apparently justified himselfe may be excused, yet the byer as the Law hath openly convicted her, so we may presume that she is legally condemned.

Now what the reason may be conjectured in these our latest, but worst dayes: that so many nefarious acts, equalling, if not farre surpassing these perpretated in former ages, should be new committed: as Catamatisme, Sodometry, Paracidy, many headed murders and the like: I can give no other reason then this; the contempt of the feare of God, and the neglect of his Sabbath.

But to leave off all forraigne prodigious acts of the like horrid nature. Which as they are numerous, so they are manifest, in History and Chronologie, and go no further then our owne nation, and these latter dayes: Hath not one brother in the heat of Wine slaine another in the Taverne? A sonne transpersed the very wombe in which he was conceived, and suffered for the fault upon the Gibbet? A man in his drunkennesse casts his knife upon his Wife, and missing her, pointed it into the brest of his innocent childe, and kild him dead in the instant: hath not the woman offered the like outrage, upon her husband in her fury, and left him dead in the place, and suffered lately for it, for remarkable example.

Within the compasse of foureteene moneths or there abouts, one *Enoch ap Evans*, upon a small difference betwixt his brother and him, tooke the advantage when he was asleepe cut his throat first, and after his headquite off with his knife, and when the mother hearing a bustling above, came into the roome to heare the cause of such a noise, he prosecuted her downe the stayers, and afterwards cut of her head with an *Hatchet*, for which he was Apprehended, arraigned, convicted condemned at *Shrewsbury*, and after, some distance from the place executed.

Since then, these grand Malefactors, who went commonly by the name of *Country Tom* and *Canbery Besse*, their fearefull murders upon three severall Gentlemen, at three sundry times, (the discourse of whose Actions, Examinations, Confession, and Sufferings, because they are already published to the view of the World, I will no longer insist upon, or make any Repetition of their hainous crimes to trouble the Reader. But to come nearer to the matter of this fact now in Agitation, I will onely remember you of Mistresse *Arden*, who caused her Husband to bee murdered in her owne House at *Feversham* in *Kent*, the memorable Cercumstances thereof deserving places in a most approoved Chronicle, may be very well spared in this short discourse. As also of Mistresse *Page* of *Plimouth*, who for poysoning her Husband, suffered with her sweet-heart Master *George Strangwich*, who had beene before time betrothed unto her: her husband being old, she yong, by which may be apprehended the misery of inforced marriage. But not to tire your patience I will onely trouble you with the poore wretched creature, who last suffered in *Smithfield* in this kinde, much commiserated, much lamented: give mee leave a little to to insist upon her cause, and compare it with this now in present,

Her injuries, and harsh and unmanly usage spurred on by the instigations of the divell, almost compeld her to what she did; which, as they would be scarce modest for me to speake, so they were almost beyond the strength of Nature for her to suffer: shee being young and tender, he old and peevish; who notwithstanding his clownish behaviour, and churlish comportment towards her, as seldome or never affording her a smooth brow, or friendly countenance, used not onely to beat her with the next cudgell that came accidentally unto his hand, but often tying her to his bed-post to strip her and whippe her,&c.

But enough, if not too much of that; she then weary of so wretched a life, which she would have bin glad to be rid off, and loath in her modesty to acquaint any friend or neighbour with her desperate purpose, who perhaps, (nay no doubt) by their good counsell might haue diuerted her from so wicked a resolution, and the divell with all catching hold upon so fit an opportunity to worke upon her weaknesse, she pondered with her selfe how she might end both their lives by poyson, which having provided and prepared to that end, shee first gave him part, and after resolved with her selfe to drinke the rest: But better motions now comming into her thoughts, and she truely repentant of what she had done, finding the confection begunne to work with him, fell downe before him upon her knees: First acknowledging the fact, then humbly desiring from him forgivenesse, withall, beseeching him to take some present *Antidote* to preserve his life which was yet recoverable: on whom he sternly looking, as he lay in that Agony gasping betwixt life and death returned her answere in this manner; nay thou Strumper and

and murderesse, I will receive no helpe at all but I am resolvd to dye and leave the world, be it for no other cause, but to have thee burnt at a stake for my death: which having said, and obstinate in that *Hethenish* resolution, he soone after expired. And this Relation I received from those of credite, who were well acquainted with the conditions of them both.

I know not how to parallell these two: Her of whom I made this Short discourse, or this miserable woman, who suffered by fire in *Smithfield* upon wednesday in the *Whitson* weeke last, being the twentieth of *May*, *Anno* 1635. the passages of whose life, conviction, and death thus followes.

The free and voluntary Confession of *Alice Clarke*, the 18. day of *May*, 1635. concerning the *Death of* Fortune Clarke, *her husband, at the time she was in Prison.*

A Iust cause, all persons may conjecture, was given on her part, of great dissensions likely to arise betweene her Husband and her selfe, unto selfe-will shee to be so addicted, disobediently to frequent the company of one *White*, of whom oftentimes her Husband hand had interdicted her his society and familiarity: which acquaintance of theirs was begun, before *Clarke* her Husband, entred into Marriage with her, and therefore with no small difficulty could be forgotten, or shaken off, such former ancient entertainments. No admonitimonitions or threats to either parties could prevaile, that proceeded from *Clarke* unto his wife, or unto *White*, of continuall private meetings betweene them: Which *Clarke* perceiving, outragiously fell from words unto blowes with his wife, the smart whereof she feeling, incontinently begot in her heart dislike, and resolution of revenge on her Husband *Clarke* for the same, a fit humour for the devill to worke on, and to her old friend *White*, to give occasion, not of dislike, but content to put in practice what she intended, which he might easily perceive by many pensive declamations, in private utter'd betweene themselves of her Husbands unkinde usage: The confirmation whereof appeares by the words that proceeded out of her owne mouth.

First, she confessed, because she often companied with *White*, that stirred up her Husbands iust anger against *White* and her selfe.

Secondly, that unawares unto them both, her Husband finding her and *White* shut up together privately in a Chamber in the house, on *Ascension-day* last in the afternoone, was thereat so with fury enraged, that hee did beate *White* going out of the doores, and after that, freshly fell foule upon her, and so cruelly added blowe upon blow upon her body, that the markes thereof were very visible on her body at this present. Her old *Love*, *White*, instantly taketh this unto heart, and in a rage (as she said) uttered these words, *That it were better for one to be hanged, then to endure so discontented a life*, and presently putting his hand into his pocket, he tooke out 4 Tokens, and gave them unto *Alice Clarke*, saying unto her, if he had had more money, hee would have given it unto her: which 4 Tokens so given unto

her,

her, she went unto *Vxbridge* forthwith, and that after-noone bought a penny-worth of *Mercury* of an Apothecary in *Vxbridge*, intending the same unto her Husband, with a further reservation, that if her Husband had not taken it, she would have administred the same unto her selfe, and so put an end unto all her sorrows, as she vainely supposed.

Thirdly, she said, that she was not the cause of her Husbands death, because shee gave not unto him the poyson whereof he died, but he tooke it himselfe violently out of her pockets, which her Husband had rifled, upon hope to finde some chinke or money there: but of such hopes he altogether was disappointed and deluded. Whether this be not a lame excuse, or strange delusion, I referre it unto the censure of the Judicious; and no further discovery of the fact, could I get from her at that time.

Shee further said, that on *Ascension-day* her husband violently attempted to drowne himselfe, which shee prevented by her language upon him: but in short space afterwards dyed that Night of the *Mercury*, taken by himselfe out of her pocket, as afore-said.

Fourthly, shee seemed to be very much afflicted in conscience, that shee was a yeare since gotten with Child by her Master, with whom shee last dwelt withall; who perceiving the same, with a small summe of money, matched her unto *Fortune Clarke* her Husband, about *Alhallontide* last, whom she could not love, or have any matter of maintenance, but relied upon her Masters former promises for the same: and hee fayling of giving her meanes, fell into folly and wickednesse. A great clog unto such a mans conscience, if it be true; to seduce a woman unto his will, and so leave her.

A SHORT TRACT VPON THE *hainousnesse of Poysoning.*

THough there be sundry sorts of *Murther* with their severall degrees, as open, or secret, acted upon a friend, a stranger, or ones selfe, yet in my opinion, I know not any of them which containes so much villany, neither including so many deepe circumstances in them, as that of poysoning: That I thinke is the reason that there are so few examples of it in Holy writ, this way either being then not knowne, followed, or practised; therefore to describe the quality of it and to aggravate it, I must wish you to consider these foure things.

First, the *Duplicem modum*, secondly, the *Duplicem effectum: Modus prior*, the first Manner, *Deliberando, Meditando*, Is an Act done by Deliberation, or Meditation, no waies carried, and hurried by the violence either of will or of passion, but done upon a cold blood, and not seldome upon fixed resolutions.

Modus posterior, Celando obtegendo, by a secret intent to hide it and conceale it from God if it were possible: so it is to the Patient under the shadow of some Physicke, or other medicine, coloured with an outward shew of an honest intent, and as far as they can from the Publick Magistrate; or else to make a distance of time, either to excuse themselves, or flye away from the hands of Justice: though

Rare

Raro antecedentem scelestum deseruit pœna pede claudo

Secondly, *Effectus prior, sensuum stupefaciendo*, by changing, stupifying, or absolutely taking away the senses, and depraving the operative Organs of the soule, and sometimes infecting all the principles of life, as the head, the heart, and the liver, howsoever altering and overthrowing the frame and constitution of mans body in generall, and making him unfit for a preparation of himselfe for death, though it be upon him, so that without the speciall Mercy of God, the party thus abused, dyes without either knowledge of his sinnes, or repentance for them.

Secondly, *Effectus posterior, creaturarum abusus*, the abusing of the Creatures, contrary to the end of their Creation: They being brought forth for the use and health of Mans Body, by this meanes they are made deadly, nay this manner of killing any, makes not onely the prime Agent guilty, but infects, and makes guilty others too, or at least, causes them to be examined strictly by the Magistrate: so that howsoever their good name for the present, is blotted and blemished, and what more is, they have but two wayes to comfort themselves, the first, is the witnesse of their owne Consciences Integrity, the second, is the Judges knowledge of their Innocence and Ignorance, by a prudent examination, of the fact perpetrated by all circumstances, and suspicious Arguments: And in this kinde the Apothecary for selling, the Messengers for buying, the Composers of it, and the deliverers of it to the party, stand in an hazard either of their lives, or fortunes, or both.

Laying aside all these together, I hope it will easily appeare what a haynous sinne it is, when it is thus committed

mitted: first, with Deliberation: Secondly, with Secresie: Thirdly, with disabling the party to fit himselfe for mercy, and with the abusing the blessings of God and their owne knowledge: and lastly, for bringing others into danger as well as themselves, yet what is more, all this done under the *Gospell*; and often, as at this present, against one whose life, credit, goods, and good name, the offender ought to cherish and maintaine to the uttermost: So I may take up that saying of *Iacob* to his two Sonnes, *My soule come not into their secrets, neither bee ioyned with their assemblies*: nor have to doe with their practises, whose conclusions are so deepely dyed with the blood of Innocents.

The second Confession of Alice Clarke *this* 10. *day of* May, 1635. *at the place of Execution, concerning the poysoning of her husband,* Fortune Clarke.

PHysitians of the Soule ought to immitate those learned Physitians of the body, frequent visitations of those sicke patients, whose diseases are desperate and inveterate; and sometimes it chanceth, that they must desire, necessity so requireth, the advice and sound opinions of others their Colleagues. Even thus it happened betweene this obdurate Malefactor and my selfe, who in Adultery was so Rooted, and insensible of the heavy burthen, and most intollerable plagues insuing for it. That at the first and second times of my visiting of her, little or no Repentance I found in her, or her heart to be touched for her

most

most horrid clamorous crimes. This is apparant, if you compare her first confession unto this, how, different in truth, how improbable the one are unto the other; nay what she confessed on *Munday*, shee was so far off to proceede in a further revealing of her selfe, that what touched her home, concerning her husbands death, she would have denied, though formerly confessed by her most confidently true.

I was thereuppon inforced to hold her unto it, and to extract the truth, and trye her spirit, called two of the Keepers of the Goale, to her unknowne, whom I appoynted to obserue and remember the speeches that passed betweene us, to verifie them unto her face, which attestation both of my selfe, and of them, shee would out-face, but could not.

Vppon *Wensday* morning, on which shee was executed, there assembled unto Newgate multitudes of people to see her, and some conferred with her, but little good they did on her, for shee was of a stout angry disposition, suddainly inraged, if you began to touch her to the quicke of her husband poysoning. Being that morning of her death accompanied and also assisted by divers of my worthy, grave, and learned brethren in the Ministery, before and at the time of her Execution, for which I doe most heartily thanke them, but that God whose worke it was, their reward for it with him is layd up in store. Like my selfe, they stood as men amazed, to perceive that none of theirs, or any other serious perswasions could for a great while prevayle with her, ioyned in opinion with me, that she was no fitting guest for the Table of the *Lord Iesus* thereupon, I made as though I would have excluded her thence, in denying the benefit of the holy Communion, of the

Body and Blood of Jesus Christ, inferring the benefit of the unspeakable blesse, by the worthy receiving of it by Repentance and Faith, and the most woefull malediction to all impenitent and unworthy receivers. Whereupon, it pleased God, so to mollifie her heart, that teares from her eyes, and truth from her tongue proceeded, as may appeare by this her ensuing Confession at the very Stake, where she was executed, unto Mr. *Cordall*, Sheriffe of *London*, relating the same with as loud and audible a voice, as possible she could, that many others besides, those present, were also witnesses of such her ensuing Confession.

First she confessed that *Henry White*, who was arraigned as a party with her, consenting unto her Husbands death, did give unto her one *Ascension* day in the after noon, foure brasse tokens, advising her therewith to goe and buy one penyworth of *Mercury*, and give it unto her Husband, saying, if that her husband were dead, she should live more quietly and contentedly with him, & after such his death, that he the said *White* would marry with her; whereupon she went unto *Vxbridge*, and that afternoone bought the *Mercury*.

Secondly, shee confessed that her Master got her with childe a yeare since, which was her overthrow, and mediated for the *Marriage*, betweene her and her Husband, whom shee could not love, nor no way affect. By her Masters perswasion, who sent her up to *London* to be *Married*, and payed the costs thereof, and further promised her maintenance during her life, if she did condescend unto his desiers, which were most unlawfull, dishonest, and unchaste, before and after her *Marriage*, with *Fortune Clarke* her Husband.

Thirdly, shee confessed, that one of *Hillinden* inticed

her

her, to run away from her Husband, with him beyond the Seas, and that ſhe did lodge in that mans houſe, and lay with him a whole fortnight, and ſpeaking unto him of her Husband, that ſhee would not forſake him, hee thereupon adviſed her to pop him up with white bread and milke, and to put ſome thing elſe into it, to choak or ſtuffe up his throat.

Fourthly ſhe confeſſed, for the *Mercury* which ſhe bought, ſhee intended it unto her Husband, but having no conuenient opportunity to diſpoſe of it, ſhe put it into her ſleeve, which her Husband as ſhe ſaid tooke it out of her hand, and then being overcharged with drink he immediatly ſwallowed it down, which ſhe perceiving, was thereat ſo perplexed, that ſhe uttred theſe words unto her Husband, that he had undone both him ſelfe and her.

And heere give me leave to note unto the World, what a deale of comfort ſhe found, after ſhee had disburdned her loaded conſcience by confeſſion, beeing demaunded at the ſame inſtant of her death, yea, or nay; that after ſuch her confeſſion, ſhee was by it the better prepared unto death, with comfort, and willingneſſe to ſuffer the ſame: Shee thus replyed with harty thankefulneſſe unto God, that ſhee had better reſolutions unto death, then formerly ſhe had, and by her countenance, which was very ruddy confirmed her inward new begotten chearfulneſſe, and that with harty prayer, and ſweet tone of voice, ſurrenderd her ſoule into the hands of the Lord *Ieſu*, who will have mercy on whom he will have mercy, unto whom wee all ſtand and fall.

Heere is nothing contained in her confeſſion, but that which true, and what ſhe uttered with her owne mouth; which I was a witneſſe off. H. Goodcole.

FINIS.

A true Relation of one Susan Higges (*STC* 13441) is reproduced with permission from the unique copy at Th British Library (shelfmark Rox.1.424). The text-block measures 125 × 254 mm. Another edition (*c*. 1630 *ST* 13044b.5) does not include the second-last stanza).

A true Relation of one *Susan Higges*, dwelling in *Risborrow* a Towne in *Buckinghamshire*, and how shee lived 20. yeeres, by robbing on the High-wayes, yet unsuspected of all that knew her; till at last, comming to *Messeldon*, there robbing a woman, which woman knew her and called her by her name: now when she saw she was betrayed, she killed her, and standing by her while she gave three groanes, she spat three drops of blood in her face, which never could be washt out; by which shee was knowne and executed for the aforesaid murder at the Assises in Lent at *Brickhill*.

To the tune of, *The worst by London Prentice*.

To mourne for my offences,
and former passed sinnes,
This sad and dolefull story,
my heavie heart begins:
Most wickedly I spent my time,
devoid of godly grace:
A lewder woman never liv'd,
I thinke in any place.

Neere Buckingham I dwelled,
and Susan Higges by name,
Well thought of by good Gentlemen,
and Farmers of good fame:
Where thus, for twenty yeeres at least,
I liv'd in gallant sort: (much,
Which made the Country marvell
to heare of my report.

My state was not maintained,
(as you shall understand)
By good and honest dealings,
nor labour of my hand:
But by deceit and cozening shifts,
the end whereof, we see
Hath ever beene repaid with shame,
and ever like to be.

My servants were yong country girles,
brought up unto my mind,
By nature faire and beautifull,
and of a gentle kinde:
Who with their sweet entising eyes,
did many youngsters move
To come by night unto my house,
in hope of further love.

But still at their close meetings,
(as I the plot had laid)
I kept in still at quarters,
while they the wantons plaid,
And would in question bring their
except they did agree (names,
To give me mony for this wrong,
done to my house and me.

This was but petty cozenage,
to things that I have done:
My weapon by the high way side,
hath me much money won:
In mens attire I oft have rode,
upon a Gelding stout,
And done great robberies valiantly,
the Countries round about.

I had my Scarfes and Vizards,
my face for to disguise:
Sometimes a beard upon my chin,
to blind the peoples eyes:
My Turky Blade, and Pistols good,
my courage to maintaine:
Thus tooke I many a Farmers purse,
well cram'd with golden gaine.

Great store of London Merchants,
I boldly have bid stand,
And shewed my selfe most bravely,
a Woman of my hand:
You ruffling Roysters every one,
in my defence say then,
We women still for gallant minds,
may well compare with men.

261

The second part, To the same tune.

But it so be it chanced,
the Countries were beset,
With hue, and cryes, and warrants,
into my house I get:
And I so being with my Maids,
would cloake the matter so,
That no man could by any meanes,
the right offender know.

Yet God that still most justly,
doth punish every vice,
Did bring unto confusion
my fortunes in a trice:
For by a murther all my sinnes
were strangely brought to light,
And such desert I had by law,
as Justice claim'd by right.

Upon the Heath of Misseldon,
I met a woman there,
And rob'd her, as from Market,
homewards she did repaire,
Which woman cal'd me by my name,
and said that she me knew; (blood,
For which even with her lives deare
my hands I did imbrew.

But after I had wounded,
this woman unto death,
And that her bleeding body,
was almost reft of breath,
She gave a groane, and there withall,
did spit upon my face,
Three drops of blood, that never could
be wiped from that place.

For after I returned
unto my house againe.
The more that I it wash'd,
it more appeared plaine: (birds.
Each houre I thought that beasts and
this murther would reveale,
Or that the ayre so vile a deed,
no longer would conceale.

So heavie at my conscience,
this wofull murther lay,
That I was sone enforced,
the same for to bewray,
And to my servants made it knowne,
as God appointed me:
For blood can never secret rest,
nor long unpunisht be.

My servants to the Justices,
declar'd what I had said;
For which I was attached,
and to the Jayle convey'd,
And at the Sises was condemn'd,
and had my just desert:
Then such a death let all them have
that beare so false a heart.

So farewell earthly pleasure,
my quaintance all adue,
With whom I spent the treasure,
which causeth me to rue.
Leave off your wanton pastimes,
lascivious and ill,
Which without Gods great mercy,
doth soule and body kill.

Be warned by this story,
you ruffling Roysters all:
The higher that you climbe in sinne,
the greater is your fall:
And since the world so wicked is,
let all desire grace,
Grant Lord that I the last may be,
that runneth such a race.

FINIS.

Printed at London for F. C. dwelling in
the Old-Baily.

Murther, Murther (Wing M3084) is reproduced with permission from the clear British Library copy (shelfmark E 172 [1]). The text-block measures 130 × 250 mm.

7

Murther, Murther:

OR,

A bloody Relation how *Anne Hamton*, dwelling in Westminster nigh London, by poyson murthered her deare husband Sept. 1641. being assisted and counselled thereunto by *Margeret Harwood*.

For which they were both committed to Gaole, and at this time wait for a tryall.

Women love your owne husbands, as Christ doth the Church.

Printed at London for *Tho. Bates*, 1641.

A bloody Relation of *Anne Hamton*, who poysoned her husband at Westminster.

Gentle Reader,

IT is not my purpose to make thee now laugh, but if possible it be to be sad, not to rejoyce but lament, not to be frolicke, but to dissolve into fountaines of teares, because a daughter of Ierusalem hath committed an abomination. Harken to me you that be wives, and give attendance you which as yet are unmarried, regard the words of Saint *Paul* which commands that every wife should love her own husband as Christ the church, not to be highminded towards him, but humble, not to be selfe-willed, but diligent, not to be like a strange woman, which wandereth abroad in the twi-light to get a prey, but to be constant and loving to him, for why? ye be both of one flesh.

A man must forsake his Father, Mother, Brethren, and Sisters, to cleave to his owne wife, and so likewise the wife for the husband. But I must tell of one who would never agree to any such pious matter.

Before I come to which relation I cannot abstaine my selfe from exclamation, let all the forrests wherein fierce lions are contained be joined in one, and privy search made, to know if ever female did the male destroy; Oh no! for though by nature they be fierce and bloody, yet doth nature so much governe them, that those which are couples, bee linkt in friendship, never disagree. Oh then thou savage woman, why unto blood wert thou addicted, as to destroy thy loving and kind husband? the relation of which, shall be divulged throughout this universe.

In the parish of Saint Margarets Westminster, dwelleth one *Anne Hamton*, in the house of *Margeret Harwood*; this *Anne Hamton* had a husband which like a loving man indeed delighted in nothing more but to see his wife pleasant: for he would often say my wife being troubled it behoveth me not to be at rest, she being pleasant I ought to be joyful: But she, most unkind woman, was of a contrary disposition; for she at her owne house, would take an occasion to be merry, when the greatest mischiefe had befallen him. Hee was a very laborious man, but she, a light huswife, when he was working shee

would

would be gossiping, with one young fellow or other, or else with such women as were like to her selfe: never was she more joyfull then when she was out of her good husbands company: what her husband got by taking paines, she spent by taking her pleasure: his mony being thus consumed, and his goods wasted, he upon a time spoke to her after this manner.

Wife, what doe you meane to doe? how dost thou intend to live? my mony you spend, which I get hardly, my goods you waste, you never got the worth of a joynt stoole, my company you hate, you must have better. O wife, wife, take counsell by me thy hitherto loving husband, forsake that company which hate not thy body, but soule, doe not drink healths to thine own confusion, nor with so greedy an appetite swallow thine own destruction; repent in time of thy wickednesse lest when thou thinkest thy selfe in security, the Lord doth cut thee off, and what will then become of thy poore soule; love me thy husband, hate those which intice thee to wickednesse, trust not to their smiling countenances, for in their hearts doe lye hid nothing but abominations. If thou wilt (I say) have my love, hate such, or else never more thinke to enjoy, that which as yet you have alwaies had.

What harme was there in all this which he spake unto her? But notwithstanding she forsooth took it in distaste, and giving him a scolding reply, shee left the roome, and went to her companion in mischief, *Margerite Harwood*, which was her Landlady, to whom she revealed the secrets of her heart, saying, that her husband was an enemy to good fellowship, and continually wrangled and brawled at her, because she affected it. In which she lyed, for hee alwayes spoke in a very loving manner unto her, except she overmuch provoked him.

Moreover she said that shee should never bee in quiet untill by some way or other she were shifted of him.

The devill finding an occasion how to accomplish a mischievous intent, alwayes makes use of it, hee knowes how to please every ones wicked humour. Wherefore he tempted the Landlady with bloody cogitations, for shee hearing her Ningles unjust complaint, she cryed out that it was her own fault, for letting such an abject villaine to live; hang him, cut his throat, or poyson him, for he is not fit to live upon the earth amongst good fellowes. To condiscend to whose counsell, she seemed very unwilling, but at length the devill got the better of her, and then she did agree to poyson him. And for the same intent she went and got five drams of poison, enough to have destroyed ten men, and mixt it amongst his food, which he no sooner had taken, but that he presently did swell very much, which

she

she perceiving, did runne to her Landlady, who askt her how much she had given him: she replyed, five drams; well done, said she, if five will not bee enough, ten shall, and thereupon they went up to see him, but he was then burst. Then did they both dissemble a lamentable cry, which caused the neighbours to come in to see what was the matter, where they did behold such a wofull spectacle as was sufficient to exhaust teares from the dryest eye composed of Pumice stone; for there did they see his nayles quite pilled of, his hands did seeme onely like two great boyles, his belly seemed as if hot irons had beene thrust into it, his visage was so much defaced by the quicke operation of the scalding poyson, that had they not well knowne the body, they would have sworne it not to have beene the man which they came to visit: they all easily perceived that he was poysoned.

A Chyrurgion being sent for, ripped up his body, and found the poyson lying round about his heart. As also there was found poyson in a paper in the window; the Chyrurgion calling for a Venice glasse put the same therein, which immediatly broke the glasse.

Wherefore they sent for an officer, and apprehended upon suspition both his wife and Landlady, whose consciences cannot but confesse that they washed both their hands in his innocent blood.

They

They are both in the Gatehouse prison of Westminster, nigh London, expecting a day of tryall, which time will not be long; till when I rest: then (gentle Reader) shalt thou have by Gods permittance a more perfect relation.

FINIS.

A Compleat Narrative of the Tryal of Elizabeth Lillyman (Wing C5647) is reproduced with permission from the unique copy at the Guildhall Library, London. The text-block measures 84 × 144 mm.

A Compleat NARRATIVE OF THE TRYAL OF Elizabeth Lillyman.

Found Guilty of *Petty Treason*:

AND

Condemned at the Sessions at the *Old Bayly* the 10th. of this Instant *July*.

To be Burned to Death,

For the Barbarous and Bloody Murther of *William Lillyman* her late Husband.

With Her

Confession and Penitent Behaviour, since such her Condemnation.

With Allowance.

London, Printed for *Phillip Brooksby*, at the Golden-ball, in *West-smith's-field*, neer the *Hospital-gate*, 1675.

Complete

She desired leave to say something to the people, which being granted her, she began in a low voice as followeth.

Good people you are come to see the sad end of a miserable woman. I have been a scandalous liver ever since I was fifteen years old, and now God almighty has taken this time to punish me for all my wickedness; I cannot but acknowledge the murder of my dear Husband, though I must needs say, I never intended it, but did it in my passion, and it is well known among my Neighbours how dearly I loved him, I pray God I may be an example to you all, aud that though I suffer this cruel Death here, I may be delivered from the pains of hell fire for ever.

And after some private prayer by the Minister, she kneeled down her self and pray'd very earnestly, which much affected the standers by, and after went cheerfully to the Stake where she suffer'd.

A

A True and Perfect Relation of the Tryal, Condemnation, and Confession of *Elizabeth Lillyman, &c.*

WHereas several Imperfect Relations and hearsay Reports may have been spread abroad concerning this unhappy woman, and that Barbarous and Wicked Fact by her committed, in Murdering her Husband: for the full discovery of the Truth thereof in all Circumstances, 'tis thought convenient to publish this compleat and Impartial Narraaive and Account of the same.

THis womans dwelling was lately, and for some Years had been, neer the *Minories*, between that and *Goodman s-fields* in the sad time of *Londons* Calamity, by the terrible Sickness, 1665. She was very busie a Nurse-keeping, or tending persons Visited with the Plague, and as 'tis supposed, got then enough to help maintain her since: for though she were from thence-forwards generally called Nurse, & pretended sometimes to take in Cloaths to Wash, yet she did not do any considerable matter of work, but lived a life somewhat extravagant and expensive for one of her condition; This man, on whom she committed this horrid murther, being the sixth that she had had.

She was Married to him somewhat above a year last past, who was a civil honest laborious person, by name *William Lilly-man*, and by profession a Cooper belonging to a Brew-house, a lusty comely man, and not above thirty years of age or thereabouts, which made her at first extreamly dote upon him, but being her self near threescore she was not a little tainted with the poison of jealousie, which often is the disturber of the discreetest marriages, and therefore might without matter of wonder prove the bane of this lascivious heart.

Baiting her controversies sometimes on that account (for which 'tis generally believ'd by their Neighbours she had indeed no occasion) till Satan takeing the advantage of her being in one of these Jealous moods (in which she used often to threaten she would do him a mischief) prevailed on her barbarously to imbrue her hands in his blood, and

bring

bring her self by takeing away his life to a shameful and untimely yet most just and deserved death. The manner and circumstances of which bloody Fact were as follows, and so appeared to the court by the Evidence on the tryal, viz:

On Tuesday the —— of *June* last, the said *William Lilly-man* comeing home in the afternoon from work to the house where they lodg'd in Swan-Alley, leading out of the Minories into Goodmans Fields, and finding his wife absent, understood she was at an Ale-house hard by in Glass-house-Yard at Nine-pins; VVhereupon having occasion to have his shooes mended he carryed them to a cobler a friend and country-man of his whose stall was just by that house where his VVife was, and took with him a peice of cold mutton, and a dryed Mackerel, intending to eat his supper there, when he came to the Cobler and had given him directions he asked him to go drink; which he consented to, promising to come very quickly, as soon as he had dispatcht a little jobb he was about; before *Lillyman* vvent into the Ale-house he asked the Cobler for a knife to cut his victuals, he having left his ovvn at home, vvho lent him a very sharp long one, which their trade commonly use to pair heels vvith; as soon as he vvas come into the ale-house he sent into the yard for his vvife, very lovingly desiring her to come and sup and drink vvith him; as she vvas coming in a Servant-maid (unluckily as it prov'd in the consequence, but very innocently intending it only for jest and merriment)

said

said to her: Ah Mistris *Lillyman*, little do you think that your Husband and I have been together and that he gave me a bottle of Ale at your house, or words to that effect, and indeed there was little reason for her to think so, for in truth there was no such thing done, nor any thing like it.

However the woman according to the nature of jealousie, takeing it in the worst sense, fell into an angry passion, possibly the sooner raised for that she was before elevated with drink, so that coming into the room where her Husband was, she was heard to say, *Do you send for me to supper, you Rascal*; (or some other ill name) I will give you a Supper; and presently afterwards being all alone with him (the Woman of the house being gone for a pot of drink, and the Maid for a Loaf for him) the said Elizabeth his Wife took up the aforesaid long knife which he had borrowed of the Cobler, and therewith stab'd him under the left papp, so that as the Surgeons afterwards testified, it pierced his very heart, and the Maid immediately returning he told her his Wife had stab'd him, and desired her to call in his countrey-man the Cobler; she hearing him talk of being stab'd, thought at first he had been but in jest, but seeing him look ill, with his hand fast on his breast began to be afraid, and called the Cobler, but before he could get in, the wounded man was got up from his seat, and coming out met him, saying, Ah Countrey-man! this wicked Woman my Wife has stab'd me with the knife which I borrowed

rowed of thee; all this while his Wife stood by, and hearing this came up to him, and said, I stab thee Love? why wilt thou say so? I have not toucht thee? and thereupon proffered to kiss him, but he with his hand putting her back said again: Ah wicked woman thou hast kill'd me: By this time, he fainting, the Cobler taking him in his arms had put him into one of the drinking rooms, and askt him where his hurt was, for as yet they saw it not; Whereupon he pointed to his left, and said, Here, here my Wife hath kill'd me; which was the last Words he was heard to utter in this world, for presently after he fainted quite away, and in short time dyed; his Wife when she saw him so very bad would have made her escape and gone out at the back door, but neighbours stopt her and sent for a constable, who carried her before a justice of peace.

At her Examination there, she behaved her self very strangely, seeming altogether unconcerned at what she had done, and laughing at it: amongst many other her silly answers, this was one, *I wish my hands may never see my eyes, if I killed my husband*; the Magistrate gravely admonished her to be serious in so sad a case, but she took little notice of it, but stiffly denyed that she murthered him, however the person being then quite dead, she was committed to *Newgate* in order to her Tryal.

And accordingly at the last sessions held at the *Old Bayly* begining on the *7th.* of this instant *July*, 1675. She was Arraigned for Petty Treason, for Killing her Husband: After the Endictment was

read,

read, and ſhe required to plead to it, ſhe fell into a kind of raveing, crying out, *ſhe muſt ſee her Husband, and ſhe would not plead till ſhe had him there:* But this vvas but a faigned Artifice or piece of Diſſimulation, and ſhe vvas at laſt brought to plead in form: vvhich ſhe did, by ſaying, *Not Guilty*: The VVitneſſes againſt her, vvere the before-mentioned Cobler, the VVoman of the houſe, and the Maid, at the ſight of vvhich laſt ſhe fell into another paſſionate fit, calling her, many baſe, ſcurrilous names in open Court; The Evidence vvas plain, as you have heard in all Circumſtances, and the Priſoner had nothing to ſay for her ſelf, but impudent Denials of the Fact, and yet confeſſed that ſhe had a vvicked intention to have done the ſaid Maid a Miſchief at the ſame time vvhen her Husband vvas Killed. So that the matter being evident, the Jury brought her in, *Guilty of the Enditment*: And accordingly ſhe received the uſual Sentence for perſons of her *Sex*, in Caſes of petty Treaſon, that is to ſay, *To be Burned until ſhe be Dead.*

The firſt night after her Condemnation, ſhe ſeemed ſcarce at all ſenſible of her condition, but on the next day, being the Lords day, ſhe began to have ſome remorſe, confeſſing then to ſome friends that came to viſit her, that ſhe had been a grievous ſinner for many years, naming ſeveral particular ſins that ſhe had been guilty of; yet ſtill denyed her ſelf to have ever been guilty of Murther or Theft; nor would confeſs the killing of her husband; ſince that ſeveral Miniſters have viſited her, and have at laſt brought her to acknowledge the Fact, and now ſhe ſeems exceeding Penitent for the ſame, being come to the place appointed for her execution, on *Towerhill*, on *Munday* the 19*th.* of *July*, inſtant.

FINIS.

A Narrative Of the Proceedings at the Sessions-House in the Old-Bayly, ... And also an Account of the Trya and Condemnation of Eliz. Lillyman (Wing N210A) is reproduced with permission from the unique copy a the Guildhall Library, London. The text-block measures 97 × 138 mm.

The following words are a transcription of the original:

2.1 A Narrative of the Proceedings at the General
2.3 the [7]th
2.8 other Enormities
2.19 evidently proved
2.22 a Swede

A

NARRATIVE

Of the Proceedings at the Sessions-House in the

Old-Bayly,

From *Wednesday* the 7th of *July* instant, to *Saturday* the 10th. Being a full and true Account of the Tryals, Examinations, and Condemnation of several Malefactors, for several Crimes.

And also an Account of the Tryal and Condemnation of *Eliz. Lillyman*, who killed her Husband, for which she was condemned to be Burned, with the manner of her Deportment at her Tryal. And likewise of *Rose Goodman*, who was condemned for stripping of Children and other Fellonious Crimes.

The Number Condemn'd was Eleven, Six to be Transported, Ten burnt in the hand, and Six to be whipt at the Carts Tayle.

VVith Allowance.

London, Printed for D. M. *Anno Dom.* 1675.

A Narrative of the Proceedings at the General Quarter Sessions holden at the Old-Bayly upon Wednesday the 7th of this instant July.

AT the Sessions at the *Old-Bayly*, there begun the *7th* of *July* instant, were Tryed a great number of Malafactors, for Crimes of various and sundry natures, as Murthers, Robberies, Burglaries, Cheats, Libellers, and other Enormities: whereby we see that Vice hath not only an infectuous quality of spreading its Venome; but that it's Poison, like that of a Viper, or Adder, doth taint the conversation of sinful Societies, with varigated and multiform tinctures of Impieties, so that it is strange to see what a speked mass of loathsome crimes present themselves at these times amongst the wicked Heard that are brought before this great Tribunal, to receive the due reward of their wickedness.

First, There were Tryed two men for Horse-stealing, they made a plausible story for themselves, but the fact was evidently proved against them, and they were found guilty of the Felony upon two several Indictments brought in against them.

The next was a *Swede* as he pretended himself to be, who had learnt the old English trick of being too familiar with mens Pocket concerns, and for the taking away

15. shillings

15. shillings out of the Pocket of his Prosecutor, was likewise convicted of Felony.

An Indictment was likewise brought against a *French* woman, formerly a Servant to a person of quality for taking away a parcel of Jewels, Rings, and other Rich commodities, (formerly mentioned in the Gazett) of several hundred pounds value, being an Alien, she had the priviledge to have a mixt Jury *de medie ate Lingue*, of *French* and *English*; she understood English pretty well, but could not speak it; The Tryal was very long by reason of the many circumstances that were brought in to confirm the evidence; The chief of which were that the same Night the Jewels were lost, she was heard walking about 1. and 2. of the clock in her Ladies Chamber, that presently after she feigned her self Sick, and was thereupon removed to another House, she staid not there long, but removed her self to *Leicester-fields*, where she was found out by a Foot-man, and appear'd to be very well, and searching her Trunk, they found some parcels of Lace that the Lady said was in the Coffer out of which she lost the aforesaid Jewels.

There were then several Testimonies given in of some debauched practices that were observed by her with one that pretended to be her Husband, for which being by the Justice sent to *Bridewell*, and there received her punishment; The Gentleman her Gallant, disowned her, and would have nothing to do with her, but these circumstances not amounting to direct proof what she was charged with, though they did too evidently prove the

the looseness of her conversation; her defence was given at large by her Interpreters, wherein she answered to several of the most material charges in the evidence given in against her, and upon the whole matter, the Jury brought her in not guilty.

There was likewise tryed that unhappy creature that kill'd her Husband at *Goodmans Fields*, viz. *Elizabeth Lylliman*; she seem'd to be a person of some 50 years of age, old both in years and wickedness; her carriage was very strange both at her Arraignment and Tryal, for after her Indictment read, and the the Clark demanded her Plea to the same, she fell into a kind of passion, and desired of the Court that she might see her dear Husband before she pleaded, which she insisted upon with seeming earnestness for some time; but this appeared to the Court to be but a mad kind of Artifice, designed out of her feigned passionate Zeal to her Murthered Husband to take off the suspicion of her being instrumental to his death, but this would not serve the turn, for upon her Tryal the Fact was evidently proved against her by several witnesses, the people of the house where they were when the Murther was done, did attest how that a little before the Murther, the party murthered, (having got a dried mackarel for his supper, went out to a Cobler that kept a Stall next adjoyning to the house, and borrowed his knife of him to dress his Fish; that while the Fish was a broyling, the people of the house being gon out of the Room, at their return, they found poor *Lylliman* with the aforesaid knife in his body, and the blood streaming out after it in this condition, nevertheless he

had

had so much strength as to go to the door, and called to the Cobler of whom he borrowed the Knife, to come to him, and then imbracing him, cryed out dear Country-man, my wife has stab'd me with the knife I borrowed of you; which words he reiterated 3 or 4 times, and then sunk down dead; The Chirurgion that searched the wound did attest that the knife was entred into his very heart; notwithstanding all which evidence, this bloody woman had the confidence to deny the Fact, and to pretend her self to be clearly innocent of it; but it was too evidently proved against her, and the whole matter being left to the Jury, they brought her in guilty of petty Treason.

A Dutch Gentleman was here Arraigned for the murther of a Frenchman; it appeared to be done in a kind of fray, for the prisoner being at a Tavern, drinking of a glass of wine with some company, one of them being the aforesaid Frenchman, would needs begin the Land-ladies health, and would have this Gentleman to pledge it, which he refused to do, whereupon the other gave him a box on the Ear, and fell upon him in a rude and violent manner, whereupon they having shut the doors to them, so that he had no way to escape his fury, he drew his Sword to defend himself, and therewith unhappily kill'd the French-man, the Jury brought him in only guilty of *Manslaughter*, so he had the benefit of his clergy.

A Gentleman was lately Rob'd near *Lambs* Conduit, behind *Grayes-Inn*, by some persons that were upon the Foot-pad that way, they took from one a Silver headed Sword, a watch, and other things of good value, two persons

ſons were taken upon ſuſpicion and arraigned at this Seſſions; whereof one of them was found guilty, the other was acquitted.

There were two ſeveral Indictments brought in againſt a Woman for the Felonious taking away of Cloaths from the perſons of two children, her Trade had been it ſeems to intice little children that ſhe found in the Streets, to go along with her, and having got them in ſome private place remote from their dwellings, and their ſtrip them of their cloaths, and after ſold them, leaving the poor children in that pitiful condition to ſhift for themſelves; thus ſhe had ſerv'd ſeveral; ſhe was found guilty upon both Indictments, and no doubt will be made an example.

One living in *Chantery-lane*, was Indicted for raviſhing a girle about 15. years of age, together with a young VVoman in whoſe houſe the ſame was pretended to be done, as acceſſary, by aſſiſting to the Fact; The fact according to the circumſtances that are uſually made uſe of in ſuch caſes, was peremptorily atteſted by the Girle and her Parents, but the witneſſes for the Priſoner, who were very many, and ſeemed to be moſt of them perſons of good account; did firſt give a very fair teſtimony of him upon their knowledge of him, and then did ſo fully teſtify by numerous circumſtances, the lewdneſs of the Girle and her mother; and that the Girle as young and innocent as ſhe ſeemed, had been notoriouſly known to be lewd, laſcivious, and diſorderly, and that they had by plain proofs only laid this deſign to get a peice of mony from him, theſe evidences being conſidered, the Jury brought him in not guilty.

Thus

 280 31

Thus we have given you a brief account of the most remarkable Trials of this Sessions, which was very great, and took up much time, holding from VVensday until Saturday following 2 a clock, the last thing remaning is to give you an account of the Several Judgements and Condemnations that past upon the Malefactors. And first those that were capable of being admitted to the benefit of their Clergy were called to the bar, and some that could read desired that benefit, others prayed Tranportation which was granted them as the Court saw cause ; The Number of these to be transported were 6 in all 3 men and 3 women ; The Number of those burned in the hand were 10 whereof six were men and 4 women, after which those who were to receive Judgement of death were set to the barre, and accordingly tyed up, which were 9 men and 2 women, eleven in all, whereof ten had judgment to be hanged, whereof several of them were for the aforementioned burglaries, one was a Pickpocket, two others for robbing upon the high-way and the woman that stripped the Children of their cloaths, After judgment, she pleaded she was with Child, and thereupon a jury of matrons were impannelled to inspect her, who returned upon their Oaths that they did not find that she was quick with Child, so she was set by for Execution with the rest of the Condemned persons. *Elizabeth Lillyman*, the person that killed her husband, her crime being petty Treason, had judgment to be burned to ashes, when she came to the Bar, she did, as formerly, passionately request to see the body of her husband before she died, saying she could not else dye in peace. But

this

this action of hers, was suspected rather as a fit of raving, then the result of a considerate mind, from one who was so apparently proved to be his *Murtheress*.

After these a pretended Printer was brought to the Bar, he had been convicted upon two several Indictments, the one for Exercising the *Mystery* of Printing, not being of the same, (but formerly a Scrivener) and the other for Printing Scandalous Libels; he pleaded for himself, that he had lived an house-keeper in good fashion, and that if he should be put to any publick disgrace, it would be the ruine of himself and a great family that he had under his charge, and pleaded the favour of the Court, who taking it into consideration, and it being the first offence that he stood convicted of, were pleased only to set a Fine upon him of 5 *l*. which he was to pay before he should be released from prison, and to prohibit him from Exercising or using the Trade of Printing for three years to come.

There were two persons that had been convicted of Forging Tickets, they had judgment to stand in the Pillory three several days, and fined.

The last were five persons, three men and two women, for petty larceny, who had judgment to be whipt at the Carts Tail.

FINIS.

Murder and Petty-Treason: Or, Bloody News from Southwark. Being A lamentable Relation of a barbarous Murder committed by a Wife upon the person of her Husband (Wing B3279A, omitting the first title) is reproduced with permission from the clear British Library copy (shelfmark RB 23.1.8837). The text-block measures 114 × 155 mm.

The following words are a transcription of the original:

3.14 (to descend neerer
3.15 the present occasion) sows such Discord and
3.16 Heart burnings, Malice and Hatred in the state
4.29 abroad to buy Stuff,
4.30 in Drink
7.1 But assoon

MURDER
AND
PETTY-TREASON:
OR,
BLOODY NEWS
FROM
Southwark.

BEING

A lamentable Relation of a barbarous Murder committed by a Wife upon the person of her Husband, on *Munday* the 25th of this instant *September* 1677.

How she stabb'd him into the Breast with a pair of Shears, so violently, that when the body was open'd, his Liver, Lights, and Heart were all found wounded and pierced through.

After which having made her Escape, being troubled in mind for the bloody fact, and confessing the same, she was the same evening taken and committed to Prison.

Licensed according to Order

London : Printed for *D. M.* 1677.

Murder and Petty-Treaſon:

OR,

BLOODY NEWS

FROM

Southwark.

AS Satan is the prime Author of all Diſorders and Confuſions in the world, ſo he eſpecially endeavours to pervert the beſt of things, and turn that into Poyſon which was intended for Antidote. Thus he mixes Tares privately with the pureſt Wheat; raiſes Diviſions and Hereſies in the beſt Reformed Churches; Seditions and Factions in the moſt happy Governments; and (to deſcend neerer the preſent occaſion) ſows ſuch Diſcords and Heart burnings, Malice and Hatred in the ſtate of Matrimony, that that excellent Institution, designed for the glory of God, prevention of Sin, and solace of Humane kind, as being composed of a sweet and cherishing power of Commanding on the mans part, a ready Obedience and Assistance on the womans, animated with mutual affection to Endear them to each other, is now become to too many, a meer Plague, the bane of Life, or a perpetual state of War; as if (like desperate Duellists) they had confined themselves to this Inclosure onely to fight the more furiously, and do one another the greater mischief.

The Person, whose unhappy Murther is here to be related, was a Tradesman. He had, 'tis said, been married to this woman about Twelve years, and had several Children by her, but all dead, as likewise divers more that she had by a former Husband; indulgent Fate seeming in kindness to take all the issue of her body out of the world, that they might not with grief behold the Tragical End wherewith she is threatned, from whom naturally they deriv'd their being.

During all this Twelve years of their Cohabitation they lived very untowardly together: But the particular occasion of this their fatal falling out, is differently related. Some say, that he had been abroad to buy Stuff, and when he came home, being a little in Drink, his Wife be-

began to chide him for that Extravagance. Others say, that he surpriz'd her upon the stairs ready to carry forth her best wearing Apparel, as resolving to live no longer with him, and that this bred the difference. But whatever the matter was, it happen'd that high words arose between them, and from words he fell to blows; insomuch that he took up a pair of Tongs and struck his Wife: who does relate her self (as 'tis reported, for I cannot learn that any witnesses were present) that she wish'd him not to strike her again: which he, it seems, not regarding, would not for all that give over his unnatural blows; whereupon she snatch'd up a pair of Shears used by persons of that trade, and in a rage stabb'd him therewith into the breast at two several places, (though 'tis thought at one blow) of which wounds he immediately after died.

Having perpetrated this bloody fact without being seen by any, when she saw him forthwith to fall and expire, she immediately runs forth, and never staid so much as to shut any of the doors after her; so that the dead body lay a considerable time before it was discovered, but at last was found by some that accidentally went in to speak with him about business. The unexpected sight of so lamentable an object, amazed at first those that beheld it; but in very little time the whole Neighbourhood was alarm'd; Officers called, and enquiry made who

should

should be the Authour of so horrid a Deed; which they soon found reason to suspect his Wife for, as well for that she was thus unusually absent, as because several Neighbours testified they heard them quarrel lately, though they could not say particularly what passed between them: Hereupon *Hue and Cry* is leavied after her, and strict search made in all probable places to apprehend her; but all in vain, had not the Lord, to whom Vengeance belongeth, and who makes inquisition for Blood, been pleased to make the Guilty her own Accuser; For though there was no Testimony abroad, yet she had a convicted Conscience within, that supplied the place of a thousand Witnesses.

These troubles of a guilty Minde continually suggesting to her ears the frightful Cry of Blood, caus'd this unhappy Wretch to wander about the Town several Hours, in intolerable Perplexity, fancying all that she met took notice of her, and that every one that overtook her came to seize her; not willing to abide in the open streets for fear of being seen, nor yet knowing where to take shelter for fear of being discovered: At last in this distraction she comes to a woman of her acquaintance, and after many Obsecrations of secrecy and silence, told her, that she had killed her Husband, and in what manner she had done it: The woman, after some wonder and reproof, makes as if she were willing to keep her councel, and procures her a

Lodging;

Lodging: But assoon as she was gone to Bed, knowing both the danger and unrighteousness of such a Concealment, declared the same to her Land-lord: Whereupon a Constable was sent for, the Criminal raised and carried before a Magistrate; where, upon Examination, she freely (as 'tis said) confessed all the Circumstances of this unnatural Murder to be, as we have herein before related; whereupon she was Committed for the present to Prison, whither she was brought on *Tuesday* Night, about Eleven of the Clock.

'Tis but a few years since a Woman near *Goodmans*-fields was made exemplary, by being burnt to Death for killing her Husband: 'Tis strange if not the Laws of God or Nature, yet that the Severity of the Punishment inflicted in such cases by the Law should not deter all women from such Traiterous attempts; for so it is, for them to rebel against and destroy their Husbands, whom the Institution of God and Laws of the Land have declared to be their Head and Governours: And if they prove unkinde, cruel or unreasonable, they ought to mollifie and amend such depravity of their

hu-

Humours by mildneſs and compliance as far as they can; to endeavour to win them by the admonitions of Friends; to be earneſt in Prayers to Almighty God to turn their hearts, and make them ſee the evil of their doings: And at laſt (if all other means prove ineffectual) to uſe ſuch Remedies for tying up their injurious hands, procuring maintenance, or obtaining Separation, as the Laws allow of.

FINIS.

A Warning for Bad Wives: or, The Manner of the Burning of Sarah Elston (Wing W918A) is reproduced wit permission from the British Library copy (shelfmark 1132.a.21). The text-block measures 90 × 145 mm.

The following words are a transcription of the original:

2.14 his ill husbandry cross carriage, ill company,
2.15 provocations, not here to be men-
3.5 designe
3.12 fortnights time
3.13 the better to prepare herself
3.14 for that terrible Death, she appeared extraor-
5.1 to bewail with tears
5.2 former Life,
5.3 communication,
5.12 he blows
5.16 destroy all the Comforts
5.17 instituted for humane
7.8 to this minute certainly tell; but
7.9 all her Miscarriages in
7.10 all good People to
7.11 Merciful God
7.13 Fiery Tryal,
7.14 which
8.2 undeservedly
8.5 petty thieveries heretofore
8.7 Actions, desiring
8.9 he that standeth should take heed
8.10 lest he fall; for once they as little as any present, thought of be-
8.11 ing guilty of any Crime that should bring them to this condi-
8.12 but confest the punishment
8.17 sentence

X·XII.

A Warning for Bad Wives:

OR

The Manner of the [illegible]

OF

Sarah Elston.

Who was Burnt to death at a Stake on [illegible] near Southwark, on [illegible] April 1678.

For Murdering her Husband Thomas Elston, the 25th of [illegible].

And likewise the Execution and Confession of [illegible] who were Executed for Robbing on the Highway.

TOGETHER

With their [illegible] the Confession [illegible]

With Allowance. Ro. L'Estrange.

LONDON, Printed for D. M. 1678.

2 A

A Warning for Bad Wives.

This unhappy woman was Convicted at the last Assizes holden for the County of *Surrey*, of Petty Treason for murdering her Husband, and received sentence to be Burnt to Death for the same. They lately dwelt in a place call'd *Fishmongers Alley*, in the Borough of *Southwark*, by Trade a Hatter, and had been married several years; but lived with much Discord and frequent Wrangling; of which some now would partly excuse the woman, and alleadge the man as the principal Cause of their Differences by his ill husbandry, cross carriage, ill company, and other provocations, not here to be mentioned. Others gave Evidence that she had threatned his Life several times before. However, most certain it was, and she never denied it, that he died by her hand: for a quarrel arising between them, and he having beat her very ſeverely, ſhe with a pair of Sizzars gave him a wound on the left part of his breaſt; whereof, without ſpeaking one word, he died. Yet all along to the laſt ſhe denied that ſhe had any murderous intention or deſigne to kill him, onely thought to do him ſome ſlight Miſchief in revenge of his Cruelty in beating her.

From the time of her receiving Sentence, which was *Tueſday* the 26th of *March*, till this present *Wedneſday* the 24 of *April*, whereon ſhe ſuffered, having begg'd a fortnights time of the Court, the better to prepare her ſelf for that terrible Death, ſhe appeared extraordinary penitent, much delighted with the company of Miniſters, and other good ſober underſtanding Chriſtians, that came to confer with her about her Everlaſting ſtate. And though through neglect of hearing God's word preached, and uſing other the means appointed, ſhe was extreamly ignorant of the nature and very foundations of the Goſpel, yet now her eyes began ſomewhat to be opened; and when thoſe Myſteries were laid forth before her, ſhe heard them gladly.

So that I know not whether we should more admire the wisdom or the mercy of God in his proceedings with this poor Creature: had she not been guilty of Blood, 'tis probable she had never known the worth of the precious blood of Christ; had she not here been [illegible] to [illegible] Flames, 'tis to be [illegible] she [illegible] escaped Everlasting Burnings. The rashness of a wicked Fury drew her into Affliction, that Affliction humbled her, and God took the advantage of her Humiliation for her Conversion. Had not one foot slipt into the mouth of Hell, she had never been in this forwardness for Heaven. There is none we see, even of the weakest Sex, so weak or foolish, but hath strength or wit enough to sin, or to make ill use of her sin, to destroy another to whom she owed both love and obedience. 'Tis onely the goodness and wisdom of an infinite God, that can make our sin good to us, though evil in it self, and can save even by Destruction: 'tis no thank to our selves or our sins, that we are better'd with evil; The work, O Lord, is thine, let thine be the Glory.

She

She was often heard to bewail with tears the ill Course of her former Life, especially her rage, unquietness and evil communication, whereby she had often provoked her Husband to be more violent and cruel towards her, than probably he might otherwise have been: For as *A soft answer turneth away wrath*, and gentle Carriage in time prevails even with the worst Natures, so passion and railing, calling of names and bitter language, especially between man and wife, are the very Bellows of the Devil, whereby he blows up such irreconcilable hatred, Feuds and Animosities, as seldom terminate in less than the destruction of one or both the parties; at least destroy all the Comforts of their lives, and turn that Society instituted for humane solace and delight, into a perpetual purgatory, or meer hell upon earth.

She spent most of the time indulged by the favour of the Court for the preparation of her Soul, in Prayer, Reading, or Conversation with Ministers, and seemed very willing to die; saying, That since she had been so unfortunate as to kill her Husband, she had never

ver been very desirous to live, but now especially she saw so much of the Worlds vanity and Heavens excellency, that she even long'd for Death.

The day appointed for Execution was this present *Wednesday* the 24th of *April*, and the place on *Kennington* Common neer *Southwark*; where a Stake being set up, she was conveyed thither on a Hurdle, being clothed all in White, with a vast multitude of People attending her, and after very solemn Prayers offered up on that sad occasion, and some few words tending to clear her Innocency as to any intent of murdering her Husband, and the horror, confusion, and surprize she was in when she saw him fall; how well she had loved him, and that even then, notwithstanding all his Abuses, she could have given her own life to have saved his: Desiring all Women to take warning by her, and to live in Love and Peace with their Husbands if it be possible; at least to avoid their Fury by going out of the way for the present, when they are in rage, rather than to stand bandying of words, or teazing them with reproachful Language; which she acknowledged had oft been her own fault: That they should remember that their Husband is their Head, and that the Apostle requires them to be obedient to them in every thing; and this not onely to the kinde and indulgent, but even the peevish and froward ought to have the same observance. She confest she had done very

ill

ill in lifting up her hand against her Husband, and offering to revenge her self of him; but protested again most seriously, that she never in her life had the least designe or thoughts of killing of him, onely it was an unfortunate Accident; and whether it came by a blow from her, or his violent running upon the point of the Sizzars as she held them out to defend her self, she could not to this minute certainly tell; but she hoped God had pardoned all her Miscarriages in that matter, and heartily desired all good People to joyn in Prayer for her: That the same Merciful God would forgive her all her other sins, and give her strength of Faith to go through this Fiery Tryal, and receive her Soul into his Kingdom. After which the Fire was kindled, and giving two or three lamentable Shrieks, she was deprived both of Voice and Life, and so burnt to Ashes according to the Sentence.

The same day there were executed at the same place two Men for a Robbary committed on the High-way: the first was *John Masters*, a person well educated, but falling into poverty, having been in prison for debt, and under other crosses, was seduced to these ill courses. The other *Gabriel Dean* by trade formerly a Pipe-maker, who sometimes pretended to be the others man; These two in *May* last, robbed a Gentleman near *Putney* of twenty pounds, but being pursued were taken, and upon evident proof condemned last assizes; *viz.* the 25th of *March* last, during all which time, their lives have been respited that they might the better prepare themselves for their end. Mr. *Masters* did protest solemnly, that he had never before been concern'd in any Robbery, and exprest himself much afflicted for his evil therein, now, but more especially for the ſcandal that might thence (though undeſervedly) ariſe to others amongſt ſome cenſorious people that delight in nothing but columny. The other acknowledged he had been a very extravagant Ill Liver, and concerned in petty thieveries heretofore. They were both extreamly penitent and devout, as far as Charity could judg by their Actions, deſiring all people to pray for them, and not to inſult over their Memory for this their Ignominious end, but rather that *he that ſtandeth ſhould take heed leſt he fall*. For once they as little as any preſent, thought of being guilty of any Crime that ſhould bring them to this condition, but confeſt the puniſhment was righteous both from God, and Man in this World, and truſted that God had pardon'd them as to the world to come; and ſo after ſeveral publique and private prayers uttered with much fervour zeal and earneſtneſs of ſpirit. They took their leaves of the world, and were hanged according to Sentence.

F I N I S.

The Last Speech and Confession of Sarah Elestone (Wing L504F) is reproduced with permission from the unique copy at Dr Williams's Library, London. The text-block measures 90 × 142 mm.

The following words are a transcription of the original:

2.3 condign
2.4 not so deplorable
2.5 a Fact
2.16 keenness, which after a little practicing of it, she became har-
2.17 den'd in it, and learn'd to swear by her Maker, and to pro-
2.24 was
2.29 another
3.1 way
3.16 husband
3.29 Marshalses
3.30 last past
3.31 to ashes … sentence

THE LAST

Speech and Confeſſion

OF

Sarah Eleſtone

At the place of Execution:

Who was

BURNED

FOR

Killing her Husband,

April 24. 1678.

With her Deportment in Priſon ſince her Condemnation.

With Allowance.

Printed for T. D. 1678.

THE

Last Speech and Confession of Sarah Elstone, &c.

Did we not make our selves miserable, God is so merciful to us, as he would make us happy; but when we with high and presumptious hands, violate the laws of nature and Grace, of Earth and Heaven, in marthering those whom through duty and affection we are bound to obey, honour, cherish and preserve: Then we need not marvel because we first forsook God that he afterwards abandoneth us to our selves and sin, and to the fruits thereof, misery, Infamy, and Perdition: And that we may see humane cruelty to be justly met with and punished by Gods upright and divine justice.

A terrible instance we have here before us; we see a wretched Wife guilty of the death of her own Husband. A sad and execrable Fact, for the which we see her rewarded with condign punishment, and with a sharp and infamous death, but not so deplorable as deserved: It is so bitter, unhumane, and bloody a Fact, that it must needs draw tears from our eyes if we have any room for pity or piety.

IN *Three-Faulken-Court*, over-against St. *Margarets-hill*, in *Southwark*, lately lived one *Sarah Elestone*, the late Wife of *Thomas Elestone*, a Felt-maker: a man very laborious in his calling, aged about forty years, and his Wife forty-six years old: they lived many years very contentedly, she assisting him in his calling in what she was able: till such time as falling into the acquaintance of some lewd women, she was drawn to commit that filthy sin of drunkenness, which after a little practising of it, she became hardened in it, and learn'd to swear by her Maker, and to prophain the Lords Day, and hate good men; such an alteration there was perceived in her, that several of her Husbands acquaintance desired him to do all that he could to reclaim her, telling him also that it was his duty, to which he answered, That he hoped God would turn her from these evil courses, but he for his part could do no good with her, for she was so obstinate, that the more he said to her the worse she was: so that seeing he could not prevail by fair means, he sought some other way, as keeping her bare of money, but then she run him in debt, and took up money at the Tally-shops, he having notice of it, told them if they trusted her any more he would not pay them: upon which she resolved of anoth-

they, which was to sell her goods, which she did by degrees, till they had scarce a Chair to sit on, or a bed to lye on. This so perplexed her Husband, that he resolved to beat her out of this wicked course, and to that end did sometimes chastize her with blows, which she was not wanting to repay; so much was their fury sometimes, that their neighbours hath been forced to part them at all hours in the night. In this like manner they lived for some years, which so troubled and disturbed the patience of the man; that oft he hath been heard to wish himself dead, or that he had been buried alive that day he was married to her, and she wicked and graceless soul would many times in cold blood threaten him, that at one time or other she would kill him; which proved to be too true, for she having been out with her Gossips, and having got a cup too much as it was thought, comes and finds her husband at work; she demands some money of him, and withall tells him, That if he will not give her some presently she would be the Death of him; he seeing her in that condition, took her and thrusts her down stairs, and shuts the door, and to work again; within a little time after when he thought her heat was over, he goes down in his shirt as he was at work, intending to drink; she meets him at the stairs foot, and with one side of a pair of Sheers gave him a mortal wound on the breast, of which he immediately dyed, upon which she presently fled: Her Husband being quickly found, Hue and Cry was made after her, and that night about twelve a clock she was taken by the Old-street Watch, to whom she confessed the fact; she had her Tryal at the *Marshalses* at the Assizes, beginning on the 22 day of *March*, last past, where she was condemned by Law to be burn'd to ashes for this horrid and bloody crime: After sentence

was

was past, she begged some time to fit and prepare her self, which was granted, as allso to two other Malefactors. Dureing her imprisonment she hath had several Ministers to visit her who laid open the haniousness of her sins, especially that of Murther: She for the most part seemed but little concerned, many times talking of other things when they prayed for her, but a day or two before her Execution it pleased God to awaken her and to discover her sins unto her, and the need she stood in of an interest in the Lord Jesus: often Remembring that saying in *Gen. 9. Chapter. 6. Verse.* *Whoso sheddeth Mans Blood, by Man shall his Blood be shed: for in the Image of God made he Man:* And *Numbers* the 35. Chapter, and 33 Verse. *Ye shall not pollute the Land wherein you are, for blood it defileth the Land: and the Land cannot be cleansed of the blood that is shed therein, but by the blood of them that shed it.*

Which made her the willinger to dye, finding that it was according both to the Law of God and Man: and hoping that the Lord Jesus would have mercy on her poor sinful Soul: Now she loved good men, good discourse, and often cryed out what should she do to be saved: when she came to the place of Execution and beheld the Fagots, she cryed, O Lord for Jesus sake let this be my last burning: O that God would give me an assurance of the pardon of my sins, and blot out the black lines of my sins with the Red lines of Christs blood. Her last words were to exhort all good people to fear God,

to

to keep the Sabbath-day, to refrain idle company, to have a care how they take the Name of the Lord in vain.

Thus with a few Ejaculatory Prayers, she concluded with that saying in *Galatians* the 5. Chapter, and the 26 Verse. *Let us not be desirous of vain glory, provoking one another, envying one another.*

Having thus said, the Executioner doing his Office, stopped the Atropos of her Speech, and her body was consumed to ashes in the Flames.

FINIS.

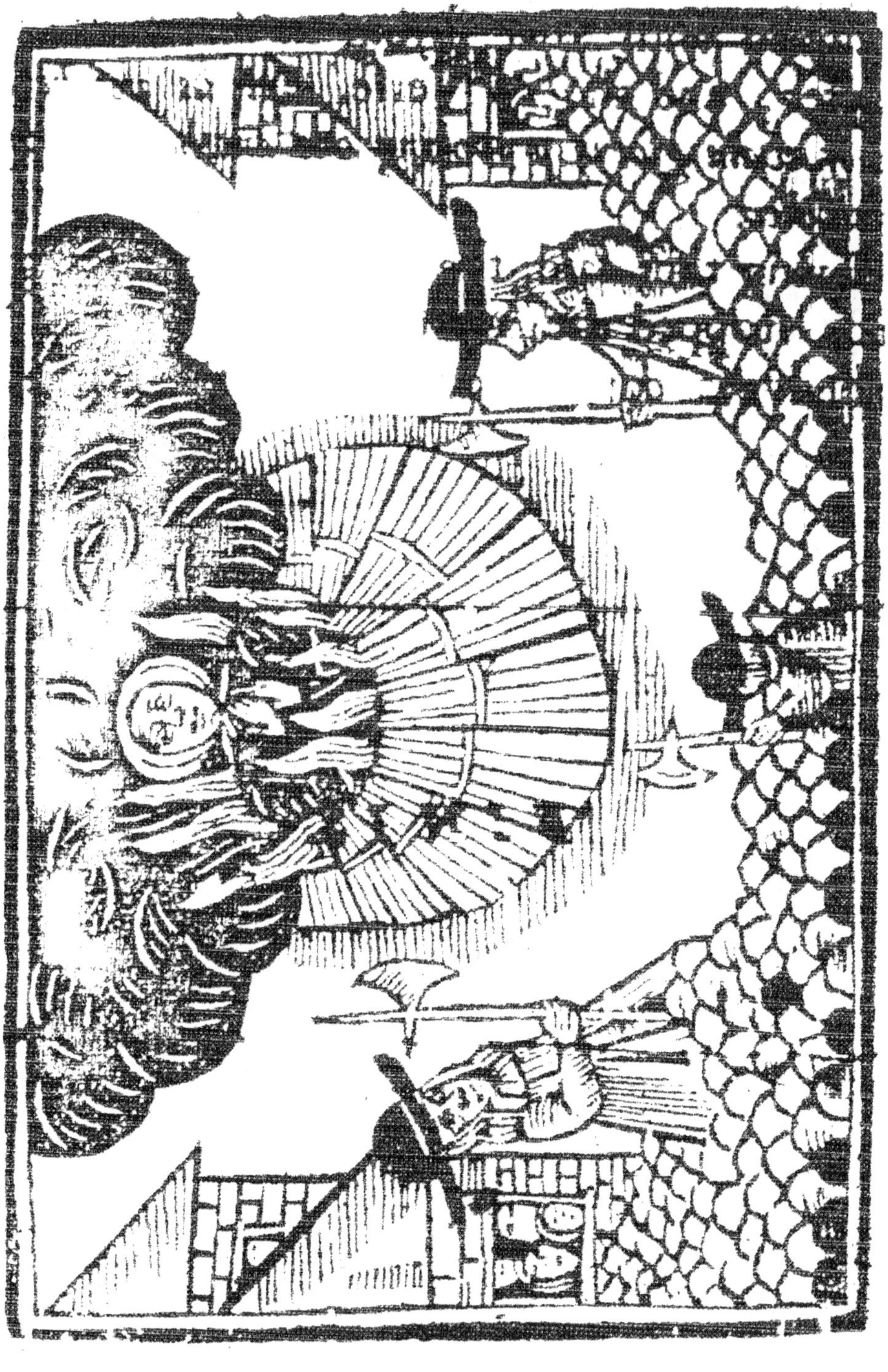

Great and Bloody News, From Farthing-Ally, In St. Thomas's Southwark (Wing G1645A) is reproduced with permission from the unique copy at Harvard College Library. The text-block measures 135 × 232 mm.

Great and Bloody News,

FROM

FARTHING-ALLY.

In St. *Thomas's*

SOUTHWARK,

Or the True and Faithful

RELATION.

Of a Horid and Barbarous

MURTHER.

Committed on the Body of *Walter Osily*, by his own Wife on the 31 of this Instant *July*. Who first strangled him with a Bow-string, and afterwards cut him with a Hatchet on the bare Head, and sliting his Nose, giving him a Mortal Wound under the right Ear, with several other Barbarous Inhumanityes, and how afterwards she discoverd it to a neighbour, as of her being Apprehended and confession before the Iustice of Peace, as likewise her Commitment to the *Marshelseas* Prison, where she remains: with several particulars relating to her Life and Conversation. August : 2: 1680

WOnderful are the prevailing Insinuations of Hell to delude poor mortals here below as may be well observed in this most barbarous and inhumane murther committed by *Margaret Osilly* upon her Husband *Walter Osilly*, The Relation of which in all its horrid circumstances being as followeth, her Husband having been abroad on Fryday at the Beargarden, to try a Dog that he had lately purchased, came home about nine of the Clock in the Evening somewhat disordered in drink, yet notwithstanding went out with her to a neighbours house, where they drank together, after that they went home seemingly well, but it proved not so, for the being no sooner entered the house but a quarrel arising between them, her husband gave her some blows, the which she to outward appearance seemed not to regard, but converting her resentments to private Revenge, the which she in time found opportunity to effect.

A He

Her Husband being over powered with drink, falling fast asleep she went to a Lodgers Chamber of hers, telling him that her Husband was dead drunk, and that he lay like a Swine upon the Flore, and that he had grievously abused her, whereupon he perswaded her to let him alone till he came to himself and then to get him up to bed; this Discourse being no sooner ended but she returned, and locking the Dores close after her, having awaked him, got him (as she since confest) to Bed; where he no sooner fell asleep but the Devil prevailing with her prompted her for to commit a Murder that has since amazed mankind, for in her search for a mischievous weapon to work her revengful Rage she chanced to light upon a Hatchet, the which she poising in her barbarous hand for some small time, at last concluded on the Tragecal Exploit, and with a down-right blow struck her sleeping Husband, who dreamed of no such force, just on the Forehead, making there a wound three inches in length and an inch in depth; but not content with that, being desperately bent on his Destruction, she repeated it with a second just under his right Ear, the which was about an Inch and a half deep which no doubt was mortal an sufficient to translate him to immortality and after that another that slit his Nose, and a fourth on his hand between his Fingers, the which he was supposed to receive in making resistance; after which, as it is verily conjectured, he lying weltring in his Blood and not presently expiring, she with a Bow-string to make all secure strangled him, and so put him out of the pain; she being resolved to perfect the Cruel Deed, and make end in Death. This Bloody exploit being acted under the Covert of darkness as near as can be conjectured about two of the Clock in the morning, she continuing with the Lifeless Corps till the Light appeared, and without doubt oft viewed the dreadful Deed her Cruel hands had done, but with what horror I leave the reader to conjecture by the Guilt. About 8 of the Clock she leaving her Husband in the bloody Bed, went to one Mr. *Fowlers* in the *Maze* Yard where no sooner entering the House, but she desired to speak with him in private, which being granted, she declared to him the horrid Murther, and how she had acted it in every circumstance desiring him to conceal it or some Report to let her bury him privately in his Ninepin Place; and after having drank there, returned home, but he being a man that detested such horrid Impieties, went instantly and acquainted

A one

one Mr. *Daniel* a Hatbandmaker, with what she related to him, who delayed not to search into the Truth of this strange report so that coming to her House he Knocked at the Dore the which she unwillingly opened, being then smoaking a Pipe of Tobacco in her Chair, but at his importunity she arose and let him in, who no sooner entered, but ask'd for her Husband, to which she replied he was gon out, but he did not believe it, for was informed that she had murthered him and that he was resolved to search, demanding the Key of the Chamber, the which after some denials she delivered to him and thereupon retird into the next Room locking her self in, upon which going into the Chamber foun the murthered Corps lie welterred in Blood all mangled on Flore, where upon he puting his Head out of the Window, called several neighbours, giving them to understand, that there was Murther done in the House, at which several came in and found the dismal spectacle, at which they started back with horror, some of them immediately running for a Constable to seise the Murtherer, whilst others watched to hinder her from making an escape, but in fine she being apprehended was carried before Justice *Freeman* where Mr. *Fowler* appeared to give Evidence against her who related what she had declared unto him, with many other circumstances, whereupon he was bound over to prosecute; It was likewise told her that for that horrid Fact she had committed she would be burnt, to which she replied, she burn'd already and that would prepare her for the Flames to come ; or words to that effect ; after a full Examination she was committed to the *Marshalsea* Prison, there to remain till she shall be delivered by due course of Law the Coroner and his Jury sitting upon the Corps returned it upon their Inquest wilful Murder, *&c.* This *Walter Osfily* was formerly her Apprentice, when upon the Death of her former Husband, she married, his time not being out when he was murthered, it was reported that he was very Familiar with her during the Life of her former Husband, and that he lay with her the night after he was Buried :

He

He having been married to her about a twelvemonth, in tha time as 'tis said, he had spent and made away of hers about two hundred pounds, which extravigance of his and the abusing her as it is conjectured were the causes for which she murthered him for which no doubt she gave him cause, being a Woman of a Turbulent Spirit, and living much at Varience with her former Husband who was a Castermaker by Trade, of which employ was also the person now murthered. May this sad Crime and cruel murther be a warning to all Christians to deter them from the like Barbarity,

FINIS.

Dreadful News from Southwark is reproduced with permission from the clear Bodleian Library copy (shelfmark Godw. Pamphlet 2209[25]). The text-block measures 130 × 235 mm.

The following words are a transcription of the original:

2.1 as by Trade an Hatter; his

Dreadful News FROM SOUTHWARK: OR, A true ACCOUNT OF THE Most Horrid MURDER committed BY MARGARET OSGOOD,

On her Husband *WALTER OSGOOD* a Hat-maker, On Saturday the 31th of *July* 1680.

Whom she most barbarously Murdered, by Cleaving his Head whilst he was asleep, cuting off his Ears, and Wounding him in several other places in an inhumane manner.

Together with her Examination and Confession of the whole Fact before the Justice of the Peace, and commitment of her to Prison till Tryal.

IN other Cases long *Preambles* may be necessary, but here is too much *matter*, and too horrid, to need either *flourish* or *Aggravation*; therefore we shall immediately come to the naked *Fact*, which being truely related, must be acknowledged one of the most dismal *Tragedies* this Age has been guilty of.

Murder at all times is a black and crying sin, no less abhorrent to Humane Nature, than punishable by all Laws of *God* and *Man*; but to find it perpetrated *deliberately*, and by one of the softer *Sex*, and by a *Wife* upon her Husband, and without any proportionate provocation; and to be persisted in, stood unto, and in effect justified, this seems to be the height of malice, and a seared Impiety.

The persons concern'd in this wicked Deed, lived in *Southwark*, in a place called *Farthing-Alley*, not far from St. *Thomas's*

Hoſpital. The Man Murdered was by Trade an *Hatter*; his Wife, by whoſe hand he was now Butchered, was formerly his Miſtreſs, the Wife then of one *Richard Cooke* of the ſame profeſſion, a man honeſt and induſtrious, but very unhappy, as it was reported, in a Wife, being too *free* and liberal of Kindneſſes both to his *Servants*, and others who courted her favour, which ſeveral were not wanting to do, ſhe being a handſome and well proportioned Woman; ſo rare it is, for *Beauty* and *Vertue*, the Indulgences of *Nature*, and the Influences of *Grace*, to joyn and keep company together.

Cook her former Husband, dying ſometime ſince, about a Month after ſhe married this *Oſgood* her man; and 'tis ſaid, was left worth by her late Husband, two or three hundred pounds, which willingly he would have diſpoſed of to other Relations, had not the importunities of his Neighbours over-perſwaded him in favour of his Wife.

This *Margaret* was now about forty years of age, and *Walter Oſgood*, whom ſhe had taken to her *Husband*, not above Twenty; whether this diſproportion in their *years*, or any other occaſion gave any grounds of Jealouſie or Diſcontent, I know not, but the Neighbours generally relate, that they were both too much to blame, each of them following looſe and extravagant courſes, whereby not only their *ſtock* was much impaired and waſted, but continual fewds and ill-language of late happened between them; inſomuch, that (as an antient Neighbour atteſts) they ſeldome went to bed without a ſtorm of Oaths and mutual Curſes.

Particularly on Friday night laſt the 30th of *July* 1680, he came home (ſome ſay in drink) about Ten of the clock, and the old Rencounters happened, yet to no ſuch unuſual degree, as to be taken notice of by the Neighborhood; farther, than that one avers, he heard the deceaſed threaten to kill his Wife, which ſhe likewiſe affirms, and as it ſeems by the bloody ſequele, was reſolved to prevent and anticipate him therein. For as ſhe afterwards confeſt, no ſooner was he laid in his Bed and faln aſleep, but the Devil inſpired her mind with a curſed *Reſolution*, and her trembling hand with ſufficient ſtrength to Murder him, which ſhe performed in the moſt

cruel

cruel and inhumane manner that (perhaps) has in any Age been heard of; for taking into her hands an old *Hatchet*, ruſty and blunt, unfit any one would have thought for ſuch a barbarous purpoſe, ſhe therewith firſt cleft his Noſe and Face, with an hideous Gaſh two or three Inches wide. The poor man thus amazedly awakened, only for a dying ſleep, did hereupon (as ſhe has ſince acknowledged) lift up his fainting hands to implore mercy from her ſavage Rage; but no *wild Beaſt* is ſo cruel as an incenſed woman; regardleſs of her own Duty, or his Cries, ſhe purſues her Revenge, and cuts him again Mortally *Croſs the Forehead* into the Skull, and not therewith ſatisfied, *ſlices* up the *fingers* of both his hands almoſt to the Wriſt, and alſo cuts off both his Ears, or ſo far mangles them, that ſhe could (as afterwards they were found) turn them over his face. Having thus mortified him, and finding the ſtreaming blood not only to run over, or through the Bed, but the Bords of the Chamber too, down into the lower room, ſhe drags him out of the bed, and wraps him up in a foul ſheet, and ſo lets him lye till morning.

No ſooner had ſhe compleated this Bloody Tragedy, but ſhe returns again to her Bed, where ſhe endeavoured to take ſome reſt, for by her after behaviour, it cannot be ſuppoſed ſhe had any ſenſe of the horrid villany ſhe had committed, and ſo ſuddenly and ſilently was this barbarous Murder perpetrated, that none of the Neighbours took notice of it.

But the next morning about ſeven a clock, the Murdereſs repairs to an Ale-houſe near her, and calling the man of the Houſe into a private Room, begins a ſuſpitious diſcourſe, as if ſhe had ſomething of importance to diſcover, and tells him, ſhe thought it was better to *Kill than be Killed*; he obſerving her Diſtracted looks and words, ſaid, *I hope you have not Killed your Huſband?* *Yes*, ſaid ſhe, *I have, come to our houſe and you will ſee it done*; then ſaid the man, *I muſt ſeize you*, No, ſaid ſhe, *You need not, I will not run away, but go home and look out things for his Burial.* Thus away ſhe went, but the Ale-houſe-keeper ſetting ſome body to watch her, went for a Conſtable, who coming into her Houſe, found her moſt unconcernedly picking of Wool (her uſual Imployment) in the lower room,

though

though the Blood was dropt through the Bords there in great abundance.

Then to a Justice they carried her, where she acknowledged the whole Fact and Circumstances, yet so far from any remorse, that she did in effect declare, were it undone, she would yet do it; and so after a full Examination, was committed to the County Goal, where she now remains.

This is the true Narrative of this barbarous Murder, which as it is almost unpresidented, so we hope it will deter all others from imitating such a bloody and inhumane Crime.

FINIS.

V

The True Narrative of the Confession and Execution Of the Prisoners at Kingstone-upon-Thames, on Wednesda the 16th of this Instant March, 1681. Viz. Margaret Osgood Burnt for killing her Husband … With … mor particular of the Confession and Burning of Margaret Osgood, of the Parish of St. Olives [sic] *Southwark, fo the horrid Murther of her Husband, on the 21th* [sic] *of July last* (Wing T2780A) is reproduced wit permission from the clear Harvard College Library copy. The text-block measures 125 × 235 mm.

The following words are a transcription of the original:

2.1 with home … whom she Marrying
2.21 an inch
2.22 tal wounds
2.43 repent her of what she had done,
2.44 Extravagencies
2.51 Murther bore such a lasting Stain
2.52 poluted Soul
2.53 Burnt according to sentence than to live with him, and

THE TRUE NARRATIVE OF THE CONFESSION AND EXECUTION Of the PRISONERS at Kingstone-upon-Thames,

ON

Wednesday the 16th of this Instant *March*, 1 6 8 1.

VIZ.

Margaret Osgood Burnt for killing her Husband.
Mary Trot for several Fellonies.

William Abbot.
Abel Hamersly.
Thomas Savioury.
} For Robing on the High-way.

Edward Turner.
William Wyer.
John Bradsham.
Richard Wilson.
} For Fellony and Burglary.

Being a satisfactory Account of all their Crimes for which they suffered, the rest being most graciously Reprieved

WITH

An Account of their Deportment in Prison, at the Place of Execution, with several other remarkable Circumstances.

But more particular of the Confession and Burning of *Margaret Osgood*, of the Parish of *St. Olives Southwark*, for the horrid Murther of her Husband, on the 21th of *July* last.

17. March. 1680/1

AMongst the many and grievous Temptations which the power of Darkness lays as Snares to deceive Souls, and bring them under his subjection; those jealousies and discontents are the pronest to work our downfals, for they often turn to dispair, whereby we make away our selves, and

s-so inevitably perish or to desperate revenge by which we destroy others the effects of the latter has been amply proved in this Tragical Exploit with which we shall Usher in this Scean of Death one *Margaret Osgood*, Wife to *Walter Osgood*, late of the Parish of St. *Olives Southwark*, Hat-maker formerly Wife to one *Thomas Cook*, with home this latter Husband was Apprentice whom she Marrying before he was out of his Time, he being Young, and she stricken in Years immediately discord was so soon between them by the instigation of the Devil which grew to such a height that notwithstanding the Mediation and Perswasion of several Neighbours, they lived as it were in continual brawling for seldom a day, or night passed but they had a falling out, which induced him to spend lavishly to keep Horses and Spannels; so that in a short time almost all that her former Husband had left her (which was considerable) was wasted, which caused her for very grief as she has since confessed, to attempt often to make away with her self, but had not power; yet, though the Devil could not bring her to destruction by one way he effected it by an other as prodigeous as the former might have been if Acted; which is as followeth, her Husband coming home somwhat late on the 21th of *July* last, and much in Drink, after some contest she got him to Bed, who presently fell asleep, not dreaming that his Thred of Life was so near Spun, when she approaching the Bedside with a Hatchet (as it is thought her heart being Armed with cruelty) and struck him on the Forehead, such a forciable blow as entered his Skull half an Inch, with that not being satisfied she gave him two mortal wounds, besides one which slit his Nose, and another under the Ears about an Inch deep, nay so far was she transported with revenge and Hellish rage that whilst he extended his dying Hands for mercy she slit one of them to the Wrist, and as if all this had not been sufficient to give him his Pasport in to the other World, she with a Whip-Cord strangled him whilst he lay weltring in his Blood; and then sitting by the Corps good part of the Night, when Day appeared she was Apprehended to the *Marshalsea*-Prison where she remained very careless and negligent of her futer state, till she was carryed in a Wagon among the other Prisoners to *Kingstone-upon-Thames*, to be tried at the Assizes holden there for the County of *Surry*, which began on *Monday* the 8th of this instant *March*, and ended on *Thursday* 11th; where upon her Trial being asked what she could say for her self, she aledged she was not (*Compos Mentis*) but *Distracted* when she commited the horrid Fact; but Mr. *Fowler* and several others who saw her the Morning after the Fact was commited; deposed upon Oath that she was as at other times and they saw no Distraction in her whereupon not being able to make any farther Defence the Jury after having received their charge, brought her in guilty of Treason and Murther, the which in case of a Wifes Murthering her Husband, the Law implyes, after which she received the dreadful Sentence to be Burnt alive, and was conveyed to the Town Prison there to remain in order to her Execution, where during the intervene of the time allowed to make preparation for another World she seemed as it were stupified with the horror of guilt; sometimes she would applause her cruelty, saying, She did not repent her of what she had done, for he had brought her to want by his Extravagancies; and at other times she would fall out into a passion, and say, it was Gods just Judgement by suffering her to run into such evil to punish her for being so wicked to her first Husband whose Bed she had suffered the latter to defile whilst the former was alive; and that she had been a grievous Offender both against God and Man; not only the Minister of the Place, but several other pious and charitable Christians came often to visit her and give her Saving advice to prepare for Immortality, intimating that she had but a short time to live on Earth, and that Murther bore such a lasting Stain that nothing but the blood of her Sacred Redeemer could cleanse her poluted Soul, to which she answered she was sorry for the Murther, but were her Husband now alive she would rather be Burnt according to sentance than to live with him, and so continued sometimes resolute and sometimes Penitent till the Day appointed for her Exe-

Execution came; which was the 16th of this Instant *March*; when being brought out of the Prison, clad almost all in White to the Market Place, or Place appointed for Execution, were being fastened to a Stake, Three Loads of Fagots were piled that she seemed as one half dead; all that she was heard to say, was to desire the People to pray for her, and to take warning by her sad *End*; after her being there near half an hour, the Executioner set Fire to the Pile, which taking reduced the miserable Wretch. It is said during her Imprisonment she did what she could to be got with Child, thereby to respite her *Execution*, but her expectation failed her; for she proved not pregnant.

Eight more that received *Sentence* were Executed at the Gallows, being Hanged by their Necks, whose Names, Crimes and Behaviours were as followeth.

Mary Troth a Notorious Offender, who had been in several Roberys, and been once before Condemned for the same; having likewise been a Publick Seller of stolen goods, was taken from the Prison and carried to the place of Execution; she seem'd very obstinate, and not in the least concern'd for her latter End, till the very last when Death's approach made her relent to think how she was entring on a state she was so ill prepared for.

William Abbot was likewise Sentenced for that he Robed *Dover* Carryer in the middle of *Kent-street*, between Four and Five of the Clock in the Morning of Silks and other Goods to the vallue of 200 Pounds; he had been tryed at the *Old-Bayly* the last Sessions, and Condemned there, where he had obtained a Pardon for the particular Fact, for which he was there Condemned, but no other, so the Carryer appearing at the *Old Bayly* the Court Ordered him to Confess where the goods were, which he refusing he was Ordered to be sent to *King-stone* to be Tried there, and being Cast, this Day suffered; his Penitence was suitable in some measures to his many Crimes, for he was more then ordinary Penitent much bewailing his Crimes and desiring all to take warning by his sad downfall.

William

William Wyer and *John Bradshaw* were condemned for breaking open the House of one *William Turner* in *September* last, and stealing thence Cloath to a considerable vallue for which they were this day Executed and dyed with great penitency desiring the company assembled to view their fatal Ends, to direct their Prayers to Almighty God for their deliverence from a second Death.

Able Hamersly and *Thomas Saviourry* suffered for the same Fact as *Abbot* did, and were exceeding Penitent, it being thought it was the first Robery they ever committed.

Richard Wilson was Comdemned for that he in *February* last, broak open the House of one Mr. *Turner* in *Southwark*, and accordingly to Sentance was Executed.

The last in this fatal Tragedy, was *Edward Turner* for breaking the House of *Thomas Stainton* in *Barmondsey*-street, and steealing Linnen and wearing Apparel to the value of Five pounds, they were both very Penitent, as indeed they were for the most part heartily lamenting their woful conditions, and beging Pardon of God for their offences, after a short Prayer, they ended their lives.

LONDON, Printed by *D. Mallet*. 1681.

The True Relation Of The Tryals At the Sessions of Oyer and Terminer ... As particularly of Elizabeth Wigenton (Wing T3063) is reproduced with permission from the clear Harvard College Library copy. The text-block measures 125 × 243 mm.

THE True Relation OF THE TRYALS

At the Sessions of *Oyer* and *Terminer*,

Held for the City of *London*, County of *Middlesex*, and Goale Delivery of *Newgate*; which began in the *Old-Bailey* the 17th of this instant *January*, and ended the 18th of the same.

As particularly of

Elizabeth Wigenton

FOR

Whipping a Girl to Death at *Ratcliffe*.

And *John Peetly*, for shooting a Gentleman in *Queen-street*. Also the Account of the Proceedings with one *John Bully* a Popish Priest. The Number of the Condemned, Burnt in the Hand, and to be Whipped, with many other material Tryals.

THE Sessions began at the *Old-Bailey*, on Munday the 17th of this instant *January*, (being put off the Wednesday before, by reason of the sitting at *Guildhal*) where were these following proceedings. *Elizabeth Wigenton* of *Ratcliff* Parish, was Tryed for the Murther of a Girl about Thirteen years of age, which was her Apprentice, the manner of the Murder being thus: She being by Trade a Coat-maker, and having set the Girl upon a Piece of Work, she had not done it so well as she required; whereupon, she beat her grievously, the which not sufficing her cruel rage, she went and got a bundle of rods, (and a man to hold her) with which, after she had bound her, she whiped her so unmercifully, that the blood ran down like rain; yet could she not be perswaded to desist, till the Girl fainted away with crying, and of her unmerciful usage in a short time dyed. Upon her Tryal she pleaded little in her own defence, onely saying, that she did not think to kill her. So that it being proved that she had been a cruel Woman by all her Neighbours, she was found guilty of wilful Murther.

Katherine Neale was Tryed for stealing about Twenty yards of Persian Silk out of a Mercers shop, which being taken upon her, she was found guilty of the Felony.

A *Jane*

Jane Yong was likewise found guilty for stealing Linnen from a Gentlewoman in the Parish of *St. Spulchres*, to the value of nine shillings.

Jane Harding, a notorious Shop-lift, was Indicted for feloniously entring the House of *Will. Smith*, of the Parish of *Botolfes* without *Bishops-gate*, and stealing Goods to the value of eight shillings and six pence, of which she was found guilty.

Jonathan Telcoat received his Tryal, being Indicted for the Murther of an aged woman; but upon Evidence it was found, that the woman being troubled with Fits, he being in the room, hit her head upon an Iron, which gave her a wound, of which she dyed; so that his being there, caused this Indictment; but upon proof that he was not near her when she fell, he was Acquitted.

John Peetly Victualler, living in *Whetstones-park*, was Arrained and Tryed for the Murder of one Mr. *Gerard*, Nephew, as 'tis said, to my Lord *Gerard*; the circumstances of which, were these: The Party killed, with several other young Gentlemen, being late abroad, on the tenth of this instant in *Holborn*, took it in their way to come through *Whetstones-park*, where spying Lights in *Peetly*'s house, they knocked hard at the door, and bid him open it, the which he refusing, one or more of them, began to break the windows, and having Linkmen with them, they threw up lighted Links, the which, as *Peetly* said, did set fire to some Linnen in a Closet, at which he being Allarumed, got his Carbine in his hand, charged with small Bullets, and pursued them up great *Queen-street*, till they came to the upper end on't, where the standing Watch had stayed them, and caused them to deliver their Swords, whenas *Peetly* thrusting among the croud, was pushed by a Watchman, and thereupon his piece went off, and shot the aforesaid Gentleman in the Thigh, of which Wound he shortly dyed: but the Prisoner pleading that the Gun went off without his knowledge, he was Acquitted.

Richard Johnson, and *John Cooper*, two Chair-men, were Tryed for the Murder of one Mr. *Washborn*, whom they killed with excessive beating, on the second of *December*; the cause of quarrel was their rushing him with their empty Chair, against the rails of *Northumberland*-house, near *Charing-cross*; so that he striking them with his Cane, they fell upon him, and gave him so many bruises, that he dyed within twelve days after: wherefore they were Convicted of Man-slaughter, there being no proof that he struck them first.

John Oliver, a French-man, who could speak no English, was Indicted for breaking into a Chamber, at *Man*'s Coffee-house at *Charing-cross*, and taking thence a Ring, some Lace, and other small matters: he pretended, as his Interpreters said, that he went there only to sleep, when he was taken upon the stairs, but being searched, the things were found about him; but for want of the Constables Evidence, who searched him, he was found not guilty, by reason none gave Evidence against him in Court, or saw the things taken about him.

Anne Ditcher, received her Tryal for stealing forty yards of Serge, and a Campaigne Coat out of the Shop of one Mr. *Hatton* in *Drury-lane*; the Discovery of the Robbery was by a little Boy, who being taken upon suspition for hankering about the Shop; confessed that he knew where the Goods were, and that he would carry him to the place where they were sold, which he did, being at a Brokers in *Southwark*. The Broaker being questioned how he came by them, brought out the woman. Upon her Tryal she pleaded she had them of a man, but he not being produced, she was found guilty of the Felony.

Anne Carter was Tryed for Felony and Burglary; for that she on the 24th of *September*, about two of the clock in the morning, drawing up the Latch, entred the house of one *Magdalen Wooff*, and coming to her bed-side, took away her purse with eleven shillings in it, and departed, the Prosecutor not daring to hinder her for fear of her life: they gave very bad Characters of each other in Court, and railed at a high rate; but in fine, the prisoner was found guilty of the Felony.

Thomas

Thomas Boys was Indicted for stealing a Shirt, a Cravat, and a pair of worsted stockings; the which being confessed by him to have been stollen from one *Edward Steevens* of *Hounslow*, he was found guilty to the value of ten pence.

Dorothy Mathews, an old Shop-lift, was Tryed for stealing about a pound and half of Silk, and near sixty yards of Taffata Ribbon, and Ferrit, from one *Elizabeth Waite* in *Holborn*. She coming into the Shop on the 19th of *October*, there being onely a little Girl in it, demanded where her Mistress was? who told her, she was gone into *London*; whereupon, she desired to see some Ribbon, which the Girl shewed her, but none would please, till she had the box of Ribbon set before her, whenas one of her Accomplices coming in, and desiring to see some likewise, held the Girl busie, till she stole the Goods aforesaid; but ere she could make her escape, being apprehended and carried before a Magistrate, the Goods were found about her; so that the proof being plain, she was Convicted of the Felony.

Eleanor Cockman was Tryed as being accessary to the Murther of one *Smith*, who was shot by one *Orme*, since dead, by reason a Watch which appertained to the Deceased, was found in her custody; but she alleadging she found it in the pocket of the dead man, whose breeches she had to wash, delivered her by the hands of his friends, she was acquitted.

Jobe Laud was Tryed for stealing a Mare, appertaining to *William Gun*, the which he had afterwards sold to one *Church*; the bargain being made at the *George* in *Leather-lane*, the said *Church* being taken upon her back, as he was riding into the Countrey; but upon this Tryal, the party from whom she was stole not appearing, the prisoner was acquitted of the Fellony.

Frances Emington was Tryed for stealing about 600 weight of Red-wood from the Royal *African* Company, which was taken from on board a Lighter, lying in the River of *Thames*, the Hatches of the said Lighter being broken open in the absence of the Waiters. The wood being taken about a Month after, as he was conveying it by the help of Porters into *Thames street*, where he pretended he had sold it to a dry Salter; and did so far impose upon his Apprentice, as to lodge some of it in his house, he being gone into the Country; so that the Fellony being plainly proved, he was found guilty.

Blanch Thomas a servant-wench was Tryed and found guilty, for Robbing her Master *William Palmer* of *St. Martins in the fields*, of the Sum of Ten pounds, which his Wife had hid between the Mat and the bed; so that as she was making the bed she found it, and converted about three pounds of it to her own use, before they missed it; but she being apprehended for the same, delivered the other moiety. Her plea was, that she found it, and therefore imagined it was lawfully hers, but that weak excuse did not serve her turn.

Thomas Underthorp was Indicted for having Two Wives, *viz. Elizabeth Toogood*, whom he Marryed at *Dukes-place*; and *Dorothy Martin*, which he since Marryed in *Worcestershire*, with whom he had a competent Portion. Both the Marriages were proved against him by several persons, the former by the man that gave him in Marriage, and by several others, the latter by the Woman herself, who appeared in Court, the former not appearing, but upon proof she was alive, he was Convicted of the Felony.

John Bully, a Popish Priest, was brought to the Barr, and his Indictment read. To which he pleaded he had been Tried for the same Fact at *Lancaster*, in *August* last, and that he ought not to be Tryed twice for the same. But in that the Opinion of the Court over-ruled him, intimating, that this Indictment being laid for his being a Priest, in *October* last, he might since the former have taken Orders from the See of *Rome*. Whereupon he had dir ction

to

to get Council, and put in his Plea, and Time allowed him for that purpose; but when he was brought to the Bar again, he made a long Apology, alleadged as before: So that at his humble Request, the Court thought fit to continue him untried till next Sessions.

The Countess of *Portland* being brought into Court in her Sedan, having been a long time sick, desired to Traverse her Indictment for Recusancy, the which was allowed.

At this Sessions there were Nine Persons that received Sentence of Death; viz. *Katharine Nevil*, *Eliz. Wiginton*, *Anne Dicher*, *Anne Carter*, *Dorothy Mathews*, *Blanch Thomas*, *Philip Demerry*, *Tho. Wicks*, and *James Dixon*. Ten Burnt in the Hand. And Five to be Whipped.

FINIS

The Confession and Execution of Leticia Wigington (Wing W2110) is reproduced with permission from th clear Huntington Library copy. The text-block measures 128 × 243 mm.

The following words are a transcription of the original:

A1r.39 Rebecca Clifford

CONFESSION and EXECUTION
OF
Leticia Wigington
Of *Ratclif*, who suffered at
TYBURN,

On *Fryday* the 9th of this instant *September*, 1681. written by her own hand in the Goal of *Newgate*, two days before her death, being Condemned for whiping her Apprentice Girl to Death.

We are fully satisfied, that the following Paper was written by this unhappy womans own hand, a while before her Death, and though at her Tryal for this horrid Fact, the Evidence against her, was full, clear and undeniable, yea which is more, though she was then so ingenious to confess her self really guilty thereof, having lain so many Months in *Newgate*, we have very great reason to judg she has been too well acquainted with that cursed crew of Popish Priests and Jesuites, who it is to be feared have debauched her with their own damnable Principles, whereby they have perswaded her to deny what she before had so fully confessed, which she does in the very words of those Jesuites who lately deservedly suffered for Treason against his Majesty, &c. who though they were Tried and condemned (as well well as her self) upon the clearest Evidence imaginable, yet *Atheistically* even with their last Breath affirmed, *That they were as innocent as the Child unborn.*

Micah the 7th Chap. and 8 9. Verses.

Rejoyce not against me, O mine Enemy : when I fall, I shall arise ; when I sit in darkness, the Lord shall be a Light unto me.

I will bear the Indignation of the Lord, because I have sinned against him, until he plead my cause, and execute judgment for me : he will bring me forth to the Light, and I shall behold his Righteousness.

THis place of Scripture I made choice of, as being somewhat pertinent to the business, and troubles and afflictions that are inflicted on me, wherefore upon my bended Knees I humbly desire all you that have been my loving Neighbours and Friends, and all other good Christians, that have heard of this horrid and dreadful misfortune that hath befallen me, and you that shall read these doleful Lines, let pity move your hearts to read them, and you that have had any hand in taking away my Life wrongfully, I pray God forgive you all ; but let me admonish you not to abuse the dead by giving out your cruel speeches by me, as you have done in my Life-time (that never did you any harm) first to Imprison me wrongfully, and that not satisfying, but to prompt on one, that was my Apprentice, *Rebecka Clifford* by Name, who was not full 12 years of age, to swear against me, she not being sensible of the danger of taking a false Oath, so that you have used me at your pleasure: I speak to you all, Rich and Poor, great and small, that have had any hand in my Death, whoever you are, for you cannot be ignorant of the great evil you have done me, (a poor friendless Creature) for you have made it your business to take away my life, who am as innocent as concerning the Murder for which I suffer as the Child unborn : but why should I reflect upon my Innocence, and the abuses put upon

A

on

on me, who am a person full of sin and corruption, when our blessed Saviour who knew no sin, neither was Guilt found in him, and yet he was buffetted and spit on and falsly accused and crucified between two Thieves, and yet he took it patiently, and was led as a Lamb to the slaughter, and as a sheep before her Shearer is dumb, so opened he not his mouth, but took the Cup of his Fathers Indignation with chearfulness, and all this for the sins of poor lost Man, and therefore why should I think it a burden to take his Yoke upon me which is made to me both easie and light, oh no, for though I were to be torn Limb from Limb, or to be burned in flames, I could chearfully undergo it to meet my Lord and Saviour Jesus Christ, for this is my comfort in all my troubles that though you kill my Body, you cannot touch my pretious and immortal Soul, that is bound up in the bundle of Life, and I thank my God, that I have good assurance of everlasting happiness in another world, though I suffer a shameful and ignominious Death here, there is laid up for me a Crown of Glory which fadeth not away eternally in the Heavens, and if this be the way that my dear Redeemer hath ordained for me to obtain it, welcome, yea thrice welcome is that Rope which is to put a period to all my miseries and oppressions which have been very numerous and great, for I have been kept a prisoner now 8 Months, where I have lain upon the hard boards having nothing but bread and water, and no more than a penny-Loaf a day neither; and my Flesh black and blew with lying upon the boards for want of a Bed, and I can say with that blessed Man of old (*David*) I have watered the boards as I laid on with bitter Tears for my manifold sins and wickedness. For though the Lord did suffer Man to be so cruel to me, it was my sins was the cause that the Lord laid this Yoke upon me; but our Saviour hath said, *Come unto me all you that are weary and heavy laden, and I will give you rest*, which promise I can with comfort say, hath been made good to me, for though my body hath wanted Food and suffered great hardships, yet my Soul hath been fed with the bread of Heaven, for though I am here confined amongst a company of poor blind ignorant and gross sinners that have not the fear of God before their eyes, yet as the Bee sucks hony out of the worst of herbs and flowers, so I through hearing their horrid cursing and swearing, do the more throw my self at the Lords Feet with a true and faithful zeal in serving him night and day, with fervent Prayers, and never left wrestling with God, and crying with bitter Tears to the Lord, till I found his lively Faith springing in my Soul. I never left lying prostrated at the Lords Feet, beging Mercy for my poor Soul till I found some assurances of his Love and favour, and now I doubt not but that when the thred of my Life shall be cut off, my Soul will be received into that Glory which no Tongue can express, neither hath it entered into the heart of Man to conceive. The Lord hath wrought great works on me, and hath been very merciful to me, but if my Lord and Saviour had been so cruel as Men and Women have been to me, I had been ere this time burning in the Flames of Hell; wherefore I do here humbly beseech and exhort all that shall read this, that you serve the Lord with ferventness of Spirit, and cease not day nor night to power out your prayses to him, that he will subdue your sins in you and to ingraft his Grace in your hearts, the Lord hath many ways to bring them that are his, home to himself; and the Lord is minded this way to bring me to him, as to let my person to suffer this shameful Death, and to be a Spectacle to the World, and be scandalized in a very gross manner, but seeing it is the good Will and Pleasure of my Redeemer, to take me to himself this way, I take it as well as though I dyed in my Bed, and imbrace it with the more Joy, considering the great Conflict my dear Saviour suffered for me, O then, how sweet is this Death to me. I have lain in this horrid place ever since *Christmas* last, in which time I have not ceased day nor night to cry unto the Lord, for mercy on my poor Soul, and crying as the Jaylor did once to *Paul* and *Silas*, *What shall I do to be saved*, I thought when I was at Liberty that I did serve the Lord well in my Family, but now I find I was nothing but a filthy bag of Corruption, and came very short of any good performances, wherefore I do upon my bended Knees, and with floods of Tears as being the last request of a dying Woman, humbly beseech all Masters and Mistresses of Families (that shall read this, that you will be careful and diligent in performing Family-duties, and to pray with ferventness amongst them that are under your care and tuition, knowing that if through your neglect any of them be lost, the Lord will require them at your hands.

I do think it my Duty (and I doubt not but it will be matter of satisfaction to some, who are my friends) to declare unto them the whole circumstance of the thing for which I am to suffer, and I do here in the presence of Almighty God, who knows the secrets of all hearts (and knows my innocence) declare nothing but the real truth, which is as follows, *viz.*

As for this *John Sadler*, I never saw him in all my Life, but a Week before he came to Lodge at my House, and that was at one *Ann Thornby's* House, and she told me, That he was a very Civil Man, and his Wife a very Honest Woman, and she asked me, Whether they should Lodge at my House? And I poor Creature, with the advice of *Elisabeth Holton*, (who was Aunt to the Girl, that was Murdered by this unfortunate Lodger *John Sadler*,) took them to Lodge in my House, by reason I had a great Charge, and an unkind Husband, who left his Ship and Living, and I having three small Children to keep, I poor silly Woman thought that I might maintain them the better with the Monny, that I should have for their Lodging, paying me but one shilling a Week, as to buy my Dear Babes bread, and to feed my two Apprentices as never got me half their Bread; but with one groat more than the shilling found us all Bread. This *John Sadler* was a Sea-man, and he and a Water-man, was a runner of Goods, and he used to have hot Victuals every day, and with dressing of my Victuals and some small releif of them by their Victuals, made me let them Lodge at my house: but I call God to be my Witness, that I did not know, but that they were Man and Wife, but as for that Sin they were Guilty of it, and not I, but since I was imprisoned here in this horrid place, I heard by *John Sadlers* Sister, that they were not Man and Wife, but that lyes at their own Door, therefore people have been very cruel to me in giving out such gross Lies of me, as to say, that I lay with *John Sadler*, and that I was a VVhore to others before; and upon no other grounds, but only by reason I did plead my Belly, which thing I was advised to, after I came into this place, that so I might save my Life. But do here in the presence of Almighty God declare, that I was never in all my Life Guilty of the horrid Sins of Adultery or Fornication, for I ever all my Life, thought that if I should be Guilty of them Sins, that I should be Damned to all Eternity, I do not speak this to justifie my self out of a Vain-glorious way, for I do confess, that I have been a great Sinner, but as for that Sin I did ever abhor it in all my Life, and should I have slandered any person in that manner, I should have feared that the Lord would have shown some heavy Judgment upon me immediately, besides the woe that is pronounced against Liers and Slanderers: and as for the Girl that Swore against me, I wish one would reason the Case with her to know whether she thinks that I am Guilty when I am Dead and gone, for she knows that *John Sadler* did this Evil, and hath given an account for his Sins, I came up when he was beating the Girl, and asked him, What he did? and she knows that when the Girl was Dead, he would have condescended to have me Bury the Girl, and he would have bought a Crape Mourning Suit and a Coffin, he said this to me, and Mris. *Thornby*, I told him, No, as for what he had done, I knew not, but I would have him go before a Justice to Answer what he had done; upon these Words, he turned to *Ann Thornby*, and the Woman who pretended she was *Sadlers* Wife, for she was by all the time, that this Man did the Murder, and then I sent the Girl to one Mr. *Robert Acton* to call him, to come and bring other Neighbours to carry this Man before a Justice, but Mris. *Acton* sent one *Thomas Millner* his Man, while this Man and the Girl was coming, this *Ann Thornby* came and told me, that her Mother and her Partner which were the Searchers, would yield to give it in that the Girl did dye a Natural Death, but I said, that I would not be Guilty of that for all the World, then this *Ann Thornby*, asked me, Where the Girl was gone, I said, to call Mr. *Acton* then said she, let me out, for I will not see him, whereupon I being almost half Distracted, I opened the Door a little, for fear *John Sadler* should make his escape; but this *Ann Thornby* clapped her Foot against the Door and ran away, and bid him run for his Life, with that, I ran and caught him by the Hair; and then the Girl and *Thomas Millner* came and found me strugling with him, and I told this young Man all that had hapned to me; and this *John Sadler*, told him, how that I was clear, and how that he would perswade me to let him Bury it, but I said no, I would have him before a Justice, then came the Woman his Wife, and *Ann Thornby's* Mother, and would fain have him be gone away with them; but I said he should not stir till he had went before a Justice, with that he said, he would go up Stairs and fetch his Gloves, and he went up and Leapt out at the Window, but I seeing the lower Window darkned, I looked up and saw him Leap out at the Window; and I run out and Cryed out, Murder, Murder, and Thieves after him, *Thomas Milliner*, and *Ann Thornly*, and the Woman as Swore to me, that *John Sadler* was her Husband, and *Ann Thornby*'s Mother were by when this *John Sadler* made his escape; and when I came in from crying out Murder and Theives after him, I thought to have kept her, but when I came in they were all gone, and this way I am cheated of my Life; for the Man ran a private way up a place which is in *Ratcliff* called the *Orchard*, and being Christmass-day towards the Evening and people were not abroad in the Streets, and I went to Mr. *Atkins*, and to Mris. *Mills*, and to Mr. *Eltons* the Apothecary, and made my Complaint, and from thence to the Girls Aunt to tell her what was befallen me, and that I had not taken these Lodgers in, but that she perswaded me to let them Lodge in my House. But they were dear Lodgers to me and mine, and to the Girl that is deceased, and when I was at *Elisabeth Heltons* House, which is the Girls Aunt, one *Gardom* a Bailiff, one as I think a little fears the Lord, caused me to be taken and brought to this horrid place, or else I had been an Evidence against *John Sadler*; and this Girl which Swore against me, *Rebecka Clifford*, Cryed by me and said, She knew that I was innocent from the Fact, for which I now dye, to the World, but shall Live in the Lord for ever; this is the whole Truth, and the last Words of a dying Woman, who truly and senserely feares the Lord of Heaven and Earth, and I could heartily wish I were as free from Committing of all other Sins, as I am of that Murder, Adultery and Fornication or Swearing, four things which I was never guilty of in my Life, though I must confess I have been a great Sinner, but I am assured, that they are washed away in the Blood of that Immaculate Lamb, which was shed to take away the Sins of all them that truly & sinserely repent, but the Lord suffered this great affliction to fall on me to draw me nearer to himself, for whom the Lord loveth he Chastiseth, even as a Father the Son in whom he delighteth, I desire all good Christians to Judge Charitably of this my Speech, and not to think that I Pen this to justifie my self; but I desire to condemn my self, that I may be Justified by my dear Redeemer: but I do this to satisfy all that are my Friends, that I dye in the faith and fear of my Creator and Redeemer; who shall change my vile body, that it may be like his glorious Body, and one chief Reason of my penning this, is to satisfy my dear Husband, whom I ever loved dearer then any thing in this World, but when he heard, that I pleaded my Belly, he was incenced against me by wicked people, who incensed him, that I was disloyal to him, and that scandal which was raised by them hindered him from coming to me, though I had not seen him in almost two years, and unkind Friends at *Deal*, kept the Letter from him which I sent, so that my Life as to this World was lost through the Treachery of unkind Friends, but as to the eternal State never more sure then now; my Husband did send up some Mony about Whitsuntide last to get my Reprieve, but but being informed that I was with Child, ordered it back again, which was occasioned by the Malice of wicked people, who did not care what scandals they did raise upon me, I pray God forgive them, and lay not this Sin to their charge, and as for the Girl that Swore against me and was the cause of my dying this shameful Death, though as innocent as the Child unborn, I pray God to forgive her, and let not my innocent Blood be required at her hands, though she hath been the cause of all this, my great Tryal and afflictions, and without the great Mercy of God, the ruins of my three poor Children, who I am afraid will be bound to curse her, but the *Lord* hath promised to be a Father to the Fatherless, and to see the needy and oppressed to have right, and as for them whoever they were that did make Ballads and Books upon me, after I was brought to *Newgate*; and raised great scandal and ignominy, and added grief to my Afflictions, I pray God forgive them all, and my dear *Husband* for giving Credit to their slanderous Reports, and not to be so kind as to come and know the Truth of the whole matter, *I* do here in the presence of Allmighty God declare, that *I* dye as innocent of the Crime for which my Body suffers, as the Child yet unborn, and *I* can truly say, that *I* am in Charity with all the Wrold, and do conclude with that excellent prayer of the Litany. That it may please the to forgive my Enemies persecutors and Slanderers, and to turn their *Hearts*; *I beseech thee to hear us good Lord.*

LONDON, Printed for *Langley Curtiss*, on *Ludgate-hill*.

A Hellish Murder Committed by a French Midwife On the Body of her Husband (Wing H1384) is reproduced with permission from the clear Huntington Library copy. The text-block measures 87 × 140 mm.

The following words are a transcription of the original:

6.3	French Midwife, living in Castle-Street
6.4	her: the
6.5	as she
6.28	Mistress went
9.3	one Yard
9.6	Ask'd What the matter was?
9.21	by her own Hands
17.1	The Enformation of Joan Rippault
17.10	him, dans l'Esgoust
17.11	Shore
17.29	her if she
24.2	St. Giles's Bone-
24.7	Ant. Matson.
24.20	Giles Malvault.

A

Hellish Murder

Committed by a

French Midwife,

On the Body of her

HUSBAND,

Jan. 27. $168\frac{7}{8}$.

For which she was Arraigned at the *Old-Baily*, *Feb.* 22. $168\frac{7}{8}$. and Pleaded *GUILTY*.

And the Day following received Sentence to be BURNT.

LONDON,

Printed for *R. Sare*, at *Grays-Inn-Gate*, and published by *Randal Taylor*, near *Stationers-hall*. 1688.

Introduction.

THE late Barbarous Murder of Denis Hobry, (what with Malice, Prejudice, Credulity and Mistake) has put more Freaks and Crotchets into the Heads and Minds of the Common People, then any Story of that size perhaps ever did in this World before: But as Fancy, Error and Invention, have No Bounds in the matter of Number and Variety; so with a respect to the Quality of These Extravagancies, it would be no less Frivolous, on the Other side, to Encounter the Passions, and the Dreams of the Multitude with Formalities of Councel and Reason: for the Exceptions are too Many to be taken Severally to pieces, and they are too Trivial (even all together) to be worth the while of a Serious Thought. And yet how Vain, and how Impossible soever, a Full, and a Distinct Answer to so many Spiteful and Groundless Shams and Misunderstandings, may appear to be; there is something yet to be done, methinks; (though but in a Complement to Common Curiosity and Satisfaction) and the shortest way of clearing all Difficulties, will be to Publish to the World a Plain and a Naked Narrative of this whole Affair; as it is Delivered, and set forth in the Informations Themselves, that have been given in Evidence upon This Cause; which I can the better undertake, for, in regard that they have all pass'd through My Hands. This Course will settle all People Right, that have a Mind to be set Right; and there's no better way in Nature to Rectify the Misapprehensions of Things, than by setting forth Matter of Fact just as it WAS; which at the same time, serves to Prove unanswerably how it was NOT. Only a word or two of Introduction by the way.

Upon the first Rumour of this Horrible Murder, there were Two Journey-men Joyners taken up, and Committed, upon

Suspicion of having laid the Body where 'twas found; but they prov'd themselves upon Enquiry, to be very Honest Men. 'Tis true They passed that way, They were seen thereabouts; Witnesses Examin'd: and Unhappy Circumstances enow for a Ground of Jealousie: But afterwards, upon the Seizure of the Midwife, and unquestionable Proofs against her, (beside her Own and her Sons Confession) the Coroners Inquest Met, according to an Adjournment, and sat upon the Body, Feb. 8. 1687. where they acquitted Mary Potron, and the Two Joyners; but Mary Hobry (the Midwife) was found Guilty of the Murder of Denis Hobry, as Principal; and John Desermeau (the Midwifes Son) was found Accessary after the Fact.

At Hicks-Hall, Mary Hobry had a Bill found against her, Feb. 21. 1687. for Petty-Treason and Murder, as Principal; and on her Arraignment the same Day at the Old Baily, she Pleaded GUILTY; but the Court with all possible Tenderness, let her know the Danger and the Consequence of her Confession, and offer'd her yet the Liberty to Depart from her Plea, and take her Tryal, if she thought fit; but she still Persisted in her Confession.

There was, after this, Another Bill found at Hicks-Hall on the same Day, against Denis Favet, and John Favet, (French-men, and Brothers) as Accessories before and after the Fact; and likewise against John Desermeau (the Son of the said Midwife) as Accessory after the Fact.

Upon their Tryal at the Old-Baily, they were All found NOT GUILTY: But the Matter had such a Face however, that the Court thought fit to put the Two Brothers to find Sureties for their Good Behaviour.

The Womans Confession has Prevented the Publick Notification of the Foulness of the Cause, that would otherwise have been made, by a Printed Account of the Tryal. So that it remains only to supply that Disappointment by True Copies of the Following Enformations, which would have been the Foundation at last (in case she had put her self upon her Defence) for the Court to Proceed upon.

THE

Midd. & West. } *The Enformation of* James Richards *of the Parish of St.* Margarets Westminster, Victualler, *taken upon Oath*, Feb. 3. 168⅞.

SAITH, That this Enformant being in Company about Four or Five a Clock in the Afternoon, Yesterday, with Mr. *Yard*, and another Person; there was a Discourse about the Dead Body that was lately found; whereupon Mr. *Yard* was saying, that there was a Friend of his missing, and that he was affraid, *This was the Man*; having heard his Wife Often say, that *she would Murther him*, or *Dispatch him*, or to that Effect. This Enformant thereupon putting it to the said *Mr. Yard*, if he could make good what he said; Whose Answer was, that he could make it good; Upon which, this Enformant advis'd the getting of an Officer to Apprehend the Woman; The Third Person Answering, that to Morrow-morning would be time enough. But this Enformant said, it was a Case would bear no Delay, and that therefore he was resolv'd to Enform with all speed; to which they Agreed: And this Enformant going then out of the Room, *Mr. Yard* follow'd, and told this Enformant, that *the Thing was too true, and that the said Woman had told him as much*; but Promised within some few Days to tell him more. Upon this, the Enformant got a Constable, and went as an Assistant to the Apprehending of the Woman, whom they found at a House in *Phenix-Alley*, and so she was taken into Custody; and Committed.

Jurat' Die & Anno supradict. coram me Roger L'Estrange. James Richards.

B Midd.

Midd. & West. } *The Enformation of* Philip Yard *of St.* Martins in the Fields, *Cook, taken upon Oath*, Feb. 3. 168$\frac{7}{8}$.

SAith, That this Enformant becoming known to the Family, and to the Person of *Dennis* Hobry in *Paris*, many Years since; and having of late been several times in his Company here in *England*, where his Wife (a Midwife) was present, became also known to the said Midwife, whom this Enformant hath heard within the Compass of *Two Months last past* (speaking upon a modest Recollection of his Memory) menacing and reviling the said *Dennis Hobry* more then *Forty several times*, Calling him *Dog, Drunken Villain*, and other the Fowlest Words of Reproche; And saying over and over upon several Occasions, *I must kill him, and will kill him, though I be Hang'd for't*, speaking the Words in *French, C'est un Chien; C'est un Yvrogne*, &c. *Il faut que Je le Tue, quoy que Je devrois estre pendue.*

And saith particularly, That upon *Thursday in the last Week*, about *Two or Three a Clock in the Afternoon*, being at the House where her Daughter Lodges, she the said Midwife took occasion to fall into a Violent Passion against her Husband, and brake out into Passions of Threatning to *Kill* him, in manner as above recited.

And saith, That on the Day mentioned in the Paragraph next above, the Wife of *Hobry*, breaking into Violences of Discourse as abovesaid, desired this Enformant to take *No Notice of any thing she had said, whatever should happen*. This Enformant demanding, what she meant by that Thing that he was not to take Notice of: She reply'd, of her calling her Husband *Ill Names*, and the like.

And saith, That Three or four days after what is abovesaid, this Enformant went to the Lodgings of the said *Hobry*, and Ask'd where he was; they made Answer, they had not

seen

ſeen him for ſeveral Days. This Enformant reflecting at that Time upon the Bloudy Menaces of this Woman toward her Husband, of the *Thurſday before*; And that this Enformant could hear no Tydings of the ſaid *Hobry* among All his Acquaintance; This Enformant had an Apprehenſion within himſelf, that ſhe might have done him a Miſchief.

On *Wedneſday Morning*, being the *Next Day*, this Enformant went again to the Lodging of the ſaid *Hobry*, to Enquire after him, and hearing no News of him yet, this Enformant Advis'd them to open the Door, for fear he might have carry'd ſome of the Goods into *France*. But the People of the Houſe would not open the Door, becauſe the Midwife that Lodg'd there had the Key.

This Enformant went the ſame Day to the Lodgings of the ſaid Midwife's Daughter, where the Mother there waited for an Opportunity of ſpeaking with her in Private, and took the Occaſion at laſt to go out of the Lodgings with her; and walking in the Street. This Enformant ſaid after this manner to the ſaid Midwife, *Heark ye; You ſpoke dangerous Words t'other day concerning what you'd do to your Husband; Have you done as you ſaid you would? For the People have been looking every where after him, and there's no ſuch Man to be found: I hope 'tis not the mangled Body that they talk of to be murther'd. No* (ſays ſhe) *'tis not that Body*. This Enformant ſaid further to her, *Why, how could you go to Work to Diſpatch a Man that you are not able to Grapple with? Oh*, (ſays the Woman) *he put me hard to't: but I won't tell you to day; 'tis not a thing to be talk'd off in the Street:* This Enformant replying, *Why, We ſpeak* French; *No body underſtands us. Well!* (ſays ſhe) *Let it alone for Five or Six Days, and I'le tell you.* This Enformant preſſing her again to tell him, till ſhe Swore ſhe would not.

And ſaith, That the ſaid Midwife going toward *Phœnix-Alley* in *Long-Acre*, where this Enformant left her, ſhe the ſaid Midwife ſaid to this Enformant in *French*, *Bouche Clos*; or in *Engliſh*, *Not a Word*.

Jurat' Die & Anno ſupradict. coram me — *Philip Yard.*

Roger L'Eſtrange.

Midd. & Weſt. } *The Enformation of* Julian Coze, *of the Pariſh of St.* Annes Weſtminſter, Gardner, *taken upon Oath*, Feb. 9. 168 7/8.

SAith, That being in Company upon *Thurſday* Laſt in the Evening with one *Yard* a *French-man*, he the ſaid *Yard* told this Enformant, that *he would never ſee the* Pariſian *more*, (ſpeaking of *Dennis* Hobry.) This Enformant asking him, *What made him ſay ſo?* To whom *Yard* replyed, that Hobry's *Wife had told him as much*: Whereupon this Enformant reflecting upon the manner of ſpeaking, and upon Hobry's being from his Houſe for ſome time, and no News of him, He this Enformant propos'd the charging of a Conſtable with her, which was done that Night accordingly; and this Enformant was Aſſiſtant to the Seiſure of the ſaid Mrs. Hobry.

Jurat' Die & Anno ſupradict. coram me — *Julian Coze.*

Roger L'Eſtrange.

Midd.

Midd. & West. } *The Enformation of* Henry Fuller, *of St.* Margarets Westminster, *taken upon Oath* Feb. 17. 168 7/8.

SAith, That being told by *James Richards* a *Victualler*, in *Long-Ditch*, that there were *Two Frenchmen* at the said *Richard's* House, that were speaking something about the *Murther'd Body*; and that one of them said, *the Woman, suspected for the Murther, had as good as Own'd it*; This Enformant being in the Office of a Constable, agreed with the said *Richards* to go to the Lodgings of the said Woman, and Apprehended her upon the Suspicion: Whereupon, *This Enformant*, and the said *Richards*, taking one *Philip Yard* along with them, and another Person then in the Company, went to the House where the said Woman Lodg'd, but missing her at Home, went according to Direction to the *Last* in *Phœnix-Alley*, where they took her into Custody. This being betwixt Eleven and Twelve at Night, upon the *Second* of this Instant *February*: And not finding a Justice of Peace up, Deliver'd her up to the *Gate-House* 'till next Morning.

Jurat. Die & Anno supradict. coram me — *Hen. Fuller.*

Roger L'Estrange.

The Enformation of Christopher Austin, *of St.* Pauls Covent-garden, *Shoe-maker, taken upon Oath*, Feb. 3. 168 7/8.

SAith, That being the Servant of *John Yzember*, (or some such Name) a Shoe-maker living at the *Golden Shooe* in *Phœ-*

nix.

nix-Alley, *Long-Acre*; the Mistress of this Enformant being ready to fall in Labour, sent her Prentice *Richard* to a *French Midwife*, living in *Castle-street*, to come and Assist her; the said *French Midwife* coming to the Mistress of this Enformant, and she not presently falling in Labour as she expected, she desir'd the Midwife to stay that Night with her, for she did not know how things might fall out. The Midwife staid accordingly, and went away the next morning; this was some Day last Week, but this Enformant doth not remember what part of the Week. The Midwife aforesaid came several times after this, to enquire how it was with this Enformants Mistress; and particularly, came *Last Night* to the House, and Supp'd there, and desir'd to Lodge there, because she did not know what Occasion there might be for her: This Enformants Mistress agreeing that she should be there that Night: The Midwife went accordingly to Bed toward *Eleven a Clock*. There came a Constable to the Door, just about the Watch crying *Eleven*; when *Richard*, this Enformants Fellow-Prentice, Ask'd *Who was there?* To which, no Answer being return'd, this Enformant call'd again and again, *Who's there? If you do not Answer, you shall not come in.* Upon this a *French-man* ask'd in *English*, if *Madame*, meaning the Midwife, *was within?* but this Enformant doth not remember the Name. Upon this, the said *Richard* above-spoken of, spake in *French* to the *French Midwife*, and told her, that somebody call'd for her to go to a Womans Labour; whereupon the Midwife went up to this Enformants Mistress to fetch the Keys: So this Enformants Mistress went down along with the Midwife, the said Midwife desiring that *Richard* might go along with her, and carry a Light. Upon this, the Boy got up, and the Midwife opened the Door; a *French-man* entering first, and bidding the Constable come in; who, upon coming in, shew'd his Staff, the Midwife seeming Surpriz'd. Hereupon, one of the *French-men* ask'd the *Midwife*, *Where her Husband was?* who Answer'd, that *she left him in Bed last Thursday*; the *French-*

man

man Answering, that *if she left him in Bed, it was with his Arms and Legs cut off*: The *Midwife*, upon these Words, deliver'd up her self before they lay'd Hands of her, and Desir'd them to make No Noise, but to go Civilly along with her. This Enformants Mistress Then did bid *Richard* ask *what the Matter was?* To which, a *Frenchman* made Answer, that he would swear, that she walk'd up and down the Room when she had Cut off one Limb, and then Cut off the rest in her own Bed. Upon giving an account hereof to this Enformants Mistriss, the Constable Commanded the *Frenchman* Last above mention'd to Assist in Carrying her away; This Enformants Mistress giving order for a Piece of Link to Light them along. And upon Discourse among them, the *Frenchman* that Spake of what he could swear, told the Midwife that he was taken upon Suspicion, and that if he were Call'd, he must *Impeach* her, and tell the *Truth*: The abovesaid *Richard*, speaking to This Enformant of some *Bloud* in the *Bed*, by which it was discover'd.

And saith, That the Prentice, *Richard* before spoken of, said to This Enformant, That This Murther if 'twere Twenty Year would be found out at Last, and This in the Hearing of the Midwife, who made No Answer. And the said *Richard* told This Enformant further; That his Master saying in the Hearing of the Midwife, that if he knew who it was that did it, he would be the first that should tell on't, adding that he never heard of such a thing in his Days; Hereupon the Midwife said, *she saw the Limbs brought from the* Savoy *in a Sack*.

This Enformants Mistress upon the hearing of the Story gave Hard words to the Midwife, and call'd her *Villaine*, saying if she had Imagin'd such a Thing she should never have come within her Doors.

And

And moreover, that the Prentice abovemention'd, told This Enformant that he Heard the said *Frenchman* say, that she had formerly Threatn'd to kill her Husband.

Jurat Die & Anno supra-dict' Coram me

Ro. L'Estrange.

The Mark of C *Christ. Austen.*

Midd. & West. } *The Enformation of* Richard Kirkham *Servant to* John Yzember, *Shoemaker of the Parish of* Covent Garden, *Taken upon Oath*, Feb. 168$\frac{7}{8}$.

SAith, That a *French Midwife* passing by the Name of *Madam Desermean*, came Last Night to the House of This Enformants Master, stayd Supper there, and was to have Lodg'd there; and That This Enformant heard his Mistress say, That the said Midwife desir'd she might stay there All Night; being Under some Disappointment at home.

When the Key of the Street-Door was Taken out, and About the Hour of Eleven, there was a knocking at the Door; And an Enquiry after a *French Midwife*, Naming the Person; and This Enformant said she was There: And upon Further Discourse, the Person at the Door said he came from one Mrs. *Richards* in *Shandois Street*. The *French* Woman Scrupled at going to Strangers; but however she would Fetch the Key; And being come down, and one of the Persons that knocked being let into The House, the *French Midwife* would have had this Enformant to go before, to see what was the matter. This Enformant went to the Door then, with one *Richards*, being one of those that knocked at the Door, who immediately made a

Sign

Sign, and a Conſtable and two others came in; and upon their Entry, One ask'd, *which it was?* To which, a *Frenchman*, one *Yard*, replyed, *This is the Woman*, pointing to the Perſon: Whereupon the Conſtable ſhew'd his Staff, and took her into Cuſtody. This Enformants Miſtreſs being Frighted at this, Ask'd *What the matter was?* To which the Midwife replyed, *Quelque Drollerie*. Or in *Engliſh*, *Some little Waggery*. This Enformant's Miſtreſs preſſing more and more to know the Bus'neſs: And ſome body asking the Midwife *Where her Husband was?* She made Anſwer, that *ſhe had not ſeen him ſince the* Thurſday *before, when ſhe left him in* Bed. And being asked, *If ſhe had not ſeen him ſince?* She ſaid, *No*. and, in *French*, that he was a Vagabond, and ſhe knew nothing of his ways, or to that Effect. It was Reply'd, *She muſt find him out*: And her Anſwer was, *How ſhould ſhe find him out, that did not ſee him once in ſix Months?* One of the *French-men* made Anſwer, *that he would be found*: This Enformants Miſtreſs asking thereupon, (as miſtruſting the Bus'neſs) *Where he was, or what was become of him?* Some One of the *French-men* replying, that *he was dead and cut in pieces*; and that *by her own Hands in her own Room, and in her own Bed*. This Enformants Miſtreſs ſpeaking furiouſly to her, *Traitreſſe*: *Que vous ayez Commiſe une Crime ſi Noire! Traitreſs that thou art to be Guilty of ſo black a Crime!* No, *Madam*, (ſays ſhe) *I am Innocent*; And ſo they Carry'd her away; and at Parting, *Well*, (ſaid this Enformant's Miſtreſs) *I believe I ſhall never ſee you more*.

Jurat. Die & Anno ſupradict. coram me.

The Mark of R *Rich. Kirkham*.

Ro. L'Eſtrange.

Midd. & West. } *The Enformation of* John Izember, *of the Parish of St.* Pauls Covent-Garden, *taken upon Oath*, February 3. 168 7/8.

SAith, That this Enformant hath known a *French Midwife*, by the Name (to the best of this Enformants memory) of *Desermeau*, for about five years last past, she having laid this Enformants Wife of several Children.

And saith, that about Ten or Twelve Days since, the Wife of this Enformant sent for the said Midwife, being, as she thought, ready to fall in Labour. The Midwife came accordingly, and the Wife of this Enformant desired her to stay all Night, to see the Event of that Illness: She stay'd, but the next morning this Enformant's Wife finding her self better, the Midwife went away, but came day by day afterward to Enquire how 'twas with her.

And saith, That the said Midwife came Last Night to the House of this Enformant, saying, that she did not care for lying at home that Night; and so she Supp'd with this Enformant, whose Wife told him, that she had agreed she should Lodge there that Night. About Eleven a Clock, the Midwife came up to this Enformants Wife, and ask'd her for the Key of the House; saying, that there was some body knock'd to call her to a Womans Labour; but she did not know the Voice, and had a mind to see who it was: This Enformants Wife thereupon going down with her to open the Door. After which, this Enformants Wife

Wife told this Enformant, that the Midwife said I do not care to go Alone with that Man, (speaking of one of the Company) Pray let your Servant go along with me. Upon this, a *French-man* that was already Enter'd the House, call'd in the Constable. And this Enformant, upon the Subject matter of this Clause, refers himself to the Testimony of his Wife, from whom this Enformant had the Relation.

Jurat. Die &

Anno supra- *Jean Izember.*

dict. coram me

Ro. L'Estrange.

Midd. & West. } *The Enformation of* Mary, *the Wife of* Tobias Hope, *of the Parish of St.* Martins *in the Fields, Sawyer, taken upon Oath,* Feb. 3. 1687/8.

SAith, That a *French* Midwife, of whose Name this Enformant cannot give a perfect Account, Lodg'd in the House of this Enformant for about Three Months last past; And that within the Compass of that time, (but the precise time uncertain) a Person that the said Midwife said was her Husband, came and Lodg'd with her, and went (as this Enformant was told) into *France*, about a Month or Six Weeks since, (to this Enformants best memory;) And that he return'd again to the House of this Enformant about Three Weeks since; and that this Enformant hath not taken

Notice of his Lodging in the House for about Ten or Twelve Days since.

But that some time last Week, this Enformant Ask'd the said Midwife how it came to pass that he did not Lodge in the House, and where he was. The Midwife's Daughter, in the Presence of the Mother, telling this Enformant, that he heard there was a Warrant out against him, and he durst not come; saying further, that *he was to go with a Lord into* New England *for Three Years:* And the Daughter saying, that *her Husband did Work for that Lord*, and that her Husband would give the said Midwife's Husband *Thirty Shillings* to Cloath him, and 'twould be a good Riddance of him. The Daughter Adding, that the Mother should keep out of the Way till he was gone. And the Mother likewise came *Yesterday morning* to the House of this Enformant, and said, that *Now he was gone, for which she was Glad with all her* Heart, *and that she came now to Lodge there again.*

And saith, That the Midwife and her Daughter came to this Enformants House upon *Last Tuesday morning*, and paid this Enformant Eight Shillings in part of Rent; and the Mother desir'd this Enformant to let her have a pair of Sheets; but this Enformant put her off 'till Saturday, and she rested contented.

At the Time next above mentioned, this Enformant Asked the Midwife and her Daughter, whether they had seen the murther'd Body? The Midwife replyed, *No, No, she did not love any such Sights.* This Enformant taking Notice of a very outragious Quarrel betwixt them, Advis'd the Woman to have a care what she did to her Husband, being affraid it might go further. The Enformant refers her

her ſelf upon the Particulars above, to the beſt of her Memory.

Jurat. Die & Anno ſupradict: coram me

Ro. L'Eſtrange.

The Mark of
Y
Mary Hope.

The Enformation *of* Elizabeth Beech, *the Daughter of* Mary Hope *above-mentioned.*

THis Enformant ſaith upon Oath, That the whole matter in the above-written Enformation of her Mother is true to her Knowledge.

And ſaith, that there is a Lock put on to a Back-Door of a Low Room where the Midwife Lodg'd, which had only a Bolt before; and that this Enformant knew nothing of it till this morning.

Jurat. Die & Anno ſupradict. coram me

Ro. L'Eſtrange.

The mark of
E
Elizabeth Beech.

Midd. & West. } *The Enformation of* Maria Anne Rippault *the Wife of* Claude Royer, *of the Parish of* St. Giles's in the Fields, *Goldsmith, Taken upon Oath,* Feb. 20. 168 7/8.

SAith, That This Enformant was told about a Fortnight or Three Weeks before the Murther of *Hobry* was spoken of, that the said *Hobry* was returnd out of *France*; about which time, the reputed Wife of *Hobry*, came to the Lodgings of This Enformant, and Discoursed to This Enformant in the Presence of this Enformants Mother to the Effect following. *Mon Coquin de Mary est encore Une fois Revenu de France*; and in *English, This Rogue My Husband is come back out of* France *again. My Cousins are stark mad upon't, but we have Complotted*, or laid our Heads together, *how to get quit of him.* This Enformant replying, *why, what will You do? How will You get quit of him?* the other making Answer, You shall hear more of That 'ere it be Long. And so she went her way.

And This Enformant being Interrogated, if she had had any Discourse formerly with the Wife of *Hobry* concerning the *Cousins* before spoken of; she maketh This Answer, That the said Wife of *Hobry* having Assisted This Enformant about five or six Months since, in the Office of a *Midwife*; among other Discourses said to This Enformant to the Purpose following, *These Cousins of Mine are good Husbands, and Industrious Men, and there are enow would Marry them, but we will keep them to our selves, for My self and my Daughter.* (who both of them had Husbands at the same time.) This Enformant Asking her *how she could think of Marrying Those Young Fellows to her Self and her Daughter, when they had*

had Husbands already? The Wife of *Hobry* replying, *Oh Never Trouble your self for that: J'ay des ruses de diable pour nous en defaire*; In *English*, *I will find out as many Tricks as the Devil himself but wee'le get quit of him.* This Enformant being at that Time Indispos'd, doth not recollect any thing further Material in that Discourse.

But This Enformant saith further, That the Wife of *Hobry* came to This Enformants Lodgings upon *Thursday next after the finding of the Body*, about four or five a Clock in the Afternoon, with the Younger of the *Two Cosins* before spoken of, whose Name, as This Enformant remembers, is *Favet*: This Enformant asking the said Woman, *He bien! vous vous estes desfaite donc de vostre Mary*; In *English*, *Well! You have got quit of Your* Husband *then?* The Woman Answer'd *Ouy*: and the *Yong* Favet (or *Cosin*) stood a little while, *Pale*, and *Surpriz'd*, but recovering Himself: *Ouy* (*dit il*) *nous l' avons envoyée aux Maroquins*; *&* *quand il reviendra il nous apportera des Diamands*; In *English*, *Yes* (says he) *we have sent him into the* Indies, *and when he comes back again he will bring us Diamonds*; speaking the words *Smiling*, and in a way of *Raillery*. And hereupon, the Wife of *Hobry* and *Young* Favet being about to go away, This Enformant ask'd them *whether they were going?* The Woman made Answer, *We are going* Home, speaking of the House where *Hobry* Lodg'd.

And further saith, That upon *Thursday above mentiond*, about Eleven or Twelve at Noon, the Mother of This Enformant said to her to This Effect, Here has been This Morning the Wife of *Hobry*, who tells me, that *she is now got quit of the Rogue her* Husband; *and that she has sent him away to the* Indies. This Enformants Mother Asking her How *she had sent him away to the* Indies? She said, That *they had made him* Drunk *with Brandy, and*

put

put him on Board, and that the Elder Favet *had lent her* Two Guinneas *to give to the People to say Nothing of it*, *Hobry* Pursuing her discourse how she had told her *Two Cosins*, that she should be the ruine of them in Taking their Money, To which she receiv'd for Answer, That *if she got but quit of her Husband, they could earn more Money.*

And This Enformant calleth also to Mind that she hath heard the said *Hobry* say, several Months since, many Times, That *she would be the Death of her Husband, and that she had it several times in her Thoughts to Strangle him, and put him into a Common-shore, near at hand to her Lodgings, but that it was too Little, for she had Measur'd it*; and she was Resolv'd to Cut *him in Pieces*, or to *Dispatch him some other way.*

Jurat Die & Anno supradicto Coram Me

Mari-Anne Rippault.

Ro. L'Estrange.

Midd. & West. } *The Enformation of* Joan Rippault, *of the Parish of* St. Giles's in the Fields, *taken upon Oath*, Feb. 20. 168⅞.

SAith, That she hath many times heard the Wife of *Dennis Hobry* exclaim against her Husband, calling him Drunkard, and Lewd Names; and that within the Compass of Five or Six Months last past, she this Enformant hath heard the said wife of *Hobry*, say (meaning her Husband) that *she would kill him*, and that *she has had it in her head to Kill him, and cast him, dans l'Esgoust*, that is to say, in *the Common Shore; but that upon measuring the Passage, she found it was too narrow for him.*

And saith, that the said Wife of Hobry telling this Enformant at a time uncertain, (but *since* Hobry's *last Return* out of *France*) that the *Villain her Husband was now return'd out of* France, *and that her* Little Cousins (speaking of the Two Brothers that pass'd under the Name of *Favet*) *were very much troubled at it*; but saying withal, (speaking of the Two Brothers) *We have been advising together how to get rid of him.*

And saith, that upon *Thursday*, in the Week when the Body was said to be found, the said Wife of Hobry came alone to this Enformant in a Low Chamber, saying after this manner to her, *My* Daughter *has bid me come and tell you something concerning my* Husband; This Enformant asking what it was; the other replyed, *I have sent my* Husband *to the* Indies, *and I have given* Fifty Guinnea's *to put him aboard, and to send him away* : This Enformant asking how she had so much Money; she replyed, *Yes, she had*

D ga-

gathered it together, saying over and above, *That a Kinsman of* Hobry *had help'd to make him drunk, and so got him aboard: And without the help of* Hobry's Kinsman, *I could have done nothing. I borrow'd two* Guinnea's *more of* Le Grand Cousin *for People to keep* Hobry *quiet in the Ship if he should be troublesom*; pursuing this Discourse, and saying further, that *she told the Two Brothers, this drawing of Mony from them would be their Ruine*: To which one of them reply'd, *Get quit of your* Husband, *and we can get more Mony.*

And further, that the Wife of *Hobry* came toward the Evening to the Lodgings of this Enformant, with the *Younger Favet* in her Company, to whom the Daughter of this Enformant said somewhat to this purpose, *Well! You have got clear of your* Husband *then?* The Wife replying, *Yes, we have sent him for the* Indies, *and the* Younger Favet, *saying thereupon, We have sent him to the* Maroquins *to look for* Diamonds.

Jurat. Die & Anno Supradict. coram me

Jane Rippault.

Ro. L'Estrange.

Midd

The Enformation of Claude Poullet *of* Long-Acre, Enammel-Painter, *taken upon Oath*, Feb. 20. 168$\frac{7}{8}$.

SAith, That about five Months since, this Enformant heard the Wife of *Hobry* talking Bitterly against her Husband to *Mademoiselle Mary-Anne Rippault*, among other matters, in Words to this Effect, *I have had it several Times in my Thought, to Strangle that Husband of mine, and to throw him into the* Common-Shore, *before my* Door; *but I have taken measure of the Place; and I find it is too little to receive the Body, unless I should cut him all to pieces: But I must do it some other way.*

Jurat. Die & Anno supradict. coram me

Ro. L'Estrange.

C. *Poullet.*

Midd. & West. } *The Enformation of* Margaret Vasal, *of the Parish of St.* Anne Westminster, *taken upon Oath*, Feb. 6. 168$\frac{7}{8}$.

SAith, That *Yesterday was Sennight*, Dame *Hobry* a Midwife came after Mass to the House of this Enformant, being formerly known to this Enformant, and ask'd to Dine with her: For *she was loth to go home to* Dinner, *because there was some body she had no mind to see.* She staid Dinner,

and

and told this Enformant that she was going into the Country the next day to lay a Lady of Quality; this Enformant telling her she would lose those in the Town that had occasion to make use of Her: *Hobry* Answering, That would make amends for all. *Hobry* had at that Time a little *Office of our Blessed Lady in her hand*, and thereupon told her this Enformant, that it was the first Present that *Hobry* had made her; upon which Words she fetch'd a Deep Sigh; and told this Enformant that her Husband had threaten'd to Dispatch her in Three or Four days.

After this, *Ah my dear Lady*, says she, *I know you well enough to be a Person that I may trust my Life in your hands*. This Enformant asking her immediately, *How your Life? Pray will you explain your self; You Fright me: What's the matter?* Well, says *Hobry*, *Upon pain of Eternal Damnation, lift up your hand, and promise you'l never discover it, but keep it as secret as if 'twere under the seal of Confession*: And fetching a deep Sigh, *I have murther'd that miserable man*, she cry'd. This Enformant calling out to her, *Miserable Wretch, what have you done*, and bid her be gone; *Hobry* begging Advice what she should do; this Enformant bad her *be gone*; *she would have nothing to do with her*; *Hobry* crying out, *She was Lost, She was mad*, and other like Words of Desperation; this Enformant seeming not to believe her: *Hobry* told her, that she had strangled him with his Crevat.

Hobry told this Enformant further, that the Landlady of the House came into her Chamber, and ask'd if it were not a Shame that her Husband should be abed at that time of day? *Hobry* telling the Landlady that he had been out Late, and bid her let him lye a-sleep, whereupon the Landlady went away.

And

And further; *Hobry* told this Enformant, that she had declar'd the Murther to her *Two Cousins*, and begg'd their help to carry him away; but they told her that for the whole World they would have nothing to do in't: And upon this, *Hobry* went away crying.

And that upon *Thursday Last*, about Nine in the Morning, *Hobry* came again to this Enformant, and this Enformant spake softly to her, *O thou wretched Creature, art thou not Content to murther thy Husband, without cutting him to pieces!* *Hobry* replying to this Enformant, that *She had not cut him to pieces.* And in Proof of it, she said, That *This was a Lord, with several Rings upon his Finger, and his Head was found in the Park.* But she said further, that *she had caus'd him to be Bury'd by two of his* Particular Friends; *and that the doing of it cost her Fifty Pieces, and there was an End of him: but for her own Part, she was a lost Woman.*

This Enformant told her, 'twas impossible for her to Bury her Husband, and no body to take Notice of it, for she could not carry him out alone; But she said *Yes*, he was Buryed, and that in Three or Four days she would tell her where he was Bury'd.

Jurat. Die & Anno supradict. coram me — *Margaret Vafal.*

Ro. L'Estrange.

Midd.

Midd. & Weſt.

The Enformation of James Lorraine, of the Pariſh of St. James Weſtminſter, Surgeon, taken upon Oath, Feb. 3. $168\frac{7}{8}$.

SAith, That about Three Months ſince, this Enformant had ſome Diſcourſe with a *French* Midwife, and ask'd her what was become of her Husband? She made Anſwer, ſhe would give a good deal to have him Drown'd or Kill'd.

And further, that on this *Laſt Wedneſday* he went to the Houſe where the ſaid Midwife Lodg'd, and miſſing of her Husband, left a Chalk upon the Door, of Direction, where *Dennis Hobry* might come to this Enformant; and according to the Appointment of the above-ſaid Direction upon the Door, the Wife of the ſaid *Hobry* came to this Enformant, of whom the ſaid Enformant enquir'd, *What was become of her Husband?* Who Anſwered, That he was affraid of an Arreſt, and durſt not ſhew himſelf: This Enformant Anſwering, that he would ſhew him where he ſhould be ſafe, and try to make up the Bus'neſs; the ſaid Midwife Anſwering, that ſhe would bring him Word the next morning. On *Thurſday morning* (Yeſterday) the ſaid Enformant met her at *Chappel*, who asking again after her Husband, received for Anſwer, That *he was gone to the* Indies, *and he ſhould never ſee him more.*

This Enformant ask'd her this Morning before two of his Majeſties Juſtices of Peace, what was become of her Husband? ſhe ſaid, *She could not tell him*; but *Such a One* would give him a particular Account of it, mentioning a Perſon, whom this Enformant took to be *Yard.*

And

And saith, That this Enformant being Interrogated if he knew any Mark about the Body of *Dennis Hobry*, to Distinguish him particularly from another Man? This Enformant saith, That he remembreth that *he had a Scar upon One Hand*, and since the Delivering of the said Evidence, He This Enformant hath been to see the said Body and Limbs, where they lay Expos'd, and told Sir *Robert Clark*, one of his Majesties Justices of the Peace, with the Officer that shew'd the Body, and other Persons that were there Present, that if *This* was the *Body*, and *Those* the *Limbs* of *Dennis Hobry*, there would be found a *Scar* upon such a Part of the Hand; and upon the Sight of the Limbs, there was a Scar to be seen upon the right Hand, as This Enformant had told Sir *Robert Clark* and Others before, who likewise saw the said Scar with This Enformant.

Jurat' Die & Anno supradict. Coram Nobis — *J. Lorraine.*

Ro. L'Estrange,
Pet. Lugg.

Midd. & West. } *The Enformation of* Anthony Matson, *Beadle of the* Dutchy-Liberty *in the* Strand.

SAith, That by the order of Mr. *Thomas Harris*, High Constable of the Hundred of *Oswalston*, This Enformant caused *Night-Men* to come and search the House of Office belonging to the House of Mr. *de Fresneau*, near *Exeter-Change*, where this Enformant attended accordingly; and saw the taking up of a Head out of the said House of Office, in a Cloth, about a Fortnight since; which This Enformant Carry'd to his own House; and there Caus'd it it to be Wash'd, and afterward by the order of the High-Constable Carry'd it to a *Body* at St. *Giles's Bone-House*. This Enformant having had the said *Head* in his Custody all the While, from the taking it up, to the Delivery of it to the said *Bone-House*.

Jurat' Die & Anno supra-dict' Coram Me *Ant. Matson.*

Ro. L'Estrange.

Midd. & West. } *The Enformation of* Giles Malvault &c. *And* Mary Hope, *Taken upon Oath*, Feb. 6. 168$\frac{7}{8}$.

THEY say Joyntly and Severally, that having been up at St. *Giles's Church* together, to see the Head of a Man that lyes there Exposed ; They These Enformants Declare that they knew the Person of *Denis Hobry*, Reputed the Husband of a *French Midwife*, and that they *Know That* to have been the *Head* and *Face* of *Denis Hobry*.

Jurat' Die & Anno supra-dict' Coram Me *Giles Malvault.*
The Mark of ꟼH *Mary Hope.*

R. L'Estrange.

Midd.

Midd. & West. } *The Examination of* Mary *the Wife of* Lewis Pottron *of the Parish of* *S.* Giles's in the Fields, *taken* Feb. 3. 168⅞.

THat she, this Examinate, was at the House of Mr. *Hope*, where her Father and her Mother lodged, upon *Wednesday* last, and her Mother likewise in Company, she and this Examinate going thither together: And that this Informant went thither to pay some Money owing for Rent, there being Twelve Shillings due, and Eight Shillings paid. And this Examinate saith, That she was not there Yesterday.

And saith, That this Examinate went to the House of the said Mr. *Hope*, upon *Monday* last in the Morning, and that her only Business was to see her Mother, and that there was no Discourse of her Father.

And saith, That upon *Tuesday*, the Mother of this Examinate, was about Noon, (as this Examinate remembers) at the Lodgings of this Examinate, telling this Examinate, That there was a great Noise in the Street about a Dead Body that was found, saying, It was a sad thing; and this Examinate answered, That she had heard of it too: And that this is all the Examinate remembers of the said Discourse.

And saith, being interrogated, If she, this Examinate, ever spake of her Husband's allowing Thirty Shillings to her Father-in-Law *Hobry*, to buy Cloaths, or to that Effect, and that if the Mony were lost, it would be a good Riddance. This Examinate saith, That she said nothing to that Purpose.

And this Examinate being asked, if she gave her Opinion for her Mother not to appear 'til her Father-in-Law was

E gone;

gone; This Examinate positively denyeth her having said any thing to that Purpose.

And saith, being interrogated, When she last saw her Father at his Lodgings at Mr. *Hopes*, That it was upon *Sunday* last was Sennight.

And being interrogated, If ever she saw her Mother in any other Lodging when she lay from Home; saith, That she hath not heard where her Mother Lodged, at any time since her lodging with Mrs *Hope*; but only once or twice, as she believeth, in *Phœnix-Alley*.

Die & Anno supra-dict' coram me,
Ro. L'Estrange.

The Mark of
X
Mary Pottron.

Midd. & West. } *The further Examination of* Mary Pottron, Feb. 5. 168⅞. *Saith,*

THat this Examinate hath several times heard her Father-in-law *Denis Hobry*, say to this Purpose; That *he would be the Death of this Informant's Mother*: And hath likewise heard her Mother say, That *Denis Hobry* had often threatned it; but that this Examinate never heard her Mother speak of any purpose she had to kill her Husband.

And saith, That this Examinate hath not seen the Dead Body of her Father; neither was she any ways Consenting or Privy to any Violence upon him; but that she hath observed her Mother to be very much Disordered in her Mind for about a Week last past. And that she, this Examinate, asking

asking her Mother what she ailed, received for Answer *She was not well*.

And being interrogated, If she, this Examinate, knoweth one *Matthew Darney* a Joyner, or one *David Foster* a Joyner also: She, this Examinate, maketh answer, That she knoweth neither the One nor the Other.

Capt' Die & Anno,	*The Mark of*
supradict' coram me,	X
Ro. L'Estrange.	Mary Pottron.

Midd. & West. } *The Examination of* John Desermeau, *Servant to* Martin Dubois, *of the Parish of S.* Clement's Danes, *Weaver,* Feb. 3. 168⅞. *Saith,*

THat upon *Monday* Morning last, the Mother of this Examinate came to his Master to have him Home with her, to speak to one that she could not understand, this Examinates Mother not understanding *English*, and about Nine or Ten a Clock, this Examinate went with his Mother to her Lodgings; but the Man she spake of did not come.

This Examinate stayed at his Mothers Lodgings about half an Hour, and went then to *Covent Garden*, where this Examinate staid 'til Seven or Eight a Clock at Night, where he spake to no Body; but about that Hour returned Home to his Mothers, and saw his Mother, and staid about a quarter of an Hour, and then went and lay under a Stall over against the *Rose Tavern* all Night. About Seven a Clock in the Morning, he went again to his Mothers, where he saw his Mother, and saw his Sister also that Morning, meeting her in *New-Street* in the *Strand*.

Capt' Die & Anno
supradict' coram
me
Ro. L'Estrange.

Midd. & West. } *The further Examination of* John Desermeau, *Servant to* Martin Dubois, *&c.* Feb. 5. 168⅞. *Saith,*

THat the Mother of this Examinate (*Mary Hobry*) hath said several times, That she was afraid her Husband would Kill her, and that he Threatned her several mornings, when he had been all night at a Debauch.

And that upon *Monday* last, the Mother of this Examinate fetched him from his Master home to her Lodgings, where she told this Informant that his Father was dead, and he must help to carry him away; shewing the Body (as it lay upon the Bed) to this Examinate; who said he would not help her, and ask'd her, *why she did such a Thing?* Whereupon she said to this Examinate, as at other times, That she was continually in fear of him, and asked this Examinate what she should do with him; and hereupon this Examinate offer'd to go away, but she hindred him from going out, and then she would have this Examinate help her to Quarter the Body, which this Examinate refused, and did not so much as touch it, but went away into the the next Room, his Mother saying *she would do it her self then*;

them; so she took a Knife, and afterwards brought the *Head* into t'other Room, where this Examinate was: Going back again, and cutting off the *Legs*, the *Arms*, and the *Thighs*, and bringing them into the Room one after another; this Examinate pressing to be gone, but she bad him stay, and not leave her alone. After this she put the Body in a Rag, and took it up with her Peticoat, and, after several Refusals to help, and to go along with her; This Examinate went with her at last, she saying she was loth to go alone, upon which she went away with the Body into *Parker's-Lane*, and there threw it behind a Dunghill.

After she was rid of the *Body*, she went back and took the *Thighs*, and carried them to the *Savoy*, and put them into the House-of-Office, and from thence returning, she carried the *Legs* and *Arms* to the same place, this Examinate going along with her.

And after that, she went back for the *Head*, and propounded the putting of it into a Common-House-of-Office; this Examinate telling her, that he was afraid to meddle with it, his Mother replying, That if she should be taken, he would be in no danger, because he did not touch it. From thence she went back again and went to Bed.

This Examinate being Interrogated, Whether he ever heard how his own Father came by his Death, and whether his Mother had ever been Question'd about it? He maketh Answer, That he hath heard it said by some, that he died of a Wound; by others, that he died of a Natural Death; but never heard any thing of it Charg'd upon his Mother.

And saith, That upon *Monday* last this Examinate asked his Mother if his Sister knew of his Fathers being Dead, who made Answer, Yes she did; And saith, That he knoweth not any such Person as *Matthew Darmy*, or *David Foster*.

The Mark of X John Desermeau:

Cap' Die & Anno supradict' coram me
Ro. L'Estrange.

This

Midd. & West. } *The Examination of* Mary Hobry, *of the Parish of* S. Martins in the Fields, *taken* Feb. 4. 1687. *Saith,*

THat this Examinate was Married to *Denis Hobry* about four years since; and that after the Solemn Marriage of the Church, he the said *Denis Hobry*, with Curses and Imprecations deny'd the said Marriage, and and cast all sort of Infamous Reproaches upon this Examinate: This being the occasion of all his Outrages, because this Examinate would not submit to a compliance with him in Villanies contrary to Nature. In the miserable Condition above spoken of, this Examinate liv'd for the space of Three Months, under Beatings and Revilings, going every day in danger of her Life.

This Examinate being brought to Desperation by this miserable Usage, retir'd into a Private Chamber, and left him, living very close for a matter of Four Months, when her said Husband going into *France*, she appeared abroad again, and followed her Affairs. This continued for about Two Years, he being most of the time in *France*.

After this Examinate had been Two years Married, and Suffer'd, and Parted as above, her said Husband came Three or Four times to her, making large Promises how good a Husband he would be, and how kindly he would live with her; and in fine, desir'd that by all means they might live together again, declaring that he had Confess'd his Sins to Almighty God, and that he would be another Man. To which this Examinate yielded, upon Condition that he should declare the same before a Priest and Two Witnesses, and own, That this Examinate was his Lawful Wife: which Declaration was Made and Sign'd before Father *Gaspar*, and Enter'd in Writing upon a Register.

This Examinate had not been above two or three days with him again, before he began to use her as formerly, and continued his Ill-usage for a matter of two Months upon the same Subject and Occasion as formerly. About that time he went away into *France*, and carried all away that he could, to the wearing Cloaths and Necessaries of this Examinate. After Three Months stay, he returned again, and upon the same Instances and Promises as before, this Examinate submitted to accompany with him again: And this way of Life this Examinate led from time to time, till this last unhappy Separation, her Husband continuing in the same way still, of Leaving her, and Coming again, and using her Ill.

This Examinate finding herself in this hopeless Condition, and under frequent Temptations of putting some violent end to her Misfortunes, she rather chose to make Tryal if she could prevail upon him to agree to a Final Separation, and prest it upon him several times with great Earnestness; but he still refused it with Outrages of Language and Actions, telling this Examinate he would be the Ruine of her.

This Informant finding herself without Remedy, in a Distraction of Thoughts, and under the Affliction of Bodily Distempers, contracted by her said Husband's dissolute Course of Life, her Frailty was no longer able to resist the Temptations of dangerous Thoughts; sometimes this Examinate was thinking to go into some other Part of the World and leave him; and other while she was tempted, to think of Extremities either upon her Husband or upon Her self; and often told her Husband plainly, That *she would Kill him if he followed that Course:* This Examinate having lamented her Condition to others of her acquaintance, and telling them she was not able to live this course of Life, and that Mischief would come on't at last. But after all these dangerous Words and Menaces, this Examinate upon Recollection, bethought her self of the Horridness of the Sin, and by God's Grace was diverted from executing so wicked a Resolution.

And

And ſaith, That this Examinate was tranſported about two or three Months ſince, to that degree of Rage and Impatience, that ſhe took a Knife once with a Reſolution to Kill her Huſband, but retracted and did not go forward with it. And that ſhe took the ſame Deſperate Reſolution again, a matter of fifteen Days after, propoſing both times to do it in the Night; but by the Grace of God ſhe was then again reſtrained.

And ſaith, That ſhe this Examinate told her Husband in the Morning, both theſe times, the Reſolution ſhe had taken over Night to Kill him in his Bed; but he made ſlight of it, and told this Examinate ſhe durſt not do it.

And ſaith, That on the very Evening before this Examinate's Husband went laſt into *France*, this Examinate ſpake to her Husband to this effect; *Hobry, you are now going into* France, *pray bethink your ſelf and lead a better Life; for when you come back again, if you Treat me as you did formerly, I do not know what Extremities you may Provoke me to.* Whereupon he promis'd this Examinate with dreadful Oaths, that he would be a good Husband to her.

The Husband of this Examinate returned out of *France*, and came to this Informant's Lodgings about three Weeks ſince, when this Informant received him after the following manner, ſaying to him, *Hobry, you are welcome, and pray will you change your courſe of Life now, that we may live Comfortably together. Yes* (ſaith he) *upon condition you will put me in Cloaths, and furniſh me with what I want.* (He having got Money in *France*, and ſpent it to the laſt Farthing.) This Informant told him ſhe could not ſupply him at that Rate, for Times were hard, and ſhe had much ado to Live and pay Honeſt Debts. This Examinate's Husbands replying to this effect; *If you do not do as I ſay, I will be a worſe Husband to you than ever I was.* This Examinate told him ſhe did not know what ſhe ſhould do with him, for his Barbarous Uſages had made her Mad. And his way was, ſo often as he asked any thing of this Informant that ſhe could not

ſupply

supply him with, he would abuse her, and say he would make her repent of it. And this Examinate hath been told by one *Yard*, that her Husband said in his hearing, That he would be the Destruction of her. This was the Course of Life this Examinate led, till this *Thursday last was Sennight*; upon which day this Examinate had no Thought of offering any Violence to her Husband, but went to Bed about her usual hour, Ten a Clock, leaving the Fore-door open for him when he should come home.

About Five in the Morning, the Husband of this Examinate came in, outragiously in Choler, and more than half Drunk. This Examinate was a-sleep, till her Husband Wak'd her with a heavy Blow with his Fist upon her Stomach, and said to her, *What! you are Drunk?* This Examinate Answering, *No; you are Drunk, you'd never come home at Five a Clock in the Morning else; you have been among base Company.* He made this Answer, *I have been among* Bougres *and Rogues, that have made me Mad, and you shall pay for't*; whereupon he gave this Examinate another violent Blow upon the Breast: With That, this Examinate turn'd from him, and fell a weeping. And this Examinate declareth in the Presence of Almighty God, That she had not as yet any Purpose or Thoughts of attempting upon his Life.

While this Examinate was weeping, her Husband took her in his Arms and Press'd her so hard, that she could not fetch her Breath, and that the Blood started out of her Mouth. Immediately upon this, he attempted the Forcing of this Examinate to the most Unnatural of Villanies, and acted such a Violence upon her Body in despite of all the Opposition that she could make, as forc'd from her a great deal of Blood, this Examinate crying out to her Landlady, who was (as she believes) out of distance of hearing her. This Examinate told him, *I will immediately Rise and Complain to the Neighbours*: Whereupon he took her Forcibly by the Arm, and threw her down upon the Bed, being before sit-ing-up to rise; and after this, Bit her like a Dog, *&c.*—— this Examinate saying to him, *Am I to lead this Life for ever? Yes, and a worse too, ere it be long, you had best look to your self*, and upon these words he fell a-sleep.

Upon this Respite the Examinate lay in Torments both of Body and of Mind, thinking with her self, *What will become of me? What am I to do! Here am I Threatned to be Murder'd, and I have no way in the World to Deliver my self, but by Beginning with him*; and immediately upon these Thoughts, this Examinate started up and took one of his Garters, which was *de Fiscelle*, or Pack-thread, put it double about his Neck *et la noua en serrant de toute sa Force*, and so tyed it, and drew it as hard as she could, *de sorte qu'il en estoit Estrangle dans un quart d' heure, sans beaucoup de Resistance.* Insomuch that he was Choak'd with it in a Quarter of an Hour, with little resistance. The Body rested there till *Monday*, only this Examinate took off the Pack-thread within a Quarter of an Hour after his Death; and in hopes that he was not yet Dead, repenting with all her Heart, that she had been guilty of such a Heinous Sin, and try'd Brandy to bring him to Life again.

Upon *Monday* Morning, *Jan.* 30. 168⅞. this Examinate went to the House of *Monsieur du Bois*, living in the *Strand*, to desire him he would give leave for the Son of this Examinate to go home with his Mother, upon occasion of speaking with an *English* Man, that this Examinate could not Understand, her Son speaking both *French* and *English*: the Youth being an Apprentice to the said *Dubois*, and of Age, Thirteen Years and an half. This Examinate took her Son with her home to her Lodgings, in Expectation of the *Englishman* before spoken of, who did not come.

This Examinate fetched her Son on purpose to have his Assistance about the conveying away of her Husband's Body; and this Examinate told her Son of a great Calamity that was fallen out; which the Child was very much surprized at, and being shewed the Body, ready to sink

down

down at the Spectacle. But this Examinate put the Boy to an Oath forty times over, to say nothing of it; and he swore he would be torn in Pieces first: And asked this Examinate, *Mother, What will you do? shift for your self, and go out of the Land, for if you are once taken you'l never get off.* This Informant answering, She had no Mony for a Voyage, and she could think of no way better than to cut off the Quarters, and disperse the Parts in several Places, so as People should not know whose Body it was: Besides, That she her self could carry them off, and dispose of them much better, her Son saying, That he was afraid to meddle with the carrying of them.

This Examinate hereupon, about Four or Five that Afternoon, having taken a Resolution of cutting off the Quarters to make it more Portable, took a Knife, and first cut off the *Head*, after that the *Arms*, and then the *Thighs*, and last the *Leggs*, some Drops of Blood coming from the Neck, but very little or none at all from the rest.

The *Quarters* being cut off by Eight in the Evening, or thereabouts, this Examinate bethought her self how to convey them away; and first took up the Body which she put into a Piece of Linnen, and carried it before her in her Petticoat: The Examinate passed through *Castle-Street* into *Drury-Lane*, and thence into *Parker's-Lane*, and so among the Dung-hills, and there left it, her Son following, to give notice if any Body came.

The *Body* being thus disposed of, this Examinate, with her Son, went back, and took the *Thighs* in a Linnen Cloth; this Examinate carrying them likewise, and her Son following in like manner, as before; and this Examinate threw them into a House of Office at the *Savoy*, and immediately went back with her Son again, and fetched the *Leggs* and the *Arms*, her Son following her to the *Savoy* again, and put them also into the House of Office.

The *Quarters* being carried away, as above, and only the *Head* remaining, this Examinate advised with her Son, What they should do with the *Head*? who advised her to throw it into the Water: But this Examinate was then afraid it would be found and known: And said, She would rather cast it into the House of Office of a Friend of hers, meaning *De Fresneau*, a *Fringe-Maker*, over against the *Savoy*, to which Place she went accordingly, her Son following her, and cast it into the Second House of Office, there being two belonging to the Place.

And saith, That upon *Tuesday* Morning last, *Mary Potter* (or *Pottron*) the Daughter of this Examinate, came to this Examinates Lodgings, and in Discourse said something to this Purpose, What is become of *Hobry*, where is he? *Yard* says he is gone for the *Indies*. This Examinate made Answer, That she had not seen him for Four or Five Days. The Examinate put her Daughter off at first, but came soon after to tell her the Truth of the Matter.

And saith, That this Examinate, thereupon, told her Daughter the whole Truth of the Matter, as is reported above; her said Daughter ready to fall down at the hearing of it; and transported with Astonishment, asking this Examinate, What they should do to keep it Private; this Examinate charging her to say nothing of it; and the Daughter replying; That she would be burned first, but that if it were any other Person than her Mother, she would discover it her self; but since her Mother was concerned, she would never open her Lips of it.

And this Examinate being interrogated, How it came to pass that she, this Examinate, being of the Communion of the Church of *Rome*, came to throw the Quarters of her Husband into a House of Office at the *Savoy*, which was a way to bring so great a Scandal upon the Religion she professed, by laying the Murther at the Door of the Professors of that Religion? This Examinate maketh Answer, That she had no Thoughts in what she did, as to that Matter,

ter,

ter, more than to part the *Limbs* and the *Body*, and hoped the Water might carry them away.

And being interrogated, If any other Person whatsoever, beside the Persons herein named, was privy to this Practice upon her Husband, or assisting to the Conveying away of the *Body*; this Examinate answereth, That there was no Person privy to the Secret, nor any Person assisting to it, besides the Persons within mentioned.

Jo. Ridley. *Mary Hobry.*

Capt' Die & Anno,
supradict' coram me,
Ro. L'Estrange.

I have heard the Information of Mrs. Mary Hobry, *consisting of Two Sheets and one Page, read in* English, *and have signed the Papers, and do hereby declare, That I have truly Expounded them in* French *to Mrs.* Mary Hobry, *according to the best of my Knowledge.*

Jo. Ridley.

J' avoue que ce qui est cerit sur ces deux feuilles de Papier, & une page, est veritable; selon ce que Monsieur Ridley *me l' a expliquee, en* Francoise.

Marie Hobry.

POST-

POSTCRIPT.

HEre's a Just and a Punctual Account of all the *Informations*, in the Cause of *Mary Hobry*; and I do here Appeal to the *Informants* themselves, That I have dealt Candidly and Conscientiously, both in the *Publishing* and in the *Taking* of them. Nay, to prevent the uttermost Spite of *Envy* and *Calumny*, they had almost all of them, as many *Witnesses* to the *Fairness* of them, as the Room would hold, where I took them: And so far from *Extorting* any *Evidence*, That the *Mother*'s and the *Son*'s, were purely *Confession*. The *Woman*, 'tis true, was examined in *Private*, for fear of any unseasonable Discovery of what she might declare: But before I put so much as one Question to her, I rendred her so particular an Account of the Points in Evidence against her, that she gave her self for *Lost*, without any Hope, either of an *Acquittal*, or of a *Pardon*; and so frankly told me from Point to Point, the whole *Series* of the Narration, as it is here set down. But still that which stuck with *other* People, stuck with *Me*: That is to say, How all this could be done without *Complices*. Now the *Boy*'s Story lay as yet in the *Dark*, and his doubling in his Tale, gave manifestly to understand, That there was a *Mystery* still *Undiscovered*. He *denyed* all upon *Friday*. Upon *Saturday*, his *Mother declared* her self. Upon *Sunday* the *Boy denyed all again*, 'till upon the Hint given him, of *his dining with his* Mother; her *drawing the Curtain of the Bed*, and *shewing him the Body of his Murdered Father*, upon that *Monday* when the *Body* was *quartered*; he fell a *Weeping*, and told an orderly Story, without any Mincing of Matters, from the very Act of *quartering him*, to the *disposing* of the *Body*, the *Limbs* and the *Head*, into those Places where they were afterwards found. This Relation of his is so agreeable to his *Mother*'s, in the

Order

Order and *Manner* of it, that it is almost *impossible* to be *False*: And to any one that duly considers the *Bulk* and *Weight* of the *Trunk* of an ordinary Man, without either *Head*, *Arms*, *Thighs* or *Leggs*, a Woman's carrying such a Burthen in the Truss of her *Petticoat*, will be found no greater a Wonder, than he shall see ten times over in *one Days Walk* betwixt the *Old Exchange* and *Westminster*.

In the Womans Story, I have done all the Right that Honestly I could to the Compassionable Condition of an Unhappy Wretch, but without Extenuating the *Horror* of the *Wickedness*. I have, since that time, Enquir'd into the *Humour* and *Character* of the *Husband*; and his Acquaintance report him at all hands to have been a *Libertine* and *Debauchee* to the *Highest Degree*, but *Drunk* or *Sober*, without any *Malice*. This is, in Fine, an *Impartial Report* of the *Case*. It falls to the *Midwife's Lot* to *Suffer Alone*, but if she had stood her *Tryal*, so that the *Evidence* against her had been left to take its Course, it would not have gone much better with some of her *Companions*, than it did with the *Miserable Creature her self*.

THE END.

A Warning-Piece to All Married Men and Women. Being the Full Confession of Mary Hobry, The French Midwife, Who Murdered her Husband on the 27th of January, 1687/8 (Wing W935) is reproduced with permission from the unique copy at the Bodleian Library (shelfmark Ashmole G 15 vol. 5 [134]). The text-block measures 285 × 370 mm.

A WARNING-PIECE
TO
All Married Men and Women.
Being the Full
CONFESSION of MARY HOBRY,
The *FRENCH* Midwiſe,
Who Murdered her Husband on the 27th. of *January*, $168\frac{7}{8}$. (As alſo the Cauſe thereof.)

For which ſhe receiv'd Sentence to be Burnt alive: And on *Friday* the Second Day of *March*, between the Hours of Ten and Eleven in the Morning, ſhe was drawn upon a Sledge to *Leiceſter-Fields*, where ſhe was burnt to Aſhes.

ALL you that Married Men and Women be
Give Ear unto this woful Tragedy,
That now befell a *French man* and his *Wife*,
Who liv'd together in continual Strife;
One *Denis Hobry* about Four years ſince
Took to his Wife a Woman Born a *French*,
Whom he Abus'd at ſuch inhumane rate,
That ſhe a thouſand times wiſh'd him ill Fate,
And thought within herſelf to end the Strife,
If ſhe were forc'd, to take away his Life:
The cauſe that mov'd him to thoſe Tyrannies,
Was her averſion to his Villanies;
At length into a private Room ſhe fled,
Intending never to Embrace his Bed,
Where ſhe remain'd four Months, and then by chance
Her Husband went beyond the Seas to *France*;
But when return'd, he Courted her again,
Tho firſt he feared it was all in vain.
He ſwore a thouſand times to pleaſe her Mind,
And prove a Husband, faithful, chaſte, and kind.
His Words prevail'd ſo much, that ſhe did yield,
Upon theſe Terms, to give him up the Field,
That he would firſt confeſs before a Prieſt
And two Witneſſes more, as he own'd Chriſt
To be his God, ſhe was his lawful Wife,
And would no more vex her during his Life.
Father *Gaſper* wrote this every Word,
Who plac'd it afterwards upon Record.
But ſcarce two days, or three at moſt, were paſt,
When he on her the old Reproaches caſt.
In two months time he went to *France* again,
And gave the Woman juſt cauſe to complain;
For, nothing that he could come at or find,
But he brought with him, and left none behind.
When three months paſſed he returned home,
And with diſſembling Words to her did come;
Whom ſhe receiv'd, expecting his good Will,
But ſoon found him to be the ſame Man ſtill.
She often beg'd of him, with weeping eyes,
A Separation, or that otherwiſe
He would be civil; who gave this Reply,
He would her ruine; which cauſ'd her to cry,
And think to take his Life, or loſe her own,
Which ſhe did often tell him in her moan.
Long ſhe endur'd, at laſt ſhe told her Caſe
To Neighbours that dwelt near about the place,
And ſaid, ſhe fear'd Miſchief would be the end
Of his ill Actions, or he ſoon would mend.
Three months being paſs'd, one time ſhe took a Knife,
With an intent to take away his Life:
But God did then beſtow on her his grace,
Which made her give her Husband longer ſpace.
So twice ſhe did intend upon her Bed
To ſtab her Husband, and to leave him dead:
And to Himſelf ſhe did declare her mind,
Who dared her in a moſt fooliſh kind.
Now he was going from her into *France*,
And ſhe told him, If that it were his chance
E're to come back, and follow the old Rule,
She muſt become unto him ſomething cruel:
Who promis'd her moſt earneſtly, and ſwore
He never would abuſe her as before.
In three weeks after he return'd again
Unto his Wife, who did him entertain;
And ſaid, dear *Hobry*, welcome thou to me
So that you henceforth a good Husband be.

I will, ſaid he, taking a thouſand Oaths,
If you'll me furniſh preſently with Cloaths.
She anſwered Him, The Times were very dear,
And hardly ſhe her honeſt Debts could clear.
He hearing her, moſt wickedly did curſe,
And ſwear he would to her be ten times worſe
Than e're he was: who then this Anſwer had
From her, That he already made her mad,
For that it was moſt commonly his way
When he did want, to threaten night and day,
If ſhe could not him furniſh, no Excuſe
Could get place with him, but ſtill her abuſe.
One *Yard* to her did openly declare,
That for her Ruine her Husband did prepare.
Thus they continued in the ſame degree,
To th' Twenty Seventh of laſt *January*;
When ſhe, about Ten of the Clock at night
Took her Repoſe, bearing no kind of Spight
Or Malice to her Husband, as before,
But open, for his Coming, left the door;
Who came at Five a Clock next Morning home,
And did in Rage and Choler fret and fome,
And to his Wife, as dead as in a grave
(With Sleep) a blow upon the Stomach gave,
Which made her ſtart; What, you are drank (ſaid he,)
If I am not, 'tis like you are, quoth ſhe:
He anſwer'd, I with Rogues all night did ſit,
Which made me mad, and you muſt pay for it;
Whereupon he gave her another Blow
Upon the Breaſt, which did renew her Woe:
To weeping ſhe immediately did fall,
And he then took her in his Arms with all
His force, till he did ſtop her Vital Breath,
So that ſhe wiſhed for a ſudden Death:
He forc'd on her ſuch barbarous Violence
In ſpight of what ſhe did in her Defence;
Forcing much Blood from her, ſhe cried out
To her Land-lady, who did not hear the Shout:
Unto the Neighbours I'll (ſaid ſhe) complain;
Wherewith he threw her on the Bed again,
And bit her like a Dog kept in a yard,
Shall this ſaid ſhe, be always my Reward?
Yea, anſwer'd he, be ſure thyſelf to keep
Well, and with that he fell in a dead Sleep;
Which ſhe beholding, and feeling the ſmart
Of his ill uſage to her; in her Heart,
What ſhall I do, (ſaid ſhe) muſt I now Die?
Or Murther him that makes me thus to Cry?
With that ſhe ſtarted full of Wrath and Evil,
Being thereto Spurr'd by th' inſtinct of the Devil,
And pull'd his Garter off his Leg in haſt,
Being a Pack-thread, which ſhe thought no waſt,
And doubling it about his Neck, ſhe drew
The ends ſo faſt, that ſhe him quickly Slew;
But ſoon Repenting, hop'd he was Alive,
And thought that Brandy would him then Revive:
When all was done, her labour was in Vain,
For Life once loſt, can ne'er be had again.
Till *Monday* following the Corps was there,
For ſhe could not convey it any where,
Untill ſhe brought her Son out of the *Strand*,
Who durſt not ſpeak againſt her courſe Command:
When he beheld the Corps lye at this rate,
He did bemoan his Mothers wretched Fate:
What will you do? you muſt (ſaid he) now Die,
Or out of *England* you muſt quickly Flie:
She told him Money ſhe had none in hand
That would buy Paſſage to another Land;
My way ſaid ſhe is to Cut off his Head,
His Thighs and Arms, now that he is Dead,
And none can tell what Country man he's then,
Though he were found by the moſt wiſe of Men.
At Four or Five paſt Noon, this Curſed Wife
Cut off her Husband's Head with a ſharp Knife:
His Arms and Thighs came off, his Legs again,
And though his Neck did Bleed, he felt no Pain.
At Eight a Clock this Night through *Caſtle-ſtreet*
And *Drury-lane* ſhe went, and none did meet,
Until at *Parkers lane* to pleaſe her will
She laid the Corps near by a naſty Dung-hill.
She did in Linnen next the Thighs convey
Into a Privy that's in the Savoy,
Where ſhe again the Arms and Legs did caſt,
Nothing remaining but the Head at laſt:
She then adviſed with her Son to know
Where they might cloſely put the Head alſo;
Who ſaid the Water was for it the Place,
But ſhe then fear'd ſome Man might know his Face;
And ſhe at laſt reſolved to this end,
To throw't into the Privy of her Friend,
A Fringe-maker, that lives by the *Savoy*,
For they do ſtill two Privies there imploy.
The Corps being found, and all the truth well known,
She did her ſelf no word of it diſown;
But did confeſs that no untruth is here,
For God will not let Murtherers go clear.
She is now Burn'd, and beggs of all Mankind
And Women too, Wiſdom by her to find.

With Allowance.

LONDON, Printed and Sold by *George Croom*, at the *Blue-Ball* in *Thames-ſtreet*, near *Baynard's-Caſtle*. 1688.

An Account Of the Manner, Behaviour and Execution of Mary Aubry (Wing A319D) is reproduced with permission from the unique copy at the Bodleian Library (shelfmark Ashmole F 5 [25]). The text-block measures 150 × 235 mm.

The following words are a transcription of the original:

2.1 the Old Baily
2.2 her Indictment
2.8 Case that rendered her Dead … Retract that Plea, and put
2.9 it fit … but she

AN ACCOUNT Of the Manner, BEHAVIOUR AND EXECUTION OF Mary Aubry,

Who was Burnt to Ashes, in

Leicester Fields,

On *Friday* the 2d Day of *March*, 1687. For the Barbarous and Inhumane Murther, Committed on the Body of

Dennis Aubry,

Her Husband, in the Parish of St. *Martins* in the Fields, on the 27th of *January* last.

And the same Day, *Daniel Sconley* was Executed at *Tyburn*.

THe late surprizing Murther of *Dennis Aubry*, the person whose Body was found in *Parkers-Lane*, his Arms, Legs, *&c.* in the *Savoy* House of Office, and his Head in another, near *Exeter Exchange*; upon strict inquiry, being known to be done, and committed by *Mary Aubry* his Wife, a *French* Woman; she upon her Examination having confessed the Fact, *viz.* That she bereived him of Life, by strangling him with a Cord, *&c.* and Cut him in Pieces, for the more private and convenient disposal of him, thereby to prevent discovery, she was thereupon Committed to Prison, where not without some Regret, which appeared by her much dejected Countenance and Behaviour: She continued till the Sessions, Holden for the City of *London* and County of *Middlesex*, *&c.* Began at the Sessions House in the

the *Old Baily*, whether being brought, in order to be Tryed for that Barbarous Murther; her Inditement was Read, wherein she stood charged, for Murthering her said Husband, by Strangling, *&c.* on the 27th of *January*, *Anno*, 1687. In the Parish of St. *Martins* in the Fields; and having Notice at large, of what was contained therein, by her Interpreter; and being demanded whether she was Guilty or not of the Fact, as laid in the said Indictment: She pleaded Guilty to the Felony, Murther, and Petty Treason; yet, the Court was so favourable to tell her, that she might, seeing it was a Case that rendered her Dead in Law by her pleading Guilty, Retract that Plea, and put her self upon the Country for her Tryal, if she thought it fit or convenient; but she still persisting to plead Guilty, her Confession was Recorded. And in the close of the Sessions, she was brought to receive Sentance of Death, as in that Case the Law requires, which was accordingly pronounced by the Court, *viz. That she the said Mary Aubry, should be carried from thence, to the place from whence she came, and thence to be drawn to the place of Execution, and there to be burnt with Fire till she be Dead.*

Sentance being past, she was reconveyed to the County Goal of *Newgate*, there to attend the time of the said Sentance being put in Execution, appearing much afflicted under the sense of so great a Crime, affecting for the most part retiredness and avoiding as much as in her lay, the concourse or company of such, especially, whom she conceived came only out of curiosity to see her, and so continued to indulge her self rather in Melancholiness than any thing that was apparent to the contrary, both before and after she was sensible the Warrant was signed for her Execution.

On *Friday* the 2d of *March*, the Day appointed for her being Burnt, *&c.* about Ten in the Morning of the said Day, the Sheriffs Officers came to demand her in order to carry her to *Leicester Fields*, the place where she suffered. When being put into the Sledg, she was with a Guard of Sheriffs Men, drawn to *Leicester Fields*, where a Stake was set up towards the North side of the *Square*, and the Wood, *&c.* accordingly prepared to perform the Execution, when about half an hour past Ten, she arrived to the place appointed, appearing very Penitent, often lifting up her Hands and Eyes to Heaven, seeming to express much sorrow for the Crime that had been the occasion of this her shameful End, and then prayed to her self; and after that, held some Discourse or Conference with a certain Person there atending when being taken out of the Slead, about half an hour after her arrival she again having Expresed much Sorrow in her manner of Cariage and Gesture as was Evident to the Spectators, she was set upon a stool prepared for that purpose; and a Rope being fastened through a Hole of the Post, or Stake, and the Noose of it put over her Neck; the stool being taken awey, she hung there for near the space of a quarter of an Hour, in which time, the Bavins and Faggots where Piled about her, and at the Expiration thereof, Fire set to them, which consumed her in about half an hour more to Ashes, *&c.*

About three hours before this Execution, one *Daniel Stonley*; who was condemned the last sessions, for Robing *Anthony Shackliffe* a Brewer, of a considerable sum of Mony, was caried to *Tyburn*, and there Executed.

This may be Printed, R P March the 2d 1687.

LONDON; *Printed by* D Mallet, *next Door to the sign of the* Star, *between* Fleet Bridge *and* Bridewell Bridge.

A Full Relation of the Birth, Parentage, Education, Life and Conversation of Mrs. Margaret Martel (Wing F2360) is reproduced with permission from the unique copy at The British Library (shelfmark 518.f.47). The text-block measures 96 × 165 mm.

The cropped lines at the bottom of p. 3 read:
[h]er) never discover'd it: and as she began, so she continu'd,
for,

The cropped catchword on p. 6 reads:
thus

The following words are a transcription of the original:

2.2 Credulity
2.3 Occur-
2.13 their Ease
2.14 than any Aversion
2.16 Rome
2.37 the Series
2.38 and Conversation
4.2 she fell
4.3 man tho not over
4.9 from City
4.22 not
4.23 as to
4.40 and borrows
7.3 part
7.4 this
7.5 ved
7.6 Squire Pvllen
7.8 tirred [?]
7.10 frivolous
7.12 the
7.16 [th]e
7.17 next
7.19 like
7.20 of … June
7.22 to [?]
7.25 [?]ine
7.26 [gi]ving
7.27 [va]lue
7.28 [sta]ntly
7.29 [of] a
7.30 [?] Silver
7.31 [Si]lver
7.32 [ev]idence
7.33 [str]ess
7.34 [an]d
7.35 [tan]ce
7.36 [not?]
7.37 [?]t
7.38 [be c]arried
7.39 [?]d
7.40 fac[?]t

F. 31

A Full

RELATION

OF THE

Birth, Parentage, Education, Life and Conversation

OF

Mrs. **Margaret Martel**

THE

Barbarous *French-Woman*,

Who was Executed over against the *Meuse-Gate*, near *Charing-Cross*, on *Friday* the 16th of this Instant *July*, 1697. for a most Bloody Murther committed by her on the Body of *Madam* PULLEN, &c.

Wherein is fully and impartially related her Youthful Roguries, Love-Intriegues, Carriage and Deportment; her Behaviour to her Parents, the true Occasion of her Coming to *England*, with her whole Carriage and Manner of Living her till the time of her Death.

To which is added,

A True Account of the Paper she delivered at the Place of Execution to the Sheriffs of *London* and *Middlesex*.

Licens'd according to ORDER.

London, Printed and Sold by *J. Bradford* in *New-street* without *Bishopsgate*, 1697.

The PREFACE.

THat I may not impose any thing upon the Credulity of my Readers, I must assure them, that the Occurrences of this French Woman's Life already appears in as many forms as Proteus had shapes, however they all concenter that she was a person but of too evil Inclination, Behaviour and Deportment; witness her last barbarous, savage and unnatural Villany.

I cannot forbear takeing notice, what a piece of Monstruous Ingratitude it appears in the Eyes of the World; An evident sign that she, and its to be fear'd too many of her Nation more, fly to our pregnant Soyl more for the love of the Loaves and Fishes, their Ease and Interest, then any Aversion Hatred or Antipathy they have either against the French Tyrant, or the damnable Heresies of *Rome*.

It is likewise worthy notice, to observe with what policy and cunningness she vail'd her *Hydra* Head of Religion to the last; appearing in her Life time, the better to ingratiate her self, as a Protestant, for belike her other sentiments were never known, till almost her last Minutes. But I cannot imagine what kindness her dying in the Romish Communion can be, for surely there is no Saintship or Cannonization, no Merit to be recorded as a Martyr, for so villanous a Butchery, unless some of her unjust, pilfer'd Plate was dedicated to the use of his Holiness, or the Shrine of some merciful *Romish* Saint.

But if Fame err not (which sometime it doth) she took *London* for a safer Sanctuary, than *Rome* it self, that common Receptacle of Spiritual Thieves, for belike (from good Hands I had it) she has formerly imbru'd her Hands in no less than the dear Blood of an Indulgent Husband and Natural Child, a villany worse than Savage, for the most bruitish Animal is tender of the Life of their Young: How she escap'd Justice for that Villany, is as unknown to me, as the veracity of the Deed it self; but thus much by way of Introduction, I shall now relate more particularly the Series of her Life and conversation, collected from the best Informations I could have.

The Life and Conversation of Mrs. *Margaret Martel*, &c.

AS nothing hath been a subject of more Horrour than the late Barbarous Savage, and Inhumane Murder Committed by Mrs. *Eartl*, so nothing can afford more variety of Remarks and worthy Observations than the whole Seris of Her Life and Conversation.

She was Born within the CITY of *PARIS*, in the Kingdom of *France*, her Parents not of the meanest Rank, Esteem and Quality, however her own unhappiness had reduc'd her; Her Education, according to the Mode of that Nation, being very Liberal; having a peculiar dexterity in what belongs to Air and Gallantrys, as Musick, Dancing, Japanning, Needle, works, and what not: greatly Loving and mightily frequently Enterludes, Masks, Balls, and such like Exercises, in which few or none ever went before her. One Pleasant fancy I shall remark in her Minority, and that was when she was about the Age of ten; A new Book in the Nature of our Academies being Publish'd, she desir'd her Father to buy one of them, which he utterly refus'd, not quoth he, *for the value, tho it is considerable, but because it tends to corrupt good manners, and to inflame the mind with Amorous desires, to say no worse*, But Madammoselle, how Earl soever it was in her years had a desire to be inform'd this, and therefore rather than to want so desireable an Help and pleasing Recreation, she even resolv'd by her finger ends to purchase Ease in mind, and so those Hours which should have been devoted to Sleep and the natural rest of the Body, she imploy'd in making Wax-work Figures for private Sale, whereby she was not only enabled to purchase her Book, but likewise to supply several such like secret Occasions. And these Intriegues she so well manag'd that Her Parents who by reason of her Inclination had a watchful Eye over her, never discover'd it, and as she

About the Age of Fourteen (to the grief of her Indulgent Parents) she fell in league with an *Italian* Comedian, a man tho not over well inrich'd with the Gifts of Mind, yet perfectly accomplished with agility of Body; as Vaulting, Fencing, Leaping, *&c.* Her Love was so hot and furious, that no perswasions whatever could over-rule her; but go she must and did along with him, tho it was apparently plain he had a wife at *Rome*. She travell'd with him from City to Town for above the space of Two Years, at which time its said her Paramour dying, she, destitute of Imploy, was reduced allmost to Swines Husks: in which condition as the Prodigal in Scripture, She turned to her Fathers House begg'd his Pardou and was receiv'd into favour.

Whilst the Impression of her sorrows were yet on her Heart, her Carriage and Behaviour was grave and demure enough; but so soon as they were worn away (as time consumes all things) she return'd like a Dog to his Vomit; and gave up her self to all the delicacy, pleasure and Effeminacy imaginable.

As I am inform'd the cause of Religion, and the preservation of a Good Conscience was not so much the Occasion of her coming to *England*, as to shield and hide her self from being ridicul'd and hiss'd at Home, not only for her Extravagant Ambitious Expences, by which she had wasted a plentiful Dowry bequeath'd to her, but also for the indirect means she took to re trieve the same. I must confess she had a Spirit above our Common Hackney Whores, as the are call'd, who Expose themselves to every Letcher for a Six penny piece; but yet she was inclin'd in time of need (*Necessitas caret Lege*) in that way to make use of her own, of which I shall repeat some Instances, as I have been creditably inform'd.

Being driven to some Necessities to support her self and and her Son, and being as unwilling to work as she was too Proud to Beg, she was fully bent to contrive some than ordinary Adventure to raise her drooping fortune in the World, and it was thus. She goes to each and every Friend and Acquaintance, with whom she had any manner of Interest, and borrows some one thing or other of Modish

dish Rigging from them; by which means she was able, like the Peacock, not only to deck and plume her self with verity of colour'd Feathers, but had also some surplassage of her Borrowings to leave as Pledges for Money: thus equipp'd and adorn'd with her Son as a Page after her, she moves to the Court, then at *Kensington*, and there takes stately and noble Lodgings, appearing at all times as a Person of no small Quality; she much frequented the Walks, Gardens, and other Places of publick Resort, where behaving her self very free and Complaisant, young Gallants, like Bees about a Honey-Pot, daily flock'd and Buzz'd about her; yet so nice and politick she was to give them no occasion, in the least, to think she was common; but on the contrary, when any made Addresses, and laid close Siege, she refell'd them with a great deal of Gravety, assuming no ordinary Gift of Modesty, the more to inflame her Suitors; at length she found she had entirely caught two Wood-cocks in her Net, and therefore was resolv'd to use them accordingly. The first was no less than Son to a Noble Earl, the second a Baron of considerable Figure, she wisely received their Addresses apart, one knew nothing of the other, till after the Expence of a great deal of time the latter, as the freest Bleeder, bore the Bell; and things brought to such a conclusion, the Nuptials being appointed, that the unwary Gentleman lodg'd all his Jewels, Rings, Plate and Treasure whatsoever in her sole Custody, not Mistrusting in the least the virtue of his bright Saint, tho to his Exceeding great cost he found the fairest face had the most corrupted Heart, for he being obliged, upon some Emergant occasions, to visit some Relations in the Country, his *Dalilah*, with all the Booty moves off; and so the poor cheated Gentleman, without enjoying any other Bliss, than the Phlematick offals of Love, the Letchery (cold comfort) of a dry Kiss, lost his *all*.

I must confess my Informer futher told me, that altho she was not so honest as to restore her borrow'd Plumes; yet she was so Cheerful as to spend that freely she had acquired so easily, and tho Interest forbad her, entertaining the Baron in her Bed, yet nature prompted her

her to the joys of *Venus*, and kind *Cupid* directed her to a jolly Hero in the field of Love, whose Service she well Rewarded: and truly she was so ravish'd with the Sweets of his Society, that she intirely forgot her self, and so spent her whole Treasure before her thoughts so imploy'd in Contriving new Scencof Love, had leisure to think of getting more.

Being tow under a cloud of Disreputation, amongst her Acquaintauce, she was unable to Borrow as afore; and therefore was forc'd to take new Methods for a Livelyhood; Hereupon it was I suppose she enter'd into the Service of the Honourable Lady *Dondanel*, where she continued not above ten or Eleven Months, at most; and then took Lodingings, in which she continu,d till the Perpetration of her Horrid Villany.

How she liv'd; that is, what Courses she now took for a Maintance, is indeed something of a Mistery, Certain it is she had no Estate; nor as I take it, received no Pension or allowance from the Government.

Her Intimacy, indeed in so worthy a Family as Squire *Pullens*, and her Familiarity with so Vertuous a Gentlewoman as Madam *Pullen* was, gives me more than Ordinary assurance that she was not addicted to such base and mean Practices as fame reports of her: And tho' by Inclination she, were not so amorous and Gamsom as her Neighbours report; yet it seems to me that Savage Barbarity was Natural and Inherent to her: for her Father was Banish'd out of *France* upon the account of Murder; And yet I must not Exclude her the Kingdom of Love neither, for being brought up under the tution of an Aunt, when she was of Age fit to enter into Religion, one of her Aunts, made all endeavours to put her into a Convent, but she so Peremptorily refus'd it, that her Aunt highly incens'd, sent her into *America*.

Such indeed was her unstable Mind; or rather uneasiness to be under any Authority that long she staid not there neither, but with her Son posted into *England*, a generous and as she thought warm Clime for Love, free from the dread of Convents and Nunneries And thus having trac'd the most Material passages of her Life, I shall now proceed to the last and very worst part of it.

On the 29th of *June* last the *Margaret Martel* Moved by an avaritious desire to support her Pride and Ambition, came to the House of Squire *Pullen*, in which sometimes before she had lodg'd the Space of 14 Months, and finding the Lady within tarred with her till towards the Evening, at which time contriving several frivolous Messages for the said Madam *Pullens* Maid, she took the opportunity with a Razor to Cut her Throat in the Closet, as the Lady was shewing her some Plate, which belike said *French* Woman had formerly pawn'd there; after this Villany perpetrated, she riffled and Plunder'd the House of several Valuable Pieces of Plate, *&c.* As shall be more fully hereafter shewn upon her Tryal. The next day after she had done this Wicked Deed, she was taken and Commited to *Newgate* where her Behaviour like the former part of her Life, was with a great deal of Assurance and Audacity, till *Friday* the 9th of *July*, at which time she was called down to the *Old-Baily*, in order to her Tryal: which was as follows.

She was Indicted on two Indictments, the first for Murdering *Elizabeth Pullen*, Wife of *Paul Pullen*, Esq; at the *Pine Apple* in *Suffolk-street*, on the 29th of *June* last, by giving her one Mortal Wound in the Throat with a Knife value 2 *d.* of the Breadth of Six Inches, of which she instantly dyed. The Second was for Robbing Squire *Pullen* of a Silver-Tankard, 2 Silver Candlesticks, 4 Gold Rings, Silver Porringer, 3 Spoons, 2 Gold Watches, 6 pair of Silver Buckles, with other valuable Goods. The first Evidence was the Maid-Servant, who said, that her Mistress being at Dinner, and near Dined, the Prisoner came and knock'd at the Door, she being her Mistresses Acquaintance, let her in, and her Mistress ask'd her, why she did not come sooner; whereupon she excused her self; to be short, after she had eat and drank, she desir'd a Letter to be carried to *Red-Lyon-Square* which Madam *Pullen* bid her go to do, in the mean while she committed her Bloody Fact, the Maid returning home, the said *French*-Woman entertain'd entertain'd her with a thousand frivolous discourses, pretending the Gentlewoman was gone abroad; which the Maid also, from her Mouth, related to her Master when he came home, whereupon he went to Bed; but the *French*-Woman tarried there till 11 a Clock, at which time, lying down on the Bed, the Maid, tho thinking little, spyed some drops of Blood upon her Petticoat, and demanding how it came, the *French*-Woman answer with a smile, and soon after went away about 12, the Maid went out to look for her Mistress, but found her not, till coming home, one of the Neighbours advis'd the Maid to break open the Door, of which it is thought the Gentlewoman had the Key, where they found her cruelly Murdered as aforesaid. Upon her Tryal, the *French*-Woman was in two or three several Tales, having little to purpose to say, for indeed most of the Goods were found in her Custody, and there was also produc'd her Bloody Petticoat and Slippers, and so the Jury half *English* and half *French* brought her Guilty of the Murder and Robbery.

Her Behaviour in *Newgate*, was now m[illegible]ed, she was twice at the Chappel once after condemnation, but it was some time before she Confess'd her Guiltiness of the Horrid fact, which thorough the perswasion of a French Divine at length she did; acknowledging the horrid Machination to be all her own.

On *Friday*, *July*, the 16th. By eight a clock in the Morning, she was convey'd from *New-gate* to the place of Execution, where to be modish, as I may say, and the better to signify her self a *Roman* Catholick she read a short Paper, and afterwards deliver'd the same to the Sheriffs; but it contain'd nothing more remarkable than what hath been said; a fresh acknowledgment of her hainous offence at the last moment of her Breath, and an Idolatrious Prayer to the Virgin *Mary*.

FINIS

A True Relation Of the Life and Conversation of Margaret Martel (Wing T2994A) is reproduced with permission from the unique copy at the Newberry Library. The text-block measures 150 × 240 mm.

The following words are a transcription of the original:

2.8 Dondanel
2.16 Murder
2.38 Publick
2.39 Penitent
2.40 Mind

A TRUE

RELATION

Of the Life and Conversation of *MARGARET MARTEL*, that Murder'd Mistress *PULLYN*.

Together with the

CONFESSION

She made of that

MURDER

In *NEWGATE*, to a French Divine, in Presence of several Witnesses: On the 12th. and 14th. of *July* last.

17. July. 1697.

THE Father of the Criminal was of *Paris*, and her Mother was of *Tours*, both of them of a considerable Family, who professed the Roman Religion; her Father having committed a Murder was banisht out of *France*, and with his Wife went into *Canada* in *America*, and she was there brought to Bed of the said *Margaret Martel* in the Town of *Quebac*.

When the said *Margaret Martel* was Five years old, she was sent by her Parents into *France*, where she was brought up in the Popish Religion, and when she was of an Age fit to enter into Religion, one of her Aunts made all her endeavours to put her into a Convent; but the said *Margaret Martel* having no Inclination at all to it, her Aunt sent her back again into *America* to her Father, but having no mind for that Countrey, she stole away and came back again into *France*; when her Aunt according to her former Resolution, endeavoured to put her into a Nunnery; but *Margaret Martel* not being able to suffer so much as the thoughts of it, did run away the Second time, and came into *England* with a Son she had.

When

When she was in *England*, she did put her Son Page to my Lord of *Essex*, where he did not long stay, but went afterwards to my Lady *Dondanel*, who took him for her Page; his Mother *Margaret Martel* being that Lady's Woman at the same time, and behaved her self well enough all the time that she staid in that Noble Family, which was Ten or eleven Months. Then the said Lady going back again into *Scotland*, and *Margaret Martel* having no mind for that Country, both she and her Son went away from the said Lady. My Lord *Arran*, Brother of my Lady *Dondanel*, took her Son for a Page for himself; and *Margaret Martel* took a Lodging for her self, where she had lived about fourteen Months when she committed this horrid Murder on the Body of Mrs. *Pullen*, with whom formerly she had lived, when she came first into *England*. She was committed to *Newgate* the next day after she had committed this barbarous Murder. At her Tryal she pleaded Not Guilty, and did desire a Mixt Jury, one half English Men, and the other Foreigners, which was granted her; and the said Jury having heard all the Evidences against her, found her Guilty of the Murder and Fellony. The next day returning she was to receive Sentence, she pleaded a great Belly but the Jury of Women brought in that she was not with Child, and then the Sentence of Death passed upon her.

She persisted a while after to assert her Innocency, and to say, that she was Not Guilty of those Crimes she was Condemn'd for; but at last a French Divine going to see her in *Newgate* ask'd her of what Religion she was; she told him, that she would dye in the Roman Religion, in which she had been brought up all her Life, upon which the Minister having told her, That of whatever Religion she was, she ought to Confess her Crime, and that there was no Mercy to be hoped for at the hands of God, unless she did confess her Crimes and sincerely Repent of them: At last after much Exhortation he prevailed with her, and she Confessed, that she had committed this Bloody Murder; and that she had Premeditated it above three Months and at last did excute it having found a fit Opportunity. She first sent the Maid upon an Errand, and then she being alone with the said Mistress *Pullyn*, she first Stunn'd her with three Blows of a Hammer upon her Head, and afterwards did cut her Throat with a Razor, that she had prepared for that abominable Use; and did after pull her into a Closet, and took all the things she had a mind to, and afterwards Lockt the Doors, and staid for the Maid in an outward Parlour, and told her, that her Mistress was gone out upon some earnest Business, and had took her Keys along with her. She desired that her Confession might be Publisht and made known to all the World: And seems now to be very Penitent beseeching Almighty God to have Mercy upon her Soul.

By divers Circumstances it is believed, she had a Mind to Murder the Maid also.

London Printed: And are to be Sold by *E. Whitlock* near *Stationers-Hall*, 1697.

The Horrible Murther of a young Boy (*STC* 6552) is reproduced with permission from the unique copy at The British Library (shelfmark 1104.b.51). The text-block measures 118 × 209 mm.

The difficulty in reproducing a readable title page is due to the poor state of the original.

The following words are a transcription of the original:

8.3 feeding
8.4 as it
8.5 this
8.6 na-
8.7 hee
8.10 cocks
8.35 He likewise asked whither she went then?
8.36 who brought

... out and how ...

... to gether ...

... were executed at Stafford the ... of August. 1606.

LONDON

... by Ed. Allde for VVilliam Firebrand ... to be solde at his Shop in the Popes-head ... against the Tauerne doore.

... 6.

A

True Relation of the cruell Murthering of a young Boy, not fully three yeares olde, whose Sister likewise had her tongue cut out of her head, hard by the rootes: which murther and massacre was done by a woman called Mother *Dell*, and her Sonne, dwelling at *Hatfield* in Hartfordshire, for which monstrous fact, they were both hanged at Hartford this last Sises. The onely witnesse to proue the Murther was the tonguelesse Childe, most mightily preserued from death, to which Childe it pleased God to lend the vse of speech, notwithstanding the want of her tongue.

IN Hatfield in the Countie of Hartford, dwelled an olde Widdowe, called Mother Dell, who had abiding with her in the house, onely her Sonne, named T. Dell: Into the house of this old woman (some foure yeares since) was seene goe in two prettie Children a Boy and a Girle, the Boy seemed not three yeares of age, and the Girle not much aboue foure. These Children were led into the said house by a wandring Pedler & his wife (or Puncke.) The going in of these children was noted by diuers, but especiallye by a Taylor dwelling in the towne called A. C. which Taylor markt them so much the more, for that they were hansomelye apparelled, and their coates made with new winges, skirtes and lags, such as he had not seene the like of before, which made him presently upon the sight of them, to make a patterne of those winges and Jagges: But doubting that he had not taken a true patterne, he watched to haue another sight of those Children, But when for two or three daies space hee could not see them, hee went to the house of Mother Dell, and did aske her for those Children? shee answered him verye shortly saying: they were safe enough, for they were gone againe with them that brought them.

With this answere the Taylor was satisfyed, because it no further concernd him then the getting of a peece of a new fashion. But within a while after, the boy was found dead in a ditch or water not farre from the Towne, with a great peece of wood tyed to his backe. The Childe being taken out, it did plainely appeare that hee was murthered before he was throwne in, The poore harmelesse Infant being found thus cruelly murthered, and none that looked on him taking knowledge of him. His pretty litle coate was taken and hanged up in divers market townes and proclamation made in euerie one of those Townes to this effect, that if any one whatsoeuer could and would tel where the Father or Mother of the murthered Childe (which wore that Coate) dwelt, he should haue fortye shillings for his paines, and his charges borne to bring him from and to the place where hee dwelt: But all this proued to little or no purpose, till at the last, this newes came to the hearing of the Taylor, who comming to the place where the Coate was to bee seene, and taking good notice of it, he presently calde to his remembrance, that, that coate was worne by one of those Children which hee had seene goe into the house of Mother Dell.

The newes of this comming to the eares of Sir Henry Butler and one other Knight, being both Justices, and both dwelling neere to that place, a warrant was made, by vertue whereof, the said Mother Dell and her Sonne were brought before them both, and strictlye examined, where they both confest ỹ two such Children as the Taylor

lor spake of, came into the house with a Pedler and his wife, and that they verily thought the Boy at that time had that coate on his backe: but all this was nothing to them, for they neither knew the Pedlar nor his wife, onely they came thether to see if they had needs of any of their ware, (as it is a common use for traueling Pedlars to cal at diuers houses) & when they had bestowed some little money with them, both hee, his wife, and those Children (which they saide were theirs) went out on the backside of the house, and what after became of them, they knew not.

Upon this their confession, they were both bound ouer to appeare and answere at the next Assizes, the Iustices hoping ere that time to finde out the actor or actors of that more then monstrous tragedy. But alas their hopes were deceiued, for the time was not yet come wherein God had decreed to bring this cruell, barbarous, and bloody masacre to light: yet notwithstanding, they were still bound ouer from Sise to Sise, almoste for foure yeares, in which time, the saide Mother Dell bestowed greate cost in altering, repayring, and furnishing of her house, which made many of her neighbors much to wõder, for that they knew not from whence shee should haue wherewith to defray that charge.

But now let vs leaue both her and her Sonne to the hel and horror of a guiltie conscience, which alwaies waytes and attends on murtherers, and let vs now speake of the poore mangled and dismembred Girle, who was now in farre worse case then her dead Brother, had not hee which prouides for the whole world, in his good appointed tyme prouided for her: For her tongue was first cut out of her head by the rootes, then was shee led by this said Mother of mischiefe and her Sonne, (at a time when they were not seene) to the side of a wood, which was sildome frequented, in which place stood an old great hollow tree, which was not very high.

Hauing

Having brought this helplesse and hopelesse child to this tree (which they ment should be her graue) the sonne got vp to the top, and rudely halled vp after him this harmles girle, who hauing seene her brother murthered before her face, had no reason to hope of life, yet did she not cease with teares and signes to begge for pitie of these pittilesse wretches, whose hearts being much harder then stone, would not relent: for this mercilesse villaine let her slippe into the tree, where they left her, in hope neuer more to see her, or heare of her.

But he that preserued Daniel in the Lions den, and made the blinde to see, the lame to goe, and the dumbe to speake, did not onely preserue the life of this childe, but also did giue vnto her an extraordinarie strength and vigor, whereby she was able, and did make such a noyse, that a man comming by that way (not by chaunce, but surlye by the prouidence and appointment of God) hearing a strange humming, and hollow crying, drawing neare to that tree, perceiued the noyse and crie to come from thence, which made him get vp to the top of it, where being and looking downe into it, he behelde that pittifull, ruthfull, and bloody spectacle: which when he had a while looked on with pittie and compassion, and hauing spoke to her, and perceyuing by her signes that she could not answer him, he made meanes to drawe her out. Which when he had done, he began (as may be easily imagined) to bethinke with himselfe, what great trouble hee might come into if hee were found with the childe, he being a stranger, as it seemes he was.

And this feare of trouble (as was supposed by the graue and wise Iudge and Iustices of the Bench, when the matter came to their hearing) made this man after he had pulled her out of the tree, to make from her with all the haste he could. But the poore soule pursued him with all the haste she could, crying and calling vnto him for succor and helpe in the best manner she could, being thereunto vrged by by paine and hunger, the least of which will force a man of a resolute and resolued spirit to breake silence, had hee vowed the contrarie: much more then being ioyned both together must they force a childe.

In briefe then, when she had lost the sight of him, God knowes what became of her, but no one man or woman can tell any certaine place of her aboade for almost these foure yeares.

Many say they haue seene such a dumbe child wander vp and downe a begging, and she herselfe hath confessed (since the time that God hath sent her vse of her speech and vtterance, that she may bee easily vnderstood by any that shall heare her) that she did beg for her foode all that time.

And questionlesse, the Lord who had reserued her, both to bring so monstrous a murder, and cruell a massacre to light, and also to make manifest his almightie power to many misbeleeuing and vnbeleeuing miscreants (Atheists I meane) he, I say, as may most euidently appeare, did both preserue her, and prouide for her.

And now the time drawing neare, wherein it pleased God to giue these wicked wretches some part of of their reward, he so directed the course of this poore wandring childe, that she came backe againe to the towne of Hatfield, where she receiued her wrongs, hauing yet no vse of speech nor vtterance, whereby she might be vnderstood. And wandring vp and downe the towne, little thinking she had beene neare the place where her innocent brother lost his life, and herselfe the instrument of her speech: but going along the streete, gasing here and there, as children will doe (yea and olde folkes too) when they come into a strange place, At last shee came by the house where this bloodie tragidie had beene acted: which house she no sooner sawe, but she knew, as did appeare by the signes of griefe and sorrow, which she made at the sight thereof. For what with her crying, and the extraordinarie noyse which shee made, shee drewe people about her, who did in some sorte

 seeme

seeme to greeue at the moane shee made: but surely they could not chuse but wonder, and desire to knowe what the sorrow and signes ment which the childe made. For one while she would gape wide with her mouth, drawing her fore finger to and fro it, as though she had beene cutting of some thing: then would she with her finger poynt into the house. And when this mother Dell and her sonne came to the doore, then her crying and her signes did seeme much to encrease, which made the lookers on to suspect much, but alas they knew not what. But at last amongst other folkes, came the Tailer before spoken of, and hee no sooner saw the child, noted her signes, and remembred the other Childe found in the water and marthered as is aforesaide, but straight he saies, that this was the other of those Children, which was ledde into that house long since by the Pedler and his Wife. Then some of the Neighbours together with the Taylor, tooke the childe and led her into the house, shee being within, stood staring wildelye round about her, at last shee spied a paire of stayres, to which shee went directlye, and comming to them, shee looked earnestlye on them, looking about the house againe, she first pointed to the stayres, and then to a Corner of the house, as who should say, these stayres did stand there.

This signe the neighbors understood well, because they knew the stayres had bene remooued and that made them thinke some foule matter would bee pickt out of her other signes. Heereupon they beganne to lay handes on the Mother and her Sonne, to haue them againe (now with the Childe) before the Justice, at which the childe seemed to reioyce.

Being brought before Sir Henry Butler, who was the next Justice, (and had examined them diuers times before concerning these Children) the Constable or Headborough beganne to tell unto his Worshippe the cause of their comming, and hauing related unto him from point

to

to point, what they had seene, the Childe marking, and understanding them well, fell to her former signes againe before the Knight. Whereupon hee did with greate wisdome and discretion, examine them aparte, one from another. But they both remained still obstinate, and in their olde tale, confessing nothing, nor would anye of them acknowledge, that they had ever seene the Girle before, notwithstanding the Taylor did still affyrme it to their faces, that that was the Girle which the Pedler and his wife led into their house long since with the boy.

The Justice assuring himselfe now, that these were the actors of that bloody Tragedy, & hoping that God would in time make it yet more plaine then it was, hee caused a Mittimus to be made & sent them to the Jayle, there to remaine without bayle or maineprise untill the Assises. And further hee willed the Constable to take the Childe backe againe with him to the Towne, and to have a great care that she might be wel looked unto, and to see the house of Mother Dell safely shut up.

All this being doone according to the Knightes commaũd, & the childes lodging & diet being much better, then it had beene long before, she began to gather both strength and spirit unto her, and to take delight to playe amongst Children.

But now (Gentle Reader) let mee intreate thee as thou readst, not onelye to admyre and wonder, but to prayse & and magnifie the mightie maker and preserver of us all, for his great mercy and might shewed to this poore childe, in this next succeeding action, which if wee looke into but with the eyes of naturall reason and humane sence, it will be thought incredible and impossible. But with God nothing is impossible, & this ought not to be thought incredible, because it was so lately and so neere unto us done, and for that the Childe is yet living in Hatfield, to affirme for truth, all that is heere written of her.

Now you shal understand, that this girle being playing with other children on the backe-side of some mans house in the towne, where cocks, hens, & chickens were feeding. It pleased God at that time, to make a cocke to be (as it were a tutor to the child, and) his first messenger of this mightie miracle, like as a bird of the same name and nature, vsing the selfe same note, put Peter in minde that he had denied his maister: from which his remembrance sprung his true and heartie repentance. But to proceede: This child being playing (as I said before) one of the cocks in the yard began to crow, and another answered him and thus they continued a prettie while. At last one of the children began (after their maner) to mocke the cockes, crying cocke-adoodle-doo: in the end this dumbe child, straining her selfe, cried as the rest had done, cocke-adoodle-doo, which made all the children amazde: and one of them that stoode next her, said: what, canst thou speake now? I that I can (said she) speaking it so plainly that they all understoode her. The hearing of this made the children breake up their play, and runne home with ioy to the house where this child was kept, to carrie newes. And when she came home to the house where she was kept, and the folke of the house finding the report of the children to be true, with exceeding ioy (after the asking of her some few questions, to which she did answere verie directly) they led her againe to the knight before named, to whom they tolde what had happened. Which when he had heard (he being furnished with the feare of God, which is indeede the true fountaine and fountation of wisedome) hee first of all gaue thankes to God, and then he did aske her who cut out her tongue? she said, the olde woman and her sonne, that killed her brother, and put her into the tree: then he asked her who tooke her out of the tree? and she saide, a man, that when hee had done did runne away from her because she could not speake to him. He likewise asked whither she went then: but alas she could not tell him: then he did aske her, who brought her

her to the old womans house first? and she said a man and a woman that had killed her father and her mother, and taken a great bagge of money from them. And she said that the man and woman had giuen a great deale of that money to the olde woman: and that the olde woman did at that time lift vp her hands thrée times, and did sweare thrée times, that she would neuer tell any body who they were. These and many other questions the Knight did aske her, to all which she did answer, with more reason and sense, then is common to one of her age.

To conclude, the Sises being come, an Inditement was prefered against the mother and the sonne, to which inditement they pleaded not guiltie, and put themselues to the ordinarie triall. Whereupon the childe was brought before the Bench, and stoode vpon the Table betweene the Bench and the Jury. Where after that the foresaid Knight had opened some part of this foule offence, the childe was asked diuerse of the former questions: to which she answered as before. The taylor likewise was there, who tolde vnto the Jurie what he had seene. Then the Jurie was willed to goe togither: but before they went, they did looke into the childes mouth, but could not see so much as the stumpe of a tongue therein. The Jurie staid not long before they returned with their verdite guiltie, whereupon they had sentence of death pronounced against them, and were both hanged at Hartfort the fourth day of August. 1606.

Thus farre (gentle reader) haue I set down briefly and truly the maner of this monstrous massacre. And how farre it hath pleased God to reueale some of the Authors: and for some secrete purpose best knowne to himselfe, to conceale the rest, which questionlesse shall be made knowne in his good appointed time, when it shall bee most for his honour and glorie. In the meane time, let me intreat all you which doe reade or heare this ruthfull discourse, to meditate (as I doe and will) on the many miseries and mischances mankinde kind is subiect to, which if you doe, questionlesse you will make lesse ioy at the birth of your children, and lesse sorrow at their death then commonly you doe, and rather seeke (in some sort) to imitate those Heathens, which did sing and daunce at the death of their children, then those Christians which doe mourne and sorrow as men past hope. As for the loue which ordinarily men beare vnto their children, it may more fitlye bee called loue to themselues, then to their children. For notwithstanding we all know or ought to know, that no one is truly happy till his end, if he die well, yet many (nay most of vs) doe rather desire to haue our children suruiue vs, then to see them fairely bestowed before vs. Neuer thinking, respecting, or regarding, what may come to them after our death: so our humors be fed in our liues And if this may not truly be said to be selfe-loue, I know not what is selfe-loue. Therefore let vs all and euery one of vs, referre and put our willes to Gods will, assuring our selues, that all things shall worke togither for the best, for them that loue and feare him.

As for the Pedler and his wife, which the child hath confest to haue robbed and kild her father and mother, they are not yet found out, nor is the place and abode of her too vnfortunate Parents yet knowne But yet all in good time, if it be the will of the Amightie, both the one and the other shall come to light. Amen.

The Most Crvell and Bloody Mvrther (*STC* 6553) is reproduced with permission from the clear Harvard College Library copy. The text-block measures 90 × 155 mm.

THE MOST CRVELL AND BLOODY MVR-ther committed by an Inkeepers *Wife, called* Annis Dell, *and her Sonne* George Dell,

Foure yeeres since.

On the bodie of a Childe, called *Anthony Iames in Bishops Hatfield in* the Countie of Hartford, and now most miraculously reuealed by the Sister of the said *Anthony*, who at the time of the murther had her tongue cut out, and *foure yeeres remayned dumme and speechlesse, and now perfectly speaketh, reuealing the Murther, hauing no tongue to be seen.*

With the seuerall VVitch-crafts, and most damnable practises of one *Iohane Harrison* and her Daughter vpon seuerall persons, men *and women at* Royston, *who were all executed at* Hartford *the 4 of August last past. 1606.*

LONDON

Printed for *William Firebrand* and *Iohn Wright* and are to be sold at Christs Church dore. 1606.

THE MOST CRVELL and bloody Murther of *Anthony Iames in Hatfield in Hartford-shire.*

HErodotus writeth of Sesostris a King of the Egiptians, that he was carried in a Chariot drawne with foure Kings, whom he before had conquered, when one of the foure, casting his eyes behinde him, looked often vpon the wheeles of the Chariot; which Sesostris earnestly noting, at last demaunded of him what he meant by looking backe so often, who replied, I see that those things which were highest in the wheeles become lowest, and the lowest as soone become highest, cogito de mutatione fortunæ, I thinke vpon the inconstancie of things. Sesostris hereupon as in a glasse beholding himselfe, waxed more milde, and deliuered the imprisoned Kings from that slauerie.

This Historie then so liuely expressing the mortalitie of mans life, that to the highest belongs a graue, assoone as to the lowest, and that man himselfe is a witnesse to himselfe, how vncertaine are his daies, (since sinne hath spread it selfe like a leaprosie ouer all flesh, and iniquitie hath gotten the vpper hand) that a Spider is able to choake vs, a haire to stifle vs, and a tile falling on our heads to extinguish vs, and in that moment when we least suspect so sudden Calamities.

Our life then is so momentarie, that in that minute wee breath, if not defended by our maker, in that minute we are breathlesse: should any flesh, endowed with that heauenly reason which God hath onely giuen to men and angels, so forget his vncertaintie, as for a little gold which is but the dregs of the earth, for vanitie, (the pleasures of the world) or for the world it selfe which is an Hypocrite, because it hath exterior apparance of goodnesse, and within is full of corruption and vanitie, which is but like to reeds, that when they shoot out first in the spring of the yeere, doe with their fresh green colour delight the eye for a while, but if we break them and looke within them, we finde nothing but emptinesse and hollownesse. forget his maker and the dignitie of his creation, who made him like to himselfe, to his owne Image and likenesse, to the intent, that as all other creatures of their owne proper natures doe loue their like, so should man set his affection on God alone, where contrarily, he being the hand of heauen, made for vertuous dispositions, conducts himselfe to vitious actions, whereby it followes certainely, that men in their liues are like children, who more delight of a horse made of reedes, and babes formed of clowtes, than in the thinges themselues, so man giues more honor to the shadowe, than to the truth, and indeede (as in this whole course) but like birds, who greedily flye to pecke vp the corne till they be caught in the ginne: or like fishes, who earnestly swimme to catch the baite, though they be choakt with the hooke: so doe many, how indirectly soeuer, hunt after riches, til they deface their bodies be the law, and condemne their soules by their sinne, as shall appeare by this following discourse.

SOme Foure yeeres since neere Deuonshey Hundred in Essex liued a Yeoman one Anthony Iames, who in repute of the world was counted rich, and by the report of his Neighbours held credible and honest.

This man in the desire of his youth matcht himselfe to an honest Countrey-maide, whose vertuous disposition equald his owne thoughts, and whose diligent care was carefully to saue what her husband brought home, as his

labour

labour did striue to procure it abroad; so that the prouidence of the one, and the care of the other, mixt such a mutuall content betwéen them, that they liued like Abraham and Sara, he louing to her, she obedient to him.

In processe of time this couple growing wealthy by their labour, proued to be as happie by their yssue, for it it pleased God to enrich them with two children, a Boy, and a Girle, that the wishes of the Father might be as wel satisfied, as the desire of the Mother, and both contented in so comfortable a blessing.

The Mother being (as women vse to say) stored first with a Daughter, and called it by her owne name Elizabeth Iames, so that when time brought the Father as happie reioycing of a Sonne, hee christened it by his owne name Anthony Iames. In the education and bringing vp of these two Children, there was a pretty louing contention betwéene the Goodman and the Wife, which of the two should proue most happie to the Parents delight, whose loue indéede was alike to them both. So that time passing away in that comfortable strife betwéene this louing couple, the Daughter had attayned to the age of Eight yéeres, and the Sonne to Seuen, in which passage the mother hauing no other yssue, was then with childe with the third, and the better halfe of her time had carried so happie a burthen.

About that season of the yéere a Faire happened in Essex, to which the Seruants they then kept, some for pleasure, the rest about necessarie businesse were sent, so that the honest Yeoman with his wife and children were onely left at home, when mischiefe like a bramble that takes hold on whatsoeuer it touches, caught this occasion, and wrought in the mindes of Nine, I cannot call them men, but villaines, and another not a woman, but a beast to make a prey of these harmelesse foure, and their increast possessions: but as *Finis est primum in intensione,*
Vltimum in executione.

So these wretches hauing fastened on this monstrous

intent made hast to the execution thereof, and so sone had attained to this wealthy Yeomans house, where finding little or no resistance, they first bound the man and the woman, and giuing the two children to two of their associats to hould, the rest fell to ransacke, where not contenting themselues with that store of riches they found, as Gold, Siluer, Plate, Rings, and other wealth, hauing made vp their packe, they consulted with themselues for their further security, to make spoyle of the owners. It was not long in question ere this hellish Iury had giuen vp as damnable a verdict, for (suspition alwaies haunting a guiltie mind,) they determined with themseules they could not bee safe from pursute, from attachment, nay from shamefull death, which they worthily deserued, without the slaughter of the father and the mother, which they presently resolued vpon, and then two of them stepping to the man, where he lay bound vpon the ground, with their daggers stabbed him in the body: who ere his speach left him, lifting vp his eyes, beg'd only this of them, take my riches, I car'd for them to bring vp my posterity, but now they are yours, I giue them you frely; then pitty my wife, bee mercifull to my children. These his last words semed to beget some remorse (seldome sene) in the men which were murtherers, which the more than monstrous woman perceiuing (as in a rage thereat) stept to his wife, and calling to him with these words; Talkest thou of pittie quoth shee, if thy eyes haue yet left so much sight to be witnes how ile be pittifull? behould how Ile performe thy peticion. So drawing out her knife, (O act too terrible to report, but the most damnablest that euer was heard of, executed by a woman) shee ript her vp the belly, making herselfe a tragicall midwife, or truly a murtheresse, that brought an abortiue babe to the world, and murthered the mother.

The good woman hauing not leaue to cry, and her husband hauing not the vse of speach, they both lift vp their hands, rowld their eyes one to another, and with that said, but silent; Farewell euer.

This

This tragicall spectacle enforced all the rest partakers in the robbery, and actors in the murther to remorce, nay euen to a repentance; that done, this horrible action had a beginning: but sinne allwaies seeking securely to shrowd it selfe in, they began now to question of their safety, and (as villaines are euer one affraid and in distrust of another) they conclude now to share their purchase, and euery knaue to shift for himselfe.

Some urged let us first kill the children, as we haue done their parents, others and the greater part glutted with the present obiect, and euen ashamed of themselues and their sinfull actions, not onely denyed, but confidently resolued they would be no further guilty in the blood of Innocents. In briefe they agréed euerie party to haue an equall portion of this ill purchased booty, which soone shared amongest them, and as it appeared, hauing more than they could tell what to doe withall, they gaue the remaine to thrée of their Consorts, of which the woman was one to conuey away the children from thence, and bestowe them in what place soeuer, while they would giue their Parents buriall.

This was as soone done as talkt of, seuen of them caried the dead couple from the house to a wood néere adioyning, and there buried them, and the other thrée are gone to trauell with the children.

These Monsters thus diuided, whether of a determinate before of ancient acquaintance, or drawne by what means soeuer, it yet rests undiscouered to the world. These two men, this woman, and these two children the next day some thrée houres before night, came to Bishops Hatfield in Hartford shire seuentéen miles from London, the children being on a horse in a payre of Panniers, the woman riding betwéene them, as it had béene to visite some of their friends, then they tooke up their Inne at one Dels house: and being brought to their chamber they called for their Hostesse, when after some other parle had betwéene them, they demaunded of her, if she would be secret in a businesse, they would unfold unto her, who presently without further

 pawse,

pawse, replied, I as God should iudge her would she, when straight they began to discouer to her their whole procee-dings, shewed her what riches they had got, and told her they were willing to make her a Partaker therein, onely they craued her aduise, how they should dispose of the chil-dren, all this was spoken in the hearing of the Girle. To which Dels wife, as by the sequell appeared soone gaue this her consent and instruction, that the Boy should be mur-thered, and his sister haue her tongue cut out.

This, thus resolued vpon, they fell to drinking, and who so merry as this diuellish company, all this while the girle sat on the frame at the tables end, and in the meane time, the boy was strayd downe the stayres, where being playing vp and downe in a lower roome, this Dels wife hauing a labourer at worke in her backside to make her bauins, called Nicholas Dracon, it was his chance to come in to call for drincke, where taking note of it, by the pretti-nes of the behauiour it vsed; his Hostesse passing by him, he demaunded of her whose child it was, who answered it be-longs to a guest or two that are now aboue, the honest labourer hauing drunke his drinke that hee came for, went backe to end his busines in the yarde, while the child (they being aboue in the heat of their cups, and not regar-ding him) strayd out into the streete, where one Meney whelpe lay: the tailor taking notice of him, especially by a greene coate with nine skirts about the wast, the fashion then being new for children, hee called the boy to him to take a patterne thereof, and hauing satisfied his desire by noting it well and taking measure of the child, the tailor as the labourer, goes backe to his worke, and the boy re-turnes to Dels house.

By this time night comming on, as the fit marke for villaines to act their villanies vnder, these wretches ha-uing supt with the children, as if no such pretence, which inwardly they intended, had lurked in their bosomes out-wardly, bare themselues faire to the little ones, and when they thought it fit time, went to bed together all in our

chamber

Chamber, the chamber hauing thrée beds in it, the men together, and the women with the children, who in the dead of the night, the time created for quiet rest, the ease of labour, and the honest mans repose; these Homesides rising from their beds, and hauing a candle ready, awaked the children, made them ready, and with flattering words told them, they must goe to their father and mother, when they poore hearts (as willing to obey, as they to demaund, little dreading they were going to such a shambles, as they had prepared for them) came downe with them, & at the staires foot stood the sonne to this Hostesse called George Dell (who belike the mother had acquainted herein) and calling to the men bad them come on and doubt nothing, for he had séene the coast was cléere, whereupon opening the backe doore, they went into the yard, where this Innkéepers wife vsed to milke her kine, & in which stood a great Stacke of wood, where deliuering the Girle to the woman, and George Dell to stay with, tooke the boy & leading him behind the pile, first stopping his mouth with Cow-dung that he might make no noyse, they slit vp his throat from one eare to another. This inhumane murther thus acted, they returne to the house, told Dels wife and her son the déed was done: quoth Dels wife, then George thou shalt conduct them to bottomlesse Pond, where for our more safety, they shall end our cause of mistrust, or feare to be discouered by throwing him in. When George Dell presently stepping to the Woodstacke, and choosing out a good big stake, he with the helpe of the rest bound thereon the dead child with a hairen rope, and George Dell himselfe taking a long Pike staffe on his shoulder, lead them the way towards botomlesse Pond, being a mile frō Hatfield, while the 2 théeues vpon the stake carried the boy, and the strumpet led the Girle in her hand.

Homicid

George Dell thus afore leading the way, the 2 théeues in the midst with ẏ dead boy, after them comes (I may rightly cal her so) the whore with ẏ sister in her hand, who (what with drowsinesse, & what with feare) séming to lag, for the night being vncōfortable to mē, it must néeds be to childrē, the monstrous femall (for no woman) began to egge her on with faire perswasion, Come apace sweet-heart, thy brother is before, and we are going to thy father and thy mother.

The poore Girle encoraged with the remembrance of her Parents names, whose liues they had extinguished from her, as if the names of them (who first gaue her life) could haue created a new motion in her, (as far as her childhood & feeble strength would giue her leaue) hastened after, and by the way cald to her with these words. Gammer, shall my mother make me ready to morrow morning, trisse me when I come from schoole, and heare me say my lesson? The diuelish Diuell answered (not hauing remorse, being remembred of the execrable act she had done) I, when she sees thee next, she shall doe all this.

The men hastening on before with ye pitifull burthen of a murthered brother, when she the diuellisht of all came after with a tender sister, and by the way began to aske her of seuerall circumstances as where she was borne, who were her parents, and what her name was? when the child answering to euerie question according to her remembrance so pretyly, that if her leader had had left in her any sparke of womanhood, who by nature are kinde, flexible, and remorseable, and not been made vp for one to be damned, she would haue pitied her.

But who are created to be Murtherers, are created to be remorselesse, and so was she, onely beguild the way with these & other such like questions, as what she walkt vpon, what she saw withall, and what she spake withall, when the innocent Child (suspectlesse that her own tongue should be her owne betrayer) according to her discretion answered to euerie one, directly pointing to her foot, her eye, and to her tongue, that with those, and by the helpe of those she sawe, went & spake. Whereupon this bloody Tygris, to make her selfe more monstrous, bad her put out her tongue that she might feele it, (being at this time come iust to a stile, where she sat downe, and told the Girle that they would rest themselues a while) when the child, (little dreading it should be the

the last time she should make vse of it, doing what she bad her) she presently caught it by the end, and with her thumbe wresting opē the childs iaws to the widest she could stretch them, she cut it out euen by the root: the Girle hereat begin-ning to make her iust lamentation, this She-wolfe holding her knife to her throat, bad her peace, or she would slit that as she had slit her tong; so that for her pain enforc't by feare (onely as the blood exceeded in her mouth she still spot out that) the woful child was quiet, when the strumpet bad her hold vp her aperne & she would giue her her tongue again, and looke (quoth she) you loose it not, for you must beare it to your brother. By this time (with their conductor George Dell) the men had discharged themselues of their burthen by bottomelesse Pond, throwing the stake & Boy they brought (& bound him withall) into a Corne field, & the child with her tongue in her aperne, and in the whores hand had ouer-taken thē, when presently went to act this last stratageme which before they had agreed vpon, & threw the Boy (as he was in his clothes) into the pond, giuing him for his requiē farewel, no other funerall rites & christian buriall, but these words; sinke there in stead of a mother-graue, ẏ dead child thus in the pond, the whore (as if she had felt her selfe sicke) not being an exercised actor in more villany, hauing forc't the child to be sad (beholding first of her brothers vntimely murther, and now of his watry graue) not resting here, made the distressed Infant take her tongue (the instrument of her speech) out of her aperne, and throw it after her bro-ther, & as it was throwne from her hand, she vttered these words, Let it goe and spare not, it cannot be better bestow-ed, they are neere a kin together.

The murthered brother thus bestowed, & his sister speech-lesse, these vilaines hauing contented Dels wife for her coū-sell, and so bountifully that where it was credibly knowne, the Lease of her Inne was (at the time of this action) at pawne for 50 l. she presently fetcht it home, and bestowed a 100. Markes more in building. The next morning before day they parted; yet in their parting this was resolued vppon betweene them, that the dumbe Girle with some little peece of mony should be giue unto a beggar to travell with, & she so disposed of, they were certen never to be discovered.

The next day in Hatfield wood (some 2 miles from Hatfield) this determination tooke effect, & a beggar for a peece of money, tooke the Wench promising to keepe her, as many such Rogues use for ones to begge withall. The childe received, and the mony payd, the 2 theeues and the whore departed: when the beggar (whether not liking the bargain least after he should pay too deere for it, of slight care or selfe-will, it is yet unknowne) he lost the child in Hatfield wood, where shortly after it was found in a hallow tree, and having received some little cherishing of some well disposed people about the wood-side, from thence it strayd to Barnet, from Barnet to London, where hapning in the dumbe manner, it used to begge at one Master Allens dore a Barber-surgeon for some releese, the Maister comming himselfe to the dore, and seeing the child make such pitiful signes to the mouth, he tooke it by the hand and led it into his shop, and opening her mouth to know the cause of the greefe it complayned of, found the tongue to be cut out, and the wound unheald, who (pitying the missfortune of the childe) of his owne charitable disposition, cured it. The mouth thus healed, for 4 yeeres space together, the Girle hath been knowne in many countreys to beg for her food somtimes about London, sometimes in Essex, but most she hath been remembred (as is certenly by divine providence of heaven, that by her these villanies should come to light) to be resident in Hartford shire, she was never knowne to speak any sillables tending to speech, only hoarsly she could mutter when any one spake to her in stead of answere Moka, moka, & so neere her tongue was cut out to the root, that the food any charitable persons bestowed on her, she had no tongue to helpe her to swalow it, but after she had chawd it in her mouth, she was faine to pull out the skin of her throat with her fingers, & gulpe it down; in this dumbe maner she continued 4 yeres. We will leave her begging for her living, and returne to

her

her murthered brother in bottomelesse pond.

This Child hauing remained three weekes in the pond, on Saint Peters day in the morning (for at that time of the yeere happened this Tragedy) some Gentlemen and others (being a hunting for Wild-foule) hapned with their dogs to beat about this Pond; when one of these dogges hauing scented the child (as where it was rose vp vnder the weeds at a banke-side) whined and cried, and by no meanes could be beat or drawne from thence, which eagernesse of the Spaniels, wrought a desire in the men to know certainely the cause thereof, and with their long staues turning vp the weeds, found there a Boy to be drowned, as they coniectured; when carying newes thereof to the towne, the bodie was by the Crowner taken vp, and layd openly for the view of all men to take knowledge of it.

The whole Countrey neere thereabouts comming at the strangenesse of the report, that a childe should be murthered and then throwne into a pond, yet none could challenge in him the right of a sonne; yet the aforesayd Henrie Whilpley, Nicholas Deacon, and diuers others of Hatfield, made testification both by apparell, and other signes (for the Boy had a red head) that this was the childe, who three weekes before was seene in Dels house, so many then signified to the Iustice: Dels wife was sent for, for her husband was a blinde man, when being demanded if such a child were not brought to her house, (as before is spoken) & who they were that brought it thether, when she constantly denied, shee knew of no such, and for certaine she could affirme, that no such child did lodge at her house, and being offered her oath, hereupon she was as redy to sweare as resolute to deny, but who knowes not lying and swearing are partners; and as inseparable companions as a theefe and a receiuer, and (as I may say) sworne brethren, that alwaies trumpe together in a sinfull societie: her oath being taken (see the iust iudgment of God, she had not power to confes that troth which would haue wrought her out of all suspition, but vtterly denying that which was so manifestly proued against her) the Justices thought it requisite (till further proofe could be had on this presumption) to bind her ouer to giue answere at the next Assizes.

When from assizes to assizes, during the passage of foure yeares shee was compeld to appeare, nothing being further found against her, but her owne deniall; whereupon the first demaund, if shee had made but this perswasion and satisfying answere, as Judge Daniell very worthyly urged against her at ẏ tryall, that keeping an Inne, shee had many guests, and many children lay at her house, of which number (for ought shee knewe) that might bee one, but who brought them, from whēce they come, or whether they will, shee is not bound to take notice of. This might haue been some instance of her innocency, but so to deny a question, the truth of which was not of sufficiency to beare her argues, a suspition and mistrust of her selfe, and prooues her to be guilty.

But to the former matter, shee hauing made her appearance at so many seuerall assises and sessions, and no instance against her, but the former, it was thought at lent assizes last, shee should haue been dismist the Court: but in ẏ meane time such is the iust iudgment of God, to the plague of murtherers, and terror of them that delight in bad, the dumbe shall speake ere they shall escape undiscouered.

For the dumbe sister of this murthered child, for when shee was in question, led (no question) foure yeare up and downe, from towne to towne, from country to country, by the hand of God was at Michaelmas last brought unto Hatfield, before whose comming thither, though Dels wife was by the grauer iudgments held in some suspition, yet was her honest carriage such to trauelors, and to all sorts of people shee had to deale withall, that generally the whole country acquited her, and held her of honest condition; for since the time of this murther it is credibly reported, that betwixt that and a hundred mile from thence, mans meat and horse meate was not to bee had so reasonable as then, nor to a trauailer better usage.

Well

Well the girle is come to Hatfield, and hauing béen there two dayes straying from place to place; the third day shée happened vpon Dels house, where, whether it were by especiall note taken before, but rather truely to be iudged by the diuine instinct of heauen, to euerye one that came by her, shée would make such pittifull action, as would haue pittied any reasonable creature to haue beheld her, as tearing of her haire, pointing to her throate, stopping of her mouth, poynting to the woodstacke, & in the motion hereof, shed teares as bitter as if her brothers former murther had béen in present action.

This strangenesse noted through all the towne, bred a wonder in the people, and the rather for that the girle by no means could be drawen from thence; at last the Bailiffe of Hatfield, taking aduise with some of his brethren, consulted together, how they might trye whether the dumbe did this, as tending to the reuelation of some concealed suit, or prouoked thereunto by ignorance, and in searching many wayes, at last it came in their minds, that their neighbor Dels wife had of long béen in question about a childe, taken vp in bottomles Pond (some foure yere since) or thereabout, whereupon they agréed to question the girle vpon what particulers, they could best thinke vpon to that purpose, and withall remembring that by commaund from the Iustices of the shire, they had reserued the murthered childes cote, and purposed to make tryall, if her remembrance could take any knowledge of it, but first resolued to tempt her memory, by shewing her diuers others.

The girle brought into a parlor amongst them, they began first to aske her of her name, as, is thy name Iohane, Alis, Agnis Frauncis, Besse, and euer as they spake her right name which was Elizabeth, shée would laugh and reioyce; on the contrary, at the naming her wrong seem discontent.

They hauing thus a knowledge of her name, began to question her further, if she neuer had had a brother; when presently she (as she accustomed before) fell a créeping, making all the former signes in the former order; then they asked her what clothes he vsed to go in, & she to the best declaration she could, made signes thereof; whereupon they shewed her many childrens Coats of seuerall colours, and euer as she happened vpon a greene, that she would kisse, and cry, euer throwing all the rest from her, with so louely and liuely action, that they were confident the murthered Boy was her brother; at last they brought to her the right coat, which after she had earnestly taken note of, the poore childe grewe to that vehement passion, as if in the sight thereof, she had seene another brother murthered. when by no perswasion, offerings, gifts, nor no course that could be taken, to part from the coate, as if for the losse of a brother, she would keepe it as a remembrance of him. All which signified to the Iustices and Knightes of the Shire, the towne had an especiall charge to prouide more carefully for her, and not to suffer her any longer to lye in the streets, and her brothers coate was giuen to her to weare out.

This wonder, the onely table-talke in the Countrey, though often brought to the widdow Dels eare, she made slight of it, (perswading her selfe belike) that with her honest report and store of wealth, the Childe hauing not a tongue to vtter any thing in her reproofe to wrest out of it, which (no question) she had done, notwithstanding all the arguments and instances against her. But see the wonderfull workes of God, an example able to make all people, that for desire of riches, honour, promotion, or what titles soeuer would be a Murtherer or consent thereunto, to loath the thought thereof, euen in the creation, and content themselues with their estate (how meane soeuer,) rather than seeke to rise by indirect meanes, knowing that a guilty conscience Salamander-like liues alwayes in fire, that his dayes are dreadfull, his nights terrible, that he that admits sinne in himselfe, kils himselfe, that to vnhonest pleasure is begot a companion repenting, and enrich himselfe with this saying,

Somnia bonorum meliora quam malorum.

And though I liue poore, I liue rich in this, that I am

vertuous

vertuous, I am not a Bond-man to my thoughts, nor slaue to my affections,

Nemo liber qui seruit cupiditatibus.

This Wench (as before is reported) being by the direction placed where she had reliefe; one day, some month before Christmasse last, going to play with the Goodwifes daughter where shee soiourned in a Parke ioyning to Hatfield (commonly called the Kings Parke) as they were in sport together, a Cocke hard-by them, fell a crowing, when the other Girle mocking the Cocke with these words, Cocka doodle dooe, Peggy hath lost her shooe, and called to her Besse, canst not thou doe so? When presently the Girle in the like manner did so; which, drawing the other child into amazement, she presently left her, and ran home crying out as she went, the dumbe Girle Besse can speake, the dumbe Girle Besse can speake. The wonder caused all the towne to gather in flocks, & ran to meet her, but the bailiffe and the Constables (more discreet than the rest) kept the Hurry from her: when she answered them to euery question directly, and forthwith began in order to reueale the former Murthers, as before is mentioned.

Speedy newes was carried to all the cheefe men in the Shire, who driuen into astonishment with the report, and the miraculous accident, that a Childe without a tongue should speake both discreetly and distinctly, to the reuealing of so monstrous a Murther, and by the crowing of a Cocke (that bird that put Peter in minde of his great sinne in denying our Sauiour and his Maister) was the Herauld to proclaime to this child, when she should speak these things, that by her the wonderfull workes of God might be glorified, and the Murthers discouered.

But the liues of the Kings Subiects, and those which til then, had been reputed honest being now like to depend on her iustification: the Iustices were very carefull to sift her by seuerall examinations, to see if they could finde her alter or trippe in any part of her former discourse, as Sir Raph Conesbye, Sir Henric Butler, Maister Auditor, and

 Maister

Master Auditor Curle, to the number of 14 Knights and graue Gentlemen of note Iustices of peace, tooke her seuerall examinations, when in the generall there could not be one found that differed in a sillable; nay though some of them threatned her with what vengeance God would stir vp for her in hell, and plagues here vpon earth, if she persisted to be a lyer, and a murtherer, both which would conclude in her (by the death of Dels wife and her sonne) if she perseuered in this testimony. Others in milder traine dealt with her, as by faire perswasions, golden promises, that frō ẏ state of a beggar, where till then she had liued, she should now be exalted and maintained by them in the same degree as their owne children, making them stand present obiects to alter her, neither of which could make her distant in any thing, but in briefe satisfied thē with this answere. I must not lye, I haue that within me bids me tell truth.

Notwithstanding this, one of Sir Henrie Butlers men (to make a further triall of her constancy herein, watching her abroad in the same Parke, where first her lost speech was reueald vnto her) attired himselfe in a bizard with hornes, and (as we commonly say) like a Diuell, and out of a thicket stept before her, & threatned her, that in that place where shee first spake, hee would teare her in peeces for belying George Dell and his Mother; when the Girle (though in common it doth appeare she should haue been frighted from her constancie) onely answered thus. Good Gaffer Diuell doe not hurt me, I speake nothing but truth, and what the thing within me instructeth me to speake. With the wonder of this Miracle (time passing away) & people comming from all places to be eye and eare-witnesse thereof, the Assizes were to be held at Hartford, where (according as they were bound) George Dell & his Mother, appeared, and being called to their triall (as in forme of law in such cases are prouided) they pleaded, not guiltie; when the Girle (as boldly in accusing, as wonderfull in speaking) gaue euidence against them, saying, that since God had lent her a speech by miracle, shee would with that inspired breath, follow the

law

law of them, & haue their bloods lawfully, who stole away her brother. Dels wife being yet asked by the Iudge, whether such lodged in her house or no? who yet continued her denyall; when the aforesayd Henrie Whelpley, Nicholas Deacon, with others, were ready to auow the being there, besides many credible persons of Hatfield, who in the life of her husband, (being a blinde man, and liuing in great discontent together) hath often heard him say: thou mayst rise a while, but a day will come when thy villanies and murthers will appeare, when thy fall shall be low ynough. Upon this euidence (the Iury going together) they were foūd guilty & a verdict returned: whereupon the Iudge according to course procéeded in sentence against them, where learnedly he instructed them, that since God had reuealed them Murtherers (as from the tongues of Babes and sucklings, that a child spake by miracle to her discouery, & that accordingly they were cast by 12 credible men of their own countrey) they would yet looke into themselues, séeing how néere they were vnto their graues, & make that more plaine which yet lay somewhat obscure, namely, who were partakers with thē in that bloody action: but nothing preuailing to molify their obdurat harts, briefly thus they replied: since the law hath cast vs, we desire to die. Whereupon the 2 of August being Saturday, hauing receiued their sentence, they were conueyed to the Goale, where being permitted to be together as long as they had stay in this world; by a prisoner that lay ouer them, was heard this conference. Mother (quoth George Dell) the law hath cast me, and I am resolued for death, I pray you (if you can) resolue the world, whether I am guilty or no? Who answered him, Sonne be contēted, take thy death patiently, it is now too late, I haue spoken what I will. The young man spending the time he had to liue, in prison & praier, and singing of Psalmes, that if the outward appearance may be a perfect witnes in earnest repentance, till Monday the 4 of August, where being with his mother, by the Iaylor deliuered to the Sheriffe, his Mother hauing by suit obtained, that she might sée her

Sonne firſt ſuffer death, they were executed at the common place of execution; the young man (though the Mother before this was beloued) the moſt lamented for.

The ſeuerall practiſes of *Iohane Harriſon*, and her daughter, condemned and executed at *Hartford* for Witch-craft, the 4 of Auguſt laſt, 1606.

AT the Aſſizes held in the beginning of Auguſt laſt in the County of Hartford, in the Kings Maieſties behalfe for Gaole deliuerie, there were by the verdict of the Countrey, Foure onely Offenders found worthy to haue deſerued death, of which 2 (as haue been ſpoken of, the Mother & the Son) for murther, and one Iohane Harriſon, & her daughter for damnable Witch-craft, wrayed time that offences ſhold come thus prodigious, that the Of-ſpring borne to be a comfort to the Parents, and the parents as much to be delighted in the Children, ſhould be cauſe of one anothers vntimely death and fatal ouerthrow.

This I. H. dwelling at Royſton in the ſayd County of Hartford, of long time hauing been ſuſpected for witchcraft; now (vpon iuſt cauſe) was apprehended, and her houſe according to the true courſe of Iuſtice, being ſearcht, there was found in a cheſt of hers, ſuch ſufficient inſtruments, (which ſhe after confeſt were helpes to her in her practiſes) that could there haue beene no other proofe nor euidence againſt her, they only had been ſufficient to iudge her vnworthy of long life. This Cheſt being opened, there was firſt taken out by the Officers all the bones due to the Anatomy of man & woman, and vnder them haire of all colours that is cuſtomarily worne; in the bottome was found a parchment lapt vp in a compas no bigger than a groat, but being open, was in breadth euery way 2 ſpans; in ẏ midſt of this

parchment

parchment was coloured (in the purest colours) a heart proportionable to the hart of a man; and round about sitting euen to the very brim of the parchment, were coloured in seuerall colours very curiously diuided braunches, on which hung dangling things like ashen keyes, and at the ends of them in some places figured, and others proportioned a mouth, in briefe the whole ioynts and artiers of a man.

This I.H. being vpon her examination, and finding such apparant witnes induct against her of her seuerall fellonies & murthers, neglected not to confesse her vtmost secret therin, that she had power (by the helpe of that parchment, man & womans bones, and man and womans haire) to inflict (by the helpe of her spirits, which she reported to haue 2 attending on her, one for men, another for cattell) in any ioynt, synnow, or place of the body, by only but pricking the point of a needle in that place of the parchmēt, where in his or her body she would haue them tortured, which torture of hers once begun in them, their paine should continue so restlesse, that a present death had bin more happier, than so lingring a calamity; and those whome she intended to kill had the same in effect. If she gaue a pricke in the middle of ẏ parchment, where she had placed the heart, which relation of her may certainely be beleeued by the seuerall consequents that she was condemned vpon. First a good countrey Yeoman (a neighbor of hers) & she falling at some words together, he calling her old Hagge, or some such like name of reproofe: She made him this answere, I will say little to thee, but thou shalt feele more from me hereafter. The honest man had scarse been departed from her halfe an houre, but hee felt himselfe, as if he had been set into your Scotch-boote, or spanish strappado, or your Morbus Gallicus, was nothing to it, sometimes in a pestiferous heat, at others, a chill cold, but at al times in continual aches, & wracking of his limbs as if the Diuell had set him on his Tentors to make broadcloth of him. In this perplexitie he continued consuming himselfe, not being able neither to goe nor stand, nor Physicke could helpe him, nor no meanes bee had to ease him.

When one of his neighbors comming in neighborly loue to visit him, he began to open his mind to him, that he perswaded himselfe, by such a one she was bewitched, and hee was as faithfully perswaded, that if he could but haue 2 or 3 good scratches at her face, wherby he might draw blood of her, he should recouer presently, his neighbour aduised him by some wile to send for her home, yet (ye betwéen them both held vnconuenient, for that either suspecting her selfe, or for not being friends she would not come) that in the night following his neighbor would haue this sicke man caried in a chaire, & lodged in his house, and in the morning his wife, (whō he knew she was good friends withal) should by some wile or another draw her theher, whā if he of himselfe were not strōg inough to scratch her, he (as he held charily) wold help him. This the next morning was done accordingly, the Witch comes, & is well scratcht, vpon which within 3 or 4 daies (as fast as the man could recouer strength) he is vp, & goes abroad; which this A.H. perceiuing, arrests him & by a triall in law for this battry had 5 š damages, and her costs of suit giuen her, the man (according as he was condemnd) paid her, which no sooner by her receiued, but ye honest man fell into his former passion, languishing a while & died: in the same maner she serued another, who méeting her out of the towne in a lane, tooke the like reuenge vpon her, & recouered. Both which blowne ouer (only a little murmurd against by a neighbor of hers) a yong womā being washing clothes in an outer rowme next ye stréet where in a wanscot cradle her child lay a sléep; when this A.H. daughter chanced to come by iust in the instant as she was throwing out a little wrinsing water, and by chaunce some of which vnawares sprinkled vpon her, which ye wench séeming moued at, called to her with these words. Do you throw your water vpon me gossip, before it be long Ile be reuenged for it. The woman (sorry for the offence, had done, followed her busines, & thought no further of it. whē on the suddē (while she was stept but into a next rowm to hāg vp some clothes) the cradle wherein her child lay, was throwne ouer shattered all to pieces, the child upon the face whelmed under it, & killed. Thus we see the Diuell hath such power on these his damnable seruants, that neither men nor infants are to be pitied by them. Not long after she had all bewitched a wealthy mans daughter in the towne, who hauing a good substantiall Yeoman to her brother, in pitie of his Sisters griefe, rode to Cambridge, and there acquainting a friend of his with his sisters affliction: the scholler told him she was bewitched, yet in regard they two had bene of an ancient friendship, & that himselfe had some acquaintance with his sister, in spight of her Incubi, her spirits, & the diuell, & al hee'd help: which according to promise he performed, and by that time her brother was returned, his sister was recouered, in reuenge of (for that her sorcery was crost, & the mayd retuct to helth by her brothers carefulnes) she caused such a plague upon all his cattell, that they all immediatly perisht, & consumed, not one of that great store he had being left, to be a remembrance of the rest: himselfe shortly after did these, & a number more at her triall were inferd against, onely one more amongst the rest, though but a homely tale, for that it made al the Bench to laugh, Ile record of her, & conclude.

How the Witch serued a Fellow in an Alehouse.

There was an honest Fellow, and as boone a companion dwelling in Royston, one that loued the pot with the long necke almost aswell as his prayers; for (quoth he) as I know one is medicinable for the soule, I am sure the other's phisick for ẏ bodie. It was this Fuddle-caps chance with 3 or 4 as good Malt-wormes as himselfe, and as sure, where the best lap was to be found, together as 4 Knaues in a payre of cards, to be drinking, where this Witch came in, & stood gloting upon them. Now this Good-fellow (not enduring to looke upon a bad face, but his owne, especially when he is Cup-shot) called aloude to her, Doe you heare Witch, looke tother waies, I cānot abide a nose of that fashion, or else turne your face ẏ wrong side outward, it may look like raw flesh for flyes to blow maggots in. Stil as the

Witch was ready to reply, hée would crosse her with one scuruy Iest, & betwéen euery Iest drinke to her; yet sweare, God dam him, she should starue ere she should haue a drop on't, since the pot was swéet hée'd kéepe it so, for should but her lips once looke into the lid on't, her breath's so strong, & would so stick in the cup, that al the water ẏ runs by Ware would not wash it out again. At last the witch got so much time to cal to him, Doest thou heare good friend (quoth she?) What sayst thou ill face (quoth he?) Mary I say (quoth she) that thou throwest in thy drink apace, but shall not find it so easie comming out. Nay, as for the comming out (answerd the fellow) I throwd it in aboue, & it shal come out beneath, & then thou shalt haue some of it, if thou wilt, because I am in hope it will poyson thée. Then with this gréeting away goes the Witch in a chafe, & the fellow sits down to follow his drink, but as the end of all drunkards, is either to ming or to sléepe. So out goes this fellow, & drawing his Gentleman Usher against a pale side, finds me a top of his nose a red lump as big as a cherry, & in his belly felt such a rumbling, as if the Tower of Babell had falne about his eares: oh the sight thereof draue his hart to an ague, & his tongue to an alarum, and out he cries, the Witch, the Witch, I am vndone, I am vndone: O God, women of Royston, helpe, helpe, the Witch, the Wicth, I am a man spoyld, helpe, I am vndone. At that word help, the Wich, in comes one of his fellowes runs in hast, & asked him what they should helpe, the Witch? Oh (quoth he) to the gallowes, for I am vndone by her. Well, yet out he runs, where for that night she would not be found, but the next morning méeting her in a lane, his pain rather increased, thā lesned, & there falls his ten cōmandements vpon her, he almost scratcht out her eyes; nay, left her not till he brought her to ẏ towne, where for this and the rest, she was apprehended, and she and her daughter, with George Dell and his Mother, worthily suffered death the 4 of August.

FINIS.

Deeds Against Natvre, and Monsters by kinde (*STC* 809) is reproduced with permission from the unique copy at the Bodleian Library (shelfmark 40 L 68 [7] Art). The text-block measures 90 × 160 mm.

The following words are a transcription of the original:

A3v.36 haue it, shee
B2v.1 And so my

DEEDS AGAINST NATVRE, and Monsters by kinde:

Tryed at the Goale deliuerie of Newgate, *at the Sessions* in the Old Bayly, the 18. and 19. of *Iuly* last, 1614. the one of a London Cripple named *Iohn Arthur*, that to hide his shame and lust, strangled his betrothed wife. The other of a lasciuious yong Damsell named *Martha Scambler*, which made away the fruit of her own womb, that the world *might not see the seed of her owne shame: Which two persons with diuers others* were executed at Tyburne the 21. of Iuly following.

With two sorrowfull Ditties of these two aforesaid persons, made by themselues in Newgate, the night before their execution.

At London printed for *Edward Wright*. 1614. 7

Deeds againſt nature, and monſters by kinde:

Tryed at the Goale deliuerie for *Newgate*, at the Seſſions in the Old Bayly, the 18. and 19. of *July*, laſt, 1614. the one of a London Cripple named *Iohn Arthur*, that to hide his ſhame and luſt, ſtrangled his betrothed wife. The other of a laſciuious young Damſell named *Martha Scambler*, which made away the fruit of her own womb, that the world might not ſee the ſeede of her owne *ſhame: Which two perſons with diuers others were executed at Tyburne the 21. of Iuly* following.

IS it not a maruell, that fire fals not from heauen to conſume an infinite number of worſe then ſauage natur'de people in this land, when vile wretches, whom God hath markt with his ſecret brand of ſecret purpoſe, ſo impiouſly attempt things againſt nature, as for example, (which God grant it may ſo prooue for our amendment) here remained amongſt vs in this Cittie a deformed creature, an vnperfect wretch wanting the right ſhape and limbes of a man though in forme and viſage like vnto one of vs, this decreped creature (as I ſaid) named Iohn Arthur, liued and maintain'd himſelfe with the charitie and deuotions of almeſ-giuing people, and by his lame and limbleſſe vſage purchaſed more kinde fauours then many others of his baſe fraternitie: money and meanes being eaſily gained by a few beggerly obſeruations, as a wretch graceleſſe, and vnthankefull for Gods blessings thus bestowed vpon him, made no good vse thereof, but spent the same in the seruice of the Diuell, as in blasphemie, swearing, drunkennes, and such like, all damnable sinnes and such as be the nurses and breeders of others: this afore-named Cripple being on a time in the middle of his drunkennes heated with lust, fell into familiaritie with a certaine woman of his owne condition, who purposing to liue as hee did, vpon charitie, and good mens almes, and seeing good benefit to come by his lamenes, vnto whom many people grew willing to giue, promised to be his associate, and as his companion and wife to beg with him. many daies and monthes spent they together, continually abusing the gifts of charitie, and wasting away the same with drunkennes in the by-places and suburbs of the Citie, which is euermore the receit of such begging vacabonds and disordred liuers, instruments of the diuell prepared still for deeds of mischiefe. This Cripple hauing not one good thought of Gods grace, so lusted after his begging companion, that he obtained the daily vse of her bodie, and continually committed so that sinne of lust & shame, making a practise thereof in the contempt of Gods Lawes, that the eye of heauen could no longer winke at them, but with a cleare sight see into their base wickednes: yea more then base in that a deformed lumpe of flesh and no perfect creature should thus abuse the seed of generation, and now and then in the fields and high-waies commit such beastly offences: but God we see hath iron hands, and will at last strike heauily, as hee did vpon these two shamelesse malefactors: For the Cripple in time surfetting vpon this his shame, and growing weary of this hated offence, as all people will doe, being not lawfully married, bgan to cast her off, and to loath her company though he himselfe might be thought the more loathsome, which she (abused woman) perceiuing, and knowing her selfe to be but his Strumpet, challenged of him the promise of marriage, and so importuned him thereunto by his former vowes and promises, and that heauen would otherwise cal his periured oathes to account,

all

all instigations of the diuell, and subtill policies to drawe them both to destruction, her importunate sutes to mariage so troubled his mind, bred such a rage in his heart, that a purpose came into his minde to rid her away by some untimely death: a motion no sooner set on fire, but the diuell was readie to bring more fewell, and neuer rested till it was all on a flame: so upon a night, a time fitting for such a dark deede, the Cripple enticed her forth into the fields neere Islington, where secretly at the Brick Kils, the lodging place for rogues and night walkers, he renewed his former familiaritie, and with a dissembling kindnes perswaded her to lodge there with him all night, which she, mistrustlesse woman, consented too, and little misdoubting his diuellish intent laid her downe upon a pallat of straw by him to sleepe which as a token of hard misfortune sodainely possessed her: The Cripple perceiuing all secure and silent, and now thinking to be rid of the shame thus daily following him, tooke the womans owne girdle, and putting the same slyly about her necke, where though nature had denyed him strength and limbes, yet by the help of the diuell, which alwaies adds force to villany, he made meanes in her sleep to strangle her, and to take away her life, as it were sodainely without repentance: therefor all people by this example ought still to be prepared for death, for hee comes as a thiefe in the night, and giues no warning: who would haue thought such an out-cast of the world, such a lame deformed creature, not able of his owne strength to help himselfe, should haue power to take away anothers life, but the diuell wee see is a cunning, and will still make the simple his strongest assisters, and those that bee the most weakest, to be of the vilest thoughts, but to conclude, the Cripple, blinded thus with his owne shame, had that ignorant opinion of the discouerie hereof, that he thought the world too simple to looke into his life, and his decreped carriage would keep away all suspition, and that no man would thinke a lame creature could be able to doe so wicked a deede: but gracelesse varlet, as hee was, too much flattered in his own opinion, the Diuell as he was first beginner of his sinne, so was hee last end of his shame, for the same morning the woman was found thus murthered, and beeing seene the night before in his company with slender examinations confessed the fact, where for the same hee had his tryall at the Sessions by a Jury of twelue men and his execution at Tyburne in the sight of many hundreds of men, women and children, which accounts him to be a Monster by kinde and the doer of a deed against nature.

Like vnto this viper of our age, wee are to place in our discourse another Caterpiller of nature, a creature more sauage then a shée woolfe, more vnnaturall then either bird or beast, for euery creature hath a tender feeling of loue to their young, except some few murtherous-minded strumpets, woemen I cannot call them, for a woman esteemes the fruit of her owne womb, the pretious and dearest Jewell of the world, and for the cherishing of the same will (as it were) spend her liues purest blood, where, contrariwise the harlot (delighting in shame and sinne) makes no conscience to be the butcher of her owne seed, nay the Image of God created in her owne body, and now and then in the conception makes spoyle of the bed of creation before it can receiue true forme. Therefore for an example likewise cast your eyes vpon this other monster of nature, which was a lasciuious, lewd and close strumpet, a harlot lodging priuately neere Bishops-gate in Bedlam at a kinsmans house of hirs, which little suspected this hir vnwomanly carriage but shame long raked vp in the ashes of secresie, though close smoking, will at last breake forth into open flame: so this graceles wanton (spending her youth in lasciuious pleasures, as many a one doth in and about this Citty) hapned to proue with child, & hauing no husband to couer this her act of shame, and withall fearing the disgrace of the world, by a diuilish practise sought to consume it in her body before the birth, but not preuailing (as God would haue it) shee was forced by nature to deliuer it aliue to the world, and so was made the vnhappy mother of a man-child

vn-

vnhappy I may name her, for her owne hand made her vnhappy. To our purpose, her lusty body, strong nature, and feare of shame brought an easines to her deliuery, and required in her agony no help of a midwife which among women seemeth a thing very strange, for not so much as the least child in the house where she lodged had knowledge of her labour, nor hardly was she thought to be with child, so closely demeaned she her selfe, but the deuill we see addes force vnto wickednes, and puts a kind of strength to nature in that kind, otherwise had she beene discouered in the childbirth.

Consider this the Child being borne with shame and she by it made a scandall to her acquaintance, renewed the remembrance of her passed sinnes, and presented present shame vnto her grieued thoughts, which troubled cogitations, by the perswasions of the Diuill, put her in mind violently to make it away, and to giue it death before the body had well recouered life, whereupon taking the poore tender babe as it were new dropt from the mothers womb, and not like a mother, but a monster threw it downe into a lothsome priuy house, therein to giue it an vndecent graue and as shee thought therby make to her selfe a ridance of a further Infamy, but God is Just and will reward shame where it is deserued, and such vnnaturall deedes, let them be acted in deserts, in the cauernes of the earth, where neuer light of day nor Sun shines, yet will they be discouered and brought to the worlds eye, so hapned it with this harlot, when all feare of suspition was past, shee safely deliuered, the Childe in the priuy smothered, and in the world no notice taken thereof, yet in the end was it thus most strangly discouered, the Tunnill of the aforesaid vault or priuy ascended vp into the next neighbours house, as in many places they doe, where by chance (as God had ordayned) dwelled an vnto ward lad that in taking delight in knauish pastimes tooke a cur Dog then vsing the house and carelesly threw it downe the Tunnell into the vault, where the murthered infant lay, and taking noe regard thereof, suffered ſered the Dog to remaine there ſtaruing and crying for food the ſpace of three dayes and nights, during which time the yelping of the dog much diſquieted the neighbours, and ſo troubled the dwellers there abouts, that they could not ſleepe a nights for the noyſe, but eſpecially the good man of the houſe, who greeued to ſee a dumbe beaſt ſo ſtarued, and for want of food thus to periſh like a kind natur'd man cauſed the priuy to be opened and the poore curre taken vp, which proued by Gods Iuſtice the only diſcouerer of the aforeſaid fact for in taking vp the dog, they were woefull witneſſes of the ſweet Babe lying all beſmeared with the filth of that loathſome place. The ſight whereof cauſed no ſmall amazement, eſpecially to the good man of the houſe, who with a diligent care (as his duty was both to God and his country) and that all ſuch inhumaine deeds might bee brought to light, made it knowne to the Magiſtrates, which likewiſe with Chriſtian care cauſed a certaine number of ſubſtantiall women to make ſearch of ſuſpected perſons, and of ſuch who were like to be the murthered Infants mother, or murtherer, amongſt many other looſe liuers and common harlots, of which number theſe by places haue too many, the more is the pitty, this aforeſaid murthereſſe came to the touch, where vpon examination, ſhe confeſſed the child to be borne with life, and her ſelfe not worthy of life, and ſo pleading guilty ſhe was brought to her triall, & for the ſame araigned and condemned by the Bench of aſſize in the old Baily the 18. and 19. of July laſt 1614. and hath ſuffred death at Tyburne the 21. following as an example, that god, either by beaſts of the field, foules of the ayre, fiſhes in the ſeas, wormes in the ground, or things bearing neither ſence nor life will by one meanes or other make deedes of darknes cleare as day, that the world may behold his high working powers, and that no malefactor can eſcape vnpuniſhed, though his deeds be as ſecret as the [illegible] of hell, beyond the thought of humane imagination, conuert vs from ſin great God of Iſrael, ſo that we neuer be endangered with the like perſwaſions, which God in his mercy grant. Amen.

The

The Cripples complaint in the Dungeon at Newgate.

ME thinkes I heare a dolefull sound,
Within this dungeon vnder ground:
Prepare thy selfe (poore soule) to dye,
For so the Belmans voyce doth cry.
  And Beggars all come ring my knell,
The Cripple now bids all farewell:
Both Crutches, Scrip, and patched gowne,
Wherewith I beg'd from towne to towne.
  Though limbes I want, and could not go,
Yet was my mind not pleased so:
But had my faults, as others haue,
Which brings me thus vnto my graue.
  In vaine delights I spent my daies,
And wrong'd my fortunes many waies:
The almes that good men gaue me still,
I wasted to content my will.
  For heauen had markt me out for shame,
Whereto I did my courses frame:
And as I was misshape by kind,
Deformed also was my mind.
  For by that sweete intising sinne,
My sodaine downefall did begin:
Wherein I set my harts delight,
On wanton women day and night.
  At last when I loues pleasures prou'd,
I hated her whom late I lou'd:
And sodaine loathing, soone begun
Ashamed sore, of follies done.
  And still desired to end the life
Of her, I promist to make Wife:
For loue so gaind can neuer last,
No sooner done, but loue is past.
  Then as my shame I hated her,
And would her death no time defer:

But arm'd with wroth in dead of night,
I traind her from all peoples sight.
That neuer more my follies great,
To my disgrace she should repeat:
Nor say vnto the world, that I
Had liu'd with her most wantonly.
For in the fieldes we two alone,
With weeping teares and bitter mone:
She crau'd amends for my amisse,
To make her Wife as reason is.
But I refus'd that honest course,
But did an act of sad remorse:
To end her shame with mine as then,
I did exceede the deedes of men.
The deuill my helper at that hower,
For he as then had strongest power:
Nor by his meanes I could not faint,
Though I was lame and limbes did want.
My heart with furious rage possest,
About her necke her girdle cast,
And forced so away her life,
Rather then make her married wife.
Neuer like deed by Cripple wrought,
For pleasures being too dearely bought,
Both old and young, both rich and poore,
Make neuer maid a common Whoore.
For doing so my life I lose,
With burthens of repentant woes,
For wanton loues are wretched things,
And with them still much sorrow brings.
Adiew vaine world, the Cripple dies,
In this my life much wonder lies:
That borne a lame deformed wight,
Should thus take pride in loues delight.

Martha Scamblers Repentance.

Poore I the poorest now on earth,
may well accuse my cause of birth:
Not being borne I nere had knowne,
This guilt that hath me ouerthrowne.
Wo worth the cause of sinne and shame,
Which staines my credit and good name:
Wo worth the traines which still are laid,
Whereby we women are betraid.
When I was won to follies will,
And tooke delight in doing ill
No thought I had of pleasures past:
But still my youth did vainly wast.
Till at the length my womb did breed,
A substance of vnlawfull seede:
Which I supposd a shame to be
(God knowes) vnto my friends and me.
And to preuent the worlds disgrace,
I sought to finde a secret place,
My shamefull burthened wombe to ease,
That way which did my God displease.
O, when my houre of labour came,
To bring to light this fruit of shame,
No Midwiues help at all I sought,
But soone my owne deliuerie wrought.
The Babe being borne and in my armes,
I should haue kept it from all harmes,
But like a Beare or Woolfe in wood,
I wisht it smothered vp in blood.
Whereat strange motions without feare,
From hell to me presented were,
And bad me bury it in a Vault,
For none aliue did know my fault.

And so my credit and good name,
Should take no spot of black defame:
And I as pure and chast should be,
From such a crime as any she.
My soule then blinded by the Diuell,
Bid me consent vnto this euill:
Where I full soone thereto agreed,
To act a more then womans deede.
The loathsome Jakes receau'd my child,
Which all misdoubts and feare exild
For being tumbled downe therein,
There well might end my shame and sinne.
But God, this deed more darke then night,
In wondrous sort did bring to light,
For by a Dog the Child was found,
As it was throwne therein to drown'd.
Three dayes and nights with yelping cry,
It troubled much the dwellers by,
Which caus'd them to release him thence,
And so found out this vile offence.
For which I surely now must tast,
Rewards for my offences past,
And dye for that accursed crime,
That makes me monster of my time.
Both maides and men, both yong and old,
Let not good liues with shame be sold,
But beare true vertues to your graue,
That honest burials you may haue.

FINIS.

A pittilesse Mother (*STC* 24757) is reproduced with permission from the clear and uncropped Bodleian Library copy (shelfmark Art 4o G 29 [4]). The text-block measures 95 × 160 mm.

4

A pittilesse Mother.

That most vnnaturally at one time, murthered two of her owne Children at Acton within sixe miles from *London vppon holy thursday last* 1616. *The ninth of May.* Beeing a Gentlewonan named *Margret Vincent*, wife of M[r]. *Iaruis Vincent*, of the same Towne.

With her Examination, Confession and true discouery of all the proceedings in the said bloody accident.

Whereunto is added *Andersons* Repentance, who was executed at Tiburne the 18. of May being Whitson-Eue. 1616. Written in the time of his prisonment in Newgate.

Printed at London for I. T. and are to be sold by Iohn Wright.

A Pittilesse Mother

That most vnnaturall at one time, Murthered two of her owne Chillderen, at Acton within sixe miles of London, vpon holy Thursday last 1616. the 9 of May being a Gentlewonan named Margret Vincent, wife of Mr. Jaruis Vincent of the same Towne.

With her Examination, Confession and trew discouery of all the proceedings in the said bloody accedent.

HOW easie are the waies vnto euill, and how soone are our mindes (by the Deuils inticement) withdrawne from goodnes, Leuiathan, the Arch-enemy of mankinde hath set such & so many bewitching snares to intrap vs, that vnlesse we continually stand watching with carefull diligence to shun them, wee are like to cast the principall substance of our reputation, vpon the wracke of his ensnaring engines. As for example, A Gentlewoman, ere now fresh in memory, presents her owne ruine amongst vs, whose liues ouerthrow may well serue for a cleare looking Glasse to see a womans weaknes in, how soone and apt she is wonne vnto wickednes, not onely to the bodies ouerthrow, but the soules danger. God of his mercy keepe vs all from the like wilfulnes.

At Acton, some sixe miles westward from London, this vnfortunate Gentlewoman dwelled, named Margret Vincent, the wife of M. Jaruis Vincent Gentleman, who by vnhappy destiny marked to mischance, I here now make the subiect of my Pen, and publish her hard hap vnto the world, that all others may shun the like occasions by which she was ouerthrowne.

This Margret Vincent before named, of good parentage, borne in the County of Hartford, at a towne named Rickmansworth: her name from her Parents Margret Day, of good education, graced with good parts from her youth, that promised succeeding vertues in her age, if good luck had serued, for being discreete, ciuell, and of a modest conuersation, she was preferred in marriage to this Gentleman M. Vincent, with whome she liued in good estimation, well beloued, and much esteemed of all that knewe her, for her modest and seemely carriage, and so might haue continued to her old age, had not this bloody accident committed vpon her owne children blemished the glory of the same.

But now marke (gentle Reader) the first entrance into her liues ouerthrow, and consider with thy selfe how strangely the Diuell here set in his foote, and what cunning instruments hee vsed in his assaylements. The Gentlewoman being witty, and of a Ripe vnderstanding, desiered much conference in religion, and being carefull as it seemed of her soules happines, many times resorted to Diuines to haue instructions to saluation (little thinking to fall into the hands of Romaine Wolues (as she did) and to haue the sweete Lambe, her soule, thus intangled by their perswasions.

Twelue or Fowretéene Yeares had she liued in marriage with her husband well beloued, hauing for their comforts diuers pretty children betweene them, with all other thinges in plenty, as health, riches, and such like, to increase concord, and no necessity that might be hinderance to contentment, yet at last there was such trappes and enginis set, that her quet was caught, and her discontent set at liberty: her oppinion of the true faith (by the subtill sophistry of some close Papists) was conuerted to a blinde beliefe of bewitching heresie, for they haue such charming perswasions that hardly the female kinde can escape their intisements, of which weake sex they continually make prise of and by them lay plots to insnare others, as they did by this deceiued Gentlewoman, for she, good soule, being

made

made a bird of their owne feather, desired to beget more of the same kinde, and from time to time made (perswasiue arguments to win her husband to the same opinion, and deemed it a merritorious deede to charge his conscience with that infectious burthen of Romish oppinions, affirming by many false reasons that his former life had beene led in blindnes, and that she was appointed by the holy Church to shew him the light of true vnderstanding: these and such like were the instructions she had giuen her to intangle her husband in, and win him if she might to their blinde heresies.

But hee, good Gentleman, ouer deepely grounded in the right Faith of Religion, then to be thus so easily remoued, grew regardles of her perswasions accounting them vaine and friuolous, and she vndutifull to make so fond an attempt, many times snubing her with some few vnkinde speeches, which bred in her heart a purpose of more extreamity, for hauing learned this maxim of their Religion, that it was merritorious yea and pardonable, to take away the liues of any opposing Protestants were it of any degree whatsoeuer, in which resolution or bloody purpose she long stood vpon, and at last (onely by the Diuels temptation) resolued the ruine of her owne children, affirming to her conscience these reasons, that they were brought vp in blindnes and darkesome errours, hoodwinckt (by her husbands instructions) from the true light, and therefore to saue their soule (as she vainely thought) she purposed to become a Tygerous Mother, and so woluishly to commit the murther of her owne flesh and blood, in which oppinion she stedfastly continued, neuer relenting according to nature, but casting about to finde time and place for so wicked a deed, which vnhappily fell out as after followed.

It so chanced that a discord arose betweene the two townes of Acton and willsden about a certaine common, bordering betweene them, where the towne of Acton as it seemes hauing the more right vnto it, by watching defended it a time from the others Cattle, whereupon the women of the same towne, hauing likewise a willingnes to assist their husbands in the same defence, appointed a day for the like purpose, which was the Assention day last past, commonly called holy Thursday, falling upon the 9. of the last passed month of May, which day (as ill chance would haue it) was the fatall time appointed for her to act this bloody Tragedie, whereon she made her husband fatherlesse of two as pretty children as euer came from womans wombe.

Upon the Assention day aforesaid, after the time of Diuine seruice, the women of the towne being gathered togeither about their promised businesse, some of them came to Mistris Vincent, and according to promise desired her company, who hauing a minde as then more setled on bloudy purposes then countrey occasions, fayned an excuse of ill at ease, and not halfe well, desired pardon of them, and offring her Maide in her behalfe, who being a good apt and willing Seruant was accepted of, and so the Townes-women, misdoubting no such hard accident as after happened, proceeded in their aforesaid defences, the Gentlewomans husband being also from home, in whose absence, by the fury and assistance of the Diuell, she inacted this wofull accident in forme and manner following.

This Mistris Vincent, now deseruing no name of Gentlewoman, being in her owne house fast lockt up, onely with her two small Children, the one of the age of fiue yeares, the other hardly two yeares old, unhappily brought to that age to be made away by their owne Mother who by nature should haue cherisht them with her owne body, as the Pellican that pecks her owne brest to feed her young ones with her blood: but she more cruell then the Uiper, the inuenomd Serpent, the Snake, or any Beast whatsoeuer, against all kind, takes away those liues to whom she first gaue life.

Being alone (as I said before) assisted by the Deuill, shee tooke the youngest of the two, hauing a countenance so sweet that might haue begd mercy at a tirants hand, but shee regarding neither the pretty smiles it made, nor the dadling before the mothers face, nor any thing it could doe, but like a fierce and bloudy Medea, shee tooke it violently by the throat, and

with

with a Garter taken from her legge, making thereof a noose and putting the same about her Childs sweet necke, shee in a wrathfull manner drew the same so close together, that in a moment she parted the soule and body, and without any terror of Conscience, she layd the liueles Infant, still remaining warme vpon her bed, and with a relentles countenance looking thereon, thinking thereby she had done a deed of immortallity: Oh blinded ignorance! Oh inhumane deuotion! purposing by this to merit heauen, she hath deserued, (without true repentance) the reward of damnation.

This Creature not deseruing Mothers name, as I said before, not yet glutted, nor sufficed with these few drops of Innocent blood, nay her owne deare blood bred in her owne body, cherished in her own wombe with much dearenes full forty weekes: not satisfied I say with this one murther, but she would headlong run vnto a second and to heape more vengeance vpon her head, she came vnto the elder Child of that small age that it could hardly discerne a Mothers cruelty, nor vnderstand the fatall destiny fallen vppon the other before, which as it were seemd to smile vppon her as though it begd for pitty, but all in vaine for so tirrannous was her heart, that without all motherly pitty, shee made it drinke of the same bitter cup; as shee had done the other: for with her garter she likewise pressed out the sweet ayre of life and laid it by the other vpon the bed sleeping in death together, a sight that might haue burst an iron heart in sunder, and made the very Tiger to relent.

These two pretty children being thus murthered, without all hope of recouery, she began to growe desperate and still to desire more and more blood, which had bene a third murther of her owne babes, had it not beene abroad at Nurse, and by that meanes could not be accomplished, whereupon she fell into a violent rage, purposing as then to shew the like mischiefe vpon her selfe, being of this strange opinion, that she her selfe by that deede had made Saints of her two children in heauen, so taking the same garter that was the instrument of their deaths, and putting the noose thereof about her owne necke she

she stroue therewith to haue strangled her selfe, but nature being weake, and flesh fraile, she was not able to doe it: Whereupon in a more violent fury, (still animated foreward by instigation of the Deuill) she ran into the yard purposing there in a pond to haue drowned her selfe, hauing not one good motion of Saluation left within her.

But heere good Reader marke what a happy preuention chanced to preserue her in hope of Repentance, which at that time stayd her from that desperate attempt, the mayd by great fortune, at the very instant of this deed of desperation, returned from the field or Common where shee had left most of the neighbours, and comming in at the backeside, perceiuing her mistris by her gastly countenance, that all was not well, and that some hard chance had happened her or hers, demaunded how the Children did? Oh Man (quoth she) neuer oh neuer shalt thou see thy Tom more, and withall gaue the maid a boxe vppon the eare, at which she laid hold vppon her Mistris, calling out for helpe into the Towne, whereat diuers came running in, and after them her husband, within a while after, who finding what had hapned, were all so amazed together, that they knew not what to doe, some wrung their hands some wept, some called out for Neighbours, so generall a feare was strooke amongst them all, that they knew not whether to goe nor run, especially the good Gentleman her husband, that seeing his owne Children slaine, murthered by his Wife, and their owne Mother, a deed beyond nature and humanity, in which extasie of griefe, at last hee broke out in these speeches. Oh Margret, Margret, how often haue I perswaded thee from this damned Opinion, this damned Opinion, that hath vndone vs all. Whereupon with a gastly looke and fearefull eye shee replyed thus, Oh Iaruis, this had neuer beene done, if thou hadst beene ruld, and by mee conuerted, but what is done, is past, for they are Saints in heauen, and I nothing at all repent it. These and such like words passed betwixt them, till such time as the Constable, and others of the townesmen came in, and according to law carried her before a Iustice of the peace, which

is

to a Gentleman named Maister Roberts of Wildsden, who vnderstanding these haynous offences rightly according to law & course of Justice, made a Mittimus for her conueyance to Newgate in London, there to remaine till the Sessions of her tryall: yet this is to bee remembred that by examination shee voluntarily confessed the fact, how she murthered them to saue their soules, and to make them Saints in heauen, that they might not be brought vp in blindnesse, to their owne damnation. Oh wilfull heresie, that euer Christian should in Conscience bee thus miscarried, but to be short she proued her selfe to be an obstinate Papist, for there was found about her necke a Crucifixe, with other reliques which she then wore about her: that by the Justice was commanded to be taken away, and an English bible to be deliuered her to read, the which she with great stubbornesse threw from her, not willing as once to look thereupon, nor to heare any diuine comforts, deliuered thereout for the succour of her Soule

But now againe to her conueyance towards prison, it being Assention day and neere the closing of the euening, too late as then to be sent to London, she was by Commandement put to the Constables keeping for that night, who with a strong watch lodged her in his own house till morning, which was at the Bell in Acton where hee dwelled, who shewing the part and duty of a good Christian with diuers other of his Neighbours, all that same night plyed her with good admoninitions, tending to repentance, and seeking with great paines to conuert her from those erronious Opinions which shee so stubbornely stood in, but it little auayled, for she seemed in outward shew so obstinate in Arguments, that shee made small reckoning of repentance, nor was a whit sorrowfull for the murder committed vppon her children but maintained the deed to bee meritorious and of high desert.

Oh that the blood of her owne body should haue no more power to pearce remorse into her Iron natured heart, when Pagan women that know not God nor haue any feeling of his Deity will shun to commit bloodshed, much more of their owne séede: the Caniballs that eate one another will spare the fruites of their owne bodies, the Sauages will doe the like, yea euery beast and fowle hath a féeling of nature, and according to kinde will cherish their young ones, and shall woman, nay a Christian woman, Gods owne Image, be more unnaturall then Pagan, Caniball, Sauage, Beast or Fowle, it euen now makes a trembling feare to beset me, to thinke what an error this unhappy Gentlewoman was bewitched with, a witchcraft begot by hell and nursed by the Romish Sect, from which inchantment God of heauen defend us.

But now againe to our purpose, the next day being Friday, and the tenth of May, by the Cunstable M. Dighton of the Bel in Acton with other of his neighbours, she was conueyed to Newgate in London, where lodging in the Maisters side, many people resorted to her, as well of her acquaintance as others and as before, with sweete and comfortable perswasions, practised to beget repentance, and to be sorry for that which she had committed, but blindnes so preuailed, that she continued still in her former stubbornnes, affirming (contrary to all perswasiue reasons) that she had done a déede of charity in making them Saints in heauen, that otherwise might haue liued to distruction in hell, and likewise refused to looke upon any protestant booke, as Bible, Meditation, Prayer booke and such like, affirming them to be eronious, and dangerous for any Romish Catholique to looke in, such were the violent opinions she had béene instructed in, and with such feruencie therein she continued that no diswasions could withdraw her from them, no not death it selfe, being here possessed with such bewitching wilfulnes.

In this danger of minde continued she all Fryday, Saturday and Sunday, the Sessions drawing néere, there came certaine Godly Preachers unto her, who preuailed with her by celestiall consolations, that her heart by degrées became a little mollified, and in nature somewhat repentant for these her most heynous offences.

Her soule a little leaning to saluation, incouraged these good

men

men to perseuere and goe forward in so Godly a labour, who at last brought her to this oppinion, as it was iustified by one that came from her in Newgate vpon the munday before the Sessions, that she earnestly belieued she had eternally deserued hell fire for the murther of her children, and that she so earnestly repented the déed, saying, that if they were aliue againe, not all the world should procure her to doe it: Thus was she truely repentant, to which (no doubt) but by the good meanes of these Preachers she was wrought vnto.

And now to come to a conclusion, as well of the discourse as of her life she deserued death, and both Law and Iustice hath awarded her the same, for her examination and free confession needed no Iewry, her owne tonge proued a sufficient euidence, and her conscience a witnes that condemned her, her iudgement and execution she receiued with a patient minde, her soule no doubt hath got a trew penitent desire to be in heauen, and the blood of her two innocent Children so wilfully shed (according to all charitable iudgements) is washed away by the mercies of God: Forgiue and forget her good Gentlewomen, shee is not the first that hath beene blemished with blood, nor the last that will make a husband wifelesse, her offence was begot by a strange occasion, but buried I hope with true repentance.

Thus Countrymen of England haue you heard the ruins of a Gentlewoman, who if Popish perswasions had not beene, the world could not haue spotted her with the smallest marke of infamy, but had carried the name of h[illegible] true [illegible] vnto her graue: and for a warning vnto you all, by her example, take héede how you put confidence vnto that dangerous sect, for they surely will deceiue you.

FINIS.

Andersons Repentance who, was executed at Tiburne the 18. of May being Whitson euen. 1616.

Written in the time of his imprisonment in Newgate.

SIgh, for my musicke was a *Syrens* song,
a fayre deceit to Shadow me in griefe:
What, saide I fayre? alas, I cald it wrong.
Vlisses know the *Syrens* danger chiefe,
Was when she sung to lul a man asleepe,
then fashiond she to sing to make men weepe.

Had I but stopt myne eares when *Syrens* sung,
and bound my selfe vnto *Vlisses* mast:
Or had I thought, alas, I am but young,
too much is all to, venture on a cast,
I might haue liu'd, and from all dangers free,
where now I dye, for life is not for mee.

Barkt in a Pinnis made by selfe conceite,
affection Captaine, ouerwhelmde with care,
Destruction neare, whom I espied too late,
incounter giuen by foule and black dispaire:
My Pinnis sunke, and sences all were dimme,
no hope of life, though still I striue to swimme.

Breake throbbing heart, eyes gush out floods of teares,
melt flesh from bone, let veynes and arthures rend:
Fly soule, and search redresse to cure thy feares,
Elizium fields cannot afford one friende,
All death, all hell, my hands with griefe I wring,
mercy may cure: forgiue fayre Englands King.

I cannot speake but kill my selfe with wordes:
I cannoe thinke but I my conscience wound.
Law stabbes mee still in euery part with swords,
Iustice commands in Fetters I be bound,
And for I was, as I haue gracelesse beene,
no life vnlesse thy mercy gracious King.

Confounding sadnesse like a load of lead,
chilles all my blood and makes my sinnewes shrinke.
Reuenge quoth wrong, let Rigor stand in stead,
Death fills the cup, and saith that I must drinke:
Still pitty pleades and thinketh death's a sting,
might it so please thy mercy gracious King.

I all confusd, and in confusion wrapt,
Implore thy mercy prostrate on my face,
Youngling was I and nouice like intrapt,
Repentance, away shall follyes chase,
No blemish blot, I hate any such thing,
If I find grace and mercy of my King.

Villaines auaunt, helhounds you are by kind,
Offensiue Varlets to a Common state,
Shame to offend so meeke a King in minde:
Presuming swaines he doth your vilenes hate,
Liue as you ought, and braue it not with bragges,
least law condemne you in your proudest ragges.

Awake for shame, and lift your eyelids vp,
sleepe not secure nor dreame of doing wrong,
If Iustice strike you cannot change her cup,
death being doome, you fall, for he is strong,
And then you curse, because you did not cease:
To vexe your King with troubling Countries peace.

Shed

Shed not the blood of any, for you know
The high Commander, God, doth so commaund:
Whose law to keepe thy Soueraigne doth intreat,
 thy health it is Gods Law to vnderstand:
Obeying God, God shall all harmes preuent,
 Keeping his peace thy King is well content.

Abate Presumption, sinne is not a iest,
 though God forbeare, yet will he surely strike:
God made thee man, make not thy selfe a beast,
 vaine man that in the worst dost take delight.
Ah stoope betimes, take well what well is spoken,
 least thou repent when as thy pitchers broken.

In budding Youth when yeares begin to bloome,
 and corage flowers the blossoms of the mind:
Fruit wanting grace fierce thunderclaps can doome,
 with lightening flasht, els beaten with the winde.
Fruit all vnkind, as bad as bad may be,
 and curst by God for an accursed tree.

Shame barraine branches for no fruit you beare,
 your leaues are greene, deceitfull are your twigs:
Christ gaue the curse then dread and stand in feare,
 the tree did wither for it bare no figs:
Beauties deceit causd Christ himselfe come nye,
 seeing no fruit he curst the tree to dye.

Might sorrowing sobs with teares redeeme whats past,
 or floods of teares suffice for foredone ills:
Behold my lookes with discontent orecast,
 whose heart doth rend, whose eyes forth fountaines stills:
And yet all this and all that longs thereto,
 is small to that which I intend to doe.

My

My heart through flesh shall issue sweating greese,
and scald my bones with salt and brinish teares:
Through flesh and bone hartes want shall begge reliefe,
on bended knees till bone my flesh out weares.
Flesh, bone and hart consumd in mourns for sinne,
still all too small, anew I must begin.

Whole lumpe of flesh, my selfe flesh blood and bone,
earths dust, clayes lumpe, all made of ash and clay,
All these are I, or else I were alone,
and soule with these inioynd to greatst dismay.
Earths dust, clayes lumpe, ash, flesh and bone abused,
soule quite resolud and yet no way excused.

Weepe flesh for sinne, Soule mourne with teares diuine,
or quell submissiue more then nature wrought:
Gods perfect image, earth to heauens combine,
soules prison earth, soules mournes, earths happies sought
Yet soule nere cease, but dround the earth with teares,
till he graunt pardon whom thy sorrow heares.

Diuine celestiall maker of Earths globe,
crownd King of Kings, most mighty power of powers:
Iust in thy iudgement cleare in scarlet robe:
sweet of all sweets in iudgement gaul to sowers,
Sweet sorrow soures with teares, if thou thinke meet,
then salue of sores with Balme shall make me sweet.

Soules chiefest dread, and bodies bitterst morne,
deathes graue, deepe hell all agonizing feares:
Accusing thoughtes hearts throb, hopes all forlorne,
element all earth, inflamed soule, heauens spheare,
Body and soule to teares re solue you still,
till iust of iusts do pardon all mine ill.

And

And all I am, in Body, Dust, Earth, Clay,
element of Ash, conceiud and borne in sinne:
Old *Adams* Childe, *Eues* Apple pluct, decay,
liues lack, Soules losse not thy mournings line;
But gush out shewers of teares in midst distres,
Harts moane, Soules groane, in one both beg redres,

Ayre, Flesh, Life, Soule, conglutinate in one,
word from his mouth, who liuing Soule did giue:
Maker of all, all made by God alone,
Breath, life, and death, by whome I only liue:
All, all in all, his mercy still appeares,
And I of him, his mercy beg with teares.

Great God remit the follies of my youth,
dread King forgiue, I will no more offend:
Nor God, nor King, but I will serue in trueth,
till *Atrapos* the daies of life shall end:
And at mine end my God shall haue the praise,
Begging of him to lengthen long his daies.

Bodies deathes feare, is no cause of my moane,
but endles feare of euerlasting death.
I wish to liue for Countries good alone,
to serue my King all daies of vitall breath:
And if his mercy be to life extended,
My life is his, till death my life hath ended.

Vnworthy far such fauour to entreate,
all is too small, all don that I am able:
Yet for thy grace in mercy is so greate,
Giue me the crumbes that doe fall from thy Table:
Who els doth starue, imprisoned in griefe,
No foode tast I, saue only thy releife.

If *Maudlins* teares did euer Christs feet wet,
and sweet her Soule with true repentant teares?
If *Peters* mourning streames did mercy get
for all his sinnes? though he his Christ forsweares:
My sad laments abounding from mine eyes,
Sweet King accept, and heare my mournfull cries.

A wounded Soule, a broken contrite heart,
creepes in greatest throng, thy vestures hem to touch:
The oyle of life, King of my life impart,
though sinnes be great, thy mercies twice as much:
Thy word my foode, for want of foode growne leane,
Spotted and foule, till Hysop make me cleane.

My Body prisond for my ill don deeds,
lawes iustice calles me to my guerdon death,
Except faire Iustice all in all exceeds,
my vitall spirits all must pant for breath:
King of my life be not so sore offended,
But let me liue, and all shall be amended.

I will redeeme my time with griefe and woe,
Ile aske forgiuenesse both of God and Man:
The like offences neuer will I doe,
but still redresse with all the speed I can:
Changing my selfe, my manners, minde and all,
Lawding his name defends me from deaths fall.

Like *Esops* Dog, I fondly lost my bone,
vaine hope of more, hath lost my selfe and all:
In floods of teares Ile helpe *Narcissus* mone,
who for a shaddow did in water fall:
The shadow his, which all to late he found,
So I deceaud, am with *Narcissus* drownd.

Learne

Learne of the Emet, equall her in paine,
shame that a Worme in vertue should surpasse:
Die to all sinne, her fauour to attaine,
and be not dull, like to the spurgald Asse,
Who can, and will not: for your willes are hidden,
Worths so obscurd, thrice worthy to be chidden.

But why delate I from my selfe to you?
Its I that mourne, I languish and lament,
Incarcered in loathsom Prison now,
hard manacled to bide all discontent:
My thoughtes disgrast, my hopes linkt to deaths fetter,
My drinke salt teares, because I liu'd no better.

The discrip-
tion of New
gate, and the
Prisoners ly-
ing there.

When I am hungry, then I feed on care,
and when I rest it is in *Plutoes* den:
My bed is griefe, my Pillow is dispaire,
my Chamber-mates, all miserable men,
Whose hopes deceau'd, and yelding to illusion,
Will, wanting grace, hath wrought me like confusion.

When *Morpheus* pitty moues me to a nap,
then *Vulcans* clattering yron chaynes awake me:
When *Tytans* mantles spread on sorrows lap,
Horror, Hells furie, sweares heel not forsake me.
Yet slumbring whiles as *Morpheus* care orequels,
Waking, me thinkes I see a thousand Hels.

And when *Aurora* lifteth vp her eyes,
and bids faire *Phebus* welcom from the West;
Then I behold more then whole worlds surmise,
men quick in hell, in torments and vnrest,
Some pine for hunger, some in cold cheynes tyed,
And Ratts like diuels do pray on some that dyed.

No misery but I both feele and see,
my cup is full of woes vnto the brimme,
My Pen cannot describe them as they bee:
amidst distresse, yet will I call on him,
In pittie shines, whose glory mercy is:
Freeing my Soule from Hell to heighest blis.

Arabian Phenix kindling vertues fire,
let mercy flame to thaw my frozen woes:
Most gratious King, quench out all coales of ire,
els Soule consum'd to cinders, sunder'd goes:
Shine still in mercy bright as sunshine raies,
life-giuing King, my Soule shall giue thee praise.

The *Publican* surprest with weight of sin,
durst not presume to cast his eyes on hie:
Gazing on Earth, his heart did neuer lin,
but *Miserere* loudly did he cry.
Peccaui Lord, this Sinners Soule confessed:
Whose note I sing, that haue no lesse transgressed.

The wandring Sonne, whose portion was mispent
with ryots, surfets, quaffing boales of vice,
Dainties all deere: in hunger now content
to feed with Hogs, this Prodigall not nice,
All tatters torne, shakt out of coulors fine,
Him need compels to keepe a strangers Swine.

The ground contents this restles to ly on,
whome beddes of downe did whilome discontent,
His head vp bolstered with some hill or Stone:
the cloudes a couering to his field-bed lent,
Where sory man oreplunged wofull lies,
His courtaines cold, and canopie the skies.

Remu-

Remunerating with himſelfe the cauſe
  of want, of woe, of hunger, and of colde:
Offence to God, the breaking of his lawes.
  then breake out teares, he could no longer holde,
But weeping ran, till he his Father ſees,
In true repentance, bending both his knees.

And with loud organe of a fainting Soule,
  Father he ſayed, I haue gainſt Heauen offended,
Gainſt Earth, & thee, whoſe power doth ſin controule,
  no worthy Sonne, ſo he his faint ſpeach ended:
Yet ſtill in ſilence pearle of teares drild foorth,
Till fathers welcome compted him of worth

His Fathers heart in pitty then relents,
  about his neck he cling'd his aged armes,
Glad in his heart his Sonne in heart repents,
  receiues him home, and with a kiſſe, he warnes
That all his friends ſhould feaſt at his free coſt,
And welcom home his Sonne ſo long was loſt.

Thriſe happy Sonne, whoſe teares renews this grace,
  and ſweet repentance was it home thee brought:
Threefold thrice double happie Fathers face,
  a Sonne to finde, whom thou ſo long had loſt:
And Sonne moſt happie in a Father kinde,
Who being loſt did ſuch a Father finde.

The ſelfeſame balme is cure for my great woe,
  the ſame repentance makes me *Abba* crie.
My ſpeach doth faint, and I can ſay no more.
  mercie redreſſe, els languiſhing I die:
Sweet ſweet of ſweets, bleſt balme, chiefe eaſe of paine,
Graunt mee my home, I will not ſtray againe.

No more ſhall folly hold my witts in thrall,
   Wiſedome ſhall ranſome Will from Follies bands:
Experience ſhall forewarne mee *Syrens* all.
   Nor ſhal Diſpaire, touch Conſcienc with foule hands
But with Repentance will I liue and die,
In Vertues bower, where ſhame can not come.

With ſinne my ſoule ſhall be no more oppreſt,
   my God and King to ſerue, ſhall be my care:
No longer ſhall my thoughts be at vnreſt,
   but dayly ſhun the place where Wicked are.
Diſcretion aye ſhall guide my Heart aright,
To ſhine mongſt men like worthy lampe of light.

My cullerd Suites will I exchange for black,
   till ſcarlet ſinnes be all as white as ſnow:
On mee ſwift Time ſhall neuer turne his back,
   nor ſhall his taſke be more my Tayres to mow:
But with repentance, furrow hopes forlorne,
Till God giue grace I ſheafe vp better corne.

My words are vowes, beleeue them all of worth,
   I cannot paint I haue forgot to gloaze:
The ſwearing tongue I haue quite cut it foorth,
   what I haue been, ceaſe further to impoſe:
And for I am as I was not before,
So God be Iudge, for men can iudge no more.

The life I led I loath thereon to thinke:
   ſay what I was, I hate my ſelfe therefore:
Giue him not Gaule that beggeth for a drinke:
   who els is kild, what need you ſtab him more,
My wounds are deepe, yet Phiſicks cure may ſpie,
A ſalue for ſoare, or els I ſurely die.

If I be raysd by him preserueth all,
  from death to life a *Lazarus* from his graue.
A *Pharaos* vassall, a persecuting *Saul*,
  but neyther now, but as my God would haue,
A Soule redeemd, and ransomd with his blood,
May liue, because the Lord hath thought it good.

And if I liue, my life I will decore,
  eiecting sinne, sweet vertue to install:
Giuer of grace, graunt grace I sinne no more,
  establish mee that I doe neuer fall,
To thee my heart, my life, and Soule, I giue,
Who after death eternally makes liue.

Direct my pathes, euen for thy mercies sake,
  guide thou my steps to shun all sinfull waies:
Keepe me from sleepe, in thee still let me wake,
  to laude thy name all time of earthly daies:
And when I earth shall be resolud to dust,
Graunt that my Soule may liue amongst the iust.

FINIS. *William Anderson.*

Natures Cruell Step-Dames (*STC* 12012) is reproduced with permission from the clear Folger Shakespeare Library copy. The text-block measures 80 × 137 mm.

The following words are a transcription of the original:

10.3	grand
10.5	in-
10.8	yee fall
10.18	your ad-
10.19	Lion
10.20	Diabo-
10.21	lus non dormat
13.10	Powre
13.18	neglect of Gods Mini-

Natures
Cruell Step-Dames:
OR,
Matchlesse Monsters of the Female Sex; *Elizabeth Barnes*, and *Anne Willis*.

Who were executed the 26. day of *April*, 1637. at Tyburne, for the unnaturall murthering of their owne Children.

Also, herein is contained their severall Confessions, and the Courts just proceedings against other notorious Malefactors, with their severall offences *this Sessions*.

Further, a Relation of the wicked Life and impenitent Death of *Iohn Flood*, who raped his own Childe.

Printed at London for *Francis Coules*, dwelling in the Old-Baily. 1637.

A Narration of the Diabolicall seduction of Elizabeth Barnes, *late of* Battersey *in the County of* Surrey *widdow, mercilesly to murder* Susan Barnes *her owne naturall Child.*

A Whole moneth, as shee confest in the publike hearing of divers persons of good repute, this Savage continued with this hellish fire kindled in her breast, violently at the last breaking forth into the unnaturall deprivation of the life of the fruit of her owne wombe. The subtill serpent Satan, that thus long time had possessed her, putteth into her minde the manner how to put in execution her diabolicall execrable intention on the innocent childe, without its least suspition, as you may perceive by the sequele of the History. To intice the childe unto its slaughter, and to goe abroad with her, she provided the 24 day of *March* last 1637. very early in the morning, an Apple Pye, a Herring Pye, Raisins

ſins of the Sun, and other fruits which ſhee carried with her; accuſtomed baits, uſed by loving Parents, to quiet and ſtill their children in their unquietneſſe, but this creature otherwiſe, to deſtroy her childe by that meanes. Theſe things being thus prepared before-hand, and the child beholding them, did ſet an edge on its affections, willingly to accompany her cruell mother, in her travell towards her long home.

The innocent Lambe and ravenous Wolfe both ſpend out the day together; with joyfull expectation, the one willingly endureth the travell and heat of the day, to goe to be placed with a kinſwoman of hers, as was pretended, but alas this was but flattery to ſhed innocent blood. Towards the evening of the ſame day, theſe her alluring kind of deadly junkets, ſhe brings with her childe, into a Wood called *Wormewall Wood*, being in the Pariſh of *Fulham* in the County of *Middleſex*, ſome 4. miles diſtance from the place where ſhe dwelt; being there in ſecret, and covered with darkneſſe, ſhe faineth unto the child this excuſe, ſaying, that ſhe was very weary, and was not able to goe any further, but muſt upon neceſſity ſtay a while, there to reſt and eaſe her ſelf, the which the poore childe, as ſhee ſaid, moſt lovingly intreated her to doe, being alſo glad of ſuch repoſe.

Being

Being ſet downe together, ſhe taketh out of her basket, the Pyes, and fruit, and ſets them before the childe, for to eate of them, which did ſo.

Thus having eaten of ſuch things formerly provided for it, being tyred with going ſo farre a journey, it being but of the age of eight yeeres, afterwards ſweetly falleth into a faſt ſleep, which was very oportune for her mothers accurſed deſigne, for that ſame night about the houres of xj. and xij. ſhee drew out of her ſheath a knife, and with that knife barbarouſly did cut the throat of the child. Soone after this bloody fact, being done by her, her eyes were opened, that ſhe beheld her miſerable condition, and that, that by her bloody hands had beene done, that could no way be again undone. She reſolved before hand, how to diſpoſe of her ſelfe after the fact committed. For ſhe carried with her the inſtrument of her owne death, as ſhe did the childs; for it a knife, ſo a halter, wherewith to end her owne life, and attempted it, but had not power to lay violent hands on her ſelfe, being mercifully thereof prevented by the all-powerfull hand of heaven: after this firſt attempt, as ſhe ſaid, ſhe was ſtrongly ſet on againe by the Devill to drowne her ſelfe, but that prevailed not againſt her, but forthwith brake out then into a great passion, as it were a fountaine of teares, humbly and heartily imploring Heavens mercy and forgivenesse for her bloody crying-fact.

Her guilty conscience, will no way permit her to rest, or shew her any place of refuge for safety; but according unto that saying of the Psalmist, it falleth upon her. *Evill shall hunt the wicked person to overthrow them*, and so it did, to the full satisfaction of all the beholders. For whither doth this affrighted Creature, run or flee suppose yee, but even unto the gates of Justice, crying, as it were there, for Justice to be rendred according to her demerit? From the wood shee flees into *Kensington*, and there hides her selfe all in straw, in the Barne of one *Disney*: and being there found, suspition of this murther was laid unto her charge, which she confest to his wife and servant, and afterwards shee was carryed unto Master *Fen* a Justice in that Towne, unto whom she confest the same fact.

This fact being rumored abroad, I went unto New-gate to visit this miserable delinquent, who at my first view of her matronlike aspect, induced me to enter into present discourse with her, to prevaile if I could possibly, to finde out the cause that moved her unto such unheard of cruelty: shee answered me me againe, none but the Devill alone tempted her thereunto, and with teares fast trickling downe her cheekes, desired my selfe, with the rest that stood by, to pray unto Almighty God, to take mercy on her poore sinfull soule, to save that from hell.

A second time I urged her, to discover the cause of that fact, and disburden her conscience, and somwhat then fell from her, thus saying, that she had spent all the estate shee had upon one that pretended love unto her, and being by that meanes become poore and indebted, knew not what would become of her, but instantly resolved on this desperate course, leaving such deep impression in her mind, with the continuance of time in not disclosing of it, that the temptation, and resolution waxed daily stronger, and powerfully wrought on her. Being demanded what she thought should become of her after the fact done, thus replyed, that she attempted to hang her selfe, but had not power, nor doubtlesse could not have such a hard heart, to kill the child, had it been but awake, as it was a sleep. For that time I departed from her, and freshly the third time indeavoured to discover more but could not, but constantly she adhered to her former confession, no whit varying.

Serious

Serious advertisements unto all good Christians, and cautions, by this ignorant sinfull womans *suddaine downe-fall.*

IF this womans house had beene set on fire, doubtlesse she would have made such an out-crie in the streets, that all her neighbours must of necessity rise, and adde unto her all help possible to quench the fire. Her heart was here set on fire by hell, musing to perpetrate mischiefe, her tongue is silent, and mouth is shut, when it should have beene wide open, to cry aloud unto God, for grace and mercy, and to crave the helpe of the effectuall prayers of Gods holy Ministers, and Congregations of his Saints here on earth, to deliver her out of the snare and bondage of Satan, whom she voluntarily obeyed. If a limbe had beene broken, shee would not rest satisfied till a Chyrurgion had beene present for to cure her.

If shee had falne suddainly desperate sicke for feare of death, hastily they post and runne to seeke for a Physitian; but her soule is sicke, and drawes nigh downward into Hell, whatcare or cure of that, where was God or his Ministers thought of all this while, blessed Saint *Paul* so soone as the Viper seized on his hand, shooke it off immediately into the fire: a whole moneth this venemous Viper, *Murder*, lodgeth in her heart; God, prayer unto him, and hearing of his Word all this while was layd aside. Cunning deluding Satan sitteth likewise on her tongue, as he tooke seizure on her heart, that he tyeth fast, not able to pray, which might have prevailed against him. Devoute Prayer is his scourge, and faithlesse faint-hearted people onely give place unto him, and sinke downe at his feet.

The Devill is but a weake faint-hearted Coward, *Resist him*, saith the blessed Apostle, *and hee will flye from you*. This kinde of evill spirit, saith our Saviour Christ, cannot be cast out, but by fasting and prayer. Our blessed Saviour Jesus Christ in the disconsolate time of his most bitter passion on the Crosse for our sakes, to encounter Satan, to comfort himselfe in that great Agony he was in, and to get the Conquest of that grand captaine of all mischiefe, prayer unto his heavenly Father in the Garden, inculcates frequently this duty unto his distressed followers, *Watch and pray*, and joynes the necessity of it, *least yee fall into Temptation*. Is a weake childe able to stand in the way of a Lyon stirred up unto fury and rage, no whit possible: much lesse is a sinnefull weake man able to grapple with the powerfull strength of sinne and Satan; and therefore pray, that power may be given unto you from above, to resist, the least of whose temptations, ye are no wayes able to resist of your selves. 1 Pet. 5.8. *Bee sober, and watch for your adversary the Devill, as a roaring Lion walketh about, seeking whom he may devoure. Diabolus non dormit*, the Divell is not idle, neither sleepes nor slumbers, but watcheth to take his advantage, seeketh which way unawares to rush in suddenly upon poore soules. By lamentable late experience, Satan hath foyled many, witnesse those weekely bills of casualties for *London* and *Middlesex*. The Devill although hee is im-

impudent and potent, the holy Apostle in the ninth verse, shewes a meanes there, to abate his pride who resist in the faith, a faithfull Christian makes him to fly, feare, and quake. In the first of *Samuel* 17. chap. 40. vers. There is mention made, that *David* chose him five smooth stones out of a brooke, with one of them hee slew *Goliah*.

Medici utuntur diversis medicamentis ad diversos morbos at Christianis contra omnia mala unicum remedium est pracationis medicina Granatensis.

Learned Physitians apply various medicines unto the nature of the disease, but unto Christians onely, one Soveraigne medicine, as an Antidote is prescribed, against all manner of malignous diseases, the onely remedy is medicine of Prayer, the healthy man prayer preserveth alive, the sicke man Prayer restoreth health: In time of warre prayer is the victorious Conquerour; In the time of peace prayer is the infallible Defender of King and people, in health and prosperity: Saint *James* 5 chapter 15. verse. *Sinnes are promised to be forgiven, and the prayer of a righteous*

teous man availeth much if it bee fervent: Precibus, non paſsibus itur ad Deum, ergo aſcendat oratio, ut deſcendat gratia: as the foot by paces carry the body, ſo the ſoule is carried up unto Heaven by Prayer; therefore let thy prayer aſcend up unto thy God daily, that hee may ſend downe the dew of his holy Spirit into thy ſoule. *Deijcitur Satan cum tu aſcenderis, aſcendis duobus modis, meditatione et oratione, meditatio quod decet docet, oratio quod deeſt obtinet, Gregory.* Satan is caſt under thy foot when thou raiſeſt up thy ſoule toward Heaven by Prayer. Two manner of wayes there are that man may climbe up unto the toppe of Heavens holy hill, namely meditation and prayer; meditation is prayers hand-mayd, Meditation inſtructeth, what becommeth the ſoule to doe, prayer ſupplies what is wanting unto the ſoule.

Good King *David* in the 5. Pſalm. ver. 3. made a promiſe unto Almighty God, and what was it. *My voyce ſhalt thou heare betimes, Oh Lord, early in the morning will I direct my prayer unto thee, and will looke up. A domino hoc iubemur orare, ut ab eo qui-*

qui secretorum cognitor est, recipiamus orationis occultæ mercedem: Chrysostom. in Math. Homil. 8.

We are of the Lord Jesus commanded this chiefely (to pray) that of him unto whom the secrets of all hearts are manifest, wee may receive openly a heavenly Reward of our Prayers offered in secreets, to conclude this, as the Psalmist advised, *Powre out your prayers before him, without which no minuite of the day can be happy unto us.* I will commend unto your daily meditations and practise that repleate zealous Collect prescribed to be read in the second Sunday in Lent, and the Lord give a daily blessing to those that doe imbrace the instruction.

The last Caution is the neglect of Gods Minister in not repairing unto him.

SInne is like a spot in a garment, at the first it may be easily expunged, but by continuance, it gathereth more and more soile uuto it, making it so difficult that it freteth the garment into peeces, before it can be cleane. Ignorant people behold their sins, through the ſpectacles of their owne fantaſies, they extend or extenuate their ſinnes as they pleaſe, thereby deceiving themſelves, ſome make ſinnes leſſer, and and others greater than they are, and it cannot otherwiſe poſſible be; becauſe, they are not able to judge of the difference being ignorant and unlettered, than a blinde man can diſtinguiſh colours.

A ſtumbling blocke into this womens way the Divell caſts, not to goe unto her Miniſter unto whom the Almighty GOD had given the paſtorall Cure of her ſoule, to reveale her minde unto him, for feare of revealing it againe, what doth GOD intruſt us with your deare ſoules? and will not you truſt us with your filthy ſinnes? to diſcover them, to disburden your heavy laded conſciences, will you not make nice to ſhew a noyſome foule ulcerated body, and ſhew the place where it paineth you moſt to the chyrurgion, to have thereby eaſe, and bee too too curious in the matters of your ſoule; your abominable ſinnes let them

alone?

alone untouched, or not confessed at all, which by confession may bee lessened, and people made wary to walke more circumspectly, and the hainousnesse of sinne being set before mens eyes, may deterre them from committing of them againe. Beloved, a weake slight and subtilty in the Devill, that with-holds the poore pensive sinner, from his ghostly comforter (Confession) what then? oh no, by no menaces, I will not doe it, hee will reveile mee, will you not blush for shame, nor hold it no blemish, to harbour wicked thoughts in your hearts, which GOD knoweth, and seeth, and in the open day of the world exorbitantly commit them, and is this a greater offence to confesse them, and to turne from them, judge yee? Our ayme of the Church of England is not such, as that of Rome, to creepe into mens secrets hearts, to hold them in awe, but discover their sinnes, to save that way their soules, and as for disclosing of such kinde of persons, let mee advise them, not in the least manner to doubt our secrecy, we have learned better

ter, and desire our Auditors to be otherwise perswaded of us. Whether is God or men wiser? the holy Spirit adviseth unto this duty of Confession, by that meanes yee lessen sinne in you, and cast out the Devill. Christ cured none but those that shewed their disease, and beleeved his power, by confession of sinne the way for the Lord Iesus is prepared, and by the prayer of the faithfull Minister unto God for the poore penitent sinner, his sinnes are forgiven him, Satan cast out, and his soule better armed against his future strong temptations. King *David* resolved saying: Palme 38. verse 18. *I will confesse my wickednesse, and bee sorry for my sinne.*

Magnus accessus ad Deum, cognitio est infirmitatis suæ, the step that we set forwards Heaven, after we have falne into sinne, is the unfaigned confessing of our downfall by sinne. *S. Luke* 15. chap. with the prodigall: *I will goe to my father, and say unto him, Father, I haue sinned against Heauen and thee.* Psal. 15. *Against thee onely have I sinned, and done euill in thy sight*, at last he prayeth, *O cleanse thou me from my secret faults, there is none whole in my body or soule by reason of sin.*

32 *Psal.*

32. *Psalm.* 5, 6 *vers. I will knowledge my sinne unto thee, and mine unrighteousnesse have I not hid. I said, I will confesse my sinnes unto the Lord, and so thou forgavest the wickednesse of my sinne.* These were the ensuing comforts and favours of God to the sinner; remission of sins for cōfessing of them. Read the 5th.Chap. of *Iames, ver. 6. Acknowledge your faults one to another, and pray one for another, that ye may be healed.* Our blessed Saviour, whē he sent his Disciples into the world, as he gave them a Commission for to preach, so likewise power over uncleane spirits, to cast them out. In a word, he gave them power of sinnes in the totall lumpe: *Whosoevers sinnes ye retaine* (saith he) *they are retained, and whosoevers sins ye remit, they are remitted.* What greater comfort could Christ pronounce, then say, *Son, thy sinnes be forgiven?* and how did the Iewes disdaine at those words, saying, *Who can forgive sins, but God only?* Christ readily replieth, and giveth them a token of the truth thereof, by the peraliptick man to rise up and walke before them, *That ye may know the Son of man hath power to forgive sins here on earth, I say unto thee, Arise, take up thy bed, and walk. Primus ad indulgentiam gradus est agnoscere delictum.* The chiefest way to obtaine mercy at Gods hands for sinns past, is to acknowledge the offences done. *Dum agnoscit reus, ignoscit Deus.* and the sinner is not readier to confesse his wickednesse, but God is as ready againe for to forgive them. *Novit Deus omnïa, vocem tamen tuam expectet, si taces Secretarius es Diaboli,* saith S. *Ambr.* God knoweth all things,

yet the voyce, and confession of penitent sinners, he regardeth, and expecteth; If a sinner be at any time silent, he is but the Devils Secretary.

The Confession of *Elizabeth Barnes*, the 26. of *Aprill*, 1637, *at the place of Execution.*

DVring the time that shee was in prison, shee concealed her Adultery, that she was begot with Child, by him on whom she had wasted her estate, and deluded with hopes of Marriage. His name, as shee said, was *Richard Evans*, a Taylor dwelling in *Battersey* in the Countie of *Surrey*: upon whose conscience lieth very heavie, his false dealing with the poore woman. I wish that hee may heartily aske God and the world forgivenes for his impieties in publicke. Through whose deceits and flatteries, this poore creatures ruine was occasioned. And so much for *Elizabeth Barnes*.

A Relation of Anne Willis, *the manner of of the murdering of her owne Child, confessed by her at the place of Execution.*

VPon an Inquisition of one of the Coroners Inquest, for the County of *Middlesex*, upon the view of the body of her Basterd-child, taken out

out of a vault in *Roſemary* Lane, by Tower Hill, by her therein throwne, being by the Iury made, returne unto the Coroner of Murder, Warrants were immediately ſent out unto all parts for the apprehending of the ſaid *Ann Willis*, who upon the ſeventh day of *March*, 1637, was taken, and brought before Sir *Thomas Iaye*, unto whom ſhe confeſſed the fact: That the Child was borne alive: there was two upon oath juſtified it, that ſhee ſaid it was alive. Oh cruell Monſters of that tender Sex. *Can a woman forget the child of her wombe? Iſa. 9.* Heavens infinite compaſſion is compared unto the Mother and Infant, the neere tye between them, and the intire care of mothers over their children! When I lift up mine eyes towards the Heavens, & againe caſt them downe to the earth; Birds and Beaſts, me thinks, do riſe up in judgement againſt theſe unnaturall cruell Beaſtes in womens ſhapes. The Swallow flieth high, and in the towring Trees, Churches, and Houſes build their Neſtes, to preſerve their yong ones o[illegible]nger; The Sparrow watcheth alone on the Houſe top, as carefull what it had hatched and brought foorth. Beaſts, ſuch as Lyons, Woolves, Tigers and Foxes, have ſecret caves and woods where they hide there young, to preſerve & foſter them alive: But theſe bloody dogs degenerate from them. O let therefore the memoriall of them periſh.

A Relation of Iohn Flood, *late of* S. Giles in the Field, *for the committing of a Rape on the body of his owne naturall child, being under the age of ten yeares.*

THis man was moſt notorious, and generally reported to be of a moſt diſſolute converſation. The fact which was layd unto his charge, fully prooved by the Teſtimony of divers grave and ſober Matrons, which ſearched the Body of the Child, and ſaid, ſhee had been abuſed by a man without all queſtion. The Honourable Judges, before whom this haynous fact was tryed, inquired to finde out the Actor of ſo horrid a deed. The Child on whom it was done, produced, nor accuſed any other perſon but *Flood* her owne Father, and related very confidently the manner of their carnall knowledge of each other, to the full ſatisfaction of all that heard her, that none but he could be the man. Being demanded the reaſon why ſhee did not immediately reveale that her Father had to doe with her, ſhee anſwered, That ſhe durſt not ſpeake of it againe unto any body, becauſe her father ſaid, If ſhee ſhould at any time tell what hee did unto her, the Devill would preſently teare her in pieces. This the child averred unto the Court before his face, at the time of his Triall.

What Flood *ſayd at the place of Execution.*

As hee impudently denied the Fact at the time of his Triall, hee perſevered to the inſtant of his death,

death, of the deniall of the fact, with many fearefull imprecations of judgements, and renunciation of Gods mercies if he were any wayes guilty: In great passionate hot termes hee brake forth against his wife, on this wise saying, That three yeeres she was conspiring to worke his downfall, wch now by her was effected. And thus this barren Tree at the Tree of execution stood and fell.

The Confession of Ioane Burs, *taken before Sir* Iames Cambell, *Knight, the* 8. *day of Aprill,* 1637.

SHee said that the Saturday before *Christmas* last, her Master having given her sharpe correction, for the stealing away of a Runlet of Wine, and expending it out in the company of Lewd creatures lazing about the City; in revenge unto her Master and Mistris, she went and bought *Mercury*, and put it into a Posset, and gave it unto them both for to drink, which did indanger their lives; but blessed be God, are both yet alive: And for that exorbitant Fact, was by the Court fined, and remaines in the Goale to this present. Being demanded why shee did so unto her Master and Mistris, Shee stood mute: but it was justified unto her face at her Triall, that these words should proceed out of her owne mouth, That if her Mistris were dead, she might afterwards have better Cloathes; And to her Master she did it, because he did beat her so cruelly. But observe in this silly Girle a passage worth note: Who perceiving the *Mercury* to worke violently on her Mistris, brought some thereof in a Paper, and shewed it unto her Mistris, saying, that doubtless her Master had put something into the Posset, that made her so sicke; craftily intending by this, to cast off all suspicion from her self; but that fastned it upon her, as just cause there was. And so much for that.

The Confession of Anne Holden, *before* Sir Iames Cambell, *the* 16. *day of* *March*, 1637.

THe said *Anne Holden* confessed, as it was in the Court read, That last Night was seven weekes, she being lodged in the house of *Iohn Atkins* at Colebrooke, was delivered of a Child, no body being with her; which said Child shee threw into a Ditch, on the Back-side of the said House, because it should not be known nor seene. But she was spared her Triall, because she is to be removed unto *Buckingham*, there to be tryed upon another Murther.

Lastly, there is one Notorious Bawd *Rebecca Smith*, who dwelt at the Seven-stars in *White-cross-street*, convicted for a Bawd; who according unto her deserts, is to be Carted about the City, and thence ought to be banisht.

FINIS.

A Wonder of Wonders (Wing B5620) is reproduced with permission from the unique copy at The British Library (shelfmark E 621 [11]). The text-block measures 110 × 172 mm.

A Wonder of Wonders.

BEING

A faithful *Narrative* and true *Relation*, of one

Anne Green, Servant to Sir *Tho. Reed* in *Oxfordshire*, who being got with Child by a Gentleman, her Child falling from her in the house of Office, being but a span long, and dead born, was condemned on the 14. of *December* last, and hanged in the Castle-yard in *Oxford*, for the space of half an hour, receiving many great and heavy blowes on the brests, by the but end of the Souldiers Muskets, and being pul'd down by the leggs, and was afterwards beg'd for an Anatomy, by the Physicians, and carried to Mr. *Clarkes* house, an Apothecary, where in the presence of many learned Chyrurgions, she breathed, and began to stir; insomuch, that Dr. *Petty* caused a warm bed to be prepared for her, let her blood, and applyed Oyls to her, so that in 14 hours she recovered, and the first words she spake were these; *Behold Gods Providence! Behold his miraculous and loving kindness!* VVith the manner of her Tryal, her Speech and Confession at the Gallowes; and a Declaration of the Souldiery touching her recovery. *Witnessed by Dr. Petty, and Licensed according to Order.*

A Wonder of Wonders, &c.

SIR,

ON the 14. of *December* last, there happened a very ſtrange paſſage concerning a Maid, *Anne Green* by name, which was got with Child, by an *Oxford-ſhire* Gentleman, the particulars whereof follow.

This *Anne Green*, Servant to Sir *Thomas Read*, being very buſie at turning of *Mault*, over-reaching her ſelf, found her ſelf to be very ill; whereupon ſhe immediatly went into the houſe of Office, remaining about a quarter of an hour, full of pain; at laſt, a Child, about a ſpan long ſprung from her, but abortive, which much impair'd her health and ſtrength; but being exceeding fearful, that a diſcovery ſhould be made thereof, ſhe laid it in a Corner of the aforeſaid houſe, and covered it with duſt and rubbiſh.

During which time, one of her fellow-Servants, admiring that she staid so long, and hearing many heavy groans, went to see what was become of her, who found her in a very sad and deplorable condition, and asking her what the matter was? she reply'd, *she was utterly undone, undone, undone*; Why *Anne*, I hope thou art not with Child? Alas, alas! *Mary*, that ever I was born, to live and die in shame and scorn: I was, but now I am clear of it; Why? what is become of it? she answered, look yonder, where it lies, and going to the place, casting off the dust, ran shrieking out into the house, acquainting her Master and Mistriss, with this sad accident; in so much, that they presently sent for her in, and demanded who it was, that had committed that foul act, and contemptible crime with her? who answered, a Gentleman of good birth, and kinsman to a Justice of Peace.

But after half an hours discourse, she was carried before a Justice, who upon examination, confessed, that she was guilty of the Act, in committing of the sin, but clear and innocent of the crime for murdering of it, for that it was dead born; yet notwithstanding, after further examination, the Justice caused her *Mittimus* to be made, inditing her to answer it at the next Assizes, and forth-with sent her to the Castle Goal at *Oxford*, where she remained till the Sessions; at which time, she was arraigned for her life, who being brought to the Bar, pleaded, *not guilty*; but after a short tryal, she was convicted for her life, and received sentence to be hanged on *Oxford* Gallowes, which was accordingly performed; and being brought to the place of execution, she fell down on her knees at the ladder foot, humbly desiring of God, that his Divine Majesty would be pleased, to shew some remarkable judgement on her, for a signal and testification to the world of her innocency, which most miraculously was evidenced to her, to the great and wonderful admiration to all that shall either hear of, or read these ensuing lines.

But before I insist upon this miraculous deliverance, it is requisite that I should communicate her speech and deportment upon the Ladder, which was with great comfort, and undauntedness of spirit by this poor soul performed, to the great admiration of the spectators.

At the going up the Ladder, she fixt her eyes on the Executioner, saying, God forgive my false accusers, as I freely forgive thee, and then turning her self on the Ladder uttered these words.

Dear Friends,

YOur business hither to day, is to see a sad spectacle, an innocent woman to be in a moment cut off, in the prime of her years, which sudden change doth not in the least strike dread or terror to my heart, but rather incites me to a motion of eternal joy and happiness; for I conceive, there is no more but this Rope and Ladder between me and Heaven, and I doubt not but that I am now going to receive that blessed Portion, which my blessed Saviour and Redeemer Jesus Christ hath purchased for me, by ransoming my soul with his precious blood, and bitter passion.

And as for this untimely end, I do unfaignedly acknowledge and confess, that it is Gods just judgement and wrath upon me, for sins long unrepented, of many judgements withstood, and mercies slighted: therefore God hath whipped me by his severe rod of correction, that he might not lose me.

I pray joyn with me in prayer, that it may not be a fruitless rod, that when by this rod I have laid down my life, by this staffe I may be comforted, and received into glory.

One thing more I desire, and to you dear Cousen, being a young man, standing at the foot of the ladder) I represent my suit, That when the doomful turn from off the ladder comes, that you would use all possible means to dispatch me of my pain; and then casting up her eyes to Heaven, being prepared for a new change of life, breathed forth her last words, saying, *sweet Jesus receive my soul*; upon the uttering of which words, the Executioner did his Office; and being turned off the ladder, her kinsman took hold of her feet, and hung with all the weight and force of his body on them, that so he might the sooner rid her of her pain.

A *Souldier* standing by, gave her 4. or 5. blowes on the brest, with the but end of his Musket, and having hung half an hour, she was cut down, (being quite dead) and put into the Chyrurgions Chest, (who had beg'd her for an Anatomy) and carried to Mr. *Clarkes* house, an *Apothecary*, where the *Physitions* met to try their skill; and having prefixed a time for the reading a Lecture over her, (being usual upon the anatomizing of either man or woman.)

When they were all met, her body was taken out of the Coffin, and laid upon a large Table, where in the presence of them all, she began to breath, which was no

small

ſmall terror nor admiration, to all that were then preſent; whereupon a large diſpute aroſe about her, and one amongſt the reſt, Dr. Petty by name, went to her, took her by the hand, and laid his eare to her temples, and perceiving life, declared that there was a great hand of God in the buſineſs, and imediately let her blood in 3 places. After which he cauſed a warm bed to be prepared for her, and a woman to lie with her, and applied ſeveral Oyls unto her, uſing many other circumſtances of art, until she recovered, which was within 14 hours: And even in the laſt minute of the 14 hour, she opened her eyes, uttering theſe words. Behold Gods providence, and his wonder of wonders, which indeed, is a deliverance ſo remarkable, ſince the ceaſing of Miracles, that it cannot be parallel'd in all Ages, for the ſpace of 300 years, And withall, it may remain upon record, for a preſident to all Magiſtrates, and Courts of Judicature, to take a ſpecial care in denounſing of ſentence, without a due and legal proceſs, according to the known Laws of the Land, by an impartial and uncorrupted Jury, either of men or women, &c. This poor Creature, which God of his infinite mercy hath evidently manifeſted his love unto, is now indifferent-well recovered, and can walk up and down her Chamber, but her neck is very sore, and black withall, her brest and stomack much bruised, yet her pain disswages daily, and divers both in City and Countrey frequent hourly to behold her. At her first recovery she seemed to be much agast, and lookt strangly, her eyes being ready to start out of her head; but by the great pains of honest and faithful Dr. Petty, she is miraculously recovered which moved some of her enemies to wrath and indignation, insomuch, that a great man amongst the rest, moved to have her again carried to the place of execution, to be hanged up by the neck, contrary to all Law, reason and justice; but some honest Souldiers then present, seemed to be very much discontented thereat, and declared, That there was a great hand of God in it, and having suffered the Law, it was contrary to all right and reason, that any further punishment should be inflicted upon her, which words brought a final end and period to their dispute and controversie; where I shall (at present) desist from reciting any further circumstances, and remain,

Oxford Jan 13. 1651.

Your obliged Servitor,
W. BURDET.

FINIS.

Newes from the Dead ('Second' [i.e. third] edition; Wing W1074) is reproduced with permission from the Bodleian Library copy (shelfmark Wood 516 [7]). The text-block copy measures 93 × 150 mm.

Newes from the Dead.

OR

A TRUE AND EXACT
Narration of the miraculous
deliverance of

ANNE GREENE,

Who being Executed at OXFORD Decemb. 14. 1650. afterwards revived; and by the care of certain hysitians there, *is now perfectly recovered.*

Together with the manner of her Suffering, and the *particular meanes used for her Recovery.*

Written by a Scholler in OXFORD for the Satisfaction of a friend, who desired to be informed concerning the truth *of the businesse.*

Whereunto are added certain Poems, casually *written upon that Subject.*

The Second Impression with Additions.

OXFORD,
Printed by *LEONARD LICHFIELD*, for
THO. ROBINSON. ·D. 1651.

Newes from the Dead.

THere happened lately in this Citty a very rare and remarkeable accident, which being variously and falsely reported amongst the vulgar (as in such cases it is usuall) to the end that none may be deceived, and that so signall an act of Gods mercy and providence may never be forgotten, I have here faithfully recorded it, according to the Information I have received from those that were the chiefe Instruments in bringing this great worke to perfection.

In the house of Sir *Thomas Read* at *Duns-Tew* in *Oxford-shire*, there lived a maid named *Anne Greene*, born at *Steeple-Barton*, in the same County, being about 22 years of age, of a middle stature, strong, fleshie, and of an indifferent good feature; who being (as she said) often sollicited by faire promises and other amorous enticements of Mr *Jeffery Read* Grand-child to the said Sir *Thomas*, a youth of about 16 or 17 years of age, but of a forward growth and stature, at last consented to satisfy his unlawfull pleasure. By which act (as it afterward appeared) she conceived, and was delivered of a Man-child: which being never made knowne, and the Infant found dead in the house of office, caused a suspition, that she being the mother had murthered it, and throwne it there on purpose to conceale both it and her shame together. Thereupon she was immediatly taken into examination, and carried before severall Justices of the peace in the Countrey: and soone after, in an extreame cold and rainy day, sent unto *Oxford* Gaole, where having passed about three weekes more in continuall affrights and terrours, in a place as comfortlesse as her condition, she was at a Sessions held in *Oxford*, arraigned, condemned, and on Saturday the 14 of *December* last, brought forth to the place of Execution: where, after singing of a Psalme, &

 something

ſomething ſaid in juſtification of her ſelf, as to the fact for which ſhe was to ſuffer, and touching the lewdneſſe of the Family wherein ſhe lately lived, ſhe was turn'd off the Ladder, hanging by the neck for the ſpace of almoſt halfe an houre, ſome of her friends in the mean time thumping her on the breaſt, others hanging with all their weight upon her leggs; ſometimes lifting her up, and then pulling her downe againe with a ſuddaine jerke, thereby the ſooner to diſpatch her out of her paine: inſomuch that the Under-Sheriffe fearing leſt thereby they ſhould breake the rope, forbad them to doe ſo any longer. At length, when every one thought ſhe was dead, the body being taken downe, and put into a Coffin, was carried thence into a private houſe, where ſome Phyſitians had appointed to make a Diſſection. The Coffin being opened, ſhe was obſerved to breath, and in breathing (the paſſage of her throat being ſtreightned) obſcurely to ruttle: which being perceived by a luſty fellow that ſtood by, he (thinking to doe an act of charity in ridding her out of the ſmall reliques of a painfull life) ſtamped ſeverall times on her breaſt & ſtomack with all the force he could. Immediately after, there came in Dr *Petty* of *Braſen-noſe-Colledge* our Anatomy-Profeſſor, and Mr *Thomas Willis* of *Chriſt-Church*, at whoſe comming, which was about 9 a clock in the morning, ſhe yet perſiſted to ruttle as before, laying all this while ſtretched out in the coffin in a cold room and ſeaſon of the yeare. They perceiving ſome life in her, as well for humanity as their Profeſſion ſake, fell preſently to act in order to her recovery. Firſt, having cauſed her to be held up in the Coffin, they wrenched open her teeth, which were faſt ſet, and powred into her mouth ſome hot and cordiall ſpirits; whereupon ſhe rutled more then before, and ſeemed obſcurely to cough: then they opened her hands (her fingers alſo being ſtifly bent) and ordered ſome to rub and chafe the extreme parts of her body, which they continued for about a quarter of an houre; oft, in the mean time, powring in a ſpoonfull or two of the cordiall water; and beſides tickling her throat with a feather, at which ſhe opened her eyes, but ſhut them againe preſently. As ſoon as they perceived any heat in her extream parts, they thought of letting her blood: & no ſooner

ſooner was her arme bound for that purpoſe, but ſhe ſuddenly bent it, as if it had been contracted by a fit of the Convulſion: the veine being opened, ſhee bled about five ounces, and that ſo freely that it could not eaſily be ſtopped. All this while her pulſe was very low, but otherwiſe not much amiſſe. Her arm being bound up again, and now and then a little cordial water powr'd down her throat, they continued rubbing her in ſeveral places, cauſed Ligatures to be made in her armes and leggs, and then ordered her to be laid in a bed well warmed: then they cauſed her neck, and alſo her temples to be anointed with confortative oyles and ſpirits, and ſo likewiſe the bottoms of her feet, and upon this ſhee beganne to open her eies and to move the lower parts of her body. About this time came in Mr *Bathurſt* of *Trinity* Colledge, and Mr *Clerke* of *Magdalen* Colledge, whoſe advice and endeavours were then and all the time afterwards concurrent with thoſe of the other two above mentioned. Then they applyed a plaiſter to her breaſts, and ordered an heating odoriferous Clyſter to be caſt up in her body, to give heat and warmth to her bowels: after that, they perſwaded a woman to goe into bed to her, and to lye very cloſe to her, and gently to keep rubbing of her. After all which ſhee ſeem'd about noon to be in a ſweat. Her face alſo began ſomewhat to ſwell and to look very red on that ſide on which the knot of the halter had been faſtned.

Whilſt the Phyſicians were thus buſie in recovering her to life, the Underſheriffe was ſolliciting the Governour and the reſt of the Juſtices of Peace for the obtaining her Reprieve, that in caſe ſhe ſhould for that preſent be recovered fully to life, ſhee might not be had backe again to Execution. Whereupon thoſe worthy Gentlemen, conſidering what had happened, weighing all circumſtances, they readily apprehended the hand of God in her preſervation, and being willing rather to co-operate with divine providence in ſaving her, then to overſtrain Juſtice by condemning her to double ſhame and ſufferings, they were pleas'd to grant her a Reprieve untill ſuch time as her Pardon might be compleatly obtained.

All this while ſhe had no ſooner opened her eyes, but preſently ſhe ſhut them again, and being call'd upon to try whether ſhe could hear or ſpeak, there appeared no ſign that ſhe could do either. Soon after, they made tryal again: bidding her, if ſhe underſtood them, to move her hand, or open her eies. Whereupon ſhe obſcurely opened her eyes. The Physitians fearing least her face might swell more & more, and a Feaver come upon her, by reason of the former suffocation, took from her right arme about nine ounces more of blood, and then ordered her a Julep, and other cordiall things to be administred upon occasion, and so left her for that night: and about two houres after she begun to speake many words intelligible.

On Sunday the 15 about 8 in the morning they return'd, and found her much amended, being able to answer to any question propounded unto her. Shee then complained of her throat, (but not much of any other part) whereunto they ordered a Cataplasme to be applyed: then she complaining of drought, a Julep was offered her, which she first took with difficulty, and at last refus'd: warm beere being given her, she disrelished it, but of cold she drank and thanked them.

All this while she lay often sighing and talking to her selfe, as if she had been still to suffer. About noone she felt an extreame sorenesse in her breast and sides, but there appeared nothing discoloured or like a Contusion. That night they ordered her a Clyster, & a Cataplasme to be applied to her breast and sides, with other means to prevent what evill might ensue by reason of contus'd blood, and so left her to rest. About 9 of the clock she laughed and talked merrily, looking fresh and of a good colour: being a little feverish, her tongue not furd nor clammy.

Munday the 16, they found that she had taken some rest, and her feaver not much encreas'd: they then tooke from her left arme about six ounces of blood more: she fainted not, but talked very cheerfully, complaining somewhat of her neck, stomack, and throat.

But before they let her bloud, having first caused all to depart the roome except those Gentlemen that were of the Faculty, they asked her of her sense and apprehension during the time of her suffering: she answered, that after she put off some of her clothes, bequeathing them to her Mother (which was early in the morning before her execution) and heard some one say that one of the prisoners was let out of the chaine to put her to death, she remembered nothing at all that had been done unto her: and that she knew not when her fetters were knock'd off, or how she came out of prison, or that she had bin upon the Gallows, neither could she remember that any Psalme had bin sung, or that she said any thing there: notwithstanding those

that

that were present do testify that she spake very sensibly: onely about a fortnight after, she seemed to remember something of a fellow wrapt up in a blāket, which indeed was the habit of her Executioner.

It is observable also, that when she came to her selfe againe, she fell into the like speeches as she had used in prison before the execution: seeming there to go on where she had so long time left off; like to a Clock whose weights had been taken off a while, and afterwards hung on againe.

That night she was fomented about the sides and other contused places, her neck being very sore, especially on the right side, where it was all black, and began to blister: there appeared also diverse spots of setled bloud on her right cheek.

Tuesday the 17 in the morning they found her pulse slow, but very unequall: her tongue not very dry nor rough: the night before she slept well; in the morning she arose, but her head was so light that she could hardly stand upright: she now complained of paine beneath the pit of her stomack: she complained also of a deadnesse in the tipp of her tongue, thinking she had bitten it in the time of her suffering: she call'd this day for some bread, which she did eate, being first toasted and moistned in beare. At night when they visited her againe, the paine of her neck and throat was decreased: the spots of setled bloud about her cheek and neck lessened, but the deadnesse of her tongue still remained. That night she slept 6 or 7 houres: and on the 18 in the morning had no feaver; her pulse was much amended; all Symptomes lessened; the paines in her breast seemed to descend into the region of the belly, being (as 'twas conceived) not in the bowells, but only in the musculous outward parts.

The 19 she was up, and did eat part of a chick. All Symptomes decreased: yet could she not goe, without the help of somewhat to uphold her. Her neck still sore, but mending. The deadnesse of her Tongue lessened. That night she slept well. About foure or five daies after, being hard frosty weather, there appeared a blacknesse over the lower part of her right arme, and upon her flankes on the same side: which by degrees waxed yellow, and in foure or five daies vanished.

By this time, the care of the Physitians was well over. The paines in her briest and side when she drew in her breath, as also the inequality of her pulse (which caused a suspition of a contusion and extravasated bloud spilt on the Lungs) being now fully ceased. The deadnesse of her tongue and sorenesse of her neck quite gone. There

remained

remained onely a giddinesse in her head when she walked or stirred her body, which in a short time likewise left her. And now being able to walk about the town, eat, drink, and sleep aswel as before this accident had befallen her, she had liberty to repair (and is since gone) unto her friends in the Country; taking away with her the Coffin wherein she lay, as a Trophey of this her wonderful preservation.

Thus, within the space of a Moneth, was she wholly recovered: and in the same Room where her Body was to have been dissected for the satisfaction of a few, she became a greater wonder, being reviv'd, to the satisfaction of multitudes that flocked thither daily to see her.

One thing more I had almost forgotten; that when the numbers of people still pressing into the house began to be too impetuous, and the Physicians had obtained of the Governour to have a Guard plac'd at the door; yet because those of the better sort could not altogether be denied admission, they thought it a seasonable opportunity, for the maid's behalfe, to invite them either to exercise their Charity, or at least to pay for their Curiosity. And therefore (themselves first leading the way) they commended it to those that came in, to give every one what they pleas'd, her Father being there ready to receive it. After a few daies the Governor (a Gentleman as much to be belov'd for his Courtesie, as hee is honour'd for his Prudence) coming himselfe to see her, did not onely contribute to her in a liberal manner, but also improved his charity with many pertinent and wholsom instructions. By this meanes there was gathered for her to the summe of many pounds: whereby not onely the Apothecaries Bill, and other necessaries for her Dyet and lodging were discharged, but some overplus remained towards the suing out of her Pardon.

And now, having done with the Sufferings, and the Cure, it will not be amisse to look back, and take a Reveiw of the Cause of them, as matter of fact for which she suffered: which (as I have said) was the supposed murther of her own Infant.

There are two things, very considerable, alledged on her behalfe, and that may seem to cleer her Innocence as to that businesse.

The first is, that the Childe was abortive or stilborn, and consequently not capable of being murthered. The other, that she did not certainly know that she was with childe, and that it fell from her unawares as she was in the house of office.

As for the first, it is evident that the child was very unperfect, being not above a span in length, and the sexe hardly to be distinguished: so that rather seemed a lump of flesh, then a well and duly formed

med Infant. The Midwife said also, that it had no hair, and that she did not beleeve that ever it had life. Besides, her fellow-servants do testifie, that shee had certain Issues for about a month before shee miscarried, which were of that nature (Physicians say) as are not consistent with the vitality of a child: the eruption of which Issues came on her after shee had violently labour'd in skreening of malt. Lastly, it is not likely that the Child was vital, the mischance happening not above 17. weekes after the time of her conception.

For the 2. that shee might not know certainly that she was with childe, it is not improbable: for shee was not 10. weeks without the usual Courses of women, before she had those continual Issues which lasted for a Moneth together: which long and great Evacuation might make her judge, that it was nothing else but a flux of those humors which for ten weeks before had been suppressed; and that the childe which then fell from her unawares, was nothing but a lump of the same matter coagulated. As for the pain, it must needs be different in such cases from that which accompanies the timely fruit of the womb: and by reason of those Issues coming from her, for so long continued a time before she could not have those throwes and passions at the time of her abortion, as women in travel are subject unto.

Adde to all this, that at her Tryall she ingeniously confessed as much as was alledged by the witnesses: and continued in the same assertions, not only before, but at her Execution, the last supposed minute of her life; and the very first words, after she came to her self again (which certainly were not spoken with design, or purpose to deceive) confirmed the same.

There is yet one thing more which hath been taken notice of by some, as to the Maid's defence; That her Grand Prosecutor Sir *Thomas Read* died within three daies after her Execution; even almost as soon as the probability of her reviving could be well confirmed to him. But because hee was an old man, and such Events are not too rashly to be commented on, I shall not make use of that observation.

It may perhaps be expected by some (and 'tis pity I can give them no better satisfaction) that I should here relate some story (like those of *Orpheus* or *Æneas* in the Poets) of what fine visions this maid saw in the other world; what celestial musick, or hellish howling she heard; what spirits she conversed with; and what Revelations she brought back with her, concerning the Present Times, or the Events of things to come. But for such matters the Ballad-makers must rest contented: since shee (as you have heard) was so far from knowing any thing whilst shee was dead, that shee remembred not what had happened to her even when shee was yet alive. Her spirits, at that time, being either so fixed or benummed with fear, as not to admit of any new Impressions; or otherwise so turbulent and unquiet, as presently to discompose and obliterate them. As we often see it fares with men that are buzz'd in the head with drink, or transported with madnesse, who, though they seem sensible enough of every present object that moves them, yet after they recover can own but little of what they did or said before.

Having here done with the Story, I cannot but reflect upon the generous attempt of those Gentlemen that freely undertook, and have so happily performed the Cure. That whilst they missed the opportunity of improving their knowledge in the dissection of a Dead body, they advanced their fame by restoring to the world a Living one: who now (deservedly) accounts it her happinesse to have fallen into such courteous and skilfull hands: not only for their successefull endeavours used in her Recovery, but for being a means to vindicate her from that foul stain of Murder, which, in most mens judgments (and, perhaps, Heaven it selfe also bearing witnesse) was so harshly charged upon her.

On

On Shee which was hang'd and afterwards Recover'd.

ORpheus, to fetch his Wife, did goe
A voyage to the Shades below
('Twas more then many a man would doe:)

The blood-leſſe Ghoſts did weepe (they ſay)
And *Pluto* groan'd, as He did play;
Yet She came back but Halfe the way.

Now we have ſeen a ſtranger ſight;
Whether it was by Phyſick's might,
Or that (it ſeems) the Wench was *Light*.

But ſure 'twill ſpoyle her Marriage-day,
For who ſo hardy to aſſay
Such an immortall *Virbia*?

Wives may deceive, and doe their beſt
To counterfeit in all the reſt;
Only let them not Dye in jeſt.

Hen. Perin Gen. Com. of Trin. Coll.

In Puellam à Diutino Patibuli Cruciatu Redivivam.

Distrahis Ecstaticam Nemesis cur dupla Puellam?
Quam denegas Superesse, non pateris Mori?
Lex vocat ad Laqueum; revocatq; in Fila Salutis
Medela; fitq; crux nova Remedium Crucis:
Mors sua Martyrium primum, Elysioq; relicto
Per tot dolores Vita Martyrium recens.
Sustinet Illa tamen Miracula sæva, Gemellæ
Βιοθανάτῳ Siremps Socia *Proserpinæ*;
Ac Fati Tropico insistens, utrinq; tuetur
Amphibia Jana Lucis, & Noctis plagam.
Sic Phœbe Zonam cùm circuit Æquidialem,
Utrumq; spectat Orbe diviso Polum:
Sic Atmosphæræ penetrans Confinia, Civis
Haud Aquila cessat Ætheræ, haud Cœli incipit:
Pyrrhæ emersit humo sic dimidiata propago.
Quam Semivivam, Semimortuam voces.

Offas ergò Cani, Junoni Ὀπτήρια *debet,*
Celebranda Threnis, & simul Genethlicis;
Mysta parentaret Cantu dum Κλαυσιγελοῖος,
Qui Flevit, & Corrisit Alternis Genis:
Comica nam Tragico commiscet Gaudia Luctu;
Ut Arcus hilaris nube Lacrymosâ nitet:
Aut Protêa velut mutatâ Luce Tabella,
Hinc Heraclitus, inde Democritus patet.

Mox proprio exoritur busto non Altera Phœnix,
Lucina sibimet, Ipsa Posteritas Sui.

At

Englished Thus.

WHY *ATE*, dost thou Double thus thy Smart?
Not suffering Her to Live, nor to Depart?
Physitians straining to Repaire what Losse
The Iudge inflicted, Multiply the Crosse:
Death wrote Her Martyr; but from Rest to Come
Back through such Paines, is Second Martyrdome.
Yet shee these cruell Miracles sustaines,
Rivall Inrolled in Proserpines both Traines;
And seated on Fates Tropick, doth survey
With either Eye the Courts of Night, and Day.
So Phœbe's Orbe in th'Equinox appears,
With Oblique Lookes viewing two Hemispheres:
Thus Eagles, when They to the Confines Fly
Of th'Atmosphære, dwell not in Ayre, nor Sky:
Such, *Pyrrha's* Unripe Issue, is displayd,
When it was yet halfe-Carcasse, and halfe-Mayd.

Pluto with Juno here might Presents claime,
While Dirge, and Caroll Consort forth her Name;
That Pantomime should Act these Obsequies,
Whose Face *Parti-per-pale* both Laughs, and Cryes:
For Shee Triumphs in Tragicomick shrowds;
As Rainebowes glister, yet in Weeping Clowds:
Or as a Protean Picture's different Site
Here shewes *Democritus*, there *Heraclite*.

Straight from her Urne this Unchang'd Phœnix rose,
Offspring Herselfe, and Midwife to her Throwes:

And

And Antedates by this Mysterious Birth
Her Resurrection :Borne-again from Earth.
Hippolytus Revived in every Part,
But 'twas by Magick, or Poëtick Art:
Sibylla Saw, then Left the Ghosts below;
But Shee did In, not From the Body Goe:
The *Shades* sent back Eurydice to *Day*,
But Fainting Shee Return'd scarce halfe the Way.
This Wonder surmounts All: See, here is bred
Posthumous Life ev'n when the Mothers dead.
Part Dyed before, part Survived after Breath;
The Embryo's Birth's Abortive, and Her death.
Orpheus, and Æsculape were here Outvyed,
'Cause both their Arts Concenter'd in one *Guide*.

Suiters Courage, All's purg'd by Sacrifice:
The Parent slaine, doth not a Virgin Rise?
Forgetfull Shee did *Gallow Lotos* Trye,
And *Lethe* tast: Let All crye *Amnesty*.
For who can think her Guilty, whom the Tombe
Does thus declare unworthy of her Doome?
Whom Law, whom Physick could not kill, whose Date
Souldiers Repriev'd, Three *Committees* of Fate?
If yee doubt still, her *Dying* Words Receive:
How e're, *Distrust* her *Risen* must Believe.

Ac Individuâ prætentat Anastase Fatum,
Terræ Genitricis Regenerata è Sinu.
Floruit Hippolytus *renovatus Membra, sed Idem*
Magicâ revixit, aut Poëticâ Manu:
Deseruit Superos, iterumq; Sibylla revisit;
At Corporis Iter fuerat, haud à Corpore:
Eurydicenq; Orbi Manes voluêre Remissam,
Mediâ tamen languebat impatiens viâ.
Natales hi cuncta premunt Mysteria; Proles
Nam Posthuma ista Matris est etiam Suæ.
Ante Ortum moritur Pars, Pars post Funera vivit;
Vitam Embryô *dat, Mortem Abortivam Sibi.*
At non Angui-dei, non vicerat Orpheos Artes,
Ni Musicus, Medicusq; foret Anastates.

Macti estote Proci, Lethum expiat omnia; Fallor?
An conditâ Parente, jam Virgo redit?
Gustabat Gabali Loton, Lethenq; *bibebat*
Obliviosa *hæc: undiq; sit* Αμνηςία.
Deniq; quis neget innocuam, stipulante Feretro;
Nex ipsa quam fatetur indignam Nece?
Quam Juris rabies, Medicinaq; perdere nescit,
Salvamq; dat Militia, Parcarum Trias?
Si dubitatis adhuc, Morienti credite: saltem
Surgenti ab Umbris Fidet ipsa Infidia.

H. B. Coll. Om. Anim.

On the Shee that was Hang'd, but not Executed.

RAre Innocence! a Wench re-woman'd! ſee
What the ſmall *Sophs* ſay to this Fallacy.
Up to the eares in death, and ſcape! no kind
Was thought more fit then to *tye up her Wind.*
Women in this with Cats agree, I think,
Both Live and Scratch after they'have *tip't the Wink.*
Henceforth take heed of truſting Females. Shee
That ſcapes *Welch Parſly*, Souldiers take for mee.

Hic Iacet—— *Quæ cùm Morte non potuit obſcurari, claruit,*
Vindicatâ nimirum Innocentiâ,
Fato Functa nec tamen Defuncta.
Converſo in Aſylum Patibulo
Tunc, cùm non minùs de Puellâ conclamatum eſſet, quàm Iuſtitiâ:
Iuſtitiâ, quam ſi non Cæcam, certè vix mitem dixeris;
Quæ cùm in alius Ventrem inquireret, Ipſa non habuit Viſcera.
Hæc verò revixit, vel ad Illius ludibrium,
Vel (quod melius eſt) exemplum.
Adiit Charontem pro formâ *(puto) nec tamen Abiit,*
Sed inhibuit Gradum. Uno oculo flevit, ſubriſit altero;
Mirum, ſi hoc non ſit δακρυγελᾶν.
Nec Vitam ſolam Medicorum artibus obtinuit,
Sed Vatis etiam beneficio Immortalitatem.
Non eſt quòd in Fœminâ plus deſideres, niſi forſan velis Conſtantiã
Ἠυποχδιασι H.B. Soc. N.C.

On one dead by Law, but reviv'd by Phyſick.

COme *Sophiſter*, diſtinguiſh, you that call
Reſtor'd Privation Supernaturall.
To ſolve your Ignorance, come view in one
An Ante-dated Reſurrection.
Some rigid ones perhaps this act will ſpell
With the ſtrange letters of a Miracle:
But know, *Phyſitians* have a larger Call,
Apollo' and *Phyſick* are collaterall.
Think not *Phyſitians Atheiſts*, ſince they doe
Profeſſe Divinity, and Practic't too.

J. Hutton Fell. of New Coll.

In Fœminam post Patibuli cruciatus reviviscentem.

LUgete Cives lugubre lugubres;
Ridete Cives ludicra ludicri:
Lugete defunctam puellam;
Plaudite, nunc rediviva prodit.

Jam non stupendum sentiat Orphea
Mendax vetustas: Eurydicen neq;
Miretur ex imo barathro
Threicio revocâsse plectro.

Quæ penè sedes viderat inferas,
Et nigra sæva regna Proserpinæ,
En! fata deludens cruenta,
Rursus adest, tumulumq; fugit.

Flevere Manes, queis comes altera
Evasit, ipsum destituens suo
Naulo Charontem, dum catervâ
Cymba gemit levior minori.

Hæc damna mœrens, ora latrantia
Compressit Orci Ianitor: & suum
Loqui dolorem nescientes
Tartareæ silüere lymphæ.

Mors, cui potentum spicula Cæsarum
Ducumq; figunt colla minacium,
Quâ fronte posthac tela promes
Fœmineo modò lusa sexu?

Ad Medicos, dissecandum corpus vitæ restituentes.

Efficitis sanum corpus, lacerare parati:
Et mox fit mulier quod modò funus erat.
Per vos posse mori viventes ante sciebam:
Jam per vos cæsos vivere posse scio.

Geo. Lee, Coll.Reg. Commensalis.

A ceux de la Messe.

Cà Catholique, que dis-tu maintenant?
Les miracles se font-ils pas? pendant
Qu' entre nous l' aveugle gaigne la veüe,
Le boiteux marche, le mort se voit en rüe.
Voy-cy la fille qui tantost estoit morte,
Elle vit à cett' heure, & tres-gaillarde se porte.

Jos. Williamson, du Coll. de la Reyne.

The Womans *Case* put to the Lawyers.

Mother, or Maid, I pray you whether?
One, or both, or am I neither?
The Mother dyed: may't not be said
That the Surviver is a Maid?
Here, take your Fee, declare your sense;
And free me from this New Suspense.

Joh. Watkins, Eq. Aur. fil. Coll. Reg.

Nondum cessârunt Miracula, dogma profanum
Mentiri Ancillæ Vita Novata docet.
Estne fides? non triste Forum, non tristior Illo
Judex, Voxq; Ipso tristior ----estne fides?
Non Crux, non Restis; non Ungula Militis, & quam
Non ferat Alcides pectore crebra manus,
Cuncta hæc particulam Vitæ non cedere cogunt,
Sed valet extremum Virgo loquuta Vale.
Sic nescit, nisi viva, Sepulchrum impura Sacerdos
Vestali caluit cui modò dextra foco.
Exili Lachesis non semper Stamine gaudet,
Et Funes *novit Parca Benigna suos.*
Hæc si non Ratio est Restim elusisse Puellam,
Quæ causa est? meritò credo fuisse Levem.

Thou

THou shalt not Swing againe: come cleare thy brow,
Thou hast the Benefit o'th' *Clergie* now;
Nor is thy *Neck-Verse* writt in Blood, which might
Confound thy Thoughts, as it must needs thy Sight.
Thus when *Apollo* keeps th' *Assises*, then
Women are sav'd by *Booke*, as well as Men.
Strange Wench! what character may fit the, best,
That still canst live, though Thou art *Hang'd* and *Prest?*

Rob. Mathew, Fellow of New Coll.

To the *Physitians.*

TO raise a Pyramide unto your skill
Were to mistrust experience, and still
Think Death a Gyant, whose vast gripe could span
And squeez to nought both memory and man.
Yee are not mortall, nor need feare to dye:
To conquer Death is Immortality.
Yee have done that. Marble may serve to hide
It's owne dust now, or tell who *should* have dy'd:
There is no other use for't. And thou Death
Vaunt not henceforth 'tis with Thy leave we breath.
Th'art vanquish't quite, and this thy Mulct shall be,
To write *Probatum* to their victory.

Ad Puellam Redivivam.

QUæ modò spes tumuli fueras tristisq; feretri,
Posthuma jam vitæ nasceris ipsa tuæ.
Ecce stupet casum Mors admirata, rogatq;
Decepit nostras quale Sophisma manus?
Nil potuit namq; illa magis te quando peremit:
Cùm tu non moreris nil minus illa potest.

Guil. Fitz-Gerald. ex Æd. Ch.

In Puellam suspensam, & dein à Medicis Anatomiam Cadaveris aggressuris, in vitam revocatam.

DUm Mors & Medici conspirant fœdere certo
Amborum ut telis una puella cadat,

Funi ut ſuccedat Ferrum, & ſuſpenſa ſecetur;
En! Ferrum & Funis, bina venena, juvant.
Unâ mulctatam, geminâ dum morte parabant
Afficere, in vitam fit rediviva novam.
Naturæ in leges, ac Gentis jura, triumphans
Eluſit Fati, Judicis atq; minas.
Nec Medici hoc, Sceleton faciunt, exangue cadaver.
Quod magis eſt, vivum cedit in Automaton.

Guil. Willis, Æd. Chr. Comm.

Admire not, 'tis no newes, nere think it ſtrange,
Twere wonder if a Woman ſhould not change:
They have myſterious wayes, and their deſignes
Muſt be read backward ſtill, like Hebrew lines.
See, theſe with Death diſſemble, and can cheat
Charon himſelfe to mak a faire retreat.
Well, for this trick Ile never ſo be led
As to beleive a Woman, though ſhee's dead.

Rob. Sharrock, Fellow of New Coll.

In puellam ὑπερέποτμον à patibulo reviviſcentem.

QUæ nuper Medicos veſpillonesq; fefellit,
Et non unius victima mortis erat,
Quàm benè Netricis *titulum meruiſſe putanda eſt,*
Cùm poterat ſtamen *ſic renovare ſuum?*

Engliſhed thus:

Thou more then Mortall, that with many lives
Haſt mock't the Sexton, and the Doctors knives:
The name of *Spinſter* thou maiſt juſtly wed,
Since there's no Halter ſtronger then thy *Thread.*

To the ſame.

Thou, thine owne *Clotho*, that knew'ſt not to feele
The darts of Death, yet woar'ſt no Buffe, nor Steele:
If with ſuch Art thou canſt thy Diſtaffe rule,
The Souldiers all to thee ſhall go to Schoole.

Dan. Danvers, Coll. Trin. Alum.

On

On the Death and Life of *Anne Greene.*

WHat Cable-thread twin'd thee thy happy fate,
That it out-lasts thy own lifes destin'd date?
Was thy Harmonious Soule strung so-so well,
As break it could not, stretcht to a Miracle?
Did'st thou indent with Rigid *Atropos*
To los't a while, and then to quit the Losse?
As cast-off Habits, when hang'd by a space,
Regaine their Fashion and their pristine grace.
Loe here's lifes *Gemini*, two lifes in one!
Or th' same in'ts Tropicall Reversion!
Time after *Stylo novo* inchoated!
From the first Sun a Parely created!
A strange Appendix after *Finis* fixt,
Or *Funis* rather: Death and Life co-mixt!
A Posthume Act after Catastrophe!
Or Antedating of the Latter day!
Death's Puzler! Selfe-surviver! thy strange fate
Do's contradictions Legimate.
Entwisted Miracles constellate here,
And complicated Wonders Co-insphere.
Thy uncouth Paradox Resuscitation
Tempts to beleeve, that from a pure Privation
Nature's propension signe's a free Regresse
To pristine Habit; tempts even to confesse
Plurality of Soules in One, since Thou
Can'st prodigally one to Death allow,
Another keep thy selfe; whilst both maintaine
Castor and *Pollux*-like alternate Reigne.
That Belgian Headsman, whose rare artfull hand
Could slice off heads, and they yet seem to stand,
Had he thee Execut'd, had sham'd his skill,
When finding thee not dead, but living still.
Perillu's Torturing Engin had but bin
A Very Bull, had'st thou first entred in.
Their Law would have some plea, were it to thee,
Who first the Malefactor Hang, then see

Whe're 'twere a just and equitable Cause,
Whether not consonant unto the Lawes.
Strange *Sophister*! that grant'st to Destiny
The Premises, Conclusion do'st deny;
Dar'st yeeld to Suffer Death, but not to Dye.
Joh. Aylmer, Schol. of New Coll.

SO sportive, *Atropos*? what, must we see
Some *Hocus*-tricks? the thread of life to be
Asunder cut, and yet entire remaine?
A Body-banish'd soule recall'd againe?
Now may the nine-liv'd Sex speake high, and say
That here they fought with Death, and won the day;
The *fatall Tree*, which first began the strife,
Sided with them, and prov'd *a Tree of life*.

Another.

DEath, spare your threats, we scorne now to obey;
If Women conquer thee, surely Men may.
How came this Champion on I cannot tell,
But I nere heard of one *came off* so well.
Pet. Killigrew, Eq. Aur. fil. Coll. Reg.

PRoh Metamorphosis naturæ dissona! fatum
Imbelle! evictæ gloria cassa necis!
Huccine, naturam, progressa peritia, solvit?
Siccine fatorum machina fracta cadit?
Euge decus medicum! sacrum inviolabile! novi
Sacratum hinc docto numen inesse Choro.
Ibimus: ire juvat; sic, sic juvat ire per umbras:
Si vixisse, mori est, ibimus: ire juvat.
Eia age Terrorum domitrix Terroris, abundè
Provida; cùm properes, ne moriare, mori.
Guil. Miles, Nov. Coll.

H*Ippolytus* was dead, and (as the straine
Of Poets tel's) was made a Man againe.
Poetick Figments are turn'd Truths, for we
Have seen a Dead Maide's Palingenesie.

He

He twice a Man; She twice a Maid: 'Tis brave;
She had one Life to Loose, and one Save.
Or else it was our *Logick* Dy'd, not she:
For from Privation a Regresse we see.
Let's non admire then *Bacon's Brazen Head*,
When we see one that speaks, and yet was Dead.
You that so much for new Inventions give,
Observe a way, found out, by Death to Live.
Catts have for every Muse a life: but Shee
For every Grace; For by this Historie
The Author doth a Third Life to her Give,
And makes her Innocence and Fame to Live.
Her Life is writt here to the life: she fell
At a cheap rate, when 'tis describ'd so well.
For, th'Author's Pen's so good, that one would Die
To be Reviv'd by such a History.

Rich.Glyd, Fell. of New Coll.

THat Life's a Vapour I'le no more complaine:
As this, so that, takes leave to come againe.
Strange metamorphosis! this *dead-live* Woman
Now differs from her selfe; and are such *Common?*

Geo. Davenant, Com of Qu. Coll.

TErnas sicne Deas, & tales decipis una?
Et vel Carnificem fœmina spreta tuum?
Illius eludas artes elapsa; sed audi,
Victricem dici te semel, esto satis.

H. Davenant, Com. Coll. Reg.

FOr certaine, she was dead! yet then
The reason how she lives agen,
Is that which so much puzles men.

Sure when her soule this clay forsook,
To'wards Pluto's court her way she took,
And came unto th'infernall brook.

It

It dranke so deep of *Lethe* there,
She had forgotten whatsoere
Sh'had suffer'd in her life time here:

Arraign'd by *Minos*, straight denie'd
That she before a Judge was trie'd,
Or sentenc'd on the Gallowes died.

No other way was left to win
Her to confesse her shame and sin
But send her back to learn't agen.

Entring her body straight, 'twas growne
So rack't and torne, that 'twas not known,
Nor yet beleev'd to be her own.

This neck was Halter-gall'd, nay more,
These sides and brest with strokes were sore,
And Hers were nothing soe before.

Her leggs (shee's sure) had shackles on,
And wonder's finding These have none;
Her selfe and they were lost and gone.

Thus what she suffer'd last, was now
The lesson she first learn'd to know,
Else no account can passe below.

If she learn't well, and not constraine
Her selfe to act it o're againe,
She may passe safe through *Pluto's* reigne.

John Dright, Ch. Ch.

(doome
ARe Fates growne kind? have they thus chang'd their
From Murtherers to supply the Midwifes roome?
Or were they not o'repowr'd, since Life had spun
Two strings unto her bow, and Death but One?

Tho. Ireland, Ch. Ch.

To the Hangman.

COme *Flesh-Crow*, tell me, what's the cause that you
Rigour to men, to Women Favour show?
Your Office you have not perform'd, 'tis plaine:
See, here's the Wench you hang'd, alive againe.

Yet,

Yet, for this once, I'le cleare you; it was not
Your *slack rope* sav'd her, nor your *fast-loose* knot.
Her fatall halter shee (to end the strife)
Untwisted spun into a thread of life.

Ed Norreys Eq. Aur. fil. Coll. Reg.

EUrydicen sileat jam fama à morte reductam,
Hippolytum taceant sæcla priora suum:
Mercurii nuper quam compulit aurea virga
Manibus, à nigro jam revocata grege est.
Arte viri domitæ Parcæ stupuêre superbæ,
Et queritur Lachesis stamine lassa novo.
Regni claustra sui vidit Proserpina rupta,
Et succum atq; herbas hoc potuisse gemit.
Porthmea pœnituit plenâ remeare carinâ,
Utq; dolos sensit, mox stupefactus, ait:
Quæ prius aufugiens in ventum vita recessit,
Tutior in medicas jam venit illa manus:
Hæ revocant animas per Tartara nigra vagantes,
Corporeisq; iterum nexibus arte ligant.
Quæ jacuit tenebris obducta, & lampade vitæ
Extinctâ, accensâ jam face clara micat.
Nunc cum sole licet cadere, & cum sole redire,
Et, si vult medicus, nec moriendo mori.

Edwin. Skrymsher Armig. fil. Nat. Max. Coll. Trin.

WOnder of highest Art! He that will reach
A Streine for thee, had need his Muse should *stretch*,
Till flying to the Shades, she learne what Veine
Of *Orpheus* call'd *Eurydice* againe;
Or learne of her *Apollo*, till she can
As well, as Singer, prove Physitian:
And then she may without *Suspension* sing,
And, authorized, harp upon thy *String*.
Discordant string! for sure thy soule (unkinde
To its own Bowels Issue) could not finde
One Breast in Consort to its jarring stroake
'Mongst piteous Femall Organs, therefore broke
Translations due Law, from fate repriev'd,

And ſtruck a Uniſon to her ſelfe, and liv'd.
Was't this? or was it, that the *Goatiſh* Flow
Of thy Adulterous veines (from thence let goe
By ſecond *Æſculapius* his hand)
Diſſolv'd the Parcæ's *Adamantine* Band,
And made Thee Artiſt's Glory, Shame of Fate,
Triumph of Nature, *Virbius* his Mate.

Chriſt. Wren, Gent. Com. Wad. Coll.

HAng up the Gallow-Tree, ſince 'twould not doo't;
The Maid was hang'd for her Abortive fruit:
Yet doe not: for, though weak, perhaps next yeare
It may, like Her, get ſtrength againe, and Beare.

Another.

If Life be but a Tennis-play, Thou then
Com'ſt from the *Hazzard* to be Toſs'd agen.
Here only was the difference, in Thine
The Game was ſav'd by playing *under Line*.

Car. Forſter, Eq. Aur. fil. Coll. Trin.

To the happy Inſtruments of the Executed Maid's Recovery.

OXFORD (the Arts Metropolis) ne're knew
A rarer feat then was perform'd by you,
Brave Æſculapian friends! whoſe Art could give
After the Execution a Reprieve.
And yet 'twas Timely too: for though grim Death
Had ſeiz'd the paſſage of her Vitall breath,
Yet you a new one made: And the ſame Veine
That let out blood, receiv'd in Life againe.
The Soule, which is in every part entire,
Can, undiſcern'd by you, to none retire:
Since you no leſſe the tracke of ſoules doe know,
Than that of Leverets in new-fallen Snow.
Others can by their Chymiſtry reduce
A Plant or flower from its duſt or juyce;
But your ſublimer Art hath done much more,
Whil'ſt humane ſoules you from their Urnes reſtore.

Yet

Yet though your skill and pity could dispence
More daies to her beguiled Innocence:
No Art removes a ruin'd Virgins shame,
Unlesse revived she, be not the same.
Thus 'tis more easy to recall the Dead
Then to restore a once-lost Maidenhead.

Kingsmill, Lucy Gent. Com. of Ch.Ch.

THou Pill too strong for fate! in whose defence
Mira'cles stept in to rescue innocence.
Death was thy *Ordeall*, and *Compurgatrix*,
And *Minos* did thy Judges doome refix.
Thou did'st *bring fort* in riddles: so, *surviv'st*
By giving breath thou Kil'dst, by dying liv'st.
Thy rude Spawn's fleeting soule did sure retire
To thee the *Damme*, as a reserve entire,
Giving thee second life, when thine was done;
Thou wer't thine owne Superfœtation.
Strange fruit o'th' cursed and the barren Tree,
That mad'st the Hangman practice Midwifery,
Nature new hatch d thee, as first Men, who tooke
Birth from harsh Entrals of a Vitall Oak.
One of the Daughters of *Deucalion*,
Thou wakest from thy *Tomb*, as they from stone.

Fr. Withins, Gen. Com. of S. Johns.

The Maids Game.

ALone this subtle Gamestresse on a day
Went to Deaths house, at *Tick-Tack* for to play.
To knowe if he was't home, or gone from thence,
His Porter, th' Hangman held her in S*uspence*.
At length he met her, plaid, and soone did spy
The Maid had left a *Blot* upon a DYE.
Death threw, and thought h'had wonn, but she said nay,
Doctors like *Doublemen* stood in the way.
After she cast, obtain'd a *Double Game*,
By putting int' one *Point* both death and shame.

W. Berkley Com. of Br. Coll.

Had I been tongue-ti'd, nor as yet had said
An Infant word, but kept my mouth a Maid,
This would have cut those Ropes, this to rehearse
Had Midwife prov'd to an *Abortive* verse,
Despightfull *Embryo* in secret plac't
By Her, by thee Shee's publikely disgrac't.
Such blowes o'th brest the standers-by her lend
As those that force tyr'd Iades to'th' journeyes end:
Had but a modest soule that under gone
T'would soon for shame have quitte its Mansion.
Yet shee's not dead, nor is her glasse quite runne,
Although her Thread be cutte her life's not spunne.
Shee lives and hath recal'd her wonted strength,
Nor is her life made short by her neckes Length.
I'le prophecy, Shee'l Lovers soone insnare
Without a Trope ther's Halters in her hayre.
Of the same cause here the effects doe fight,
One thing both hang'd and sav'd her, shee was *Light*.

Walter Pope è Coll. Wadh.

Dum sacer Eurydicen Orpheus deducit ab orco,
Flectit ad infernum lumina retrò Lacum:
Sic Correpta statim, nigras revocatur in umbras
Rupta nec est Fidibus restituenda Fides.
Tutius effugium sua fata dedêre puellæ:
Quin & Apollineâ fit rediviva manu.
Sic valet ulterius Medicus quam Musicus; Ille
Imperat Infernis, Supplicat iste Diis.

Strange *Metamorphosis* Ovid never wott!
A maid chang'd from, yet to her selfe is brought:
He *Pythagoricall* migrations chants,
How humane soules *inoculate* with plants.
When Hers loath to *divorce* her antient *Mate*
(*Scepticke* in *Love*) resumes her former state;
And as halfe choak't in double prison walls
One of her Body, th'-other of the Gaole.
Shee takes a gentle flight in freer Air,

And

And ſtraight returneth home more *debonnaire*.
New birth's noe *Probleme* now: for we have ſeen
A *ſenſleſſe Corps* quickned with Life has beene.
And that not by a *Miracle*, but Art
With *broken winded* Nature, playing part.
The great inchanting Orpheus who could bring
From Hell Eurydice by a *fidle ſtring*;
Yet Let her ſlip againe: And breaking's Truſt
His *Magicke-muſicke Nerve*, in ſunder burſt.
Apollo ſcornes to make ſuch *Emp'ricke Cures*:
Here's one now dead *alive*, *alive* endures.
Her *fatall thread* was Cut: Yet Plutoes bands
Could her not raviſh, from his ſacred hands.
Yea though a knife had Cut the *Siſters Twine*,
His *Plantan Leafe* would that together *joyne*,
See Orpheus, See, thy *wonder-working Lyre*,
Holds noe Compariſon with thy Heavenly Sire.

W. Hatley, of Saint Johns Coll.

QUam penè abſtulerat glomerato ſtamine, vitam
Tibi reddit Eumenidum manus:
Dum petit erranti cultro tua fila ſalutis,
Scindit Capiſtros Atropos.

TErgeminus diræ dormiſcit Janitor Aulæ,
Et Furiæ infernam deſeruêre Domum:
Quaſq; creat, ſentit mors jam quaſi mortua pœnas:
Virbiaq; è propriis pullulat Exequiis:
Fabula naſcentem Materno funere Bacchum
Ne jactet, virgo hæc funere nata Suo eſt.

Guil. George, Æd. Chriſti Alumnus.

SEarch for a pleaſant now delight,
To celebrate her births day's right:
It is a birth when after Death
The body gaines his former breath.
O! who'le pay him that dig'd the pitte?
The hungry grave hath loſt a bitte,

And yet still gapes, alas! I feare
Death it selfe will be buryed there.
Shee's sicke, and melts in her owne wo,
The female Sex should cheat her so.
(That she could not decieve the same,
In whom the first deceit found game.)
Either Physick conquers Death,
Or Physitians coine new breath;
Or *Atropos* hath lost her knife:
This was a hanging *to the Life*.
O! Wench reforme in thy new age,
Write Vertue in this second page:
The first shewes Characters of Vice,
O! live well once, who livest twice.

Theodore Wynne Fell. Com. Jes. Coll.

HEre lies—'t must not be so. Here Goes a Shee
That lost her life to lifes recovery.
Here Goes She, whose last Snuffe of vitall breath
Was blowne Out and In, by one blast of Death.
Whilst thus her Innocence Fate justifies,
Wee'l write on her Accuser, Here He *Lies*.

Car. Capell, Armig. Coll. Winton.

IUgglers we'have seene cut a Thread, whole: Thy *Line*
Of life was so: just such a Trick was Thine.
Hocus Pocus, fast and loose, dead and gone,
Here agen: Women have more tricks than one.

Hen. Capell Armig. Coll. Winton.

THou Sophister of Fate, that canst deny
A faire dispute by an *Amphiboly*;
Reade Hebrew-wise thy Neck-verse, make to be
In thine own doom an *Infra-pollency*:
Insert st no Negative, and yet canst state
An affirm'd sentence Illegitimate.
Sure *Minos* Jury was for these too *Grand*,
That did thy Doom re-eccho, did withstand
Thy Epilogue, and make it for to be

But

But a new Prologue to Virginity.
Thy Mate ſhall be no *Proteus*, yet in thee,
Although but one, will be Polygamy.
Thou canſt intombe a Wife-hood, and yet riſe
A Virgin out of th'aſhes, Phœnix-wiſe.
Ceaſe would the Romans th'wonder to extoll
Of th' Head found freſh; Thine had been *Capitoll.*
Caligula his bloudy wiſh would check
To cut off *Rome*, had thine but been the neck.

A. Spence of St. *Joh.*Coll.

WHat hath the Law its power loſt
Since th' Engliſh tongue hath it engroſt?
Or did old *Juno* owe a ſpight
To Fate, and it for to requite
Sit croſs-leg'd charming Her alive,
And hence Death prove ſo *Abortive*?
Sure *Venus* was in th' Horoſcope,
When She was ſtrugling with the Rope:
And kept out Death from entring in,
To ſhew that *Cupid* cannot ſin.
If ſo? then might She well eſcape,
Love ſuffers not a ſecond rape.
Strange Beaſt! what all her Riders fling?
Could not Death rule Her in a ſtring?

Sam. Chriſtopher of S. Joh. Coll.

IUſtice would cut, but Fate unedg'd the knife,
Unravel'd the vex'd thread, and repreiv'd life,
Bad the aſtoniſh'd Siſters ſpin more years,
New-cloath their Diſtaffe, and lay by their Shears.
Wonders long ſince were in their Sepulcher,
Yet did One miracle revive with Her.

Joh. Hall, Eq. Aur. fil. Coll. Reg.

SHe liv'd, and in the Cord made Fate deſpair,
Safe, as Sea-Surgeons in their Cable are.
Whoſe ſcruples pallie-Juryes weigh amiſſe,
The Gallowes her exacter Balance is.

Yet,

Yet, that loose Flames some penalty might meet,
She thus did penance in her winding-sheet.
May this not-still-born Gibbet-issue thrive!
The first the knife ere Midwif'd there alive.

Will. Bell.

DEath's Metamorphos'd and hath chang'd his name,
And nature too; then Death with Life's the same.
This *Wench* as free of Soule as *Body* try'd
More then by living, to spight Death, and di'd.
Thus *Hells Purveigher* over-charg'd growes dull,
Or (which is all as strange) he's mercifull.
Or rather Justice with it selfe at strife
Judg'd the *Wench* worthy both of death and life.
The crime was hainous, but (if you know all)
T'was not soe *High* as to be *Capitall*.

T. Arthur, *Comm. Ch. Ch.*

I'le stretch my *Muse*, but that a verse
I'le *hang* upon thy *living hearse*.
Chime in yee witts, and rhyme a Knell,
For *Death* herselfe is lately fell.
Never was yet this *meagre fiend*,
Soe baffled by the woman kind.
Nan playes a prize with death, shee mounts
The stage, and there brave soule recounts
Her former prancks, and then Comes on
The *Fury* with her *hempen thong*;
As boldly she *enters the list*,
And though by one unhappy *twist*,
Her *thread of life* did snap in twaine,
Yet by this foile she lives againe
And doth defie the *fatall Spinster*,
And all the brood of *Pluto's* Minster.
Have you not known how variously
A *vapour* betwixt Earth and Skye
Doth dance, till by contrary flame
It's frighted to its forme againe?

Thus,

Thus *Meteor-like*, shee hung betweene;
(Was't not a wonder to be seene)
But th' *burning-feaver* of the rope,
Which puts all others out of hope,
Restores her to her to selfe; shee is
Alive by *Antiperistasis*.
But soft! *Physitians* doe not thinke,
I at your commendations winke.
'Tis you against the Fatall Vote
Gave this first heard of *Antidote*.
Had sage *Hippocrates* this seene,
His leading *Theme* had alter'd beene;
For such the wonder is, that you
Have made Art long, and Life so too.
Who will not rather henceforth cry
Pray let me be *Anatomy*?
What foole will feare an after-slaughter,
Since you have *raised* up this *Daughter*?
Clergy looke to it, for since shee
Was rob'd the *benefit* of thee,
Physitians straight did part the strife
And *writte her in the booke of life*.
In *India* say Authors good,
A tree doth beare cloath, drinke and foode.
A wonder sure! but is't not much
The *Gallow-tree* should bring forth such?
Startle not reader in beleife,
'Tis made not only *Tree of life*;
But by *Phisitians Chymick* paines
Unto her both Repute, and Gaines.
Soe that hereafter it will be
Thus to be hang'd, good huswifrie.

Ant. Wood, Schol. of Mert. Coll.

On Anne Green *her execution.*

Sure Death abhorres the colour, all have seene
That Death is blacke, and therefore loves no *Greene*:
A happy colour, in what Prædicament
Will the Logicians put this Accident?
Shee had her Neck-verse; 'tis a currant signe
Shee could not read, her verse was but a Line.
Againe; upon this deed to set a crowne;
Sh'ad been cut-up, if not so soon cut downe.
Read this thou youthfull, *Read*, and be afraid,
Shee's a maid twice, and yet is not *dis-maid*.
O Paradoxe! if truth in thee can lye,
No wonder if the maid could live and dye.

Joh. Mainard, of Magd. Coll.

Are fates dread engines, and his Armory
(Muskets and Ropes) but Masque and Mummery?
Sure Cupid (changing armes once more with death)
Turnd hangman to preserve his Martyrs breath.
Nights Queene (who once her selfe did suffer rape)
Pitty'd her Paralell, and let her scape.
Thou Paradox of fate, whom ropes reprieve,
To whom the hangman proves a gentele Shrieve,
Death's after birth: Thou by thy Posthume fate,
And penitence truly art regenerate.
Sterne Bassaw's by the bowstrings slender twine
Want vent for mighty soules: Thy fœminine,
Wrastles with death in a more firme embrace
Of Sinewy cords, yet never quits the place.

Rich. Garrard Gent: Com: of S. Joh. Coll.

FINIS.

A True and Sad Relation Of Two Wicked and Bloody Murthers (Wing T2581A) is reproduced with permission from the unique copy at The British Library (shelfmark 1132.g.55). The text-block measures 105 × 158 mm.

The following words are a transcription of the original:

7.10 are
7.13 to preach repentance … Jesuits
7.15 sent to
7.16 stles as they call themselves,) Answer'd
7.17 very well … unto them
7.18 altogether unnecessary to force them, for
7.19 Desire to go voluntarily
7.20 made of strong

A True and Sad Relation Of Two Wicked and Bloody Murthers,

The one done by the Earl of *Pembrook*, and his Company, upon a Gentleman, a Constable, and a Watchman, at *Turnham-Green*, Five Miles from *London*, on *August* the 16*th.* at Night.

The other was done by one

Jane Lawson,

The Wife of *James Lawson*, living at *East Barnet*, upon her self, and Two small Children, the one a Boy between Two and Three Years old, the other a Girl about one Year and a half old; on *Wednesday* the first of this Instant *September*, 1680. full of horror and amazement.

The Circumstance of which is very true, and sad to Read.

ALSO,

A strange Account of Two

PROPHETS,

lately at the City of *Tholouze*, in *France*, *With their Nine* Prophecies.

Printed for *J. Clarke*, in West-smithfield, 1680. With Allowance.

A true account of three very Remarkable Circumſtances, &c.

ON *Thurſday*, being the 19th. of *Auguſt*, 1680. between the hours of Eleven and Twelve at Night, the Earl of *Pembrook*, comming in a Hackney-Coach with three more from *Windſor* to *London*, and at *Turnham-Green*, within five miles of the City: the Conſtable and his Watch for them parts, ſtopped the Coach, and demanded *Who was there?* to which the Coachman replyed, It was the Lord *Pembrook*: with that ſome in the Coach bid him drive on: but the Coach-mans anſwer was, *They ſtop my Horſes*, which made them cry out in the Coach, *They be Thieves come to rob us*: they preſently replyed, *We be the Kings Watch, and in his Name we command ye to ſtand, and tell us who you be*: With that they ſwore, *God Dam um*, with many more Oaths, *they would make um know who they were*: and on the other ſide of the Coach that was from the Watch, the ſaid Earl and his Company came out with their drawn Swords, and both parties met behind the Coach, and people being up at a Houſe juſt againſt the place where this fray was, ſome Company being drinking there, and one Gentleman which was the Kings Meſſenger, that knew the Lord *Pembrook* very well, came to perſuade him into the Coach, and had not ſpoke three words to the ſaid Lord, but he run his Sword into his Belly juſt above the Nable: with that the Gentleman ſnatcht a Bill from one of the Watch-men, and with it knock'd the Lord down, took away his Sword, only ſaying theſe Words: *My Lord, you have Killed me, I can Kill you if I will, but I will not*, ſo ſet his foot upon his Sword and broke it, then dropt down dead; ſome of the company, while this was doing run the Conſtable in three ſeveral places of his left ſide, ſo that in five days he Dyed, and two of the Watch-men was Wounded, ſo that one of them is ſince dead: they were all taken and had to a *Tavern* to be ſecured till morning: but they call'd for Wine, and made ſome of the Watch-men drunk, then throw'd Gold and Silver about the Room, and ſo while they were ſcrambling one upon the other, made their Eſcape, and is not heard of to the Writing of this, which is *Septemb.* the 6th. 1680. *The other Murder was at* Eaſt-Barnet, *which is as follows*.

James Lawson, a person of an indifferent estate, and a good Neighbour, (or at least-wise so reputed) being an Inhabitant and Parishioner of the Parish of *East-Barnet*, in the County of *Middlesex*, within a small Mile of *Whetstone*; happened to come home on *Wednesday* the first of *September*, at Night very late, being much in drink, a thing he was very seldom addicted to by the observations of the Neighbourhood, who are ready to attest they have seldom or never seen him disguised: As soon as he came in, he immediately calls for his wife, who with a small Child in her arms came to meet him lovingly, but upon discovery of his error, began to School him at an extraordinary rate, insomuch that the Neighbours came in to pacifie her, imagining the words she gave him would not be put up without blows from her Husband, which was a thing to which he was never enclined: having used several Arguments to reconcile them (or at least wise the woman) for her Husband neither gave her ill language, or once offered to oppose her unreasonable womanish Fury (which is conceived incensed her the more.) The Neighborhood departed all, except two intimate acquaintance, rance, who knew the womans temper as well or better then her Husband, and likewise their condition in the world, which was not so high but that she would ruine him if she continued this course: At which she began to rage extreamly, and abuse them in an extraordinary manner: insomuch that seeing there was no good to be done with her, they took their leaves and were ready to depart, when just in the interim comes the own Mother of this woman, who began to be no less angry with her then the rest, telling her she had long time been a woful Spectator of her unworthy actions to her Husband, and that she found the cause lay not so much in him as in her self, and withal told her, if she used this Trade for so small an occasion, he was a mad Man or worse if he did not leave her, although she was her own Daughter, and then, quoth she, what will you do? Mother, quoth she, I will do well enuff without him or you either, no question of it: the old woman being somewhat angry to hear such an undutiful expression from her own daughter, began to reply as followeth: Daughter, quoth she, to my knowledge *James* is no common drunkard, and if a wife be the first that should divulge her Husbands infirmity, especially when it is so

seldom,

ſeldom, certainly you are to blame more then he. I would willingly reconcile this Difference if I can, you ſee you want for nothing neither at home nor abroad, neither for your Belly nor Apparel, according to his ability, therefore ſuch a ſmall fault ought rather to be winckt at, then proſecuted in this violent manner by a Wife to a Husband: beſides, what would you ſay if this uproar of yours ſhould take away your husbands livelihood amongſt his Neighbors, for you muſt conſider it is them he lives by, Truly, I tell you you act very imprudently, if he looſes his imploy you may e'n go a begging: pray Daughter, ſaid the old woman, take not my Counſel unkindly, I hope I adviſe you for your good, and you will find the comfort your own, if you accept it, but otherwiſe I know not how you and Three ſmall Children will be maintained without his labour: Mother, replies the unnatural Daughter, you may preach at home as long as you will, but in my Houſe you ſhall not, and with that thruſt both her and her Neighbours out together: the old woman onely replying, I pray God you do not repent you had taken my counſel: they were no ſooner thus thruſt out, but the Woman reviles her Hnsband with the names of Drunkard, Hell-

Hound,

Hound, Jackanapes, and idle Raſcal, which ſo much incenſed the Man, that he told his Wife if ſhe held not her Tongue the ſooner, he would make her: but ſhe ſtill replying, he gave her two or three good cuffs on the Ear, whereupon ſhe takes up Two of her Children, and told him that neither ſhe or them would trouble him longer, and thereupon goes out of the Door: The Man minds her not, ſuppoſing ſhe had been gone to her Mothers, as ſhe commonly uſed to do in theſe Freagues: Whereupon after about an hours time, he follows her, but not hearing of her at her Mothers, he returns home, where he found his Dog violently Barking at the Well, and ſo looking into the ſame, found the Bucket was let down, (a thing unuſual) which he drew up, and in the ſame both his Children dead; whereupon he immediately goes out and tells the Neighbors of the accident, who upon ſearch likewiſe found his Wife: Whereupon the Man run quite Diſtracted, and it is thought will continue ſo to his Dying day.

A Letter from Tholouze *in* France.

A Few Days ſince arrived in this City Two very Antient Men, who call themſelves Apoſtles, and they ſay they have the Spirit of Truth: No perſon at any time ever ſaw them enter into this City: They go in ſuch an extraordinary ſtrange Habit as never was ſeen before in any Country in the World. They walk about the Streets Preaching and Exhorting the people to Repent, and do Pennance, and to quit their evil lives, becauſe they ſay that God is angry againſt the *Romans*; They ſay that this City is as another *Sodom*, and that the Iniquity of this People is mounted up to Heaven, and that within Three Months (if they Repent not, and amend their Lives) this City ſhall be Deſtroy'd by Fire as *Sodom* was. They have continued ſtill in this City Preaching from Day to Day; they go with their Feet bare, and their Hands and Eyes always lifted up to Heaven; They have not been known to ſleep ever ſince they came hither; they have been often forbidden by the Magiſtrates to preach; but they anſwer'd, they were ſent on the behalf of God, to move the people to Repent and do pennance; whereupon they were cauſed to be put into priſon, where ſeveral *Jeſuits*, and Learned Men went to viſit them, and Diſputed with them in the *Latin*, *Greek*, *Hebrew*, and *Chaldean* Languages. They certainly know thoſe that live a Wicked Life; And when any ſuch come before them, they particularly Exhort them to Repent, and amend their Lives. Their Food is nothing but Bread and Water; they lift up their Hands

and

and Eyes continually towards Heaven, and are continually exhorting the people to Repentance; They preciſely nominate the Day that our Saviour ſhall come to Judgement in: And when they were asked how long time ſhall yet paſs before the general day of Judgement? they anſwered, That the World ſhall have an end in the Year *One Thouſand Six Hundred and Ninety*; But about two or three Years before that time, all the Chriſtian World ſhould be troubled with Wars; they ſay they are much above a *Thouſand Years* of Age; And being ask'd from whence they came, they anſwer'd, they came from *Damaſcus* a City in *Gallilea*, and were ſent by God to preach Repentance to the World. The *Jeſuits* have obtained of our Magiſtrates that theſe Men ſhould be ſent to *ROME* to the *POPE*; But theſe (Apoſtles as they call themſelves) anſwered, *That they knew very well all that muſt happen* [illegible]; *And that it was altogether unneceſſary to force them; for they had a great Deſire to go voluntarily to* ROME: their Chains were made of ſtrong and heavy Iron. And when they were in the Streets, & their Chains very ſtrongly faſtened on their Legs, they brake them in pieces before the people.

They Propheſſed that
In the Year 1681, *ſhall be Wars over all.*
In the Year 1682, *ſhall be no* Pope, *and Rome ſhall have no*
In the Year 1683, *they ſhall Preach throughout the World.*
In the Year 1684, *ſhall Jeſus Chriſt be known to Mankind.*
In the Year 1685, *a great Man ſhall riſe.*
In the Year 1686, *a great Earthquake ſhall happen.*
In the Year 1687, *all* Africa *ſhall burn.*
In the Year 1688, *The four parts of the World ſhall be greatly Aſtoniſh'd. And,*
In the Year 1689, *ſhall be the time when God ſhall Judge the World,*

Finis.

The Cruel Midwife (Wing C7419A) is reproduced with permission from the unique copy at The British Library (shelfmark 1132.f.66). The text-block measures 98 × 163 mm.

The following words are a transcription of the original:

4.26 Mistriss) left … likewise

The CRUEL MIDVVIFE.

Being a True Account of a most Sad and Lamentable DISCOVERY that has been lately made in the Village of POPLAR in the Parish of STEPNEY.

At the House of one Madame *Compton* alias *Norman* a Midwife, wherein has been discovered many Children that have been Murdered. Particularly Two that were lately found in a Hand-Basket on a Shelf in the Sellar, whose Skins, Eyes, and part of their Flesh were eaten by Vermin: The Skelliton of Six others that were found buryed in the Sellar; with the design of digging for others in the Garden. With he manner of the Discovery.

ALSO

An Account of the Seizing or Apprehending, Behaviour, and Commitment to NEWGATE, of Madam *Compton* alias *Norman*, the Midwife, on the Account of Murthering these Infants.

Licensed according to Order.

L O N D O N,
Printed for R. *Wier* at the *White Horse* in *Fleet-Street*, 1693.

The Cruel Midwife of Poplar, *&c.*

EVery thing is carried on by a natural Instinct, to the Preservation of it self in its own Being: And by the same Law of Nature even the most brutish amongst the Bruits themselves, may be observed to retain a special Kind of Indulgence and Tenderness towards the young The Monsters of the Sea draw out their Breasts, and give Suck to their Young ones. The barbarous Cruelties of some Midwives, Nurses, and *even* Parents to young Children, may assure us, That there are greater Monsters upon the Land than are to be found in the Bottom of the Deep; and if some of these may extenuate their Inhumanities, by I know not what Vertuous Pretences, yet the Barbarities of the rest must be wholly imputable to their savage Nature, and the bl dinefs of their Disposition.

The Gentlewoman, who is the chief Subject or Occasion of the following Narrative is by Name *Crompton*, or least generally known among the Neighbour-hood by no other Name than Madam *Crompton*; she came to live at *Poplar*, which is near *Stepney*, about Two Years since, taking a large House, where none but

Per-

Persons of considerable Rank had li-ved before, bringing with her at first only a Maid Servant, going for a Midwife of great note to Persons of Quality; here she had not continued long, before she was observed to have several Children of divers Ages; but all the time of her living in this Place has been very private, not in the least associating herself with any of the Neighbourhood, or coming to Church, *&c.* but her Maid Servant would often be in Discourse, with some of the adjacent Neighbours Maids, being always very inquisitive with them, but she would never communicate any thing of her Mistresses Domestick Affairs. The Midwife herself was scarce ever seen in the Neighbourhood, not so much as to stand at the Door, but steping into the Coach early in the morning, and coming home in a Coach in the Night, and seldom or never were any Visitants seen to come thither, but only some Gentlemen and others often in the Evening or Night, except it were some of the Parish for the Kings Taxes, the Ministers, Poor or other Duties, which generally, if she hapen to be at home she readily paid them at the Door, or sent the Maid to them with the money and many complesant Words; she was observed to be often from home for several days together, yet so much

was

was her maid servant her Confederate & Creature, that the Affaires of the House was kept so private and obscure from the Neighbours, that they could not tell how many Children she had in the House, or how often changed, or otherwise disposed of: *Mrs. Crompton* is between Fifty and Threescore Years of Age, and her maid has often declared upon several Occasions, That her mistress has been a *Midwife* above Thirty Years; and 'tis generally said that she she has followed this barbarous Infant murmurdering Trade so long, the truth of which is best known to the Omnipresent God, the searcher of Hearts, who can bring the most hidden Things of Darkness to light, and from whom no Secret is hid, who for Reasons best known to his Providence, permits some Persons Sins to go before to Judgment, that is to be punished in this Life, and others to come after, that is, reserved to the Tribunal of the great Day.

Mrs. *Crompton* going out of Town the beginning of the last Week, on *Friday*, pretty early in the Morning, the Maid-Servant (no doubt by the Order and Appointment of the Mistress) left the House likewise, leaving at home a Boy about Seven Years of Age, and a Girl about Six Years Old, with a little Infant

in

in the Cradle; leaving with them for Food only a piece of Cheese and Water, not any Beer or Bread, but bid the Boy, in case the young Child cryed, to give it some Water, and she would return in a little time; all which the Boy has since related: The Children continuing in the House alone most part of the Day, and no Maid returning, grew very impatient, and particularly for want of Sustenance, *&c.* and the Boy bringing of it into an outward Room next the Street, a Neighbour's Son passing by, and hearing the Child cry, called to the Boy to know what was the matter; to whom he declar'd, after some time, the Reasons: That they were left all day alone in the House, without Victuals, and that the young Child was almost starved; after which, Neighbours being called, the Constable and Masters of the Parish were sent for, some of whom coming and entring the House, examined the two Chilgren, who declared as before mentioned; and farther, besides the Infant in the Cradle, the Boy declared there were two more that lay Dead in a Hand-basket upon a Shelf in the Cellar; another lay Buried in the Garden, and a Fourth in the Cellar: Upon present search, they found the Two Children in the Hand-basket as the Boy had said,

they

they being most lamentable Objects of Humane Misery, looking at first sight, were liker the Carkasses of Catts or Doggs, than Humane Creatures, all their skin being off, as likewise their Eyes and part of their Flesh eat with Vermin, stinking in a lamentable manner.

On *Monday* being 21*st.* Instant, the Coroners Inquest were Impanell'd, and coming to the House where the Dead Bodies lay in the Basket, after viewing of them, they ordered some Labourers (according to the Words of the Boy) to Dig in several soft places of the Cellar where they perceived the ground had been broken, where, after some time, they Dug up six several Skeletons of Children of several Ages; upon which Night coming on, the Coroner Adjourn'd the Jury till the next Day, resolving to have the ground in the Garden likewise to be broken up before they brought in their Verdict, many of the *Spectators* took several of the Bones and carried them away, some of which are now to be seen at the *Ben-Johnson's* Head, near *St. Brides* Church by *Fleetstreet*.

Who were the Parents of these Children, or upon what account this Midwife had the keeping of them, is not certainly known, though it's it's generally conjectured, and that not without a great deal of Reason, that these were those commonly called *By-blows*, or *Bastards*, which she undertook, for a certain Sum of Money agreed on, to ease the Parents of, by keeping them as long as they lived. It's hoped our Grandsire Time, that brin gs all things to light, will unvail the Darkness of this hidden Mystery of Iniqnity, and expose the Truth as the Sun at Noon-day; In the mean time great care is taken and search made in order to discover the Midwife or her Maid.

Postscript.

TUesday, *August* 22. This Day the Coroner's Inquest met again, but were adjourned till *Monday*, on the Account that they had done digging in the Garden, and other ports for Children, and for other Reasons. This Day likewise about One in the Afternoon, our Madam *Compton*, alias *Norman*, was Apprehended near *Covent-Garden*, and with the Assistance of the Constables and Beadles, being led between two Men, attended with a numerous Croud of People; she was carried to the Petty Sessions of *Bloomsbury*, where she was Examined before their Majesties Justices

of

of the Peace there ſitting; who likewiſe took ſeveral Affidavits, by which ſhe is vehemently ſuſpected (if not poſitively charged) to have Murthered ſeveral Children that were put to her to Nurſe; upon which ſhe was from thence Committed to *Newgate*, by the Warrant or Mittimus ſigned by the Worſhipfull Juſtices of the Peace then on the Bench.

When our Doughty Midwife was firſt ſeized, all the way ſhe went to the Juſtices, and when ſhe came before their Worſhips. ſhe was obſerved to carry her ſelf with a great deal of Confidence, not ſeeming in the leaſt concern'd, or much denying the Fact. It has been obſerved that ſeveral Gentlemen and others have been ſeen to enquire at ſome of the Adjacent Ale-houſes concerning ſome particular Children.

F I N I S.

For Product Safety Concerns and Information please contact our EU representative GPSR@taylorandfrancis.com Taylor & Francis Verlag GmbH, Kaufingerstraße 24, 80331 München, Germany

Batch number: 10731486

Printed by Printforce, the Netherlands